Spying on the World

Spying on the World
The Declassified Documents of the
Joint Intelligence Committee, 1936–2013

RICHARD J. ALDRICH, RORY CORMAC
AND MICHAEL S. GOODMAN

EDINBURGH
University Press

© editorial material and organisation Richard J. Aldrich, Rory Cormac and
Michael S. Goodman, 2014

Documents in Chapters 2–16 and 18–21 reproduced by courtesy of the
National Archives, London
Document in Chapter 17 reproduced by courtesy of the National Security Archive, George
Washington University, Washington DC
Document in Chapter 22 contains public sector information licensed under the Open
Government Licence v2.0

The authors would like to thank the British Academy for generously funding this project

Edinburgh University Press Ltd
The Tun – Holyrood Road
12 (2f) Jackson's Entry
Edinburgh EH8 8PJ
www.euppublishing.com

Typeset in 10.5/12.5 pt Miller, Courier, Arial and Times New Roman by
Servis Filmsetting Ltd, Stockport, Cheshire,
and printed and bound in Great Britain by
CPI Antony Rowe, Chippenham and Eastbourne

A CIP record for this book is available from the British Library

ISBN 978 0 7486 7856 3 (hardback)
ISBN 978 0 7486 7857 0 (paperback)
ISBN 978 0 7486 7858 7 (webready PDF)
ISBN 978 0 7486 7860 0 (epub)

The right of Richard J. Aldrich, Rory Cormac and Michael S. Goodman to be identified
as authors of the editorial material in this work has been asserted in accordance with the
Copyright, Designs and Patents Act 1988 and the Copyright and Related Rights Regulations
2003 (SI No. 2498).

Published with the support of the Edinburgh University Scholarly Publishing
Initiatives Fund.

CONTENTS

1. Introduction: The Rise of the Joint Intelligence Committee ... 1
2. Origins of the Joint Intelligence Committee ... 10
3. World War II and the Role of Intelligence in Strategic Planning ... 31
4. A Post-War Intelligence Machinery ... 61
5. Origins of the Soviet Threat ... 121
6. Sigint Targeting ... 148
7. The Berlin Blockade ... 156
8. Chinese Intervention in the Korean War ... 168
9. Estimating Soviet Capabilities ... 208
10. Counterinsurgency ... 224
11. The Suez Crisis ... 240
12. The Cuban Missile Crisis ... 251
13. Vietnam ... 267
14. The Soviet Invasion of Czechoslovakia, 1968 ... 295
15. The Rise of International Terrorism in the Middle East ... 341
16. Northern Ireland: Direct Rule ... 352
17. The Falklands War ... 372
18. Changing Requirements at the End of the Cold War ... 380
19. War in Iraq: Weapons of Mass Destruction ... 389
20. War in Iraq: Aftermath ... 399
21. The Joint Intelligence Committee and the National Security Council ... 409
22. The Syrian Civil War ... 417
23. Through the Looking Glass: Illusions of Openness and the Study of British Intelligence ... 424

Appendix: Chairmen of the Joint Intelligence Committee ... 436
Document Sources ... 438
Bibliography ... 440
Index ... 445

1

INTRODUCTION: THE RISE OF THE JOINT INTELLIGENCE COMMITTEE

For more than half a century, the Joint Intelligence Committee or JIC has been a central component of the secret machinery of British government. It represents the highest authority in the world of intelligence, acting as a broker between the realms of the spy and the policymaker. According to Britain's most experienced Whitehall watcher, Peter Hennessy, the JIC and its supporting staff constitute 'the most sensitive of all the "black boxes" in the Cabinet Office'.[1]

The official guide on this subject, entitled *National Intelligence Machinery*, claims that the JIC aims to 'provide Ministers and senior officials with co-ordinated inter-departmental intelligence assessments'.[2] This rather broad definition can be better understood by a description offered by one former JIC Chairman, Sir Percy Cradock, who calls it the 'final arbiter of intelligence'.[3] The JIC also acts as the government's watchdog – monitoring global developments in an attempt to provide early warning. From the early Cold War days, the committee compiled regular reviews on activities around the Soviet perimeter. It has watched for impending wars ever since. In addition, during the Cold War, the JIC drew up a target list of subjects on which intelligence was urgently required by policymakers. This was then used to guide the activities of the intelligence services in their activities, ranging from agent running to communications monitoring and overhead photography.

The JIC was established in 1936 as a military body to serve the Chiefs of Staff. It performed strongly during the Second World War and its status was upgraded from sub-committee to full committee shortly after 1945, since when it has been involved in almost every key foreign policy decision taken by the British government. During the Cold War the role of the JIC expanded again – not least because intelligence was such a vital component in assessing the character and nature of the Soviet Union. In 1957 it was brought within the Cabinet Office, a move that, according to officials, was 'a reflection of the broadened scope and role of intelligence'.[4] This ensured that the JIC was now at the centre of not just defence policy but also broader foreign policy and that it contributed to a growing culture of national security policy at the centre of government.

Today the JIC enjoys a remarkably high profile and since 2001 has often constituted a current political issue. Intense controversies surrounding the Iraq War and weapons of mass destruction, together with the Hutton Report and the Butler Report, ensured that the then JIC Chairman, John Scarlett, found himself centre-stage in a major political controversy. Even as an abbreviation, the initials 'JIC' are known to all and its importance is public knowledge. Moreover, the passionate interest evoked by the release of the government dossier *Iraq's Weapons of Mass Destruction: The Assessment of the British Government* and the subsequent furore underline the public demand for more information about the precise connection between the core executive of British government and the intelligence services.

This dramatic growth in public interest has had a direct impact on the attention given to the workings of the JIC. For example, an internet search conducted by Dr Julian Lewis, a Conservative MP and member of the Intelligence and Security Committee, revealed that

> in the 10 years from 1982 to the beginning of 1992, which includes the first Gulf War, there were just 99 references to the JIC in British newspapers. Even in the 10 years from the beginning of 1992 to the beginning of 2002, which includes the events of 11 September, there were only 431 such references. However, in the 18 months from January 2002 until [July 2003], in that year and a half alone there have been a massive 502 references.

In Lewis's words, these figures implied that the 'the JIC has become a matter of common currency and political controversy'.[5]

The JIC and the Intelligence Community

How does the JIC fit into the broader intelligence community? How does the JIC work in practice? Partly as a result of the neglect of intelligence in wider writings on the British governmental system as a whole and partly as a result of the fragmentary nature of archival releases, the committee often gets treated in isolation by commentators. In reality, the JIC lies at the heart of a Whitehall intelligence machine. The committee is involved at the start and end of the intelligence process: it has traditionally set the requirements and priorities for the collection agencies, and it disseminates intelligence assessments to consumers under its own name (although it does not itself write the assessments).

The British system contains three primary intelligence agencies responsible for collection: the Secret Intelligence Service (MI6), the Security Service (MI5), and the Government Communications Headquarters (GCHQ). After collection, validation of sources is carried out within each agency. Intelligence must then be analysed. This stage tends to take place within Defence Intelligence. Part of the Ministry of Defence and created in 1964, Defence Intelligence is Whitehall's largest analytical body and conducts all source analysis from overt and covert sources. It is therefore a core, but often overlooked, player in the Whitehall intelligence machinery. Defence Intelligence also has some collection responsibilities in support of military operations.

Assessment then takes place inside the central intelligence machinery housed within the Cabinet Office. As mentioned earlier, the JIC does not write JIC assessments. During the Second World War, a body known as the Joint Intelligence Staff was created to act as the committee's drafters. This group was strengthened and renamed the Assessments Staff in 1968. Consisting of around thirty individuals seconded from relevant government departments, the Assessments Staff collate and assess incoming intelligence from all sources. Having done so, they compose the intelligence report. The Assessments Staff, however, are not subject experts. Each assessment is therefore discussed in what are known as Current Intelligence Groups. Here experts from across Whitehall scrutinise and challenge the assertions. Once approved, papers are sent up to the JIC for further scrutiny and comment, before dissemination to consumers.[6] Most intelligence, unless it is particularly time sensitive, is then disseminated by the JIC.

Aside from the committee approach, the JIC system is also defined by a quest for consensus. The JIC does not rely on dissenting footnotes (as the Americans do), but instead aims to issue reports expressing an agreed interdepartmental viewpoint. On the one hand this prevents the policymaker from becoming his own intelligence analyst, from being able to cherry-pick the most desired evidence, and from bickering with colleagues over what constitutes the most accurate intelligence. On the other hand, it leaves the committee open to accusations of providing bland 'lowest common denominator' assessments. Using the declassified documents in this volume, readers can make up their own minds about which depiction is more accurate.

Strengths and weaknesses in assessment

Since its creation, the JIC has gradually increased in prestige, status and closeness to policymakers. It has evolved from a sub-committee of the Chiefs of Staff to lie at the heart of Whitehall's core executive. After a slight dip in policy impact at the turn of the century, the JIC's intelligence assessments are now read by the highest levels of government.

Certain academics have questioned the future of the committee. Philip Davies, for example, has suggested that the government has 'effectively abandoned' the tried and tested JIC formula. He has asked whether the committee has entered its twilight years.[7] Whitehall insiders are quick to argue the opposite and insist that the JIC is in excellent health for the future. The JIC may well be 'just a committee' and historians should be wary of misty-eyed nostalgia, but it is certainly an important one in terms of the relationship between intelligence and policy. It is also a committee (and part of a broader system) which has long been admired and indeed copied by British allies around the world.

The growing importance of the JIC is clearly underlined by the increasing rank of its chair over the decades. Although the JIC's evolution is characterised by a remarkable ascent of the Whitehall hierarchy, numerous highs and lows have punctuated the committee's history. Many will be brought out within this volume. Overall, the JIC's record is broadly successful. Indeed, it would not have reached its seventy-fifth anniversary – quite an achievement for a government committee – in 2011 had it demonstrated a history of failure. Successes within these pages include the JIC's performance during the Second World War when military consumers drew upon intelligence to inform strategically important offensives. Similarly, the committee was accurate on Suez and deserves credit for anticipating the nature of the Cuban Missile Crisis. Furthermore, its performance on irregular threats gradually improved as it became more experienced in assessing and understanding the issues involved. It was one of the first government actors to recognise the importance of non-traditional security issues and by the late 1970s had even broadened its scope to consider the threat of radioactive accidents at nuclear power stations.

Traditionally, the JIC has been most impressive in terms of providing cumulative, regular and cautious advice to military and political consumers. This background material gradually increases consumer knowledge and understanding to ensure that policymaking discussions are well informed. It would, however, be an oversimplification merely to state that intelligence informs policy. Indeed, policy is often devised independently of intelligence, rendering intelligence important only in aiding the operation and execution stages. Either way, intelligence is vital to at least one stage of the policymaking cycle.

A second area of traditional JIC strength is detail and analysis. The joint intelligence machinery receives a vast amount of intelligence from all available sources: human, signals, imagery, open and so on. This includes both qualitative and quantitative data. Staff must therefore assimilate this range of material, which may be contradictory, into a coherent report. Indeed, the committee has a strong track record of crunching data and reducing a great deal of intelligence into a manageable product for busy consumers.

The committee's history also includes numerous intelligence failures. Broadly speaking, these revolve around forecasting and warning. For example, the JIC failed to predict a number of Cold War confrontations, including the Berlin blockade, the Korean War and the Soviet invasion of Czechoslovakia. It failed to warn of any early post-war insurgencies or of the Irish violence – although these are notoriously difficult phenomena to predict. Many of these intelligence failures can be ascribed to mirror-imaging. Korea, Czechoslovakia and the Falklands War are certainly instructive examples. Slow to learn lessons, the JIC continually applied Western values and thinking to foreign leaders, using home-grown cultural assumptions about a reluctance to use military force in place of hard intelligence. Despite offering broadly accurate strategic assessments regarding the Falklands, for example, the JIC misread the Argentineans and assumed a process of escalation in a way that was inherently unlikely. This case is particularly concerning given that the JIC was explicitly warned about this particular cognitive trap just twenty-nine days before the invasion.[8]

Other notable failures include the Iraqi WMD fiasco, which has been blamed on a number of factors from groupthink and overcorrection to poor validation of sources. A further potential cause of failure is that of perseveration, or the danger of getting stuck in an assessment rut. If the JIC merely reports each week that a given situation has changed little, consumers become blind to the potentially large change over a longer period of time. This has occasionally proved problematic and has required the intervention of particularly sharp minds to correct. Underestimating the Argentine threat to the Falklands is a case in point. When the committee is used effectively, however, this potential danger can actually become a strength of the JIC's all-source assessment function. In the case of assessing Middle Eastern terrorism, for example, the JIC used its interdepartmental authority effectively to overcome precisely this phenomenon, which was occurring at departmental level.

If the JIC is poor at warning of impending crises, its performance is generally impressive after they erupt. The committee has provided authoritative, regular and balanced briefings to consumers including at the highest levels of Cabinet. This is a pattern throughout the committee's history. Crises and conflicts bring out the best in the JIC.

Producers and consumers

Accuracy of JIC assessments is only one half of the story. The most precise and insightful intelligence is rendered useless if it is not read by those making policy decisions. Impact is therefore vital. Broadly speaking, there are two main schools of thought regarding producer–consumer relations. The first, a traditionalist approach, argues that the two should be kept separate. Intelligence must be apolitical and simply inform policymakers of the neutral facts from which they can make judgements. Distance would ensure objectivity of intelligence by reducing the dangers of politicisation.

This approach is too idealistic. In practice, intelligence assessments are rife with ambiguity and uncertainty. Political concerns permeate every aspect of intelligence work, from requirement setting all the way through to assessment and dissemination. Moreover, if intelligence is too distinct from policy, then the intelligence community struggles for relevance, becomes isolated and produces superfluous material.[9] Knowledge of current national policy and its impact on the wider international environment can also be a vital input into future forecasting.

The second, an activist approach, is more realistic. It argues that some level of interaction between the two camps is vital to ensure that intelligence is relevant, timely and useful.[10] This position does, however, increase the risk of politicisation and the abuse of intelligence by policymakers. It should be noted, however, that overt politicisation is rare. It more frequently takes the form of subtle pressure and, according to former JIC Secretary Brian Stewart, includes bias, prejudice, closed mindsets and the fear of harming one's career or losing friends amongst peers. But politicisation can also be caused by ignorance, complacency, arrogance and lack of moral courage.[11] Although a danger of the 'activist' model, it can be overcome by better communication, trust and openness between producers and consumers.[12]

Moreover, there is a distinction, albeit a fine one, between politicisation and policy contextualisation. Policymakers should not dictate analysts' conclusions and analysts should not withhold assessments which contain bad news. However, policymakers *should* be able to request intelligence assessments that address the issues currently under policy consideration. To ensure timeliness and relevance, intelligence should be brought 'within the realm of politics' by presenting and packaging assessments in ways that effectively engage policymakers' concerns.[13]

The JIC sits firmly in the 'activist' camp. For much of its history, it has brought together the intelligence and policy communities. Sitting at the interface of the two, the JIC has certainly aided the policy relevance of intelligence over the years, whilst smoothing over the inevitable tensions between the two communities. Indeed, each group has inherently different objectives, pressures and working patterns. Elected policymakers operate in the short term and desire papers which are concise and free from ambiguity, and allow decisive and speedy action. The analyst's professional imperative, however, is to produce an objective paper that reflects reality in all its complexity (as well as to ensure that intelligence is read).[14] In bringing together policymakers and intelligence officers, the JIC helps enhance interdepartmental harmony and create a sense of community cohesion.

This ethos of cooperation permeates the theoretical foundations of the JIC. It owes itself largely to the intimacy of Whitehall and the uniqueness of the British Cabinet government, relying on consensus, interdepartmentalism and collective responsibility. Whitehall is geographically small, allowing analysts and policy officials to easily meet their counterparts in different departments. This ease of face-to-face communication is in contrast to the United States, for example, where the CIA is based outside Washington DC.[15] Michael Herman, another former JIC Secretary, has described how some business was conducted through such informal Whitehall channels as the Cabinet Office mess. It is here, he states, that consensuses were built up and information flowed horizontally across the otherwise strict vertical lines of Whitehall hierarchy. He recalls how after JIC meetings on Thursdays he would head to the mess to 'drink red wine and dissect the day's performance of the JIC's Heads of Agencies'.[16] This intimacy and informal communication helped build trust between members of the JIC, and to overcome the traditional intelligence–policy divide.

Making an impact

Thanks to its remarkable record of policy relevance, the JIC has gradually acquired impact at the highest levels of government. Again, however, this broad trend masks some fluctuation between high and low points. The first major high was in May 1940, when the Chiefs of Staff began to look towards the JIC for advice. By 1942, military plans, such as Operation Torch, drew heavily upon JIC assessments. This continued after the war. For example, the Chiefs of Staff accepted (flawed) assessments on Korea and used JIC intelligence as a briefing document when dealing with the Americans. This pattern continued even after 1957, when the JIC moved to the Cabinet Office.

Given the importance of Soviet nuclear and missile capabilities, JIC assessments on this topic became a core part of post-war military planning. In short, the committee maintained impact. However, the Chiefs of Staff doubted certain JIC estimates, and discrepancies existed between the producers (the JIC) and the consumers (the Chiefs of Staff) over Soviet capabilities until the mid-1950s. Regarding Suez, tactical intelligence was appreciated by the military, but strategic assessments were marginalised by senior policymakers despite the accuracy of the intelligence provided.

Senior policymakers became increasingly interested in irregular threats. Cabinet committees welcomed the JIC's appraisals of Middle Eastern terrorism, whilst Edward Heath was personally briefed on JIC papers assessing Northern Ireland. The rise of terrorism on the JIC agenda in the late 1960s altered the purpose of intelligence. Intelligence to counter terrorism not only intends to inform decisions but also leads to direct intervention. Terrorism makes intelligence more active. Closer relations between the intelligence community on the one hand and policy and operational actors on the other are vital.

The relationship between intelligence and policy is symbiotic. The JIC has evolved over the years to ensure that its product is tailored to policy needs and is easy for the busy minister to quickly consume. It even engages in periodic feedback surveys to enhance the impact of its intelligence. Certain officials, such as Burke Trend, Cabinet Secretary from 1963 to 1973, and JIC Chairmen such as Patrick Dean and Denis Greenhill, went to great lengths to ensure intelligence is relevant and has impact.

Impact is, however, a two-way street. Some policymakers are far more intelligence literate than others. Some have had huge appetites for intelligence. Others have expected too much of intelligence and have treated the JIC as a crystal gazer. Still others have marginalised the JIC altogether. Winston Churchill was a notoriously keen consumer of intelligence. He had a voracious appetite, including not only raw intelligence but also daily JIC reports. Similarly, Margaret Thatcher had a deep interest in the secret world. Such was her desire to know more about how the system worked that in 1980 she became the first Prime Minister to ever attend a JIC meeting.[17] David Cameron is also highly conscious of JIC material and begins each meeting of the National Security Council with a briefing from the JIC Chairman. The benefits of an interested Prime Minister extend beyond JIC impact on Number 10. Once ministers realised that Thatcher was reading JIC reports, they decided that they should probably pay attention to them too.

Conversely, Eden famously marginalised the JIC over Suez. Fifteen years later, Harold Wilson also failed to heed JIC assessments – this time over sanctions and Rhodesia.[18] Indeed, Michael Palliser, one of Wilson's private secretaries, recalls 'not always' showing JIC assessments to the Prime Minister.[19] It appears that Tony Blair and Gordon Brown were also less interested in JIC material – although Blair developed a sudden keenness when his first crisis erupted in the late 1990s and it seemed that the Provisional IRA ceasefire was breaking down.[20] Working beneath the National Security Council, the JIC now once again has impact and access to the highest levels of government.

In the mid-1990s, the decision was taken to declassify and release most of the highly secret papers of the JIC. These are now in the National Archives. The process began with the JIC material for the Second World War and more recently has extended to provide JIC material for the period up to the early 1980s. This volume reproduces some of the core documents from the committee's rich history. It places them within their historical and policy context to provide readers with an original insight into the secret workings of Whitehall.

Notes

1. Peter Hennessy, *Whitehall* (London: Secker and Warburg, 1989), p. 391.
2. *National Intelligence Machinery* (London: The Stationery Office, 2006), p. 23.
3. Percy Cradock, *Know Your Enemy: How the Joint Intelligence Committee Saw the World* (London: John Murray, 2002), p. 260.
4. *Central Intelligence Machinery* (London: HMSO, 1993), p. 11.
5. Dr J. Lewis MP, Security and Intelligence Services Annual Debate, July 2003. Available at http://www.julianlewis.net/speech_detail.php?id=80 (last accessed 14 October 2013).
6. Michael S. Goodman, 'The British Way in Intelligence', in Matthew Grant (ed.), *The British Way in Cold Warfare: Intelligence, Diplomacy and the Bomb, 1945-1975* (London: Continuum, 2009), pp. 127–40.
7. Philip Davies, 'Twilight of Britain's Joint Intelligence Committee?', *International Journal of Intelligence and Counterintelligence* 24/3 (2011), p. 428.
8. Michael S. Goodman, 'Avoiding Surprise: The Nicoll Report and Intelligence Analysis', in Robert Dover and Michael S. Goodman (eds), *Learning from the Secret Past: Cases in British Intelligence History* (Washington, DC: Georgetown University Press, 2011), p. 274.
9. Michael Handel, 'The Politics of Intelligence', *Intelligence and National Security* 2/4 (1987), p. 7; Roger Hilsman, *Strategic Intelligence and National Decisions* (Glencoe, IL: Free Press, 1956), pp. 163–5.
10. For more details on this debate see Jack Davis, 'The Kent-Kendall Debate of 1949', *Studies in Intelligence* 36/5 (1992), pp. 91–103.
11. Brian Stewart, *Scrapbook of a Roving Highlander: 80 years round Asia and Back* (Newark: Acorn, 2002), p. 269.
12. Robert Gates, 'Guarding against Politicization', *Studies in Intelligence* 36/5 (1992), pp. 6–9.
13. Richard K. Betts, 'Politicization of Intelligence: Costs and Benefits', in Richard K. Betts

and Thomas G. Mahnken (eds), *Paradoxes of Strategic Intelligence: Essays in Honor of Michael I. Handel* (London: Frank Cass, 2003), pp. 60–1.
14. Michael I. Handel, 'Leaders and Intelligence', in Michael I. Handel (ed.), *Leaders and Intelligence* (London: Frank Cass, 1989), p. 10; Richard K. Betts, 'Policy-Makers and Intelligence Analysts: Love, Hate or Indifference?', *Intelligence and National Security* 3/1 (1988), pp. 184–5.
15. Gregory F. Treverton, *Reshaping National Intelligence for an Age of Information* (Cambridge: Cambridge University Press, 2003). p. 213.
16. Michael Herman, 'Up from the Country: Cabinet Office Impressions, 1972–75', *Contemporary British History* 11/1 (1997), p. 85.
17. Ian B. Beesley and Michael S. Goodman, 'Margaret Thatcher and the Joint Intelligence Committee', History of Government blog, 1 October 2012, https://history.blog.gov.uk/2012/10/01/margaret-thatcher-and-the-joint-intelligence-committee/ (last accessed 14 October 2013).
18. Cradock, *Know Your Enemy*, pp. 234–9.
19. Peter Hennessy, *The Secret State: Whitehall and the Cold War*, rev. ed. (London: Penguin, 2003), p. 292.
20. Private information.

2

ORIGINS OF THE JOINT INTELLIGENCE COMMITTEE

ON TUESDAY 7, July 1936 seven individuals sat around a large table in Whitehall. As the clock struck eleven, the first ever meeting of the Joint Intelligence Committee (JIC) began. Earlier in the year, a decision was made to create a central clearing house for intelligence: the JIC. In fact the first steps towards an integrated governmental approach to intelligence assessment occurred previously, in December 1923, with industrial and economic intelligence, but this would take years to become truly effective. The realisation that a wider-reaching interdepartmental intelligence assessment system was needed came from the military but was channelled through Sir Maurice Hankey, the creator of the Cabinet system of government.

Whilst it might have been Hankey who converted the concept of centralised intelligence assessment into practice, the stimulus for change came from military quarters. On 22 July 1935 the Director of Military Operations and Intelligence (DMO&I) in the War Office, Major General John Dill, wrote to Hankey about the need for a better system of coordinating intelligence:

> We find an increasing tendency for certain specific aspects of intelligence to develop, in which two or more separate Departments are equally interested, with the result that the danger of uneconomical duplication in the collection and recording of such intelligence is tending to increase.[1]

The underlying problem was not solely one of duplication, but of providing the best possible intelligence for planning purposes.

'Intelligence', as it was understood at this point in the 1930s in the United Kingdom, was synonymous with the military. The three separate branches of the military – the War Office, the Admiralty and the Air Ministry – each had its own dedicated intelligence staff and communication between them was patchy at best. Intelligence was collected individually, assessed separately and, by and large, used for internal purposes. Separate to these were the 'civilian' intelligence agencies, MI5 and MI6. These were largely staffed by ex-military individuals, and the heads of both had spent their careers in the army and navy respectively. Encompassed within MI6 was the code-breaking outfit, the Government Code and Cypher School (GC&CS). Both organisations had a broader remit than mere military matters but, nonetheless, military concerns remained dominant. The third element of intelligence at this time, albeit not recognised as such, was political reporting, located within the Foreign Office (FO). This was partly obtained via diplomatic channels and partly by the private networks created by the head of the FO, Sir Robert Vansittart. The net result of these three elements was twofold: that 'intelligence' was far more concerned with gauging capabilities than it was intentions; and that there was little attempt to coordinate activities.

For Dill, the key was to ensure that intelligence was best optimised and utilised for planning purposes. For Hankey, the importance was, in his words, that 'arrangements [could be made] for facilitating touch between all the departments who obtain information on any particular subject'.[2] From their correspondence it is clear that they referred specifically to the three services' intelligence directorates. Indeed, when the JIC was created as the solution, it did not include MI5, MI6 or the FO as members.

Possible ideas for a 'Joint Intelligence Committee' were debated throughout late 1935. Integral to these discussions and proposals throughout, Hankey was able to take advantage of his central position in the Whitehall machinery. He was the secretary to the Committee of Imperial Defence (CID), the powerful forum chaired by the Prime Minister and attended by senior ministers. In addition, he was the secretary to the Chiefs of Staff (COS) Committee and chairman of the Deputy Chiefs of Staff (DCOS) Committee: he therefore filled a vital role in linking the ministerial, official and military components of the government and was a central figure in pushing ideas forward.

In October 1935 Hankey ensured that the idea of a central intelligence committee was discussed in both the COS and the DCOS committees. Despite some initial differences of opinion there was a consensus that some sort of change was needed. To resolve matters, a special 'ad-hoc sub-committee' was created, designed to foster proposals. Its membership comprised Hankey as chairman and the three military officers responsible for intelligence in the services: Dill, Vice-Admiral William James and Air Vice-Marshal Christopher Courtney.

The resulting report, entitled 'Central Machinery for Co-Ordination of Intelligence', is reproduced below.[3] Fundamental to the subsequent creation of the JIC, it was disseminated on 1 January 1936. The report's conclusion was that 'our intelligence organisation requires some modification to cope with modern conditions'. The 'modern conditions' referred to the duplication that was becoming increasingly problematic and common. Furthermore, it was recognised that the 'eventuality of war' required an efficient intelligence system. As such, Hankey's committee suggested that 'direct and permanent liaison between the many departments' was needed. Their proposition was that the existing interdepartmental forum for intelligence on industrial matters be expanded and that a separate services' intelligence committee be created.

The report was passed between the DCOS and COS committees and the CID and, despite some redrafting, was approved. Much toing and froing followed, including the creation of the Inter-Service Intelligence Committee (ISIC), but such measures proved short lived. On 16 June 1936 the COS committee met to discuss progress. At the meeting Hankey proposed to 'extend the functions of the Inter-Service Intelligence Committee in order to enable that body to assist the Joint Planning Committee (JPC) when the latter required co-ordinated intelligence'. The COS wholeheartedly approved.[4] The title accorded this new body was 'Joint Intelligence Sub-Committee'.[5]

The JIC was, from the outset, a sub-committee of the COS committee. In contrast to the ISIC this increased its importance and positioned it firmly at the centre of government, where it was drawn into the orbit of the COS planning machinery. The JIC thus had a wider scope, not only absorbing the roles and remit of the ISIC, but also acting in an advisory capacity to the JPC and the Joint Planning Staff.[6] The new JIC comprised seven representatives: six were from the military and the seventh was Desmond Morton, a former MI6 officer and later Churchill's intelligence adviser. The FO had shown interest initially in the JIC but, it would seem, wanted to see how it performed before becoming involved.

The JIC members themselves were aware of this gap. Two years after its creation the then chairman, Brigadier Frederick Beaumont-Nesbitt, put out a paper, also reproduced below, arguing that 'here surely is a deficiency which could and should be made good'. He recommended the existing committee be enlarged, with the 'inclusion of a senior FO representative, who would also be asked to act as Chairman'. This proposal was reinforced not only by the increasingly political content of deliberations, but also because it would stop any 'vested interests' from becoming 'too powerful'.[7]

The COS reaction was, perhaps, unsurprising. Any committee that reported to them, it was suggested, should not have an FO chairman.[8] Yet the general reaction to Beaumont-Nesbitt's proposal was supportive, not least within the FO itself. Whilst such deliberations were underway the German army, in March 1939, marched into Prague and Neville Chamberlain, the Prime Minister, promised support to Poland in the event of German aggression. Within the FO a Situation Report Centre (SRC) was created. Unlike the JIC, which had produced long-term strategic assessments up to that point, the SRC was designed to produce tactical summaries. By June, with the prospect of conflict looming, the FO chairman of the SRC, Ralph Skrine-Stevenson, produced a paper on the coordination of intelligence in time of war. Like Beaumont-Nesbitt's proposals of a year earlier, he argued that the present system was not effective and that the FO should take an increased role. This time it hit a nerve. With rapid progress and some careful manoeuvring behind the scenes, the ideas were ratified at various levels within Whitehall. The result was that on 3 August 1939 the SRC and JIC were amalgamated and the FO assumed the chairmanship, a position it would hold until the Franks Report in 1983.[9]

The JIC had assumed several new roles. It now had responsibility for producing both short-term and long-term intelligence assessments. Furthermore, it was now accountable for overseeing all administrative arrangements relating to the intelligence machinery in its totality, and for taking the lead in highlighting any deficiencies in the existing system. This, then, was the shape that the JIC would take as events in Europe worsened.

```
                    Cab 54-3 extraction
(THIS DOCUMENT IS THE PROPERTY OF HIS BRITANNIC MAJESTY'S
GOVERNMENT).
S E C R E T.
D.C.O.S. 4.
(Also paper No: C.O.S. 420 (D.C.).)
                                              COPY NO.17
              COMMITTEE OF IMPERIAL DEFENCE.
              CHIEFS OF STAFF SUB-COMMITTEE.
         SUB-COMMITTEE OF DEPUTY CHIEFS OF STAFF.
    CENTRAL MACHINERY FOR CO-ORDINATION OF INTELLIGENCE.
                         REPORT.
```

General

We have been instructed by the Chiefs of Staff Sub-Committee to investigate and report on a suggestion that some central machinery is now required for the co-ordination of certain types of intelligence.
2. The field of intelligence which it is now necessary to cover in time of peace in order to be properly prepared for the eventuality of war with any Great Power has been almost immeasurably extended and complicated by reason of –
(1) The extent to which modern war involves the whole of the resources of the nation; and
(2) The vast extension of the zone of operations that has been brought about by the advance of aviation.
3. As a result of our discussions we have formed the opinion that our intelligence organization requires some modification to cope with modern conditions. There are certain types of intelligence which can neither be comprehensively collected nor intelligently interpreted unless special arrangements are devised to establish direct and permanent liaison between the many departments, military and civil, who are in a position to make

contributions to the general stock of information on the subject in question, and to give expert advice, each from its own technical viewpoint and experience, as to the significance of the material thus collected.

Industrial Intelligence

4. The first type of intelligence of this nature relates to industrial resources and, consequently, the potential war capacity of foreign countries. In 1929 the study of this problem necessitated the setting up of the Sub-Committee on Industrial Intelligence in Foreign Countries, composed of representatives of the Treasury, Foreign Office, Board of Trade and the Defence Departments, whose terms of reference are:-
(1) To establish direct liaison for the interchange of information and reports in regard to industrial intelligence in foreign countries between the Board of Trade and the Service Departments;
(2) To deal with all matters arising out of this interchange which may require joint discussion; and
(3) To discuss the significance of the more important information.
In addition a permanent whole-time staff was found to be essential to study this vast and complex problem, and the Industrial Intelligence Centre has been working very satisfactorily since 1931.

Other types of intelligence

5. Industrial Intelligence, however, is not the only type of intelligence calling for special treatment, and for the last two years there has been considerable interdepartmental discussion on the arrangements necessary for the central collection, collation and interpretation of intelligence relating to air targets in foreign countries.
There may also be other types of intelligence which, as a result of further experience, will be found later to need special treatment, but at present we have no recommendations to make on them.

Air targets in foreign countries

6. As regards air targets in foreign countries, we consider that our aim should be to ensure that the Defence Departments are in possession of such information as will enable our Air Forces to obtain the maximum effect on an enemy nation, by means of air attack, against those objectives the destruction or dislocation of which the Government consider would contribute most towards the attainment of the national aim.

7. We consider that this problem opens up a vast field for the collection of intelligence, which cannot be covered by the present intelligence branches of the Defence Departments. Before, however, putting forward any recommendations, we consider it advisable to state what the problem involves.

8. Briefly the problem can be considered under three heads:-
(i) Selection of target groups;
(ii) Collection of information;
(iii) Registration of information.

Registration of information

9. Dealing with the registration of information, we consider that this should be carried out in such a way as to facilitate the selection of suitable targets for the Government's approval and to have immediately available all information which the Air Forces require to take immediate action against those objectives which the Government may decide are to be attacked. This information must, therefore, be tabulated and filed to conform to Air Staff requirements: the responsibility for selecting the method of registration to be adopted should, therefore, rest with the Air Ministry in discussion with the staffs of the other Defence Departments.

Selection of target groups

10. Air targets may be classified as -
(1) Military objectives (in the accepted sense of the term).
(2) Industrial targets.
(3) Non-military targets.

We attach as Appendix I a list showing the sub-division of targets in the industrial group.

Non-military targets are those which may be attacked in order to produce moral effect, whether the ultimate aim is to break the national will of the enemy or to stop work in particular localities. These targets include:-

(i) Crowded industrial areas where air attack would produce great moral effect.

(ii) Essential services, i.e., water supply, sanitation, fire fighting.

(iii) Centres of Government.

The reference to targets of this nature in this Report is not intended to prejudge the question as to whether or not they would, in the event of war, be attacked. If, however, it is possible that as a measure of reprisal or otherwise it were decided to do so, we must clearly be prepared beforehand by collecting the necessary information.

Collection of information

11. It is essential to collect as much information as possible regarding the groups of targets referred to in the preceding paragraph. Whilst purely military targets can be dealt with by the Defence Departments in consultation, each industrial target presents a specialist study of which the Intelligence Branches of the Defence Departments have little or no experience, and it is necessary to mobilize as much technical data as possible regarding them. The lines of investigation concerning them must follow similar channels in each group and the information produced so as to comply with registration requirements. In order that this may be done effectively, certain definitions have been evolved in the Air Ministry which we attach as Appendix II, and which should be applied when necessary.

Suggested organization

12. We are of opinion that the problem goes far beyond the bounds of the Defence Departments and includes questions which can only be dealt with in association with industrial experts and those connected with the public services. We suggest that it is undesirable, if

it can be avoided, to set up any fresh organization if the needs can be met by adaptation of existing machinery. We believe that the Sub-Committee on Industrial Intelligence in Foreign Countries is a suitable body to which the work might be referred, though that Committee and such sub-committees as it may form may require to co-opt additional members to deal with specific subjects.
13. If our proposal is adopted we are of opinion that the suggestions regarding the future composition of the Sub-Committee on Industrial Intelligence in Foreign Countries should emanate from that Committee itself, but we put forward the following suggestions for their consideration:-
(a) A primary need will be to decide whether the target groups mentioned in paragraph 4 are generally suitable or whether amendment is needed.
(b) Having settled the target groups to be studied, the next step is to obtain the Information required for registration. Since expert knowledge of each group is essential it would appear to be desirable to set up a number of sub-committees each charged with the study of one or more of the target groups enumerated in paragraph 9 and Appendix I, under chairmen nominated by the main committee, with the power to co-opt experts either from the Services or civil life.
(c) Each sub-committee should be in the closest possible touch with the registration branch at the Air Ministry, in order to ensure that the information which is being obtained is in the form required for registration and in order that the registration staff may indicate where gaps lie in the information provided. To ensure that this is done it is suggested that the Secretaries of the Sub-Committees should be provided by the Air Ministry and the Committee of Imperial Defence and organized on the lines adopted for the Supply Committees of the Principal Supply Officers Committee Organization, viz., Permanent Secretary or Secretaries to the Sub-Committees provided by the Air Ministry working with a Joint Secretary from the Committee of Imperial Defence, the latter being responsible for co-ordination.
14. We have not referred to the question of co-ordinating Service intelligence, but it would seem that the necessary co-ordination can be effected by an inter-Service Intelligence Committee composed of representatives of

the three Service Intelligence Staffs, meeting at the request of one of the members. It is suggested that the Committee should be composed of
Admiralty - Deputy Director of Naval Intelligence.
War Office - Head of M.I. (1) General Staff.
Air Ministry - Deputy Director of Intelligence.
15. Close liaison will, no doubt, be required between the Sub-Committee on Industrial Intelligence in Foreign Countries and the Air Raid Precautions Department of the Home Office. That Department should be in a position to give valuable information on the question of air targets and should be represented on any new organization.

Recommendations

16. Our recommendations therefore are:-
(1) That the scope of the Sub-Committee on Industrial Intelligence in Foreign Countries should be enlarged to include "Air Targets Intelligence"; it being understood that other types of intelligence may subsequently be added.
(2) That in view of (1) above, the Sub-Committee should have the power to co-opt additional members or call on such persons as they considered necessary to deal with specific problems.
(3) That as a first step its terms of reference should be altered to read as follows:-
(a) To supervise co-ordinated interchange of information and reports between the Defence Departments and other departments concerned in regard to:-
(i) Industrial Intelligence in Foreign Countries.
(ii) Air Targets Intelligence.
(b) To deal with all matters arising out of this interchange which may require joint discussion; and
(c) To discuss the significance of the more important information.
(4) That the Sub-Committee on Industrial Intelligence in Foreign Countries should themselves put forward proposals as to any alterations which their additional responsibilities may necessitate in the composition of the Sub-committee.
(5) That the above proposals should be regarded as provisional and experimental.
(6) That the co-ordination of Service Intelligence

should be carried out by an inter Service Intelligence Committee, composed as under, meeting at the request of one of the members-
Admiralty - Deputy Director of Naval Intelligence.
War Office - Head of H.I. (1) General Staff.
Air Ministry - Deputy Director of Intelligence.

                (Signed) M.P.A. HANKEY (Chairman).
                    "   W.M. JAMES, Vice-Admiral D.C.N.S.
                    "   J.G. DILL, D.M.O. & I.
                    "   C.L. COURTNEY, D.C.A.S.

2, Whitehall Gardens, S.W.1.
1st January, 1936.

APPENDIX I
INDUSTRIAL TARGETS
So far as the investigations by the Air Staff have progressed, the following groups appear to be essential: they are not placed in order of priority nor are they likely to be final:
(i) Electricity supply, i.e., power stations, grid system, etc.
(ii) Gas supply, including gas grid and coke ovens.
(iii) Oil supply, including depots, hydrogenation plants, etc.
(iv) Steel industry, including special steels required for armaments.
(v) Factories for and reserves of explosives, incendiary material, poison gas and their keys, e.g., nitric acid, chlorine, ammonia, etc.
(vi) Factories for and reserves of munitions, including projectiles, torpedoes, mines, bombs, S.A.A. guns, rifles, machine guns.
(vii) Factories for and reserves of motor vehicles, including tanks and tractors.
(viii) Factories for and reserves of special alloys, machine tools.
(ix) Transportation, i.e., railways, roads; water-ways. Transportation is common to targets in all three groups so that the key points in the various transportation systems, though remaining constant, will be applicable to the majority of industrial groups.

(x) Shipyards, shipping in harbour and shipbuilding establishments.

APPENDIX II
DEFINITIONS
(i) <u>"Key" industries</u> are contributory industries which are more profitable for air attack than the industry which they supply. For instance, the whole output of the aircraft engine industry of a country might depend upon the output of one magneto factory. This factory would, therefore, be the "key" industry to the aircraft engine industry.
(ii) <u>Basic industries.</u> These include coal and steel production on which the industry as a whole of a country largely depends. They cannot be classified as "keys" as defined above.
(iii) <u>"Key" services</u> are public services, such as electricity, gas, transportation, on which industry depends and which may present more profitable targets for air attack than the industry itself. For instance, the destruction of one power station might cause the output of a group of factories to cease.

* * *

The War Office
Whitehall
S.W.1

Colonel L.C. Hollis,
Committee of Imperial Defence,
Richmond Terrace,
WHITEHALL, S.W.1.

21st December, 1938.

Dear Hollis,

As promised on the telephone last night I am sending you herewith a copy of my Paper, which for want of a better title I have called "The Organization of Intelligence". It does not pretend to cover all the ground or to deal in detail with every aspect of the problem. It will, however, give you I hope sufficient indication of the lines on which I suggest we might organize. I am convinced that something of this nature is required; we here in the War Office - and to a great extent at the Air Ministry and Admiralty - spend a great deal of our time in dealing with material which more rightly should be handled by the Foreign Office. Equally, at the Foreign Office they must have to cope with a number of Reports that are not strictly speaking political. What I mean is the type of Report which would have a bearing on Government policy, or preparations, for war. What I suggest we want, therefore, is a small organization, whose task is to handle this very considerable mass of information which falls between the true political and the military. I would describe it as Military/Political. I cannot see that my proposals would infringe in any way, either on the Service Departments or on the Foreign Office - rather should they lighten the burden of all of them.

I would emphasise, as I have done in my Paper, that the proposed Bureau would be solely advisory. It would have no executive power whatsoever. I emphasise this as I feel certain otherwise we shall meet great opposition from vested interests, who will be frightened that an organization of this nature will become too powerful. That is also the reason why I suggest that the Foreign Office representative should act as Chairman.

The reception of my proposals up to date - the Paper has only gone to D.M.O. & I., D.D.M.O., M.I.2., M.I.3. and S.I.S. - has been on the whole very encouraging. The D.M.O. and D.D.M.O. both agree on broad lines, though the D.M.O. suggests that "salt will have to be put on the tail of many people in Whitehall ere it goes through". I have not had D.D.M.O.'s final comments, but hope to get them after Christmas. Nor have I seen the comments of M.I.2. and M.I.3.; but Dennys tells me that having discussed it very fully with his three sub-sections, they have come to the conclusion that it is a practical proposition and would mean, in their case, a reduction of some four officers. Menzies, who I believe discussed it with his Chief, is also in agreement, while insisting that a representative of S.I.S. should be part of the permanent body, since so much of the material that they would deal with would be supplied by his organization.

I should be most grateful if you and Ismay would now consider these proposals, and let me have your views in due course. I should also much value your advice as to how we should then proceed. Possibly the most diplomatic method might be to endeavour privately to enlist the sympathetic support of the Foreign Office before giving any wider circulation.

As you said last night this proposal, if proved acceptable, might considerably modify our present ideas with regard to the Middle East Bureau. For the moment, therefore, I feel that the latter should be left where it now is, in a state of suspended animation. Nevertheless, I think that at an early date after Christmas we must decide what we are going to do about this M.E. Bureau.

There is one other point on which the J.I.C. will also have to adjudicate, and that is to decide which Service should be responsible for the collection and collation of Air Defence Intelligence. At the moment this is not done satisfactorily, chiefly because in several foreign countries air defence comes under the control of the Air Ministry concerned, whereas in others this is not the case. The result is that for some countries Military Attachés are collecting this information and passing it home, in others this duty falls on the Air Attaché. It is not going to be very easy to find a satisfactory solution without overlapping, but the matter cannot be allowed to remain in its present state.

THE ORGANISATION OF INTELLIGENCE

The object of this Paper

1. The object of this paper is to discuss the existing Intelligence organisation; to ascertain whether this system produces the best results; and, should it appear as a consequence of this investigation, that some more efficient procedure is desirable, to submit proposals designed to make good the apparent defects.

2. It will simplify study of this subject if, at the outset, a distinction is made between the two main divisions under which Intelligence can be broadly classified. The first can be described as Military Intelligence – using the term Military in its widest sense – and the second as Political Intelligence.

The former includes all that technical data (e.g. armament, equipment, organisation of the armed forces etc.) which is of special interest to the three Defence Services. The latter comprises information on the system of government, economic and industrial conditions and the general trend of policy in foreign countries. Such matters are primarily the concern of the Foreign Office, though influencing to a lesser, but nevertheless considerable extent, other Government Departments. (For instance, it is clearly impossible to produce a well-balanced military appreciation without adequate knowledge of the political background).

3. Reduced to essentials, therefore, every Intelligence organisation, whether at the War Office, Admiralty, Foreign Office, or elsewhere, is normally handling two different categories of information. One is of particular interest and usually the immediate concern of one, or at most two Departments. The other, in varying degree, the concern of all Departments.

4. For the purposes of this paper - which is intended to deal with the wider aspects of Intelligence - there is no need to examine in detail the methods employed in the collection and collation of items falling within the first category. This is of local interest, and should be dealt with locally. It is in the second category - Political intelligence - which is common to all Departments, that overlapping and wasted effort may occur. And it is proposed, therefore, to confine discussion to this aspect alone of the problem.

The present system

5. The sources through which this Political Intelligence is obtained are many and various. They range from the Daily Press and the speeches of foreign statesmen, through Diplomatic and other official memoranda to Secret and Most Secret reports. And all these, with only few exceptions, are received by each Intelligence Directorate. How the latter deal with them is their affair; but every item has to be examined - if merely superficially - and its value assessed. This in itself means time; and frequently, where the Service Departments are concerned, it must mean wasted time. For much of this information is quite outside their province. True, it is of interest and widens the general knowledge of the officers dealing with it; but, too often, it may mean less time available

for what is their first task – the collation of information of definite military value.

6. Under the present system such a state of affairs is inevitable, since no single Department is responsible for first assimilating this mass of material and for subsequently passing it on to other interested parties in an easily digestible form. It is not the task of the Foreign Office; though it is this Department which requires, and takes, the lion's share. It is certainly not the task of the Service Departments, which only have an indirect connection, and which would indeed be guilty of a trespass should they attempt to do so. Yet every Department, for its own purposes, must, at the moment, be prepared to analyse the international political situation. There may be as many readings of the situation as there are commentators: there is certainly no doubt whatever that for some at least the time thus spent could have been better employed.

7. The disadvantages of this procedure become even more marked when, for example, a General Staff paper is called for. In nearly every case a political background will have to be produced on to which the military appreciation can then be hung. Provided that this appreciation is to be circulated only within the War Office, the War Office cannot be accused of exceeding its responsibilities. But, if it is to have a wider circulation, there is always the possibility that the political assumptions will be found not to be in accordance with Foreign Office views. And in such matters, it is this Department that must be the decisive factor.

8. That these and kindred difficulties have been recognised is shown in the recurrent demand – a demand, however, that has been invariably refused on the grounds of impracticability – for a Ministry of National Defence and a unified General Staff. Nevertheless, and in spite of these refusals, some measure of satisfaction has been given during the past ten years to the requests for closer co-operation. The Imperial Defence College has been established, the Chiefs of Staff sub-committee of the Committee of Imperial Defence has been set up, while yet other additional sub-committees embracing the Defence Services have been added from time to time as the need for them became apparent. Moreover, it is through these sub-committees, on which all interested parties

are represented, that agreed decisions are reached and agreed recommendations are submitted to the full Committee of Imperial Defence and to the Cabinet.

9. This is a perfectly natural and logical process, and it might have been expected that among the first sub-committees to be formed would have figured one to co-ordinate all Intelligence matters. This committee to be responsible for keeping world political developments under continuous observation, and for issuing, from time to time, a political summary or a memorandum that would form the basis of all major political or military appreciations. Such, however, is not the case. All that at present exists is a Joint Intelligence sub-committee (henceforth referred to as J.I.C.), with somewhat ill-defined duties and which meets only at infrequent intervals. Here surely is a deficiency which could and should be made good.

10. It has been proved by experience that, to enable the Chiefs of Staff sub-committee to function satisfactorily, a lesser body is required to prepare the material necessary for their deliberations. To meet this want the Joint Planning Committee has been called into being. Subsequently, the need for whole-time staff officers attached to the J.P.C. became apparent and, since their appointment, have constantly proved their value. Similar treatment might, with equal justification, be accorded to the analogous Intelligence Committee.

11. It seems, therefore, that to be logical the C.O.S. Committee should be provided with a J.I.C. complementary to, and working in the closest touch with, the J.P.C. In its present form the J.I.C. does not, and in fact cannot, fulfil this role; nor, it is believed, would the addition of a permanent staff officer from each of the Service Departments give it the wider scope that might be so profitably employed. Something more comprehensive seems to be demanded, and in the following paragraphs proposals will be submitted for developing this organisation on suitable lines.

The proposed system

12. It must be clearly understood from the start that the suggested organisation is designed to be purely advisory. It would take no decisions, nor lay down any

policy. Equally it would in no way interfere with the complete liberty of action of any particular Department. These points deserve to be emphasised to allay apprehension which a scheme of this type may, quite naturally, raise.

Its principal task would be to sift all that political intelligence material, which hitherto has been dealt with by several departments, and, as the result of these labours, to compile a reasoned analysis of international affairs, either, periodically, in the form of a Secret summary, or, as and when required, in the form of a political appreciation. (The above would be the normal but doubtless it could be asked to undertake special investigation of particular subjects).

13. Having defined its main duties it is now necessary to set out the suggested composition of this organisation. For this it is considered advisable to maintain the J.I.C. as a foundation round which to build. Thus the three Deputy Directors of Intelligence (Admiralty, War Office, Air Ministry) would continue to exercise general supervision and to form the connecting link between the proposed new organisation and the three Services. But, in view of the increased responsibilities that will be assigned to it in the future, it is important to strengthen this controlling body by the inclusion of a senior Foreign Office representative, who would also be asked to act as Chairman. (At present this duty devolves on D.D.M.I.)

14. It is not intended that these representatives of the four Departments most nearly concerned, should do more than guide the labours of the revitalised J.I.C. The work of collating the reports received, and of preparing the periodical summaries and appreciations, would be undertaken by a special staff drawn from all interested Government Departments. How the personnel will be provided, and the general allotment of duties, is best shown by a diagram. This is attached as Appendix A. The size of this staff and the suggested lay-out have been arrived at arbitrarily based on experience in the M.I. Directorate of the War Office. Obviously, it is only possible to lay down a definite establishment and conduct of work as the result of actual experience.

15. Opponents of these proposals will undoubtedly protest that a considerable increase of staff is entailed, and

this, moreover at a period when it is difficult to select suitable personnel and when, in any case, it is inopportune further to augment their number. It is contended, however, that this may not ultimately be the case; since, if this organisation achieves what it is hoped to be capable of doing, it might then be possible to reduce the staffs of the several Intelligence Directorates. Under existing conditions it is quite certain that a great deal of valuable time is wasted daily through handling reports, which have no military significance and have only a political value. In the future all such reports would be the responsibility of the staff of the J.I.C. Furthermore, there should be an additional saving of time and labour for the M.I. Directorates if they no longer have to compile political appreciations as they are now compelled to do. Collectively, this should mean a considerable lightening of the burden, and the eventual possibility of effecting some reduction in personnel.

16. It may be argued that to remove this political side from the M.I. Directorate is to deprive it, and the War Office (Admiralty and Air Ministry) of essential information. Actually this would not be the case, since the J.I.C. summaries would adequately meet this need, and indeed, in an improved form since these summaries would represent a joint opinion and not that of one Service only. Furthermore, should a political appreciation be required by War Office (Admiralty and Air Ministry) this could always be called for by the Deputy Director of Intelligence, and this also as an agreed production should have an enhanced value.

17. A final word may be desirable as to the methods of circulating intelligence reports and other information under the system here envisaged. What is proposed is broadly as follows. No change would be made in the case of purely military reports. These would go as hitherto direct to the Department/Departments interested. Where, however, these primarily military reports contained items of political interest, copies or relevant extracts would be passed to J.I.C. for consideration. As regards political information contained in Foreign Office Telegrams, Official Despatches and memoranda from H.M. representatives abroad etc., this would always be passed to J.I.C. except in such cases as were only for action by a Department. Eventually, it might be possible to cease

circulation of such items to M.I. Directorates, though in the early and experimental stages of the new procedure, it would be preferable to continue the present system, but on the understanding that where political intelligence was concerned no action by M.I. Directorates was necessary. (The case of F.O. has not been dealt with as conditions are so dissimilar from those in Service Ministries).

18. Such, in general terms, is the system it is suggested might be introduced. It is fully realised that much inter-departmental discussion will be necessary if final agreement is to be reached. Nevertheless, it is believed that, given a fair trial, it will go some way towards remedying an obvious lack in the machinery of the C.I.D., and will also provide a speedier and more efficient instrument for dealing with certain aspects of current international problems than is possible under the methods obtaining today.

The study of Propaganda

19. An additional argument in favour of these proposals is to be found in a memorandum by Sir Stephen Tallents dealing with his experiences as Director General designate Ministry of Information during the crisis last September (M.I.C.15). In this memorandum Sir Stephen Tallents states that: "The outstanding lesson, however, taught by the September rehearsal in the Ministry's sphere, was the lack of machinery for securing the prompt, wide and efficient conveyance of British news and views to potentially enemy peoples."*

He goes on to argue that it is essential to build up a nucleus organization in peace that will be capable of carrying out: "such continuous study of conditions and opinion in enemy countries as will ensure, at a moment which may come suddenly and will certainly be critical, a

---

* In this connection the following extract from a recent memorandum of M.A. Berlin (No.1130 d/d 2.11.38) is significant.
  "I believe that propaganda in Germany, as far as it may affect military matters, is receiving wide study and attention. We know, for instance, that at the Wehrmachtsakademie, which corresponds to our Imperial Defence College, considerable time is devoted to the study of this subject both by civilian and military students."
  It is fair to assume that the propaganda instrument has been allotted a prominent place in the scheme for "total war".

just assessment of the vulnerable points in enemy public opinion and the lines on which they should, through all available channels be attacked."

20. To fulfil this object Sir Stephen Tallents proposes the creation of a centre that would: "while conducting part of its work in secret, be able also to work openly and in normal conditions. This means that some peace-time 'cover' must be secured for it, whether by its attachment to some regular organization, or possibly through the recognised interest in German affairs for other peace-time purposes of the man in charge of it".

It may also be added, to complete the picture that the "existing agencies" through which he proposes to collect the material necessary for his purpose, are the Foreign Office, Admiralty, War Office, Air Ministry, the S.I.S. organization, and the B.B.C.

21. The case for a reorganised and enlarged J.I.C. must stand or fall on its own merits; but it is at least noteworthy that all of the "existing agencies" cited by Sir Stephen Tallents - with the sole exception of the B.B.C. - are already represented, either directly or indirectly, in that body. Moreover, in the reconstituted J.I.C. could be found, - or so it would seem - not only the ideal cover that is being sought for, but also a permanent staff handling daily the very type of data that is required. By the addition of one more section to that organisation the peace-time propaganda nucleus, that is so urgently needed, could most readily be provided.

22. It is doubtless a simple matter to criticise this scheme, both in its indirect connection with a potential Ministry of Information, and also, more directly, in its original purpose as a common centre for the collation and distribution of Political Intelligence. Yet it would be difficult to deny entirely that, something on the lines set out above is either illogical or would contribute nothing to promote increased efficiency. No claim is made that these proposals are final and that there are no alternatives. They are tentative suggestions put forward as a basis for discussion and criticism, from which it is hoped agreement in principle might result. Once that has been achieved agreement on matters of detail should not present an insoluble problem. All that is now asked, is that criticism should be unbiased and constructive.

Notes

1. Dill to Hankey, 22 July 1935, TNA: CAB 54/3.
2. Hankey to Dill, 29 July 1935, TNA: CAB 21/2651.
3. DCOS 4, 'Central Machinery for Co-Ordination of Intelligence', 1 January 1936, TNA: CAB 4/24.
4. Minutes of the 178th Meeting of the Chiefs of Staff, 16 June 1936, TNA: CAB 53/6.
5. JIC 1, 30 June 1936, TNA: CAB 56/2.
6. For more see Edward Thomas, 'The Evolution of the JIC System up to and during World War II', in Christopher Andrew and Jeremy Noakes (eds), *Intelligence and International Relations, 1900-45* (Exeter: University of Exeter Press, 1987), pp. 223-4.
7. See Beaumont-Nesbitt's report and cover note to Hollis, 21 December 1938, TNA: CAB 21/2651.
8. DCOS 41st Meeting, 14 July 1939, TNA: CAB 54/2.
9. JIC 32nd Meeting, 3 August 1939, TNA: CAB 56/1. In fact, Foreign Office incumbency of the chairmanship was longer than this: if those chairmen who were diplomats seconded to the Cabinet Office are included, then the FO and its FCO successors only relinquished the role in 2001.

3

WORLD WAR II AND THE ROLE OF INTELLIGENCE IN STRATEGIC PLANNING

DESPITE PRODUCING A series of useful assessments, the pre-war JIC had been hindered by its limited impact and relative aloofness. The German invasion of Norway in early 1940 resulted in the start of what would be a change of fortunes, with the JIC becoming increasingly prominent and central to planning. As a predominantly military committee the JIC was well placed for its strategic role. Operation Torch, the plan for the invasion of north Africa in 1942, was the first occasion on which the JIC was efficiently used for what it had been created to do: provide the intelligence input into a large, strategically important military offensive.

Three events were crucial for the JIC's profile in April 1940: first of all, the German army invaded and quickly overran Norway; secondly, back in London, Winston Churchill assumed the position of Minister for the Co-ordination of Defence; and thirdly, Victor Cavendish-Bentinck, the JIC Chairman, was invited to take part in discussions with the Joint Planning Committee (JPC). Within a month the reverberations from these events would be felt to great effect, leading to a dramatic rise in the JIC's stature.

The fall of Norway was the catalyst. Whitehall had received no forewarning of the invasion and, deeming the issue an intelligence failure, officials wanted to know why. As Maurice Hankey conceded, 'It is no use crying over spilt milk ... nevertheless, it is a good thing to look back on our mistakes – and this is by no means the only one – in order to try and rectify them in the future.'[1] In a subsequent post-mortem, the speed – or lack thereof – at which intelligence reports were transmitted to planners was identified as one crucial factor.[2] On 10 May 1940, Chamberlain resigned and Churchill took over. One of his first moves was to ask who was in charge of intelligence and this, together with the failure over Norway, gave the JIC a new direction and impetus. Firstly, the sub-committee was instructed to initiate its own assessments when it saw fit (as opposed to waiting for a formal instruction to do so). Secondly, it would move closer (metaphorically, not physically) to those planning the war effort. These efforts coincided with the JPC taking an increased interest in intelligence matters and requesting a JIC input into its planning.

From May 1940, the JIC accordingly began to play a greater role in the war effort. Not only did the planners begin to look to the JIC for advice but so too did the Chiefs of Staff. It was perhaps this factor, more than any other, which allowed the JIC to escape from the creative vacuum that had characterised the pre-war period. Thus, by late 1940 the JIC was producing, in addition to its mainstay long-term assessments, a series of daily and weekly tactical forecasts, including:

1. the daily 1030 summary for the War Cabinet
2. the daily 1600 Situation Report
3. the daily 1630 JIC Intelligence Report
4. the daily 0700 and 1800 War Cabinet Map Room summaries (the former being a summary of information on force dispositions, the latter a more domestic operational summary).[3]

The JIC's efforts, output and significance were assisted greatly by the introduction in late 1941 of the Joint Intelligence Staff (JIS). It comprised two teams of drafters, easing constraints on JIC members' time, so that the JIS spent their days writing the assessments themselves. An important development in the history of the committee, the JIS remained in place until 1968. The creation of a further subordinate body, the Intelligence Section (Operations), strengthened the JIC's role in planning, for it was designed to 'collate intelligence for operational planning'.[4] By 1942, then, not only had the JIC become firmly entrenched in Britain's war efforts, but the additions of Ultra decrypts and the US entry into the war meant that intelligence was firing on all cylinders.

By 1942 the war had truly become a global conflict. One of the biggest questions facing British military planners concerned the future direction of the war. The German army had become bogged down in Russia, yet Stalin was adamant that a new Allied western front be opened up in order to divert German resources and effort. Many of the American planners were keen to support this in the form of a cross-Channel offensive, but their British counterparts favoured, and eventually had approved, a move into French North Africa.

The JIC had first been involved in plans for an invasion of north Africa in December 1941, then codenamed Operation Gymnast.[5] An assessment of 'German intentions' in January 1942 suggested that increased forces were being sent to the Russian front, whilst in north Africa attempts would be made to bolster Rommel's forces in order to seize and exploit oil reserves.[6] Throughout the first half of 1942 the JIC, and the JIS, continued to produce a torrent of papers for the military planners, covering various aspects of the invasion and predicting what sort of resistance might be expected.[7] The increased pressure and requirement for assessments was such that the JIC was forced to start meeting twice weekly from March.[8] To underline just how crucial the JIC had now become to planning, a new study was begun that concentrated on 'the probable strength, efficiency, equipment, training, and morale of the Axis forces in 1942, economic factors, morale on the home front, and the bearing which these may have on the Axis plans of campaign for this year'.[9]

By the summer of 1942, and after acrimonious discussion, the Americans finally conceded to the British plan to invade north Africa before concentrating on north western Europe.[10] A JIC report in July suggested that if the Germans could be driven out of north Africa that year, then it would seriously hamper their military efforts the following year. This assessment was important for two reasons: firstly, British planners wanted to open the front in 1942, not later, and the JIC paper supported the idea that time was of the essence; and, secondly, it reinforced the belief that a successful attack in north Africa would keep open important shipping and supply routes.[11]

As planning continued for the invasion, now codenamed Operation Torch, the JIC continued to issue assessments. One constant throughout was the belief that if the Allies attacked north Africa, then Germany would have to transfer reinforcements from other areas. Furthermore, given the assumption that Germany would need to rest parts of its army for maintenance and recuperation in late 1942, it would be realistic to expect a quick and decisive victory.[12]

An example of the sort of assessment produced by the JIC is reproduced below.[13] The paper was originally prepared for the planners but was considered so important that it was also passed to the COS, who approved it unreservedly. The lengthy report covered several crucial aspects: the reaction to an invasion in north African countries; the levels of resistance to be expected; the critical importance of achieving surprise; and the effect if delayed. These were vitally important questions and, unsurprisingly, the paper was well received.

The assessment was symbolic of the papers produced at this time. In addition to specific papers on how an Allied attack would affect Germany's war efforts more broadly, the JIC also issued tactical analyses, based on Ultra decrypts and for the specific use of the planners and force commanders.[14] Topics included forecasts of German troop dispositions, the nature of the opposition to be expected, and suitable locations for the invasion. As the date for the invasion approached, the JIC's work took on greater importance, with a series of papers focused on whether or not the Germans were aware of Allied plans.[15] By and large, these various types of assessment have proven to be remarkably accurate.

In the early hours of 8 November 1942, the weeks and months of preparation were put into action when British and American forces launched a multi-pronged attack on the coast of north Africa. In the aftermath General Dwight Eisenhower, responsible for Allied forces in north Africa, personally asked for his gratitude to be conveyed to the JIC. He congratulated the committee on the 'invaluable help given', particularly 'the regular flow of information [which] has enabled planning to be kept up to date'.[16] Operation Torch was the first military plan that involved the JIC in a detailed and central way. Information provided under the JIC umbrella ensured that those responsible for strategic planning were kept abreast of the most detailed intelligence available. Here was a JIC that, for the first time, was properly and effectively integrated with those it was designed to inform.

> Circulation of this paper has been strictly limited.
> Issued for the personal use of File
> TO BE KEPT UNDER LOCK AND KEY
> It is requested that special care may be taken to ensure the secrecy of this document.
>
> **Copy No. 39**
> *Circulated for consideration of the Chiefs of Staff*
>
> JIC(42)304(O)(FINAL)
> AUGUST, 1942.
> WAR CABINET
> JOINT INTELLIGENCE SUB-COMMITTEE
> OPERATION "TORCH" – INTELLIGENCE APPRECIATION
> Note by the Secretary
>
> The attached report, which has been forwarded for the consideration of the Chiefs of Staff Committee, is circulated in Final form. Will departments please return all previous drafts to the Secretary.
> (Signed) DENIS CAPEL-DUNN.
> Great George Street, S.W.1
> 7TH AUGUST, 1942.
>
> *Circulated for the consideration of the Chiefs of Staffs*
> JIC(42)304(O)(FINAL)
> AUGUST, 1942.
> WAR CABINET
> JOINT INTELLIGENCE SUB-COMMITTEE
> OPERATION "TORCH" – INTELLIGENCE APPRECIATION
> Report by the Joint Intelligence Sub-Committee
>
> NOTE: This paper was prepared in the first instance for the Joint Planning Staff, but we consider that the Chiefs of Staff committee should see it. Its form does not lend itself to a summary of conclusions such as is normally included in appreciations of enemy intentions.

In this report we appreciate the scale of opposition likely to be met by an Allied expedition against French North Africa this year. We would like to draw special attention to the important factors given in Part III (page 11).

PART I - REACTIONS OF COUNTRIES AFFECTED

France
1. The Vichy Government will remain subservient to the Germans and will order resistance in French North Africa and may support that resistance with the French Fleet. It is unlikely that this will lead to a declaration of war on the united Nations by the Vichy Government. They will be reluctant to burn their boats with America. An added deterrent will be their fear of air bombardment.
2. The arrival of the Allies in force in French North Africa and their rapid success must appear to the majority of the French people as the first step in the liberation of their country. The revival of hope inspired by this will increase the embarrassment of the Vichy Government and add to their difficulties of internal security.

French North Africa

3. The civil authorities and the military command in French North Africa will comply with Vichy French orders to resist until they can plead force majeure. Their forces will lack the zest to fight or the means to prolong resistance. Many of them will have an underlying sympathy for the Americans.
4. The French Command in North Africa must have doubts as to the sympathies and will to fight of many under their command. Although discipline may tell in the initial stages, in face of a resolute Allied thrust with powerful forces, resistance is likely to collapse speedily. Once resistance has collapsed the French, even though they may not enthusiastically collaborate, are unlikely, by sabotage or otherwise, seriously to interfere with consolidation by the Allies.
5. It is unlikely that success in Algeria will be immediately followed by the surrender of Tunisia and Morocco. As far as the French are concerned the will to resist

is unlikely to vary as between Morocco and Algeria or between specific points in Morocco itself.

6. The native population as a whole may be expected at the outset to welcome the Allied forces as deliverers from the French rulers. Subsequently when hostilities have died down the natives may become disillusioned though this disillusionment may be offset to some extent if economic benefits are forthcoming. This would not extend to native troops.

Spain

7. It has been Spain's consistent policy to keep out of the war. The predominant influence however would be Germany's ability to bring military pressure to bear. If in the absence of this pressure the Franco Government wished to react against successful Allied landings in North Africa, there would be powerful influences in Spain which would exercise a restraining influence at least in the early days of the operation. Spain has not yet recovered from the Civil War and is in no position politically, militarily or economically to fight a War of national effort. The Allies have a powerful weapon in Spain's knowledge of her dependence upon the goodwill of the Allies for supplies of the essentials of life.

8. Immediate Spanish reactions would, therefore, probably be confined to reinforcing Spanish Morocco while waiting to see how the operation progressed. If it were swift and successful and Spanish territory were respected, the Spaniards would be unlikely to take any provocative action. If and when, however, Germany could concentrate on the Spanish frontier powerful land and air forces, she could probably force the Franco Government to accede to her demands for passage of troops. In such circumstances that Government would probably prefer to throw in their lot wholly with the Germans rather than to adopt half measures.

9. In the meantime Spain would be unlikely to risk an open breach with the Allies by allowing the Germans to operate from air bases in the South. Although German pressure upon Spain would no doubt be intensified if the Allies extend their present use of the Gibraltar aerodrome to include offensive operations against North Africa, there is no reason to suppose that this in itself would seriously influence Spanish policy. The Spanish Government

would, of course, consider it necessary to fire at British aircraft which flew over Spanish territory.
10. Faced with Allied invasion of North Africa and with increased German pressure, the Franco Government would be in a difficult position. Until the Germans can give military support, and provided our operation is successful, the Allies will be able to put stronger pressure on the Franco Government than the Germans, with German support the Franco Government, Fascist in character and avowedly favourable to the Axis, would, if forced to a decision, side with the Germans. In the opinion of the Foreign Office it is impossible to say whether an alternative government would result in more or less resistance to German pressure. It is impossible to say whether Spanish Morocco and the Canary Islands would follow the lead of the Franco Government.

Italy

11. The Italian Government, although anxious to gain a footing in Tunisia, which they have long coveted, would be doubtful of the effect on the French of the arrival of Italian troops there. For military reasons the Germans are unlikely to use Italian troops.
12. The Italians will be preoccupied with the threat to the homeland. The "Fleet in being" complex will persist. The Italians will not he prepared to denude the Home Front of air force defences in face of the threat of heavy scale bombing of their cities.
13. Italy's participation is likely, therefore, to be confined to the operation of air forces based on Italy, Sicily and Sardinia, and to naval forces operating within range of their own shore based aircraft. In addition, defences in Sardinia and Sicily would he strengthened.
14. Although the Italian Government and Military Commands will continue to conform to German strategy, there will be some in Italy who will covertly welcome the Allies' action.

Germany

15. The arrival of Allied forces in strength in French North Africa, particularly if it takes place as early as October, would face the Germans with a difficult

strategic situation. They are unlikely by that time to have been able to disengage from the Russian front for immediate action in a new theatre of war any substantial land and air forces. They cannot ignore the possible repercussions of the Allied action in France, Italy, the Balkans and even Spain. They cannot be certain that the Allies will not attempt a landing on the continent of Europe. In short, they cannot afford to weaken garrison troops in occupied territories. On the contrary, they may find it necessary to increase them and to keep a more vigilant eye on unoccupied France and Italy. They might even have to occupy the former and stiffen the latter by garrison troops.

16. Rommel's position, if he is still operating in Egypt will be difficult. The need to maintain him there will limit the possibilities of a German move into Tunisia.

17. Short though the sea passage to Tunisia is, the Germans will not, in the light of past experience, relish being dependent on sea communications, with Italian convoys manned largely by Italian crews and escorted by the Italian Navy. Recent events have shown that the Germans suffer from delay, hesitancy and even non-cooperation on the part of the Italians.

18. Germany will be most anxious to avoid the additional military commitment of occupying and garrisoning unoccupied France and will therefore wish to avoid acting without official French concurrence. Even with such concurrence, she will anticipate that her troops will not be welcomed by the French in North Africa. Even if, as is probable, she has obtained French agreement in advance to move German troops to Tunisia in the event of an Allied landing in North Africa, the need to rely to some extent on French co-operation will lead to delays, difficulties and misunderstandings.

19. Whatever military action the Germans decide upon they will undoubtedly bring all possible pressure to bear on the Vichy Government to put up maximum resistance in North Africa. They will not, however, put demands to the Vichy Government with which even that Government could not comply without risk of losing control of the French people.

20. They will exert such pressure as they can against Spain to interfere with Allied operations and will almost certainly protest violently if the Spaniards allow the

WORLD WAR II AND THE ROLE OF INTELLIGENCE

Allies to use the aerodrome at Gibraltar as an operational base. They may press the Franco Government to declare war against the Allies and to accept German naval and air co-operation. They would probably, however, not feel confident of being able to persuade the Spaniards to declare war or even to acquiesce in the use by them of air bases in Southern Spain until they were in a position to back such demands by force.

PART II - ENEMY FORCES LIKELY TO BE MET
INTRODUCTION

A - <u>FRENCH</u>

21. <u>Naval</u>
(a) The following are the total forces considered to be normally in full commission:-

MEDITERRANEAN	WEST AFRICA
1 Battlecruiser	4 6" Cruisers
4 8" Cruisers	6 Contre torpilleurs
3 6" Cruisers	5 Destroyers
17 Contre torpilleurs	19 Submarines
9 Destroyers	
22 Submarines	

A large part of this fleet is based on Toulon but would be available for operations in North African waters.

(b) Other heavy units exist but are not considered to be effective. They are:-

(i) The 26 year old battleship "PROVENCE" (modernised in 1933) now being used for training purposes at TOULON. Reduced crew but armament fully effective. At least 5 days to prepare for sea.

(ii) The battlecruiser "DUNKERQUE" believed to be under repair at TOULON until January, 1943.

(iii) The battleship "RICHELIEU" at DAKAR Could be used as a fighting unit though her maximum speed is probably only 23 knots.

(iv) The battleship "JEAN BART" at CASABLANCA with only one 15" turret.

(c) The efficiency of even the better units is estimated being not more than 60% by British standards. Oil fuel stocks are known to be low.

(d) It is believed that the Fleet would obey the

orders of Vichy Government and would fight. Their activities, however, would be in defence of French North Africa.

22. <u>Military</u>

(a) The French forces in North Africa, details of which are given in Appendix 'D' may be summarised as the equivalent of:-

MOROCCO .... 4 divisions
ALGERIA .... 3 divisions
TUNISIA .... 1 division.

Increase in the above from reserves in North Africa is likely owing to lack of equipment.

(b) The bulk of the troops are disposed to defend landings or near the ports of North Africa. The major concentrations are located at TUNIS, CONSTANTINE, ALGIERS, ORAN, FEZ, MEKNES, CASABLANCA and MARRAKECH. Owing to difficult and inadequate lateral communications, the great distances involved (CASABLANCA to ORAN is some 500 miles, and ORAN to ALGIERS is 250 miles), and also to the shortage of coal, petrol and any rapid major redistribution of forces would be difficult.

(c) Troops are poorly equipped and are particularly short of A.F.V's, also of field A.A. and anti-tank artillery and ammunition for all arms. It is estimated that there is only through ammunition for about three weeks' sustained fighting at maximum. This position could be improved by the release of stocks in France at present under Armistice control. Few units, except mechanised cavalry and tank units, are motorised.

(d) It is estimated that, at the most, the equivalent of ten ill equipped French divisions from Metropolitan France might be available for transfer to French North Africa, but only a few rather ill equipped units are likely to be sent.

23. <u>Air</u>

(a) The French air force in North Africa, details of which was given in Appendix 'A', amounts to approximately 500 aircraft of all types. It would be possible with German consent to reinforce this from unoccupied France with an additional 120 aircraft.

(b) The types of French aircraft are obsolescent, the best fighter being the Dewoitine 520 with a performance slightly inferior to the Hurricane I, and the bombers with a similar performance to Blenheims.

(c) Stocks of bombs, ammunition and petrol are believed to-day to be adequate for some two months intensive operations. There is reason to believe, however, that during the next month or two these stocks may be further increased from Unoccupied France.

(d) Serviceability is high, probably about 70 per cent. The standard of training is not high, due to limitations on flying caused by necessity to conserve petrol. Morale is good. Lack of M.T. would hamper operational efficiency of squadrons as ground staffs could not be quickly moved.

(e) Lack of combat experience and indifferent organisation is likely to prevent the French air force from carrying out sustained operations in face of modern Allied machines and technique. Doubts of the French High command as to the sympathies of individual pilots are likely also to be a hampering factor.

B - SPANISH

24. The Spanish Fleet is now disposed as follows:-
Ferrol:
    18" Cruiser
    16" Cruiser
    8 modern Destroyers and 3 older Destroyers
    2 Eolo class minelayers
    2 Vulcano class minelayers.
Cartagena:
    6 modern Destroyers and 1 older Destroyer
    1 Vulcano class minelayer
    1 modern Sloop
    5 Submarines
6 M.T.B's are based on Cadiz, 1 at Algeciras, and 1 at Tangier; 1 Vulcano Minelayer in Canaries.

25. The activities of the Fleet are strictly limited by the fuel shortage, but it is thought that there may be an accumulated reserve sufficient to enable the Fleet to operate for a short period. Discipline is the best of the three services and there is a wholesome respect for the British Navy.

26. The general feeling is friendly, especially among the officers, many of whom have personal connections with us.

27. It is considered that the friendly Spanish Fleet will take no action at all unless Spain declares war against the United Nations, and even then will only carry out a purely defensive role such as the convoying of coastal traffic.

28. The Army in SPANISH MOROCCO is organised in an army of two corps and comprises some 135,000 men, including 14,000 in labour battalions. (See Appendix 'E'). Reinforcement of up to 25,000 men might possibly be sent from SPAIN following our landing in NORTH AFRICA. There is a great lack of modern equipment, including M.T. and the standard of training is low. Though ill-equipped by modern standard, the troops can be expected to fight well for any cause in which they believe.

29. The Spanish Air Force consists of some 460 aircraft of all types. Its fighting value is negligible. Through lack of aviation spirit it has for some time been virtually grounded.

C - ITALIAN

30. The normal effective strength of the Italian Navy (Ships in commission) is as follows:-
    2 15" Battleships
    3 12.6" Battleships
    3 8" Cruisers
    6 6" Cruisers
    2 5.3" Cruisers
    4 Destroyers
    42 Torpedo boats
    60 Submarines
    90 M.A.S.

2 additional 15" battleships under construction, of which one may by October be in commission.

31. The Battleships are concentrated at Taranto, Cruisers detached to Messina, Naples and/or Cagliari (Sardinia) and Navarino (Greece).

32. Naval morale has risen slightly recently with German stiffening and consequent on the reduced threat from our fleet, the Italian naval surface forces have been showing more enterprise than formerly. If faced, however,

with an equal or superior force they are not likely to show any more aggressive spirit or resolution than they have done in the past.
33. The Italian army is unlikely to be used for operations in French North Africa. Its main preoccupation is likely to become defence and reinforcement of Sicily and Sardinia.
34. Particulars of the Italian air forces likely to be used are dealt with in Appendix 'C'.

D - GERMAN

35. German naval surface forces are unlikely to move to the Mediterranean. Their forces already in this area as:-
   Submarines - 16-20 operating in Eastern Mediterranean off Libyan and Egyptian coast
   E-boats - 7-10 operating off North Africa.
Both U-boats and E-boats are more efficient and enterprising than the Italians.
36. The German land force will in October still be fully committed in Occupied Europe, Libya and Russia. There is unlikely to be a strategic reserve in Europe which is not already committed, and everywhere the army will be at full stretch.
37. Germany is unlikely, therefore, to redispose her land forces strategically merely to counter a possible Allied assault on North Africa. This depends, however, largely on the success of the Allies' cover plans and upon whether the Germans can be kept guessing as to the threat to the Continent, by deceptive action and if possible by diversionary raids. It is not until she definitely knows that the assault is about to take place that she will be constrained to take counter action.
38. There exists the possibility, however, that by October, Russia will be in a sufficiently weakened state for Germany to have pulled out up to, say, 10 divisions and to have brought them back to Germany ready to counter any Allied action which she might expect in Europe during the autumn. This must certainly be her aim, and its fulfilment is entirely dependent on the way the Russian campaign develops in the next two months. This strategic reserve would be likely to be held centrally in Germany or France.
39. By October the German Air Force, which will have

been heavily engaged on the Russian Front for nearly 18 months in addition to operations in the Western and Mediterranean areas, is likely to be at a low ebb. Although the first-line strength may be maintained at some 4,000 aircraft, it will be a force without depth and in need of a period for re-equipment. It may be found to be weak in strength, low in serviceability and difficulty will be experienced in making forces available for sustained operations in a new theatre of war.

PRE-ASSAULT PHASE

40. It is difficult to know whether the Germans will attempt to reinforce the Central Mediterranean area effectively prior to the date of assault. A great deal will depend on the effectiveness of strategic surprise, both as to objective and time. Although the German High Command is bound to be aware some considerable time before the date of assault that a large-scale operation is being planned and although they will suspect French North Africa as a possible objective, they may be uncertain as to the exact locality of the attack until a very late stage.

41. Commitments elsewhere and the limited nature of their resource will, it is thought, prevent them from actually moving reinforcements to the Central Mediterranean area until they are certain that French North Africa is the real objective. We think it reasonable to assume, therefore, that no move is likely to be made until Day -4, by which date air reconnaissance will have disclosed the direction in which the convoy is sailing.

42. Meanwhile the French, faced with the possibility of attacks against the Mediterranean or Atlantic North African Seaboard, or possibly both, will be in a state of alertness but are unlikely to change the disposition of their force until it is known for certain which is the area of the main attack. They may rush over to North Africa some extra equipment supplies as a precaution.

ASSAULT OR 1ST PHASE (say D minus 4 to D 14)

43. At any time after D minus 4 we must be prepared for a move of the Toulon squadron to Oran with the concurrence of the Germans. At the same time, the French may

dispose their available submarines in the Eastern and Western approaches to the Straits of Gibraltar. Surface forces based on Casablanca will probably put to sea and, in face of overwhelming force, would probably retire to Dakar. The force at Dakar is unlikely to play any part.

44. Whilst it is possible that the Italian Fleet may endeavour to interfere with our convoys, it is not likely that they will risk bringing their heavy forces to the westward outside the protection afforded by shore-based aircraft. There is a danger from submarines to our ships on passage and when lying off beaches, but it is not considered that the number of submarines in the area could be materially increased during the period of the initial assaults. A subsequent build up of the scale of attack is to be expected.

45. So far as land forces are concerned, the only serious opposition likely to be met is from French forces already in North Africa, the dispositions of which are shown in Appendix "D". The mobility of these forces will be restricted by lack of M.T. and petrol.

46. In addition to the French air forces based in North Africa, attacks will be sustained from German and Italian air forces based on Sicily and Sardinia. The estimated scale of these attacks is set out in Appendix "D".

2ND PHASE (say D 15 to D 30)

47. Assuming the fall of Oran and Algiers, Allied troops not engaged in mopping-up operations in Algeria are likely to encounter the next serious opposition in Tunisia. If success in Algeria has been rapid and overwhelming and it has become known that the expedition is predominantly American, French resistance in Tunisia might be half-hearted or even collapse altogether. We cannot, however, count on this.

48. The Germans will have every incentive to attempt to forestall the Allies in establishing themselves in the key position of Tunisia. Their ability to do this will depend both on the rapidity of the Allied advance and on the forces they can make available* in the time.

49. The quickest means of reinforcement would be by air. No trained German air landing formations, however, are

---

* See Appendix "F"

likely to be available other than those already in Libya. Transport aircraft at the expense of other duties could be made available at short notice to ferry between 2,000 and 2,500 troops per day from SICILY to AFRICA, if they were all devoted to carriage of personnel, and all but light equipment were taken by sea. The transport aircraft could be assembled within about 48 hours of the decision to do so. Italian troops would be available immediately, but it is unlikely that these would be used in view of possible French reactions.

50. One German Infantry Division and the lorried infantry of an armoured division from France could begin to reach SICILY after one week, when a flow of 2,000 men per day could start. On this assumption approximately 14,000 lightly armed infantry might be available in TUNISIA in 14 days from the order to move.

51. Germany is heavily engaged and will continue to be heavily engaged in supplying Rommel's forces. She will therefore have only limited air transport to spare. In any case Germany would be unable regularly to supply and maintain by air any considerable forces in TUNISIA. For regular maintenance sea transport would have to be used. Further, the operation of transport aircraft from SICILY whose aerodrome facilities will be fully utilised for operational aircraft would prejudice reinforcement of the latter. Accordingly a steady flow, for any length of time, of 2,000 troops per day by air may not be practicable.

52. The scale and timing of any possible enemy sea-borne reinforcements are set out in Appendix "F", which shows that first elements might arrive in TUNISIA about two weeks after the assault. A complete division could not arrive and be operationally effective before about four to seven weeks after the assault.

53. If by the end of a week from the date of the assault the German High Command are faced with a situation in which the Allies are well established in Algeria and are developing a threat towards TUNISIA and Rommel is fully engaged in the East, they are likely to hesitate before attempting to forestall the Allies by themselves moving against TUNISIA. The German assessment of the threat from aircraft and light naval forces based on Malta and Algeria would affect their decision.

54. Whether or not an attempt is made to move land forces

into TUNISIA, it is not considered likely that during this phase the enemy would operate air forces in TUNISIA (with the possible exception of some fighter aircraft if land forces are moved in) since no advantage could be gained by moving long range bomber and other types from their already well-established bases in SICILY and SARDINIA.

55. The establishment of Axis air forces in Southern Spain and the Balearics is considered improbable during this period. Operationally there would not be sufficient advantages to base aircraft on the Balearics which would be deficient in fuel, bomb-stocks and facilities generally.

THIRD PHASE - LONG TERM POLICY

56. Assuming that French resistance had been overcome and that the Allies were established in Tunisia during the Second Phase, the alternatives open to the Germans if they were to attempt to recover the position would be combined operations based on Sicily or a move through Spain with a view to closing the Straits, and subsequent operations through Spanish Morocco. For maintenance and supply reasons we do not consider that a counter-offensive based on Tripoli (L) is a possible course of action.

   (a) <u>Combined operation from SICILY</u>
   Once we were established in TUNISIA the Germans would have to stage a large scale combined operation in order to turn us out. This operation could not be mounted before the Allies were in too strong a position to make it too hazardous to attempt.

   (b) <u>A move through SPAIN</u>
   Formations would have to be withdrawn from Russia for this operation. The size of the force required will depend on the attitude of Spain. The following estimate is made of the time taken from the date of the decision to move, allowing for resting and refitting.

	Forces Required	Time required to reach Southern Spain
Should Spain resist	14 divisions	3 to 5 months
Should Spain acquiesce	6 - 8 divisions	2 to 3 months

NOTE: One to two divisions might be made available from France and, with Spanish acquiescence, might reach Southern Spain in 3 to 4 weeks.

We assume that, if the Germans entered Spain from the North, we would have to occupy Spanish Morocco. The above forces would therefore constitute no immediate threat to North Africa, but only to GIBRALTAR. A threat to ALGERIA or SPANISH MOROCCO (apart from air forces based on Southern Spain) could only arise through a combined operation. In face of powerful Allied air defences in Spanish Morocco, we do not believe that the Germans would attempt this combined operation but would have to be content with the threat they themselves could mount against the Straits of Gibraltar with their air forces in Southern Spain.

PART III - IMPORTANT FACTORS AFFECTING THE COURSE OF THE OPERATION

57. As a result of the above appreciation, we are impressed by the following factors which are likely to exercise an important influence on the course of the operation:-

a) Date. The date by which the operation takes place is all important. Whatever the result of this summer's campaign in Russia, the Germans are bound to start withdrawing substantial land and air forces for resting and refitting some time this Autumn, and we cannot count on this being delayed, at any rate so far as Air Forces are concerned, later than mid October. By the beginning of November Germany's fears of invasion of the Continent this year may be at rest.

b) Initial success. Neither French North Africa nor Spain will risk incurring German displeasure until they are satisfied that the Allies mean business and have the forces to establish themselves firmly in North Africa. French resistance, therefore, and Spanish independence in face of German pressure will be influenced by the initial success of the Allies. Last but not least, Germany's difficult position as to whether or not to risk moving troops into Tunisia will be governed by the speed of the Allied approach to Tunisia. The importance of overwhelming force, to gain initial success, must be stressed.

c) <u>Strategic Surprise</u>. Initial success, in turn, is largely dependent upon strategic surprise. Until Vichy and the German High Command are convinced beyond doubt that the expedition is destined for French North Africa, no German troops or air forces are likely to be moved there. In face of their other commitments and subject to paragraph (a) above, it is unlikely that any troops would be moved to a preparatory assembly area such as Sicily.

d) <u>Use of U.S. Troops</u>. There is no question but that the will to resist invasion by U.S. Troops would be weaker than the will to resist invasion by the British.

e) <u>Preparatory steps</u>. French North Africa may provide scope for discreet preparatory moves, particularly by the United States. If found practicable, personal contact, bribery, infiltration of personnel under guise of commercial relationship and even some form of Trojan Horse, methods should facilitate the initial assault but such steps must be very discreet, as strategic surprise is of primary importance.

f) <u>Allied Policy towards Franco Government</u>. In the initial stages the Franco Government have more to fear from Allied action than from German.

g) <u>Propaganda</u>, allied to military strategy, towards France, French North Africa and Spain will be of the utmost importance.

h) <u>Supplies to North Africa</u>. Since one of the difficulties of our operation will be communications and supply, any arrangements that can be made to time the arrival of ships from North America carrying oil and coal so as immediately to precede or coincide with our assault, may be of great subsequent assistance to ourselves. Between now and the time of the operation, however, it would be important that French North Africa should not receive supplies likely to stiffen French resistance.

58. The following Appendices are attached:-

Appendix "A" - Strength and Dispositions of French Air Forces.

Appendix "B" - Strength and Dispositions of Spanish Air Forces.

Appendix "C" – Strengths and Dispositions of German and Italian Air Forces.
Appendix "D" – Distribution and Strength of French Land Forces.
Appendix "E" – Distribution and Strength of Spanish, Moroccan Army.
Appendix- "F" – German Land Forces Available to Oppose the Operation.

(Signed)   J. H. GODFREY
(")   F. H. N. DAVIDSON
(")   C. E. H. MEDHURST
(")   C. G. VICKERS
(")   C. BRAMWELL
(for V. CAVENDISH BENTINCK)

Great George Street, S.W.1.
7TH AUGUST, 1942.

Appendix "A"

FRENCH AIR FORCES

1. The estimated strength and disposition of the French Air forces in North Africa at the beginning of October are likely to be as follows:-

	Fighter	Bomber	Recce	Naval	Total
TUNISIA	33	–	13	29	75
ALGERIA	69	51	21	6	147
MOROCCO	152	122	26	–	300
	254	173	60	35	522

2. Faced with the possibility of attacks against their Mediterranean and Atlantic North American seaboards, it is unlikely that the disposition of the French Air Force would be substantially changed, at any rate until it was known for certain which was the area of the main attack.

3. The above forces might be reinforced by some 3 bomber and 3 fighter groups (29 L.R.Bs. and 78 S.E.F.) despatched to North Africa from Unoccupied France either immediately prior to the date of the assault, if the French had obtained reliable intelligence as to the projected operations, or immediately after the assault.

Part of these reinforcements might become available within two days and the whole force within 10 days of the decision to transfer them.

4. The types of French aircraft are obsolescent, the best Fighter being the Dewoitine 520 with a performance slightly inferior to the Hurricane I and the Bombers with a similar performance to Blenheims.

5. Stocks of bombs, ammunition and petrol are believed today to be adequate for some two months intensive operations. There is reason to believe, however, that during the next month or two these stocks may be further increased from Unoccupied France.

6. Serviceability is high, probably about 70 per cent. The standard of training is not high, due to limitations of flying imposed by necessity to conserve petrol. Morale is good. Lack of M.T. would hamper operational efficiency of squadrons as ground staffs could not be quickly moved.

APPENDIX "B"

SPANISH AIR FORCES

The estimated first line strength and disposition of the Spanish Air Forces at the beginning of October, 1942 are likely to be as follows:-

Region	Bomber	Fighter	Recce.	Seaplanes	Total
Peninsula	115	183	12	6	316
Belearics	12	18	–	11	41
Spanish Morocco	–	17	39	7	63
Rio de Oro (and Canary Islands)	11	28	–	3	42
	138	246	51	27	462

The fighting value of the Spanish Air Force is negligible. Since March 1942 the Air Force has been virtually grounded owing to lack of aviation spirit and although within the last few weeks activity has very slightly increased, it is not thought that there will be any improvement in the fighting efficiency by the beginning of October. Serviceability is not above 35%.

APPENDIX "C"
GERMAN AND ITALIAN AIR FORCES.

1. The scales of attack given in this appreciation are based on that normally attained by the German Air Force. Experience during the last 12-18 months indicates that neither strength nor serviceability are maintained in the Mediterranean area as efficiently as in other theatres. The figures which are given therefore probably represent the maximum which it is possible for the G.A.F. to reach, and no account has been taken of the likely diversion of aircraft against Malta or for shipping escort to Libya which are incalculable factors today.

2. The scales of attack to which the assaulting forces are likely to be subjected fall into three phases:-
   First Phase. During the approach to the objective and for a period of approximately a fortnight thereafter before reinforcements can begin to be operational in the Central Mediterranean.
   Second Phase. While the Allies are still in process of consolidating their position in Algeria and extending their operations into Tunisia.
   Third Phase. If the Allies succeed in establishing themselves in North Africa, up to and including Tunisia, so that the Germans, in order to evict the Allies if they so decide, are forced to mount combined operations based on Italy and Sicily through Spain.

First Phase

3. Estimate of the Axis Air Forces likely to be available in the Central Mediterranean during the First phase.

	SICILY		SARDINIA.	
	G.A.F.	I.A.F.	G.A.F.	I.A.F.
L.R. Bombers	105-165	100+	30	50-100⁻
Bomber Recce.	15	10	5	20
Dive Bombers	-	15	-	-
S.E. Fighters	30	120	-	30
Coastal	-	50	-	30
	150-210	295	35	130-180

+ including 30 torpedo-carrying aircraft
- including 30-50   "   "   "

Estimated strength - 90 percent of I.E.
Estimate serviceability - 50 percent of I.E.

4. <u>Reinforcements</u> (taken into account in the higher figures above)

On its becoming clear by D minus 4 that the operation was likely to take place against the French North African Coast, a reinforcement of 60 German long range bombers could be moved from the Western Front and become operational from Sicily by D 3 to D 14.

The Italian reinforcement of Sardinia up to a maximum of 100 long range bombers, of which 50 would be torpedo bombers, could be effected by D minus 2 and would be operational during the whole of the First Phase.

5. <u>Scale of Effort</u>

The average daily scale of effort per 24 hours by the combined Axis forces during the First Phase is estimated as follows:-

<u>oran</u> - 30 sorties by long range bombers and torpedo carrying aircraft.

or <u>ALGIERS</u> - 100-120 sorties by long range bombers and torpedo carrying aircraft.

or <u>TUNISIA</u> - 120-140 sorties by long range bombers and torpedo carrying aircraft. In addition up to 15 Dive Bomber sorties and 120 S.E. Fighter sorties

<u>CASABLANCA</u> - Out of range for all types of aircraft.

Second Phase

6. <u>Estimate of the Axis Air Forces likely to be available in the Central Mediterranean during the Second Phase</u>.

	SICILY		SARDINIA	
	G.A.F.	I.A.F.	G.A.F.	I.A.F.
L.R. Bombers	165-195	100	30	100
Bomber Recce.	15	10	10	20
Dive Bombers	-	15	-	-
S.E. Fighters	30	120	-	30
Coastal	-	50	-	20
	210-240	295	40	180

Estimated strength 85-95 percent of I.E.
Estimated serviceability 45-50 per cent of I.E.

7. <u>Reinforcements</u> (taken into account in the higher figures above)

There would be a further increase between D14 and D21 of 30 G.A.F. long range bombers operating from Sicily, raising the total G.A.F. long range bomber force to 225 aircraft. Otherwise there would be no change in the forces available during the first phase.

8. <u>Scale of Effort</u>

These reinforcements would not affect the scale of attack on ORAN, but would increase that against ALGIERS and TUNISIA by up to 10 sorties per 24 hours in each case.

9. <u>Move to Tunisia</u>

It is not considered likely that the Axis would operate air forces in TUNISIA, with the possible exception of some fighter aircraft if German land forces were moved there, since no advantage could be gained by moving long range bomber and other types from their already well-established bases in Sicily and Sardinia.

10. <u>Balearics</u>

The establishment of Axis air forces in Southern Spain and the Balearics is considered improbable during this phase.

<u>Third Phase</u>

11. <u>Estimate of the Axis Air Forces likely to be available in the Central Mediterranean during the third phase</u>

The forces likely to be engaged during November and December are estimated as follows:-

	SICILY		SARDINIA	
	G.A.F.	I.A.F.	G.A.F.	I.A.F.
Long Range bombers	195-255	100	30	100
Bomber Recce	15-30	10	10	20
Dive bombers	0-30	15	-	-
S.E. Fighters	30-80	120	-	30
T.E. Fighters	0-15	-	15	-
Coastal	50	50	-	20
	290-460	295	55	170

Estimated strength - 80 percent of I.E.
Estimated serviceability - 45-50 percent of I.E.

12. **Reinforcements (taken into account in the higher figures above).**

During the Third Phase, estimated to cover the period November - December, it is considered that the G.A.F. in the Central Mediterranean could be reinforced as follows:-

	November	December
Long Range Bombers	30	30
Dive Bombers	-	30
S.E. Fighters	20	30
T.E. Fighters	30	-
	80 aircraft	90 aircraft

After December any increase of the G.A.F. in Sicily would be unlikely in view of the restricted aerodrome accommodation, whilst shipping and supply difficulties would make the establishment of any greater forces in Sardinia improbable.

13. **Effect of Postponement of the Operation form the beginning of October to the beginning of November**

The postponement of the operation to the beginning of November would make it possible for the G.A.F. to strengthen their forces available throughout the First phase by approximately 30 long range bombers and 20 S.E. fighters, but would not affect the Italian Air Force. Thus throughout the First Phase, if in November, the G.A.F. would consist of:-

	SICILY	SARDINIA
L.R. Bombers	195	30
Bomber Recce	15	5
Dive Bombers	-	-
S.E. Fighters	50	-
	260	35

During the Second Phase G.A.F. reinforcements could come into operation at an earlier stage but would not differ materially from those already given. This would result in a more rapid increase in the scale of effort and by the end of the Second Phase this could be approaching that likely to be attained towards the end of the Third Phase with the operation beginning on 1st October.

14. G.A.F. Operations in Spain

Even assuming Spanish acquiescence it is unlikely that air attack would be encountered from the G.A.F. during the first week of the operation. A striking force of not more than 60 long range bombers could however become operational during the second week. These would be at the expense of reinforcements to Sicily unless the Germans were prepared to reduce even further their depleted forces on Western front.

By February, a force of some 450 aircraft could be made available to support a move by land forces through Spain and to support combined operations thence against North Africa.

APPENDIX "D"
FRENCH LAND FORCES IN NORTH AFRICA.

	MOROCCO	ALGERIA	TUNISIA
Infantry Regiments	13	14	3
Cavalry Regiments	4	3	2
Mechanised Cavalry Regiments	2	4	1
Field Artillery Regiments	3	4	1
A/A Artillery Regiments	1	1	1
Tank Battalions	2(?)	-	-
Engineer Battalions	2	-	-

In addition - Coast Defence and A/A Artillery at ports.

APPENDIX "E"
SPANISH MOROCCAN ARMY

	EASTERN ZONE	WESTERN ZONE	TOTAL
Army Troops	4,000	27,000	31,000
Labour Units	2,500	11,500	14,000
IX Corps	–	40,500	40,500
X Corps	27,500	–	27,500
Khalifian Troops and Civil Guard (500)	5,500	11,500	17,000
	39,500	90,500	130,000

Note 1: The inter-zone boundary runs southward from VALHUCEMAS. The bulk of the troops in the Western zone is located in the western half of that zone.

Note 2: Khalifian troops are Moors, owing allegiance to the Khalif, and constitute a valuable reserve. In addition, some 40,000 of the army are Moorish troops and Foreign Legionaries – Spain's best fighting material.

APPENDIX "F"
GERMAN LAND FORCES AVAILABLE TO OPPOSE THE OPERATION

1. German troops could be brought from:-
    (i)   Libya
    (ii)   The Aegean area
    (iii) Germany
    (iv)   Occupied France
    (v)   Russia.

The speed of movement will depend on a number of factors, such as the degree of readiness of the troops, the availability of rolling stock, the collection of shipping, and communications generally. The estimates of the timings given below have taken these factors into account so far as it is possible.

In all the above places the troops already there are likely to be a minimum for requirements with little or nothing to spare.

2. Germany might, however, make any of the following areas:-

(a) <u>From France</u>, using French or Italian ports.
1 Armoured Division, which may only be partially re-equipped and rested (from Russia).
1 Infantry Division.
The first elements could arrive in Tunisia about two weeks after our assault had taken place. A complete division would not arrive and be operationally effective before about four to seven weeks after the assault. The second division could be operationally effective some 10-12 weeks after the assault.

(b) <u>From Libya (and Aegean area.)</u> – unless Rommel has met with unexpected success, there will be no German troops available with which to reinforce Tunisia. Units in Italy en route to Libya might be diverted to Tunisia.

(c) From Germany – At a pinch, German could form the equivalent of one weak composite mobile division from the various depot and training formations in Germany. There is also the possibility that one newly raised S.S. Division destined for either the Balkans or Russia might be diverted to North Africa.

These formations could reach North Africa on the same timing basis as those from France.

(d) From Russia – In October, Germany is unlikely to be able to spare more than 2-3 Infantry Divisions for operations in North Africa or Spain. These would probably require some rest and re-equipment, especially for African conditions. They could not be operationally effective, even without rest and re-equipment until two to four months after our assault.

There exists the possibility, however, that by October Russia will be in a sufficiently weakened state for Germany to have pulled out up to, say, 10 divisions for operations in other theatres. The formation of such a strategic reserve must be the aim of the High Command, and its fulfilment is entirely dependent in the way the Russian campaign develops in the next two months.

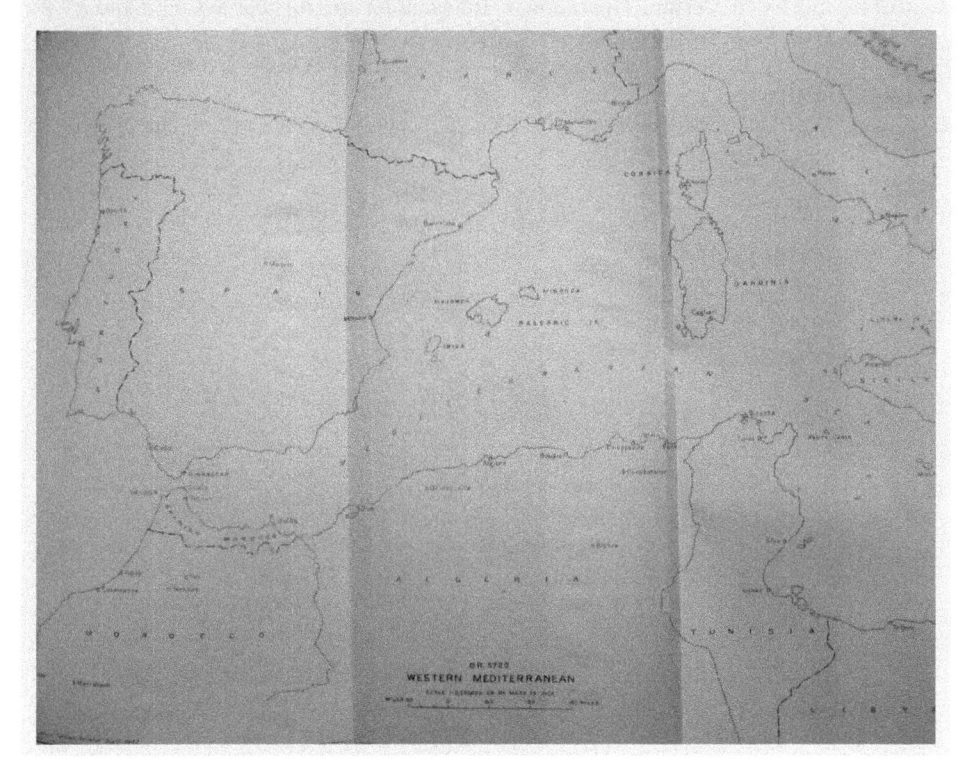

WESTERN MEDITERRANEAN

Notes

1. Hankey to Hoare, 24 April 1940. TNA: CAB 127/375.
2. COS(40)352, 'Urgent Intelligence Reports', 13 May 1940. TNA: CAB 80/11.
3. JIC(40) 29th Meeting, 15 May 1940, TNA: CAB 81/87. Details of the additional yet separate services' intelligence summaries are given in JIC(40)60, 'The Production of Intelligence Summaries by the Joint Intelligence Sub-Committee and Service Departments', 15 May 1940, TNA: CAB 81/96.
4. JIC(41)470, 'Intelligence Section (Operations)', 24 December 1941, TNA: CAB 81/105.
5. JIC(41)462(0), 'Operation Gymnast – Cover', 8 December 1941, TNA: CAB 81/105.
6. JIC(42)34(Final), 'Germany's Intentions', 25 January 1942, TNA: CAB 81/106.
7. For instance, see 'Operation Gymnast – Scale of Air Attack', 10 March 1942, TNA: CAB 119/74.
8. JIC(42) 11th Meeting, 31 March 1942, TNA: CAB 81/90.
9. JIC(42)113(Final), 'Axis Strength and Policy, 1942', 10 April 1942, TNA: CAB 81/107.
10. Michael Howard, *Grand Strategy: History of the Second World War, Vol. IV: August 1942–September 1943* (London: HMSO, 1972).
11. JIC(42)265(Final), 'German strategy in 1942/3', 16 July 1942, TNA: CAB 81/109.

12. JIC(42)299(0)(Final), 'Operations in a Certain Country', 3 August 1942, TNA: CAB 81/109.
13. JIC(42)304(0)(Final), 'Operation "TORCH" – Intelligence Appreciation', 7 August 1942, TNA: CAB 81/109.
14. JIC(42)320(0), 'A Certain Operation – Information for the Force-Commander', 20 August 1942, TNA: CAB 81/109.
15. JIC(42)432(0), 'Recent Intelligence Affecting Operation "TORCH"', 3 November 1942, TNA: CAB 81/111.
16. JIC(42)431(0), 'Letter by Brigadier Mockler-Ferryman on a Certain Operation', 30 October 1942, TNA: CAB 81/111.

4

A POST-WAR INTELLIGENCE MACHINERY

BY 1943 THE JIC had become an integral part of the war effort, having demonstrated its worth in the planning for Operation Torch. Indicating its new-found prestige, the committee had spawned regional offshoots around the world and had provided the model for foreign JICs. In London, too, it had generated a number of subordinate bodies, encompassing everything from support for operations to a special sub-committee on carrier pigeons. Its most important body was the Joint Intelligence Staff – the two teams of drafters that produced the JIC assessments. Presiding over this intelligence empire was a committee of seven full-time members: a Foreign Office chairman, the chief of MI6, senior representatives from MI5 and the Ministry of Economic Warfare, and the directors of intelligence in the War Office, Admiralty and Air Ministry. Throughout the second half of the war the JIC met at least weekly, and held frequent meetings with the Chiefs of Staff Committee and the Joint Planning Staff.

Following the successes of Torch, the JIC was instrumental in providing the intelligence background to the planning for subsequent invasions, including the invasions of Sicily (Husky) and north west France (Overlord). From 1943 onwards it also fulfilled a further role: beginning to plan for the post-war world. One of the problems that had beset pre-war intelligence, despite the JIC's creation, was the intermittent connectedness of the intelligence 'community' and the slowness with which Germany, Italy and Japan had become intelligence priorities. By 1943, however, the increased reputation of the JIC allowed it to proffer its own opinions in such a way that those in Whitehall took note. Furthermore, in his exalted role as Chairman, the diplomat Victor Cavendish-Bentinck proved an indispensable figure at the heart of the intelligence and policy worlds. Perhaps the greatest measure of the wartime JIC's esteem was that it survived.

The committee itself began to look towards the post-war world as early as 1943, a point that predates higher-level conversations within Whitehall on the same subject. The initial discussion was started by Cavendish-Bentinck. He presented his vision for a post-war JIC to committee members in October 1943.

A core question centred on whether the JIC should remain a subordinate body to the COS or, as Cavendish-Bentinck suggested, move outside that reporting chain and assume a broader range of subject matter, not just that of a military concern. This idea, as it transpired, would be too revolutionary for his colleagues: in fact it was not implemented until almost fifteen years later when, in 1957, the JIC moved into the Cabinet Office. Despite Cavendish-Bentinck's best efforts back in 1943, it was extremely difficult, and understandably so, to anticipate a world in which the COS were not the fulcrum.

What did the JIC actually do? A 1944 definition of the JIC's work, endorsed by the committee itself, offers a glimpse:

> The Joint Intelligence Committee in addition to its responsibility for co-ordinating the product of the various collectors of intelligence into the form of agreed advice on enemy intentions, has the additional responsibility of watching, directing and to some extent controlling the British Intelligence organisation throughout the world, so as to ensure that intelligence is received at the most economical cost in time, effort and manpower, and so as to prevent overlapping.[1]

Cavendish-Bentinck, now assisted by Denis Capel-Dunn, the very able wartime JIC Secretary, drafted further documents on the JIC's post-war structure. Their vision encompassed not just the committee itself, but how it should become the centrepiece of Britain's post-war intelligence machinery. This was no self-appointed task. Indeed, the instruction had come from the top, having been signed off by Sir Edward Bridges, the Cabinet Secretary.

Their subsequent report – reproduced below – offered a rare semi-official definition of intelligence. As it stated, 'intelligence is, however, of high importance as a servant of those conducting military operations. It is no more. It cannot win battles, but if it is absent or faulty, battles may easily be lost.' Here was the centrepiece of their argument: not only was the JIC vital but intelligence, as a whole, would be just as crucial after the war as it was currently. In order to make the intelligence machine as effective as possible, the authors argued, 'inter-departmental co-operation' was crucial. The reasoning was straightforward:

> The machine . . . should ensure that the agency best fitted for the collection of a particular type of intelligence continues to collect it. It should ensure that, as far as possible, no other agency should collect the same material from the same source. It should ensure that the material collected is collated with other material bearing on the same subject, so that the best possible evaluation may be made. It should ensure that the information, when received and collated, is made available to all those with a legitimate interest in it and whose work will profit from its receipt. It should be controlled at the top by a strong inter-service and inter-departmental body, representing the needs of producers and consumers of intelligence.

The JIC, perhaps inevitability, was the means to achieve this. Thus, 'we believe that no Department, however experienced and well staffed, has anything to lose by bringing the intelligence directly available to it to the *anvil of discussion* and appreciation among other workers in the same field'.[2]

Members of the JIC continued to revisit these ideas. A revised draft was issued in September 1945, now based on the knowledge that the war was successfully over. By this point neither of the original authors were involved: Cavendish-Bentinck had departed to become ambassador in Warsaw; Capel-Dunn had died in a plane crash on the way back from Montreal. It was accepted that pre-war failings of the intelligence machine had 'led to the need for rapid and largely improvised expansion under the imminent threat'. Furthermore, having now 'set our house in order', the JIC made five recommendations as to the future of British intelligence:

1. An intelligence organisation must be centrally directed and fitted to the system of command.
2. Its collecting agencies must cover the world.
3. Its collating staffs must work as far as possible on an interservice basis.
4. All commanders must be provided with intelligence staffs able to give them the intelligence picture which they require for their tasks.
5. London has been the focal point of British intelligence during the war and should remain the hub of the intelligence organisation.[3]

The report received widespread support: the COS, and Bridges in particular, were effusive in their praise. The report was important in the subsequent creation of the Joint Intelligence Bureau (reformed into the Defence Intelligence Staff in 1964) and it helped install the JIC at the apex of British intelligence. A subsequent report in 1947, written by retired Air Chief Marshal Sir Douglas Evill, labelled the JIC as 'indispensable'.[4] The following year, largely as a consequence, the JIC was elevated to full committee status, the chairman's rank was raised and, for the first time, a proper charter was issued which outlined the central role that the JIC was designed to play:

The Joint Intelligence Committee is given the following responsibilities:-
(i) Under the Chiefs of Staff to plan, and to give higher direction to, operations of defence intelligence and security, to keep them under review in all fields and to report progress.
(ii) To assemble and appreciate available intelligence for presentation as required to the Chiefs of Staff and to initiate other reports as the Committee may deem necessary.
(iii) To keep under review the organisation of intelligence as a whole and in particular the relations of its component parts so as to ensure efficiency, economy and a rapid adaptation to changing requirements, and to advise the Chiefs of Staff of what changes are deemed necessary.
(iv) To co-ordinate the general policy of Joint Intelligence Committees

under United Kingdom Commands overseas and to maintain an exchange of intelligence with them, and to maintain liaison with appropriate Commonwealth intelligence agencies.[5]

Thus, by 1948, the JIC was equipped to deal with the post-war world.

```
      The circulation of this paper has been strictly
        limited. It is issued for the personal use of

TOP SECRET                                        Copy No. 10

                        10 January 1945
                    THE INTELLIGENCE MACHINE
          Report to the Joint Intelligence Sub-Committee
                                                         Page
I.—Introduction                                             2
II.—The Existing Organisation                               5
III.—Organisations whose Policy is now under the
Direction of the J.I.C.—
The Inter-Service Topographical Department                  6
The Intelligence Section (Operations)                       8
The Inter-Service Security Board                            8
The Combined Service Detailed Interrogation Centre          9
The Central Interpretation Unit                            10
IV.—Departments and Organisations not Directed by
the J.I.C. which deal with Intelligence—
The Political Warfare Executive                            11
Postal and Telegraph Censorship                            13
The Secret Services                                        13
The "Y" Services                                           15
The Special Operations Executive                           15
Secret Communications                                      15
R.S.S.                                                     16
V.—The Post-War Intelligence Organisation                  16
ANNEX A.—Survey of Activities of the Information and
Records Branch of Imperial Censorship                      20
ANNEX B.—Chart of proposed Central Intelligence
Organisation.

                        I.—Introduction.
THE Joint Intelligence Sub-Committee invited us to pre-
pare a report on the post-war organisation of intelli-
gence. "Intelligence," in the military sense, covers all
```

kinds of information required for the conduct of war. By natural extension, it has come to cover also security — preventing an enemy or a potential enemy from obtaining information which might help him or harm us. With the coming of total war, the meaning of warfare has been extended to cover a wide area, embracing such fields as those of economic warfare, political and psychological warfare and deception. Those responsible for these latter forms of warfare, no less than those directing our main operations at sea, on land and in the air, require intelligence. Intelligence covers also the means by which information is conveyed, *i.e.*, communications.
2. Before the present war, the Intelligence Branches were not much favoured parts of the Staff in any of the three fighting Services. Indeed, it would be foolish to pretend that even now, in the sixth year of the war, intelligence has not many critics. Intelligence is, however, of high importance as a servant of those conducting military operations. It is no more. It cannot win battles, but if it is absent or faulty, battles may easily be lost. It is important, therefore, that the Intelligence Branch, no less than the branches responsible for the supply of ammunition, fuel and food, and the branches responsible for reinforcement of the forces in the field, should be as efficient as we can make it. Yet no one would be so bold as to contend that our Service Intelligence Staffs entered this war adequately equipped for the task confronting them. There existed no sufficient trained cadre of intelligence officers. Our topographical information was woefully lacking. Fortunately, there existed in the product of the Government Code and Cypher School one certain channel of first-class information, but its full value could not be got unless the machine at the centre was properly equipped to collate and assess it against cognate intelligence from other sources. In the War Office in peace time there was no separate Directorate of Intelligence, and in the Air Ministry the peace-time intelligence organisation was, frankly, not impressive. In the Admiralty, the position was rather better. There existed a system of naval reporting centres in ports all over the world. Moreover, the Naval Intelligence Division, even in peace, was a senior division of the Naval Staff under the direction of a senior officer and, accordingly, carried more weight within the Navy than

did the parallel organisations in the other two services. In no Service was there a school of intelligence. There was a tendency to employ officers in intelligence, not because they were particularly suited to the work, but because they possessed a language qualification. In the Army, at any rate, intelligence was a dangerous branch of the Staff for an ambitious officer to join.

3. It is sometimes forgotten that the Directors of Intelligence in the Service Departments are in a different position from that of any of the other heads of divisions. The Directors of Intelligence are responsible to their Chiefs of Staff and, as members of the J.I.C., to the Chiefs of Staff Committee, for advice in war as to the probable intentions of the enemy, and in peace as to the development of warlike actions or policies on the part of foreign countries. In addition to this responsibility the Directors of Intelligence are the heads of great organisations with world-wide ramifications. This combination of advisory and administrative function places upon them a heavy burden.

4. While we believe that it is right to record the situation described above, so that it may not be reflected in the conditions obtaining in the future, we recognise that the decision to allow the Intelligence Branches, which had achieved much in the last war, to wither in the period between the wars, was a natural decision. The fighting Services had terribly scanty financial provision out of which to ensure the security of the country and the Empire. Those in control could not be blamed if they decided that as there was not enough to go round, ships, aircraft, guns and warlike stores must be brought before intelligence. We all hope the country will have learned its lesson and that, in future, it will be publicly recognised that it is poor economy to save on the armed forces to such an extent as to encourage potential enemies to become actual enemies, and then to pay at shortage rates in life and treasure for our unreadiness. It would, however, be rash to assume that the lesson will be remembered. Therefore, "taking the worst case" as we are taught to do in our appreciations for the Chiefs of Staff, it is clear that we should strive not merely to ensure that our Intelligence Service after the war is the most efficient possible, but to ensure that it is as economical as can be without sacrifice of efficiency.

5. One of the most vivid of the impressions we have gained in the course of our association with the Joint Intelligence Sub-Committee, and, particularly, during our recent enquiry, has been of the great volume of the available material and of the number and variety of the Departments and organisations interested in it as producers or consumers of intelligence, or both.

6. Intelligence reaches this country in war-time through many channels, of which the following are the principal:-

(a) The reports reaching the Foreign Office from our Diplomatic and Consular officers abroad.
(b) The reports reaching the Service Ministries from Naval, Military and Air Attachés, Naval Reporting Stations, the interrogation of prisoners of war, captured documents and equipment, &c.
(c) The product of the "Y" Services.
(d) The product of the Government Code and Cypher School.
(e) The reports from agents of S.I.S.
(f) The reports received through the channels of the Security Service, including the interrogations of persons entering the United Kingdom.
(g) The product of Postal and Telegraph Censorship.
(h) The product of aerial photographic reconnaissance received in the Air Ministry.
(i) The reports reaching the Dominions Office from our High Commissioners in the Dominions.
(j) The reports reaching the Colonial Office from our Governments in Colonial and Mandated Territories.
(k) Reports to S.O.E. from their agents.
(l) The foreign press-reading organisation of P.W.E.

7. In addition to these official channels, a deal of information reaches this country both in peace and war through private channels. There is correspondence between the representatives of British commercial and financial organisations abroad, and their head offices in this country. There is the information obtained from the correspondence of individual scientists and academic figures as well as that of learned societies. Learning knows no boundaries. There is the information collected by newspaper correspondents abroad and by private travellers. In war-time, much valuable information is drawn from this mine of unofficial intelligence. In peace-time, however, much of it is wasted as far as the Government machine is concerned. Even the information reaching this

country through official channels, as outlined in the last paragraph, has rarely, till recently, found its way to all those who could put it to the best use.

8. War-time relaxation of financial control and the urgent need of the different organisations engaged directly in military operations to be sure of getting quickly the intelligence they require, have resulted in some overlapping of responsibilities and duplication of work which should not be acceptable or permissible in peace-time, and should, if possible, be avoided in war. The remarkable diversity of controls during most of the war both in intelligence producing and intelligence consuming organisations, has fostered the tendency to duplication. The three principal fighting Services, though they have their own Ministries as in peace, are operationally directed by the Chiefs of Staff Committee under the ultimate control of the Minister of Defence. S.O.E. (which developed into an intelligence producing agency) has, however, been under the ministerial direction of the Minister of Economic Warfare; the Political Warfare Executive under that of the Foreign Secretary and the Minister of Information; the S.I.S. under that of the Foreign Secretary; the Security Service, until recently, under the Chancellor of the Duchy of Lancaster, though now under the Foreign Secretary; and the Postal and Telegraph Censorship Department, under the Minister of Information. There were, no doubt, excellent reasons for the decisions that led to this state of affairs. It may well have been right under the pressure of war to avoid the dislocation that any attempt at rationalisation would have caused. Goodwill, and the national genius for making the best of anomalies, has produced remarkably good results from this strange machine. None the less, we believe that a more symmetrical organisation could have done at least as well at less cost. Certainly, if we are to plan an organisation for peace capable of ready adaptation to the needs of a future war, something simpler and more economical must be devised.

9. In the international field it is now generally recognised that the price of peace and security in the modern world is some surrender of national sovereignty. Hence such experiments as the League of Nations and the Dumbarton Oaks concept. The pressure of war has led to the remarkable innovation of the Combined Chiefs of

Staff and the various integrated Allied Headquarters. It is, however, noteworthy that this country, which has taken the lead in these directions, pays perhaps more regard to responsibility of Ministers to Parliament for the conduct of their Departments. Yet, in defence matters, the war has brought about a considerable degree of inter-departmental co-operation through the machinery of the Chiefs of Staff organisation. We believe that few now would contend that this development has been anything but advantageous. If, therefore, in this report we recommend its extension, involving the surrender of some departmental sovereignties, we do so in the firm belief that it is essential. We recognise that each Department affected could make a convincing case for the retention unimpaired of its own sole authority, but we are confident that whatever disagreement there may be with our individual recommendations, any objective study of the problem confronting us would have led to the same general conclusion, namely, that we cannot afford to start another war unprovoked with the necessary intelligence; and that we cannot afford in peace (or even perhaps in war) the kind of intelligence organisation we have to-day.

10. We have not, in this report, dealt in detail with the internal organisation of the intelligence directorates in the three Service Departments. To have done so would have destroyed the balance of the report and laid us open to the charge of making proposals on insufficient evidence and superficial enquiry. We have preferred instead to propose a certain amalgamation of existing inter-service and inter-departmental bodies so as to provide a central intelligence agency and to leave it to Departments to work out the alterations in their own organisation that would be possible and desirable were that proposal accepted.

11. Enquiries under other auspices have been or are being made into the two principal branches of our Secret Service, and we do not, therefore, propose in this report to deal in detail with this aspect of the problem, save in so far as it is necessary for our purpose. We believe, however, that there will be general acceptance of the contention that the secret vote should be relived of as much as possible of the expenditure on intelligence. A great part of the expenditure now, in war-time, borne

on the secret vote for, for example, P.W.E. and S.O.E., represents acknowledgeable activities. The more that expenditure on intelligence can be placed on the public vote, the less temptation there will be in future to raid the secret vote in times of financial stringency. It is because we are convinced of the need for the strongest possible Secret Service in peace-time in preparation for our war needs, that we urge that everything possible should be done to protect the Secret Service from having to bear responsibility for activities that need not of themselves be regarded as secret.

12. As regards the other peace-time intelligence producing Departments, there is one general observation that we desire to make. Whereas in the Service Departments intelligence is the sole responsibility of certain officers specially selected for dealing with it, in the Political Departments, e.g. the Foreign Office and the Colonial Office, the officials who receive, collate and assess information are also responsible for formulating policy. This is not necessarily a bad thing, but the system does possess a serious weakness. One who is concerned in devising and recommending policy, and in assisting in its execution is likely, however objective he may try to be, to interpret the intelligence he receives in the light of the policy he is pursuing. To correct this possible weakness, it is clearly desirable that some quite objective check be placed on all intelligence received. So far as intelligence affecting the conduct of the war is concerned, the problem has been to some extent solved in the Foreign Office by the establishment of the Services Liaison Department, whose function it is to take part at all levels in the deliberations of the J.I.C. in the preparation of intelligence appreciations, and to interpret to the Planning Staffs the foreign policy of His Majesty's Government. This departure has justified itself in war, and we hope that it will be decided to continue it in peace. We believe that no Department, however experienced and well-staffed, has anything to lose by bringing the intelligence directly available to it to the anvil of discussion and appreciation among other workers in the same field.

13. To sum up, the machine that it is our task to devise should, we suggest, have the following characteristics. It should ensure that the agency best fitted for the

collection of a particular type of intelligence continues to collect it. It should ensure that, as far as possible, no other agency should collect the same material from the same source. It should ensure that the material collected is collected with other material bearing on the same subject, so that the best possible evaluation may be made. It should ensure that the information, when received and collated, is made available to all those with a legitimate interest in it and whose work will profit from its receipt. It should be controlled at the top by a strong inter-service and inter-departmental body, representing the needs of producers and consumers of intelligence.

II. The Existing Organisation.

14. The Chiefs of Staff Committee receive their advice on intelligence matters from the Joint Intelligence Sub-Committee, which is the principal inter-service and inter-departmental body dealing with intelligence and security. The J.I.C. is composed of an Assistant Under-Secretary of State from the Foreign Office, as Chairman, together with "C," the three Service Directors of Intelligence, one of the Directors of the Security Service and the Director-General of the Economic Intelligence Organisation, which, until recently, formed part of the Ministry of Economic Warfare, and has now been absorbed by the Foreign Office.

15. Under the J.I.C. a number of inter-service bodies have grown up during the war, such as I.S.T.D., C.S.D.I.C., and C.I.U. Owing to the lack of any central organisation to which they could all be attached, these bodies have been grafted on to existing Departments or fathered on to some particular Minister as an individual. Their policy has, however, been generally directed by the J.I.C. The authority acquired by the J.I.C. has come about largely through force of circumstances. The J.I.C. has never been formally invested with any executive authority. Yet in practice it has been found convenient that it should acquire such authority, and no objection has been raised in any quarter. It would be disastrous if the lessons in co-operative working between the Services which have been learned during the war should be lost in peace. Yet we must face the prospect of the disappearance of most of

these inter-service bodies unless some central home can be found for them in peace. Departments, particularly Defence Departments, struggling to carry out their own individual responsibilities in peace time within a rigid financial provision, will be most unwilling to bear the cost of inter-service organisations from which they only derive a partial benefit.

16. In war the J.I.C. has developed into a forum of discussion of all matters of common "intelligence" interest to its members, and thus into a kind of Board of Directors laying down inter-service intelligence and security policy at home and abroad. It has come to be consulted in the establishment of similar organisations in the Middle East and Iraq, and at the various Combined Allied Headquarters. Its representatives at Washington form with the United States J.I.C. (which has been modelled on it) the "Combined Intelligence Committee" which reports to the Combined Chiefs of Staff.

17. While it may be that in peace the composition of the Committee may have in some respects to be modified, we are satisfied that the organisation has sufficiently justified itself and shown sufficient vitality for it to be right to recommend that it should be the controlling body for the inter-service and inter departmental machine that we advocate, and that so far as possible all intelligence producing and using agencies should be represented on it or have access to it according to their needs.

18. We have, during the war, formed within the Joint Intelligence organisation a whole-time staff responsible for preparing for the Joint Intelligence Sub-Committee the appreciations required by the Chiefs of Staff and other authorities of enemy intentions and capabilities, and for giving advice on these matters at all times to the Planning Staffs. It was not until the spring of 1943 that the Joint intelligence Staff was set up. Before then the appreciations of the J.I.C. were prepared on an *ad hoc* basis. Experts from the different Departments concerned were summoned to meetings, and the Secretary drafted reports as a result of their discussions. This was a clumsy system. It resulted in delay in the production of reports and in considerable interference with the work of Departments. Moreover, the permanent Planning Staffs established in the Cabinet Office

had no Joint Intelligence advice at their own level. Each Planner sought the opinion of the Intelligence Directorate in his own Ministry. Frequently one or other of the Directors of Intelligence found himself in disagreement with the intelligence assumptions upon which the Directors of Plans advised the Chiefs of Staff. Now the Joint Intelligence Staff is composed of whole-time officers from the three Services and both the political and economic intelligence sides of the Foreign Office. This Staff works in offices adjoining those of the Joint Planning Staff. The Joint Intelligence Staff is thus constantly informed of operational events and requirements, and the Joint Planning Staff is equally constantly provided with intelligence advice. This system has worked so well in war that we urge that it be retained in peace, in whatever shape the Joint Staff organisation emerges after the war.

19. While the Joint Intelligence Staff is well equipped to prepare for the J.I.C. papers on enemy intentions generally, there exists no similar inter-service body to draft papers for the J.I.C. on enemy technical developments. Each of the three Intelligence Directorates has within it a technical section, but we are not satisfied that this is enough. We believe that there should be more interdepartmental discussion on technical intelligence. With the perfection of modern weapons, the responsibility as between the Services for watching particular developments is increasingly ill-defined. Moreover, now that on the operational side the Joint Committee on Research and Development Priorities and the Joint Technical Warfare Committee have been established, it is desirable that inter-service technical intelligence should be similarly integrated.

20. The information of military importance collected by the agencies referred to in paragraph 6 is collated separately in "country sections" or corresponding divisions in the Departments concerned. Generally speaking, each Department considers that it requires the information for its own special purpose, and therefore employs its own separate staff to study and interpret it. In war time, the final interpretation of most of this intelligence is made by the J.I.C., who use the Joint Intelligence Staff for the purpose. Before the war, no such final interpretation was ever made. Each Department reached its own

conclusion, and, unless the matter was of sufficient importance to be brought either to the Cabinet or to the Committee of Imperial Defence, each Department proceeded on its own interpretation, which might well differ from that of other Departments. It is as well to remember how recent has been the growth of the appreciating organisation as we know it to-day, since, unless a positive decision to retain it is made, it is highly likely that in peace it will be allowed to disintegrate.

21. It should be noted that the J.I.C., which grew up as a Sub-Committee of the Committee of Imperial Defence, has no representation from a number of intelligence-producing agencies, e.g., Postal and Telegraph Censorship, P.W.E., S.O.E. and the Colonial Office. This is because some of those agencies were set up to meet special needs during the war and were not, at the time of their creation, brought within the framework of the Joint Staff organisation which has grown up under the Chiefs of Staff. Others which existed before the war were not represented on the J.I.C. at the time of its foundation because it could not be foreseen how it would develop under the impetus of war. In later paragraphs of this report we consider in some detail the various intelligence organisations now in existence, including those which have grown up during the war, and discuss the extent to which it is proper that their activities should be continued in peace time, and the organisation in which these activities should be conducted.

III. Organisations whose Policy is now under the Direction of the J.I.C.

22. Apart from the Joint Intelligence Staff, there are now the following inter-service organisations whose policy is directed by the Joint Intelligence Sub-Committee, but which are administered by one or other of the Service Departments:-
The Inter-Service Topographical Department (Admiralty).
The Intelligence Section (Operations) (War Office — but housed in the Offices of the War Cabinet).
The Inter-Service Security Board (War Office).
The Combined Services Detailed Interrogation Centre (War Office).
The Central Interpretation Unit (Air Ministry).

The Inter-Service Topographical Department.
23. At the time of the German invasion of Norway, when a rapid division had to be taken to send forces to that country, it was found that only a small part of the intelligence required by the Commanders of those forces was ready to hand. It was as a result of that experience that the Chiefs of Staff, upon the recommendation of the J.I.C., authorised the establishment of the Inter-Service Topographical Department at Oxford. Owing to the fact that there existed no central organisation upon which the new Department could be grafted, it was necessary to invite one of the Service Departments (who were the principal consumers) to undertake the formation and administration of it. A branch (N.I.D. 16) of the Naval Intelligence Division had been engaged since 1915 in the production of geographical handbooks on various parts of the world. The purpose of these handbooks was to supply, by scientific research and skilled arrangement, material for the discussion of naval, military and political problems, as distinct from the examination of the problems themselves. By the end of 1918, upwards of 50 volumes had been produced in handbook and manual form, as well as short-term geographical reports. These handbooks acquired considerable popularity not only in Naval circles, but in the other Services and in Embassies and Legations abroad. The Admiralty had been able to secure the services of distinguished figures in academic life in the preparation of the books. The present series is very comprehensive and though produced by the Admiralty is of interest to nearly all Departments, and would indeed be suitable for general publication — though we understand this might involve some copyright difficulties. Perhaps largely because of their experience in organising their own geographical section, it was upon the Admiralty that fell the responsibility for organising the new Topographical Department. A Royal Marine officer was given charge of the Department, and a large inter-service and civilian staff has been employed. The principal function of the Department has been the production and keeping up to date of handbooks in the I.S.I.S. series and also special reports called for at short notice by Theatre and Force Commanders. The handbooks are designed for the use of Commanders, and provide up-to-date information covering the topography, details of

the administration, the economy and the defences of areas which may become the theatre of military operations. While the Department is administered by the Admiralty, its policy is directed by the Joint Intelligence Sub-Committee through a Topographical Sub-Committee composed of the Deputy Directors of Intelligence and officers of comparable position in the other Departments concerned. The priorities given to the work of the Department are laid down from time to time by the Directors of Plans, who are in a position to judge of the areas which may become operationally important.

24. A separate report is being prepared by the Topographical Sub-Committee on the peace-time requirements of the Services from the Topographical Department. This report will be of considerable value as a yardstick by which to measure peace-time defence requirements for intelligence generally. At the same time we think that the Inter-Service Topographical Department should be regarded as the nucleus of the Central Intelligence Agency whose creation after the war we believe to be desirable and which is outlined later in this report. The information that has been amassed by the Department since its creation, on a wide variety of subjects, not all of them directly related to defence, is of great volume and, we believe, of much potential value. To take one example. Before the United Nations turned to the offensive in 1942, a broadcast appeal was made over the wireless to the general public to send in copies of photographs in private possession covering all parts of the world. The response to this appeal was remarkable, and much valuable data was collected. The Department now possesses a library containing 600,000 photographs, all indexed and cross-indexed, which must be the most comprehensive collection of its kind in the world. Another task the Department have undertaken is that of maintaining an index of people possessing special knowledge of different parts of the world. This is known as the Contact Registry. The Department itself, in building up its reports on topographical information about foreign countries, naturally found it necessary to get into contact with as many people with accurate knowledge of the areas concerned as possible. Therefore, in April 1941, they set up a registry, recording the essential particulars of all civilian refugees who reached this country

and claimed special knowledge, topographical or otherwise, of places abroad. From this beginning there has grown up the present index, to which contributions have been made by the Services, the Civil Departments, shipping companies, industrial concerns, British Chambers of Commerce, tourist agencies, learned societies and universities. The present index of contacts covers nearly all parts of the world and includes particulars of over 70,000 people. Here again the information in the Registry is indexed and cross indexed and is a mine of potentially useful information.

25. It is because the information already recorded in the publications of I.S.T.D. and that to be found in their files and in their registries seem to us to provide the best possible basis for the Central Bureau we have in mind, that we recommend that the Bureau should be built up around the organisation of the Department.

Intelligence Section (Operations).

26. This body is a clearing house for factual intelligence of all kinds. The Joint Planning Staff, Force Commanders, numerous branches of the Service Departments concerned with operations, Combined Operations Headquarters and many other organisations all require detailed intelligence on numerous questions. In the past it was found that the Intelligence Branches in the Service and other Ministries often received from a number of different quarters the same request in a number of slightly differing forms within a short space of time. It was, therefore, found convenient to institute a kind of information bureau, to which any duly authorised authority was entitled to go to seek factual intelligence. The result has been a noticeable reduction in duplication and a considerable saving of time. It will be evident that a good deal of the material produced by the Intelligence Section (Operations) is the kind of material that is also produced by the Inter-Service Topographical Department at Oxford, and that the material acquired by I.S. (O) and given to its customers is also the kind of material that finds its way into I.S.T.D. In fact, it is probable that if I.S.T.D. had been in London instead of at Oxford, it would not have been necessary to establish I.S. (O) as a separate organisation. The central secretariat of I.S.T.D. would seem to have been the appropriate body to

deal with this work. If our recommendation that I.S.T.D. should form the nucleus of a Central Intelligence Bureau is accepted, we believe that it will be unnecessary for I.S. (O) to continue its separate existence. In any case, it is doubtful whether I.S.T.D. could remain at Oxford owing to problems of accommodation. They now occupy premises which will shortly be required by the University and College authorities. In parenthesis, we would point out that the fact that there was a demand for such an organisation as I.S. (O) is a strong argument for the maintenance of the principle of factual intelligence being available for all authorised consumers in a central place.

27. As a matter of convenience, I.S. (O) has been found accommodation in the Cabinet War Room, alongside the Joint Planning and Intelligence Staffs. Though it is an inter-service body with representatives from the three Services and from the Political and Economic branches of the Foreign Office, its general administration is in the hands of the War Office, who provide the necessary junior staff.

The Inter-Service Security Board.
28. "The inception of security measures during the preparatory stages of an operation planned at home is the joint concern of the Admiralty, War Office and Air Ministry. Co-ordination is effected by the Joint Intelligence Sub-Committee through the Inter-Service Security Board."* The I.S.S.B. has fulfilled, during the war, a most useful task in dealing with the day-to-day problems of operational security. They meet daily and are served by a strong secretariat, established in the War Office. A link with the Civil Ministries is provided by the Advisers to the Panel on Security Arrangements in Government Departments, who are *ex officio* members of the Board. The Board's principal function is the coordination of measures for preventing leakage of information to the enemy in connexion with special operations. They have developed a close liaison with the parallel organisation in the United States, and with Supreme Headquarters, Allied Expeditionary Force. They also maintain close contact with the London Controlling

---

* Manual of Combined Operations, 1938 (Amendment 3, 1942).

Section, whose operational deception measures have to be closely co-ordinated with our security policy. Local inter-service Security Boards have been established in the different theatres of war.

29. While in time of war there is clearly need for such an organisation as the I.S.S.B., we do not consider it necessary in peace-time. The normal machinery of the J.I.C. should be competent to deal with the inter-service security problems that will then arise. Arrangements should, however, be made for the re-creation of the Board upon a resumption of hostilities.

30. It is convenient to deal under this head with another organisation which deals with military security matters, though it does not come under the J.I.C., and forms no part of the Chiefs of Staff organisation. At the time of the fall of France, when this country lay under immediate threat of invasion, a body was established called the Security Executive, under the Chairmanship of Viscount Swinton. Its function was to advise on the measures to be taken against any possible "fifth column." In practice, it extended its function very widely and has provided a useful forum for discussion and agreement between civil and military interests affected by the rigid security restrictions that it has from time to time been necessary to impose. It is unnecessary in this report to examine in detail the functions that the Security Executive came to perform, since during the last two years it has largely ceased to perform them, and it now exists practically only in the form of its junior committee known as the Liaison Officers Committee, who advise on such questions as the entry into this country of foreign technical missions, the restrictions on the publication of official statistics, and a number of similar minor matters. The Liaison Officers Committee are at present more than usually active, since they are engaged in recommending the "unwinding" of a number of restrictions that it is now possible to relax. The Secretariat of the Security Executive also is responsible for the direction of some aspects of the work of an organisation established in Washington called the British Security Control, which did most valuable work before the United States came into the war in dealing with the security of merchant shipping in the Western Atlantic. This arose through Viscount Swinton having been given a personal responsibility

under the then Lord President of the Council for certain of the activities abroad of the Secret Services.

31. It will be seen that the inter-service and inter-departmental organisation for security in war, though it has been remarkably effective, has followed no clear-cut plan. The principal agency for general security at home is, of course, the Security Service. An inter-departmental body under the Chairmanship of the Secretary of the War Cabinet, called the Panel on Security Arrangements in Government Departments is, as its name implies, responsible for ensuring co-ordination in the security practice of Government Departments in this country and, so far as possible, with Government agencies in the United States and the Dominions and Colonies. On this body the Service Departments are represented, and co-ordination with the J.I.C. is effected in the person of the Chairman and the Secretary, who is also the Secretary of the Joint Staff. The Inter-Service Security Board does come under the J.I.C., and though its responsibilities are primarily connected with operational security, its work necessarily affects many civil authorities. The Security Executive, on which again the Service, as well as the Civil Departments, are represented, is concerned primarily with the impact of the security measures made necessary by war-time conditions on the general public.

32. We believe that the lesson to be learnt from our experience of security during this war has been that an attempt to draw a distinction between military and civil security must fail, and that it would be wise so to arrange things in future that a single authority be established to deal with these problems. The Joint Intelligence Sub-Committee, since it includes representatives not only of the Services, but of the Foreign Office and the two principal Secret Intelligence organisations, is probably best fitted for the task. It is true that as the J.I.C. is part of the Chiefs of Staff organisation, it might be thought that it would give excessive weight to military considerations. We believe that it should be possible to give satisfactory guarantees to avoid this criticism being justified in practice.

The Combined Services Detailed Interrogation Centre
33. This organisation, which is administered by the War Office under one of the Deputy Directors of Military

Intelligence, is responsible for the maintenance of certain camps in which selected prisoners of war are detained. Measures are taken at these camps for overhearing and recording the conversations of the prisoners. Each Service Department maintains a section responsible for analysing the reports produced in the Centre. The collation of these reports has provided much valuable operational, technical, economic and political intelligence. While it is hard to see much scope for such an organisation in peacetime, it is clear that the experience gained must not be lost, since it is bound to be of value in any future war. It may be that the technique which has been developed will, however, be of value to the security authorities in peace-time. It might, therefore, be possible both to obtain immediate advantage and to provide the nucleus for a war-time organisation if S.I.S. or the Security Service were to be responsible in peace for research in this field. We cannot make a firm recommendation on this matter in the absence of a decision as to the organisation of our Secret Services in peace-time. We wish, however, to record our opinion that steps should be taken to ensure that we do not lose the profit of our experience.

The Central Interpretation Unit.
34. Air photography has proved a valuable aid not only to tactical reconnaissance, but to intelligence generally. For example, air photographs, since they provide an accurate and permanent record of the study of a particular area at a certain time can, by comparison with photographs subsequently taken, indicate the effect of damage by bombing, shelling or sabotage, and the degree of reconstruction that an enemy has been able to carry out. They can similarly provide most useful information as to particular developments, both military and industrial. They provide the quickest and, in the case of any inaccessible country, the only way of obtaining material for the construction of new maps. The Central Interpretation Unit, which is administered by the Royal Air Force, is under the policy direction of the J.I.C. It is so closely linked with the Royal Air Force organisation for taking aerial photographs, that it is necessary to consider the two together. The present photographic reconnaissance organisation provides every branch of the Government at war with such information as can be

extracted from photographs. The organisation has five tasks to perform—
(1) To decide on the priority of the demands for reconnaissance and the manner in which particular tasks shall be carried out.
(2) To fly the necessary sorties in order that the photographs be taken.
(3) To carry out the technical processing (developing, printing, &c.) of the photographs.
(4) To undertake the first interpretation of the photographs.
(5) To carry out the distribution of the photographs and their interpretations to the interested authorities.
35. The Air Ministry have established a special Photographic Reconnaissance Group (No. 106) to carry out the necessary flights. The decision on priorities is at present carried out by an inter-service committee subordinate to the J.I.C. The remaining functions of the organisation are those of the Central Interpretation Unit. So high a degree of efficiency has already been achieved that in favourable conditions of weather the customer who urgently requires information can be provided with the prints and interpretational reports within 24 hours of the photographs being taken.
36. It would be invidious, even if it were possible, to assess the relative values of different types of intelligence. All are complementary. Intelligence obtained by one means may give to intelligence obtained by other means a value which it would not otherwise possess. Yet in sheer volume, the product of aerial photographic reconnaissance has probably provided the greatest single contribution. It requires but little imagination to recognise that the scope of this particular branch of intelligence will greatly extend in the future with the development of aircraft of improved performance and the technical advance that is to be expected in photography. There are few branches of governmental activity in peace or war which may not in future benefit from the products of photographic reconnaissance.
37. While the principal part in aerial photographic reconnaissance must, we recognise, be undertaken by the Royal Air Force, since it is they who have to operate the aircraft, the interest of the consumers is so considerable that we do not believe that any one Ministry should

be burdened with the exclusive responsibility for the general control and direction of this branch of intelligence. Moreover, the interest of the consumers will be such that is to be hoped that they will be able to exercise influence in obtaining the resources in aircraft, technical equipment and personnel which the organisation will require. In proposing that the organisation should come under centralised control for general policy, while remaining under the operational control of the Royal Air Force, we are not, we believe, making any very revolutionary proposal. We have in mind that the policy direction should be in the hands of the Joint Intelligence Sub-Committee. In this case the J.I.C. would normally operate through a special photographic reconnaissance committee, on which all consumer, as well as operational, interests should be represented. It is for consideration whether the Photographic Reconnaissance Organisation ought to enter the commercial field and be available to provide material, not only for Government agencies, e.g., the Ministry of Town and Country Planning, the Colonial Office, &c., but also for industrial and commercial concerns. It would be right, if this proposal found favour, for His Majesty's Government to buy out the principal independent company working in this field in peace time. If the organisation did undertake non-official work, the revenue obtained would provide useful relief to the expense of the intelligence organisation as a whole, or could be used towards meeting the expense of research and development in aircraft production.

38. The organisation we have in mind would cover the needs of the United Kingdom, India, Burma and the Colonial Empire. It should, however, be possible to make mutually satisfactory arrangements with the Dominions whereby it undertook certain work on their behalf in return for relief in some non-Dominion areas which could conveniently be covered by organisations within the Dominions. It is hoped, shortly, to come to an arrangement with the United States whereby they undertake the principal responsibility for aerial reconnaissance in the Far Eastern war. It would undoubtedly be in the common interest if a similar rationalisation of responsibilities between ourselves and America could be maintained in peace.

39. While, as we have said, we recognise that the

operational control of flying units can hardly be vested in any inter-service committee and must remain with the Royal Air Force, we believe that the Central organisation might well take over such responsibilities as the following:-
(1) The training of photographic reconnaissance interpreters, pattern makers and model makers.
(2) The School of Photography and the Photographic Interpretational Wing of the School of Military Intelligence.
(3) The Photographic Reconnaissance Development Unit and the Army Photographic Research Centre.
(4) The Technical Organisation required for the selection and installation of photographic equipment in reconnaissance aircraft.
40. A development of the existing organisation has been that No. 106 Group has undertaken the responsibility for certain high-speed courier air services. This has followed from the need to distribute the product of aerial photographic intelligence without delay to consumers in war theatres. During recent international conferences No. 106 Group has flown urgent despatches between the United Kingdom and the scene of the Conference, e.g., Moscow and Athens. It is evident that the need for this Service will exist in peace. We understand that the Foreign Office are already considering the advisability of equipping certain of their missions abroad with aircraft. The need for a high-speed courier service, however, is likely to be felt by other Departments, including the Service Departments and the Colonial and Dominions Offices. It is for consideration whether it would not be economical for such a service to remain the responsibility of the organisation charged with the distribution of air photographs and in peace time be directed by the J.I.C. in common with secret telecommunications — with which we deal later.

IV.— Departments and Organisations not Directed by the J.I.C. which Deal with Intelligence.

The Political Warfare Executive.
41. The intelligence organisation of the Political Warfare Executive was started when an intelligence requirement became apparent for the production of

leaflets and clandestine broadcasting. The clandestine broadcasts are designed to give the impression of coming from inside enemy or enemy-occupied country. It was therefore necessary to ensure that they should be based on the most accurate intelligence, so as to carry conviction. P.W.E. also undertook on behalf of other organisations responsibility for training certain agents. This created a need for further detailed information. With the growth of P.W.E. it became necessary to provide a considerable volume of intelligence as the background for policy-making and for the output for open, as well as clandestine, broadcasting. In course of time, P.W.E. Intelligence accumulated much detailed information about contemporary administration and political conditions in German Europe. This in turn led to a somewhat anomalous arrangement under which the hand-books on these subjects required by those planning for Civil Affairs tasks were prepared and produced by P.W.E., since P.W.E had the information and it was not so readily available elsewhere. The present P.W.E. intelligence organisation, which is a large one, is designed to carry out the following tasks:—

(a) The provision of background intelligence (political and social) in enemy and enemy-occupied countries on which to base political warfare policy and action, for propaganda output.

(b) The service of quick information for immediate use in propaganda.

(c) The provision of intelligence on governmental and administrative machinery (this relates principally to the requirements of Civil Affairs).

42. While it is evident that in any future war the technique of political warfare will play a considerable part, it is uncertain how far it will be thought necessary for His Majesty's Government to engage in open or secret propaganda in time of peace. The tendency will certainly be to close down on these activities. At the same time, it is important that the benefit of the experience gained in this field during the present war should be preserved and that plans should be laid for the creation of an appropriate organisation for war purposes. Here again it is to be hoped that if war comes again it will be possible for political warfare to be conducted under some more closely integrated arrangements with the

staffs dealing with other forms of warfare than at present. The only reason why P.W.E. found it necessary to build up the considerable intelligence organisation now in existence was that they could not obtain their needs from any one other source. We have had the advantage of visiting their organisation and studying some of their files. We were impressed by the volume of the material that had been collected and the care that had been taken in collating it. A considerable effort is made to provide other interested organisations with the product of the P.W.E. intelligence, in the form of intelligence summaries made up of extracts from the enemy, enemy-occupied and neutral press, and of summaries of broadcasts, &c. Similarly, a fair volume of material collected by other agencies finds its way to P.W.E., there to be collated and assessed for political warfare purposes.

43. While the reason for the creation of this organisation is easy to understand, it is, in our opinion, highly regrettable that any such organisation should have been necessary. It provides a vivid example of the expense that results from unco-ordinated effort. The handbooks produced for Civil Affairs cover, in some respects, a rather different type of material to that included in the operational handbooks of I.S.T.D. At the same time, we find it hard to believe that, had it been administratively possible for a single organisation to meet both needs, a considerable economy in man-power and effort would not have resulted.

44. We think it is useful to record that the P.W.E. intelligence organisation possesses some 7,000 files and records of some 190,000 personalities. The files cover a wide range of subjects, of which the following are examples:-

(1) Public opinion abroad as to foreign and domestic issues and the organisations or forces moulding it.
(2) Enemy propaganda output and the policy underlying it.
(3) Political parties and activities.
(4) The machinery of Government, central and local.
(5) Social and cultural organisations and influences.
(6) Economic information to illustrate living conditions.

45. While some of the information in this great library is of ephemeral interest, much must be worth preserving. We understand that P.W.E. will shortly be closing down

that part of their intelligence organisation which provides material for Civil Affairs handbooks. We think it would be regrettable if these handbooks were not kept up to date and the work of maintaining the files were abandoned. We recommend, therefore, that these records, as a temporary measure be handed over to I.S.T.D. and that, pending the creation of a Central Intelligence Bureau, I.S.T.D. should accept responsibility (and should take over the necessary staff from P.W.E.) for keeping alive such part of this work as it is desired to preserve. It is recognised that, if the files are to be handed over to I.S.T.D., it will be necessary to arrange for the continuation of the flow of material from which they have been built up. Certain of the records of P.W.E. should, we believe, be handed over to other organisations for them to examine and, where necessary, to retain. For example, the personality records should, we suggest, be handed over to S.I.S., and the files relating to social and economic intelligence be accepted by the Enemy Advisory Branch of the Foreign Office.

Postal and Telegraph Censorship.
46. The Postal and Telegraph Censorship Department is, in its present form, a war-time creation. It is, in our opinion, in many ways a model of what an intelligence collecting and disturbing organisation should be. At the same time, its position in the war machine is as anomalous as that of many of the other organisations with which we have dealt. It is controlled by a Director-General who is responsible to the Minister of Information in his personal capacity, though not to the Ministry of Information. There exists an inter-departmental committee on censorship at the official level. Although its primary functions are the collection of intelligence and the prevention of intelligence from reaching the enemy, the Censorship Department is not represented on the Joint Intelligence Sub-Committee, nor is it part of the Chiefs of Staff organisation. In practice, the Department has worked in close contact with the J.I.C. as well as with the Service Departments individually, and owing largely to the efficiency of its administration and the wisdom with which it has been directed, it has given general satisfaction and met with very little criticism.
47. The Information and Records Branch of the Postal

and Telegraph Censorship organisation has aimed at providing for simultaneous distribution of the product of censorship to all interested Departments in accordance with the requirements submitted by and agreed with those Departments. It has been so devised as to operate with great speed and flexibility. The user Departments appoint officers, provided with small staffs who serve within the Censorship organisation and there handle the volume of material and ensure that all divisions within their Departments receive what they require. Censorship Stations in all parts of the globe are provided with what are called "allocation lists," which are continually revised by an Allocations Committee. Annexed to this report (Annex A) is a detailed description of the method of working of the Information and Records Branch of Imperial Censorship. This method appears to us to provide a simple and speedy method of ensuring that the collectors of intelligence know what to look for and that intelligence received goes to those interested in receiving it. From the Annex it will be seen what a formidable volume of material is dealt with by censorship, and how rapidly it has been found possible to deal with it.

48. Save for the needs of the Security Service and the police, censorship has no place in the life of this country in peace-time. The complex but remarkably effective system whereby practically no cable traffic in the world escapes the control of our censors could not be maintained in peace. The internal censorship carried out unobtrusively, has revealed much useful information during the war, but since its legal basis was something very like one of those "general warrants" on which the Courts since the days of John Wilkes have frowned so heavily, there can be little likelihood of retaining it in peace. It therefore behoves us to ensure that the records of the Postal and Telegraph Censorship Department are preserved and that machinery be devised which can be rapidly set in motion and expanded in an emergency. We believe that censorship is just as much an instrument of defence intelligence as, for example, C.S.D.I.C., and that the present divorce of the Department from the central defence organisation cannot be justified. The nucleus of the war-time censorship department should in peace have its home in the Central Intelligence Organisation whose establishment we recommend. There would, we believe, be

much to be gained by closer integration of censorship with other intelligence producing agencies — and this could be achieved by the method we advocate. Censorship is concerned with the product of intercepted wireless traffic and hence with the activities of the "Y" Services and R.S.S.; with the product of cryptography and hence with the Government Code and Cypher School; with the technique of secret inks, and hence with some of the technical activities of S.I.S.

The Secret Services.
49. We understand that other authorities have been or are being made responsible for detailed examination of the working of the two main branches of the Secret Service, and will submit recommendations as to their future. It would therefore, be inappropriate for us to attempt in any way to cover the same ground. There are however, certain general points which have come to our notice and which we feel it useful to record. It is stated in an earlier paragraph that we believe that it should be axiomatic that the Secret Services should not be called upon to provide intelligence that can be obtained by acknowledgeable means. We recognise that there is a certain type of intelligence relating to the internal security of this country itself which is not, and may not become the responsibility of the Defence Organisation. Subject to that, we doubt whether any case can be made for the retention of the present system, under which the responsibility for counter-espionage is divided between two authorities with no better basis for division than that of geography. The work of foreign agents is not limited by political boundaries, and it can only hamper the effectiveness of our machine for such boundaries to determine the means by which we combat the activities of foreign agents.
50. We think it safe to say that after the end of the present war, by far the most important intelligence requirement for a country such as ours will be accurate information rapidly acquired of scientific and technical developments in other countries. Our geographical position, our enormous commitments and our limited man-power will make it essential for us to obtain a technical lead over the rest of the world in compensation for our weaknesses in other directions. That being so, we will have to husband our resources in intelligence and ensure that

the different branches of the Secret Service, if the Secret Service remains divided, shall not bid against each other for the limited amount of technical talent that will be available.

51. While we do not propose in this report to make specific recommendations for the organisation of liaison between the fighting Services and S.I.S. and the Security Service, we do wish to record our conviction of the importance of careful selection of officers of high quality from the Services before attachment to these bodies. Whether or not the criticism is justified, it is unfortunate that in the early days of this war there existed an impression in Whitehall which came to our notice, that certain of the officers lent to the Secret Services by the Service Departments were officers for whom it was not easy to find employment elsewhere. If that were true, or even appeared to be true, the effect on the prestige of the Secret Services and therefore on the support they enjoy, must have been deplorable.

The Government Code and Cypher School.

52. In this war the value of the product of the Government Code and Cypher School has been beyond price. While it is true that we cannot be sure that we will be able in future to retain this great advantage over our competitors in the same field, we have no doubt that it is of high importance that research in cryptography in peace time should be energetically pursued. Here again, however, some pulling together of the strings appears to us to be desirable. We can see no case for the S.I.G.I.N.T. Board, which under C.'s Chairmanship is made up of members of the J.I.C., remaining apart from that organisation. It can only be to the interest of the consumers of intelligence generally, no less than that of the cryptographers, that a single high-level organisation should deal with the policy directing this specialised branch of intelligence as well as all other work in the intelligence field. The School, though it is, and should in our opinion remain, under the direction of "C.", is not a part of S.I.S. We are not satisfied that there is any valid case for the school continuing to be carried on the Foreign Office vote. By far the greater part of its work in war is carried out for the Defence Services. In peace the proportion of political to military work will

shift, but we feel that it would be both logical and advantageous for the expenses of the school to be borne on whatever vote carries the other inter-service and inter-departmental intelligence agencies.

53. There has been during the war a natural tendency to insist that each cobbler should stick to his last, to refuse to permit S.I.S. to circulate their appreciations of the intelligence they produce or G.C. and C.S. to contribute views on the meaning and importance to be attached to the messages they have decyphered. In view of the rather haphazard way in which these various organisations have grown up and of the different authorities to which they are now responsible, this has probably been the right policy. We do believe, however, that it should be possible under a new dispensation to obtain value from the contributions of many outside the Foreign Office and Service Departments in the assessment of intelligence received. The experienced cryptographer can make useful deductions from the cyphering characteristics of the traffic with which he deals, just as R.S.S. have developed a remarkable skill in analysis of signalling characteristics. The telegraph censors, with their unrivalled knowledge of commercial signalling traffic, have also something to contribute to the appreciators, the interceptors and the decoders. We have had the advantage of seeing appreciations written within S.I.S., which under the present rules cannot receive a general circulation, which struck us as being valuable and important.

54. Apart from the positive value to be obtained from the seeking contributions [sic] from all who offer them, there is advantage in stimulating those working in particular parts of the intelligence machine to an interest in the wider picture to which they are contributing. This would induce a healthy rivalry and should do much to counteract the ill-effects of a mechanical routine. We discount the argument that any such policy would endanger the security of the highly secret material in question. It is not by treating intelligent men and women as robots that security is best assured.

The "Y" services.
55. At first sight, it appeared to us anomalous that permanent Interception stations should be maintained separately by the three Services, the Radio Security service

and the Post Office. We understand, however, that the requirements of the three Services differ so greatly, and the technique involved varies so much, that any proposal to provide a single interception service for all users would fail to secure support. None the less, the fact that the Radio Security Service does attempt to cover for its purposes the whole field of interception, leads us to believe that there is an area of common interest in which the specialised techniques of the Services should not be concerned. We are not qualified, nor have we had the time to make sufficient study, to express a firm opinion on this matter, but we believe that there is a sufficient *prima facie* case for a separate enquiry to be justified into the possibilities of economy in this direction.

The Special Operations Executive.
56. The Special Operations Executive, during the period before it was placed under the operational control of the several Theatre Commanders, had to build up a considerable intelligence organisation of its own. This was the inevitable result of its separate existence. Moreover, since it is an organisation which employs agents, it is natural that a considerable flow of intelligence from foreign countries has found its way into S.O.E. headquarters. Arrangements are made for this information to be available for other organisations, but only on condition that it is distributed to those organisations by S.I.S. This is a sound arrangement under existing conditions, since only thus can a check be put upon the information by the wider intelligence resources of the latter organisation. Despite the real contribution that S.O.E. has made during this war, we cannot believe that the experiment of running special operations as a separate military function outside the direct control of the Chiefs of Staff and under the direction of a non-service Minister, will be repeated. We understand that it is likely to be proposed that the nucleus of a Special Operations Organisation should be maintained within S.I.S. With this proposal we cordially agree. The intelligence requirements of those responsible for special operations in any future war should, we feel sure, be met in the same way as the intelligence requirements of any other body engaged in military operations.

Communications.
57. The present Secret Communications Organisation dates back only to 1938, and first took the form of linking up the London headquarters of S.I.S. with its chief representatives abroad by a special wireless network. At the same time the foundations were laid of an organisation for designing and producing wireless transmitting and receiving sets for the special purposes of S.I.S. The history of the subsequent development of the Special Communications Organisation is fascinating, but it would be out of place in this report to do more than indicate its present responsibilities. These may be summarised as follows:-
(a) *Direct Communications* — Machinery exists to-day not only for communication with the fixed branch establishments of S.I.S. in different parts of the world, but also for communication with many S.I.S. agents equipped with light portable sets capable of the requisite range. At the terminal points of the main line system to the branch offices of S.I.S. further networks radiate to sub-stations operated by agents.
(b) *Interception* — This is the function of the Radio Security Service, which is dealt with separately below.
(c) *Distribution to Theatre Commanders, &c.* — It will be evident that much of the value of the product of the Government Code and Cypher School would have been lost were it not possible to transmit it by most rapid means and under conditions of the highest secrecy to Theatre Commanders. Moreover, when military operations are unsuccessful, the normal signal communications of armies in the field may collapse, as occurred at the time of the fall of France. Therefore, it was found necessary to set up a channel for conveying urgent operational intelligence to the fighting commanders by special channels of communication. The system has reached a high degree of efficiency, and has the added advantage of providing a specially secret signals link for certain communications by the Prime Minister, the Chiefs of Staff, &c.
(d) *Production* — Nearly all the equipment used by the Special Communications Organisation is designed, developed and produced within the organisation itself, and the results achieved have been impressive. At the same time it is to be noted that the S.O.E. have carried out a similar policy of designing and manufacturing their

own communications equipment. While we recognise that in communications with agents S.I.S. are concerned more in the provision of efficient receivers and S.O.E. in the provision of efficient transmitters, we doubt whether the country is so rich in technicians and qualified artisans as to be able to afford this division of effort. In the Services, the Signals Directorates are, for good reasons, not controlled by the Directors of Intelligence. Therefore, it might be difficult under existing arrangements to bring about a complete centralisation of research, development and production of radio equipment. We do feel, however, that consideration should be given in future to means of devising economies in this direction.

(e) *"Black" Broadcasting* — The Special Communications Organisation provides, maintains and operates the equipment with which the Political Warfare Executive carries out a large part of its distribution of propaganda. The technique of conveying the illusion that broadcasts in fact made from this country are made from stations established in enemy, or enemy-occupied country, has reached a high degree of efficiency. We have not yet seen the full capability of this technique. The very high-powered transmitter that is used for certain "black" broadcasts may before the end of the war play an important part by carrying out the "intruder" operation known as "Aspidistra." It is hard to see how use can be made of this technique in peace-time, but its value in this war has in our opinion been sufficiently proved for it to be right that the Secret Communications Organisation should continue research in this field and should make preparations in peace to enable it to carry out similar responsibilities in any future war or international emergency.

The Radio Security Service.
58. The organisation from which the Radio Security Service has grown was originally established to act as policemen of the air to detect illicit wireless communication. In developing our own secret communications channels, experience was gained which showed the need for a protective security organisation to ensure that the messages passed over these channels did not become compromised. Now the Radio Security Service is responsible for a general inter-service scrutiny of wireless traffic to cover all

communications not covered by the other "Y" Services. In particular, the Service intercepts and passes to the Government Code and Cypher School, which interprets and distributes a mass of valuable information originating from the enemy secret services. The knowledge that has been acquired by R.S.S. of methods of identification of signals traffic by characteristics of procedure and technique is now considerable, and has made a valuable contribution to intelligence and to the work of interpretation of intercepted communications generally. The experience that has been gained must not be lost, and the technique must in peace, as in war, continue to develop.

V.—The Post-War Intelligence Organisation.

59. In paragraph 13 above, we gave an outline of the characteristics which our post-war intelligence organisation should, in our opinion, display. The proposal which we now put forward is designed to create an organisation possessed of those characteristics. At the head of the organisation and directing its general policy we propose should be the Joint Intelligence Sub-Committee. The J.I.C. should remain directly responsible to the Chiefs of Staff, though we think that the practice that has grown up, of the Committee giving advice on request to other Departments and authorities, should be preserved. Under the J.I.C. we propose that there should be a system of standing sub-committees dealing with all the various aspects of intelligence. We think it essential that all the intelligence authorities should be brought under the J.I.C. umbrella. In addition to these sub-committees, we propose the establishment of a Joint Intelligence Bureau. Into this bureau should be fed information from all existing intelligence sources. Within the bureau, this information should be brought together and reproduced in the form required by the different customers of the intelligence machine. We have in mind that each intelligence-producing organisation should continue to collect intelligence from its own sources, but should not normally receive intelligence from other Departments or organisations save through the medium of the Central Bureau.

60. In peace-time, a certain limited amount of officially acquired intelligence is made available to the general

public either in the form of official publications, such as the commercial reports issued by the Department of Overseas Trade, or in answer to direct enquiries generally addressed to that Department by particular commercial firms. We believe that there is scope for a considerable extension of this practice. It is evident that the revival of our export trade after the war will be as difficult as it is important. It is no part of our responsibility to make recommendations to this end, but we believe that we can serve both the interests of defence and the wider economic interests of this country in peace-time by providing a comprehensive intelligence agency. Even in war, much of the information which is of value to the Foreign Office and the Defence Services is in no way secret. We propose, therefore, that the Central Intelligence Bureau should be available, not only to Government Departments and agencies, but also to the general public. While its services, like those of any other Government agency, would be provided free of cost to official customers, there is no reason why members of the public making use of it should not pay for its services. His Majesty's Stationery Office make a charge for their publications, as does the Ordnance Survey for those of its maps that are made publicly available. This proposal would have a twofold advantage. In the first place, as has been said, it should provide trade and industry with much information which should assist them in their normal business. Secondly, it should provide a revenue which should assist the Defence organisation in meeting its expenditure on intelligence.

61. We fully recognise that no Department or Service can absolve itself from direct responsibility for the technical assessment of the intelligence relating directly to its own constitutional responsibilities. We are satisfied, however, that there is a wide field of common interest where it should be possible to avoid duplication of effort. This field covers some highly secret matters as well as a large area of matters which are hardly, if at all, secret.

62. If the J.I.C. is to take over the responsibility for the direction of the kind of organisation that we have outlined above, it may be that its constitution should be to some extent modified. In particular, the Board of Trade should, we think, at any rate in peace

be represented. In any case, the Foreign Office, "C" and the Directors of Intelligence must clearly continue to be members. Separate representation on the J.I.C. of the Economic Intelligence Organisation within the Foreign Office should not, in our opinion, be necessary. Representation of the Security Service must evidently be a matter to be decided in the light of the decisions taken on the future of that body.

63. A committee as large as the J.I.C., while competent to lay down policy, is evidently unsuited to the day-to-day administration of a large organisation. This task requires the whole time services of a single individual aided by a competent departmental staff. Here a special difficulty confronts us. We have little doubt but that the best arrangement would be for "C," who is the head of S.I.S. and G.C. and C.S., the Chairman of the S.I.G.I.N.T. Board and the ultimate head of the Special Communications Organisation, to accept responsibility for the direction of the new Central Intelligence machine. Since the Central Bureau will, if our recommendations are accepted, be the principal clearing house for the product of "C's" organisations, it would, in our opinion, be both administratively convenient and correct from the point of view of security for "C" to be in charge. At the same time, "C" for obvious reasons may not be a public figure, known to the world at large. Perhaps it would be possible to arrange for a deputy to be appointed to "C," who would be responsible to him for the public side of his activities, but would bear a title which would not disclose to the outside world that he was a subordinate. In the following paragraphs we refer to the head of the organisation as the "Director-General." We propose that the Director-General and, in his absence, his deputy, should be *ex-officio* members not only of the J.I.C., but of all its various sub-committees, though it should not be necessary for them to attend all sub-committee meetings. The Director-General would have the services of a permanent secretariat common to the J.I.C. and its sub-committees. The secretariat should be responsible, under the Director-General, for ensuring the co-ordination of the activities of the different branches of the national intelligence machine. The sub-committees we have in mind are the following, but the list is not intended to be exclusive. Moreover, there

should be power to establish *ad hoc* sub-committees when need arises.

The S.I.G.I.N.T. Board.
64. This Board should be composed as at present, but its responsibility should cover not only G.C. and C.S., but also Special Communications and R.S.S., and ensure co-ordination between them. Should it, in future, be found possible to bring about some further integration of the "Y" Services, it would be proper that it should be under the Board.

Joint Intelligence Staff.
65. We have in mind that a Joint Intelligence Staff should exist as at present to draft strategic intelligence appreciations for the J.I.C. and to advise the Planning Staffs. Its members would take their instructions, as at present, from their own Ministries.

Joint Technical Intelligence Committee.
66. We propose that there should, in future, be established a permanent committee representative of the technical sections of the three Service Departments, which should be responsible for giving joint advice on foreign technical developments in the defence field to the Planning Staffs and the research and development organisations working under the Chiefs of Staff. In the light of experience it could be decided whether this committee should itself be served by a whole-time inter-service staff on the lines of the Joint Intelligence Staff.

Security Committee.
67. This Committee as its name implies, would advise the J.I.C. on all questions of military security in peace, and form the nucleus for the war-time Inter-Service Security Board. We propose that it should have sufficient contacts with the remainder of the Government machine for it to be unnecessary at any future date to re-establish anything on the lines of the Security Executive.

Photographic Reconnaissance Committee.
68. This Committee should, under the J.I.C., be responsible for the policy direction of aerial photographic reconnaissance and for the production, interpretation

and distribution of aerial photographs. If it is agreed that a special air communications service can properly be run by the Intelligence Organisation, its policy direction should be in the hands of this sub-committee.

War Planning Committee.
69. We contemplate that a sub-committee with a small staff should be charged with planning and making all preparations for the expansion and modification of the intelligence machine that would be required for war. Such war-time needs as censorship and political warfare intelligence should be catered for by this sub-committee.

General Intelligence Requirements Committee.
70. This sub-committee's task would be to lay down the priorities to be accorded to the nation's "intelligence effort," to co-ordinate the work of the different collecting agencies, to allot responsibilities between those agencies and to exercise general supervision over the Central Intelligence Bureau described below.

The Central Intelligence Bureau
71. We propose that the inter-service, inter-departmental intelligence organisations, such as the Postal and Telegraph Censorship, I.S.T.D. and the intelligence side of P.W.E., should find their home in peace-time in the Central Bureau, which should be so constituted as to permit of their expansion in time of war to fulfil their full functions. It would be wrong to attempt to produce a detailed blue-print at this stage, of the bureau, but there may be advantage in providing a rough outline. We have in mind that the bureau should be organised on the lines of the Information and Records Branch of the Postal and Telegraph Censorship Department. That is to say that it should provide machinery, through liaison sections staffed by the consumer Departments, for conveying the needs of the consumers to the bureau, who would be responsible for ensuring that the information was collected by the agency best fitted to collect it. The bureau would also be responsible for ensuring that the material it produced was distributed to all those with a legitimate interest in it. The bureau should be divided into two parts, one of which would deal with secret information, and the other with information that is not

secret. It is suggested that in both its secret and its non-secret parts the bureau should be organised both by geographical areas and by subjects. We have in mind that information required as a basis of high policy by, for example, the Foreign Office or the Chiefs of Staff should be collected and collated in the first instance in the non-secret branch of the bureau. It should then be tested in the light of any secret information that is available. The next stage, if appropriate for inter-service or inter-departmental assessment, would be for the material to be dealt with by the Joint Intelligence Staff, and the final assessment would be made by the Joint Intelligence Sub-Committee itself. The bureau would be responsible for providing in the shape of memoranda or reference books such factual information as was required. It will be for Departments to determine how far they will wish to maintain their own collating and appreciating machinery once the Central Bureau has been established. We believe that if our recommendation is accepted, the central machine will sufficiently justify itself to encourage Departments to refrain from duplicating its work.

72. Our proposals are illustrated in the Chart attached to this report (Annex B).

Ministerial Responsibility.

73. The centralised intelligence machine described in the preceding paragraphs will be a fairly large organisation, and it will be necessary for its expenses to be carried on the vote of some Department, though we believe that some of its expenses may be met from revenues produced by itself and that, in any case, its creation should result in some saving. Much will depend on the organisation of which the Joint Intelligence Sub-Committee itself forms a part. If we revert to a system similar to that which existed before the present war, with no central defence organisation other than the Committee of Imperial Defence and its sub-committees and secretariat, it would perhaps be most convenient for the Treasury vote to carry the unified intelligence organisation. The Treasury carries the vote for His Majesty's Stationery Office, which is an existing semi-autonomous Government agency. On the other hand, if a Defence Ministry were created, it would be logical for the intelligence organisation to form part of that Ministry.

(Signed)
V. CAVENDISH-BENTINCK.
DENIS CAPEL-DUNN.
Offices of the War Cabinet,
10th January, 1945.

ANNEX A.

GENERAL SURVEY OF ACTIVITIES OF THE INFORMATION AND RECORDS BRANCH, IMPERIAL CENSORSHIP.

The main function of this Branch is to ensure that basic intelligence material from the public communications system is properly selected and made available for use in the Government Departments served by this Branch with the minimum possible delay.

Military, Naval, Air Force and financial material is handled by specialist sections, which are not included in the organisation of I.R.B., but which work in close liaison.

In order to carry out this function, I.R.B. has to ensure that—

(1) The Requirements of user Departments are properly disseminated to and understood by various branches of Censorship.

(2) The channels along which the material flows are clear and defined.

(3) The material is adequately recorded.

I.R.B. is not an intelligence section, that is to say, they do not collate the material, except in certain specially defined categories, where experience has proved that collated reports provide the most economical result, *e.g.*, conditions in enemy and enemy-occupied territories, and other similar categories of material.

Information material arrives in I.R.B. in the shape of—

(1) Letter submissions, reports and information slips from United Kingdom Postal, British Dominions, British Colonial and Allied Censorships.

(2) Telegrams from United Kingdom Telegraph Censorship, Dominion, Colonial and Allied Censorships and from the organisation responsible for monitoring commercial radio communication circuits.

(3) Reports of telephone conversations.

In order to deal with this the following organisation has been evolved:—

1. *Cable Section* (the full title of this is "Translation, Scrutiny and Sorting of Telegrams Section").

The three principal classes of telecommunications are handled:—

(1) *Terminal Telegrams*.—These are screened by the censor on duty in the telegram office before being forwarded to I.R.B.

(2) *Transit Telegrams*.—All transit telegrams are sent to I.R.B. They are then scrutinised against Watch Lists and examined.

(3) Copies of all monitored *Radio Intercepts*.

Material of interest under (1), (2) and (3) is passed to the appropriate liaison sections for allocation to Government Departments.

NOTE.—The total traffic through the Cable Section amounts to about 75,000 items a week. These are handled by some 60 linguists and cablese experts.

Overseas stations screen messages before sending copies to I.R.B.

NOTE.—In most urgent cases the routine can be by-passed by Senior Officers, and the copy passed direct to the Department or Section interested.

2. *Liaison Sections* (Trade and General).

These two Sections deal with the information liaison between Censorship and Government Departments and are responsible for the final allocation of information material.

They are divided into the Trade Liaison, which deals with all the Government Departments responsible for Trading Controls, and the General Liaison Section, which deals with all Government Departments of a non-trading nature. There is inevitably some overlap in certain categories of information and officers of the Trade and General Sections exchange opinions and determine between themselves which will handle borderline cases.

The material handled by these two Sections includes letter submissions from British Dominion, Colonial and Allied Censorships, telegram copies passed to them by the Cable Section and reports of telephone conversations.

United Kingdom Postal Censorship submissions are allocated direct by Postal Censorship and only come to I.R.B. for mechanical distribution in Records Section (see 6 below).

Each Liaison Section is in charge of an Assistant Censor.

Each Section has its own Reports Sub-section.
Senior Officers of these sections act as liaison officers and establish and maintain personal contacts with their respective Government Departments.
They are responsible for seeing that the Government Department is satisfied with the information which has reached it, and that Censorship is satisfied that the requirements of the Government Departments are fully understood and being acted upon.
A consistent and persistent effort is made to keep the information requirements of Government Departments within bounds.
It has been found by experience that Government Departments are inclined to make use of the Censorship machine as an administrative convenience regardless of the nature of the Censorship's limitations.
It is therefore one of the responsibilities of liaison officers to protect Censorship from undue demands by Government Departments.
The Trade Section is staffed with gentlemen experienced in foreign and home trading affairs.
The General Section, whose interest can be divided into:—
(1) The Security Services;
(2) The Propaganda Ministries;
(3) The Domestic Ministries, *i.e.*, Home Office, &c.;
(4) The Ministries for Colonies, Dominions and the Foreign Office;
(5) The Services;
is staffed with ladies whose background knowledge enables them to deal with questions relevant to their work. The General Section also compile reports on home opinion and conditions in enemy-occupied territory, and other matters derived from the information passing through this Section.

3. *Requirements Officer.*

This gentleman is the Secretary of the Allocation Committee, which, in turn, is composed of:—
(a) The Requirements Officer,
(b) The A.C. of the Trade Liaison Section,
(c) The A.C. of the General Liaison Section,
(d) The A.C. of the Control Section,
(e) The Chief Postal Censor's representative,
(f) The representative of the Chief of the Overseas

Section, Secretariat. (The Chief of the Overseas Section, Secretariat, is the channel for correspondence with Overseas, Dominion, Colonial and Allied Censorships. It is a separate organisation within Imperial Censorship and is responsible to the Director-General through the Secretary.)

The Requirements Officer clarifies requirements received from Ministries, and consults with other members of the Allocation Committee as to the *form* in which requirements are passed on to examiners through the Allocation List. His work is internal to Censorship, outside contacts being maintained by the Liaison Sections. Informal consultation is maintained in the interval between Committee meetings. The Requirements Officer depends directly from Liaison Censor, who is *ex officio* Chairman of the Allocation Committee, at the same level as the A.C.'s of the Trade Liaison Section, the General Liaison Section and the Cable Section.

4. *Control Section.*

This Section reviews all the products of Censorship received by I.R.B. from whatever source they may come, and assesses their value, with the object of estimating the efficiency of the Censorship machine, particularly in its information aspect. It divides its activities geographically into regions.

(1) The United Kingdom. (Control and review is maintained by correspondence supplemented by personal contact.)

(2) The Eastern Hemisphere. (This includes all territories in which Imperial Censorship operates or has affiliates, in Europe, Asia, Africa and Australia.)

(3) The Western Hemisphere. (Including the United States, Canada, British Colonies and the Independent American Republics.)

The activities of this section have to do with control in the broadest sense. The work of Censorship is kept up to the standard required by means of advice contained in reports and memoranda. This section depends directly on the Deputy Chief Officer and has a finger in practically everybody's pie.

5. *Central Watch List Section.*

This Section is a clerical Section whose function is to produce names supplied by the Departments for

Watching in the form most suitable for the work of the Department.

Names suspected by Censorship are always checked back with Government Departments.

1. Watch List Names comprise—
(a) those contained in M.E.W.'s War Trade List (about 20,000 names) and Supplements;
(b) those submitted by Ministries, Departments, …}
Services … … … … … … … … … … … … … … … … … … …}
approximately
(c) those submitted by Chief Postal Censor… … … …}
5,000.
(d) those submitted by "Security" … … … … … … … …}

2. All names are issued, in the form of lists or otherwise as experience has found to be the most convenient form to:—
(a) Sorters at P.O. centres;
(b) Postal Censorship;
(c) Telegraph Censorship;
as follows, viz.:—

(a) *For Sorters.*
Duplicated copies (from a stencil) containing *all* names listed in paragraph 1 are supplied on foolscap sheets, about 30 names to a page; these sheets are known as "Masters" and are stuck on thick cardboard at the P.O. centres for convenience of handling. A separate "Master" is maintained for each country. The letters picked out are passed to a special scrutiny room where they are bundled and passed to the Censorship Section concerned, *i.e.,* Trade, Private, Security or Services. These "Masters" are kept up to date by manuscript from Supplements issued by Central Watch List Section and when any sheet or "Master" becomes too congested it is restencilled. The "Masters" used by the sorters in the first stage give no indication whatever as to the Ministries, &c., for which the names are on watch; the copies of the "Masters" used in the special scrutiny room referred to merely have a code letter against each name, to indicate the class of mail into which the letter falls, *i.e.,* Trade. Private, Security, War Trade List, &c.

(b) *For Postal Censorship.*
Four lists are issued, viz.:—
(1) The printed War Trade List and Supplements
(2) The T.M.L. (Trade Miscellaneous List) and Supplements.

(3) The P.M.L. (Private Miscellaneous List) and Supplements.
(4) The Security List and Supplements.
In addition to these four main lists, Postal Censorship receives the following advance notices of names which are coming on "watch," which notices give the "story" connected with the watch and enable Examiners to recognise the type of correspondence required from the body of the letter, viz.:—
W.L.M.'s (Watch List Memoranda) on names submitted by Ministries, Departments and Services. Issued by I.R.B. H.Q., who receive the requests.
S.L.A.N.'s (Security List Advance Notices). These concern Security names only. Issued by Central Watch List Section.
M.L.A.N.'s (Miscellaneous List Advance Notices). Refer to names submitted by C.P.C. and are issued by C.P.C. H.Q.
The T.M.L., P.M.L. and Security Lists do not contain the full stories as given by the Advance Notices, but reference numbers to the latter are given against the entries on the list. (Q) appearing after the W.L.M., S.L.A.N. or M.L.A.N. reference number indicates to the Examiner that the respective Advance Notice must be consulted, whereas (U) placed after the number signifies that there is no need to consult the Advance Notice, since all letters are wanted without any restrictions. (The W.L.M.'s are issued in the form of copies made by the "Banda" process. S.L.A.N.'s and M.L.A.N.'s are duplicated copies from a wax stencil).
On the four main lists is indicated against each name the Ministry, Department or Service for whom the watch has been put on. Recently, for Trade Tables only, of Postal Censorship, a card index has been introduced, which contains all names on the T.M.L., P.M.L., Security List and *Supplements* to the War Trade List. This index is being issued, as an experiment, in place of those separate lists and Supplements.
A further change which will take place in the near future is the amalgamation into one combined list of the P.M.L., T.M.L., and Security List, for use on Postal Censorship Tables, other than Trade, instead of those three separate lists.

(c) *For Telegraph Censorship.*
(1) A "Kalamazoo" Binder containing names (on strips) from Ministries, Departments, Services and Security.
(2) Main War Trade printed List.
(3) A supplementary "Kalamazoo" Binder for names from War Trade Lists Supplements pending their inclusion in the main List.
(The strips on the "Kalamazoo" Binder (1) have brief notes of any qualifications to the "Watch," thus obviating the necessity which would otherwise exist, of referring to W.L.M.'s and S.L.A.N.'s.)

6. *Records Section.*

1. *Receipt and Release Section.*—(This includes also (A) Distribution and (B) Records Sections.)
Receipt and Release is divided as follows:—
(1) *Mail In Table.*—Handles all incoming letter submissions.
(2) *Ministerial Returns Clerical* Table.—Handles, on return, all submissions and/or originals sent to Ministries for action. Transcribes the action given onto Records copies.
(3) *Ministerial Releases Examiners Table.*—Central point for the release, condemnation, &c., of letters emanating from any British Censorship Station which have been submitted to, and returned with, action by Ministries. All letters are examined for Censorship violations which might conflict with Ministerial decisions.
(4) *Ministerial Reminders Clerical Table.*—Handles matter of "reminding" Ministries of outstanding submissions requiring action. Reminders are sent weekly.
A. *Distribution Section.*
1. *Letter Distribution* divided as follows:—
(a) Main split of records into five (5) main Ministries, for convenience in handling only.
(b) Trade and General. This is also sub-divided for Foreign Office, B.B.C., Ministry of Information.
2. *Cables and Reports Distribution* (also reports from overseas stations).
3. *Photostat Section.*
4. *Re-submission to Ministries Sections.*
5. *Dispatch to Division of Reports.*—Washington to Ottawa and other main Censorship Agencies.
B. *Records Section.*
This Section has three main files:—

(1) Sender file;
(2) Numerical file;
(3) Card index of addresser.

The Records Section receives two copies of each submission. One of these is filed by sender, the other by records number which is put on the submission by the originating unit.

Prefixes are used by different units and consist principally in groups of 3 letters (for example, a submission from Palermo, Italy, might be numbered ITA/PAL 234), *i.e.*, the submission originates in Italian Censorship, the Palermo station. A card file for addresses is cross-indexed to the sender file.

Notes.—Some *subject matter* folders are maintained for submissions which are of purely temporary interest and will be referred to only for the preparation of reports. Submissions regarding letters of complaint about the slowness of the mails at Christmas time is one example of the material contained in the Subject Matter folder. (Registered letters and originals are never put in Subject Matter File.)

Third Party Files.—No attempt is made to maintain Third Party Files.

Action copies of submissions of held originals are kept in Receipt and Release Section. Numerical receipts are filed in Records Section.

Ministries' and Departments' actions in regard to submissions are forwarded back to unit originating submission for their information. (This is a matter of morale. For the same purpose D.A.C.'s occasionally visit I.R.B.).

Cables filed only by numbers. These are sorted into terminals, transits, wireless intercepts (received from monitors) and cables received by mail (from Ottawa, Malta, &c.). Cables can be located only by number, and consequently requests for copies can come only through some Ministry or Department to which an allocation of that same cable has been made.

Telephone intercepts are handled in the same manner as cables.

Reports are filed by stations preparing them and by number. *Captured Mail* is filed separately. It is divided into *Italian* and *German*. This mail is received in bags which in turn contain bundles of letters. Each bundle is numbered in London.

When a numbered bundle is sent to files, it is called a Transfer. Reference to letters in different bundles is therefore made by "Transfer Number." All letters bearing the same transfer number are filed in the same file. The Control Section's reviews of stations' work is facilitated by this filing system.

Alphabetical Filing Guides.—Underline names of addressor and addressee as guides for the filers, and is therefore responsible for seeing that all correspondence relative to individuals or companies is properly filed together. This is important, especially in the case of individuals and companies operating on an international scale, where some variation in name occurs, as between one country and another (for example, Svenska Tandstiker becomes Swedish Match Company in English). All their correspondence is filed together.

Counter-Espionage Section.

This Section was established as a result of a Conference held at Miami, Florida, in August 1943.

It works under the executive control of the Chief Officer, I.R.B., who is Chairman of the Censorship Counter-Espionage Committee which consists of Chief Officer, I.R.B., the Deputy Chief Postal Censor and the head of the Secretariat.

The function of the Committee is to co-ordinate Censorship action on all counter-Espionage matters.

The function of the Section is to ensure that all information concerning Counter-Espionage which would assist in the detection or interception of communications of enemy agents is made available to those Overseas or Allied Stations handling the material in which these communications may occur.

There is a special Censorship Liaison Officer in Section V, M.I.6 and, in addition, the Officer-in-Charge maintains close contact with M.I.5, the Trade and General Liaison Sections in I.R.B., and with specially appointed Counter-Espionage Officers at certain agreed Overseas Stations.

Through the office of the Director, Western Area, New York, it is in close touch with its opposite number in United States Censorship, known as the Technical Operations Division.

FLOW OF MATERIAL THROUGH I.R.B.

I.—*Submissions, Information Slips, Reports.*

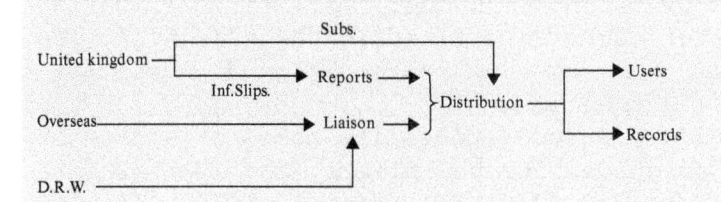

```
                         Subs.
United kingdom ─┐
                ├──► Reports ──┐
        Inf.Slips.             ├─ Distribution ──┬──► Users
Overseas ───────┴──► Liaison ──┘                 │
                                                 └──► Records
D.R.W. ─────────────────────────┘
```

United Kingdom submissions by-pass Liaison and go direct to the Users allocated by Postal Censorship. They are, however, seen by Reports. Information Slips go only to Reports where they are collated and embodied in reports on special topics. Overseas and D.R.W. submissions are allocated by Trade and General Liaison Sections and are seen by Reports.

II. —*Telegrams.*

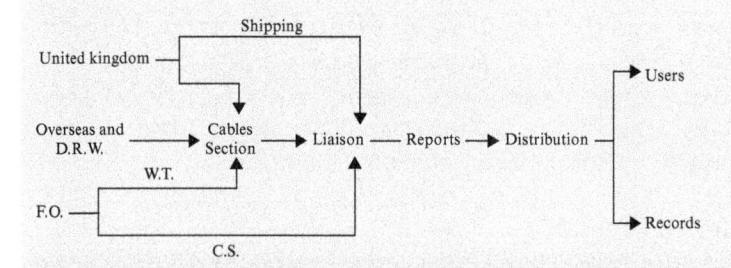

```
                    Shipping
United kingdom ──────────────┐
                             │                           ┌──► Users
Overseas and      Cables     ▼                           │
   D.R.W.    ──► Section ──► Liaison ── Reports ──► Distribution
             W.T.     ▲                                  │
F.O. ────────────────┘                                   └──► Records
                C.S.
```

W.T.s are Wireless intercepts; C.S.s are W.T.s selected, decoded and translated by the Foreign Office. Cables Section scrutinises for Listed names, sorts the telegrams into categories, e.g., Oils and Fats, Metals, Textiles, Chemicals, rejects obviously useless material, translates messages in foreign languages and, as Cables Section, does not allocate, passes the telegrams on to Liaison for allocation. Shipping telegrams go direct to Liaison, by-passing Cables Section so as to save time.

III.—*U.K. Telephone Intercepts.*

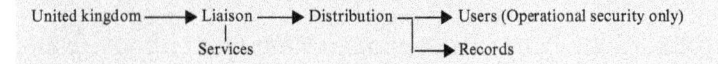

```
United kingdom ──► Liaison ──► Distribution ──┬──► Users (Operational security only)
                      │                       │
                   Services                   └──► Records
```

As Telephone intercepts are used for Operational security only, they are allocated by Liaison in collaboration with the Services.

IV.—Requirements.

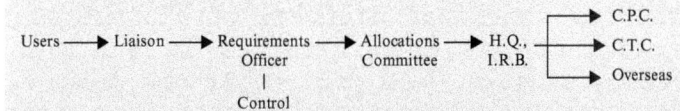

```
Users ──▶ Liaison ──▶ Requirements ──▶ Allocations ──▶ H.Q.,  ──┬──▶ C.P.C.
                      Officer           Committee       I.R.B.  ├──▶ C.T.C.
                          │                                     └──▶ Overseas
                       Control
```

The Users inform Liaison of any change they wish to be made, or Liaison suggest changes to the users. Liaison passes the new requirements or amendment to the Requirements Officer, who studies them from the Censorship angle. As Chairman of the Allocations Committee he submits them to that body for discussion by the members, who include representatives of the C.P.C. (and of the C.T.C. and Overseas if necessary), and representatives of Liaison and Control Sections. A version agreed unanimously by the Committee and the User is finally arrived at and this is issued by H.Q., I.R.B., to the C.P.C., the C.T.C. and Overseas, who transmit it to their officers in the form best adapted to their needs. In postal Censorship it appears as an amendment to the Allocation List. If Control, in its Reviews of U.K. submissions, finds weaknesses in the A.L., it passes the information to the Requirements Officer who takes appropriate action to have the A.L. amended if necessary.

V.—Watch Lists.

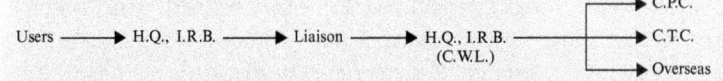

```
Users ──▶ H.Q., I.R.B. ──▶ Liaison ──▶ H.Q., I.R.B. ──┬──▶ C.P.C.
                                        (C.W.L.)      ├──▶ C.T.C.
                                                      └──▶ Overseas
```

Users fill in a form giving all the relevant particulars of the firm or person to be watch-listed. This is vetted by H.Q. and Liaison and passed back to H.Q. for the Central Watch List Section which again checks up and incorporates the names in the appropriate List.

VI.—Action.

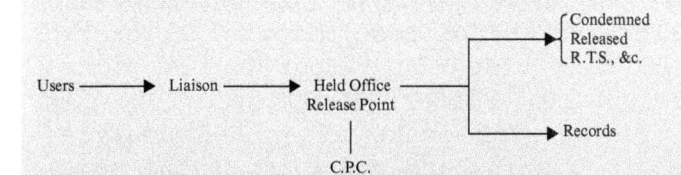

```
                                          ┌─ Condemned
                                          ├─ Released
                                          └─ R.T.S., &c.
Users ──▶ Liaison ──▶ Held Office ────────┤
                     Release Point        └──▶ Records
                          │
                        C.P.C.
```

A submission "For action" is returned by the User to Liaison with the former's recommendation for disposal. This recommendation is vetted by Liaison who pass the slip to Release Point which works in contact with an A.C.

at Holborn representing the C.P.C. who is alone ultimately responsible for the final disposal of all postal matter. If the original has been retained in I.R.B., Release Point obtains it from Held Office; if the original has been submitted, it has come into Release Point with the submission slip. Release Point then carry out the action recommended and approved.

VII.—*U.S. Liaison Mission in I.R.B.*

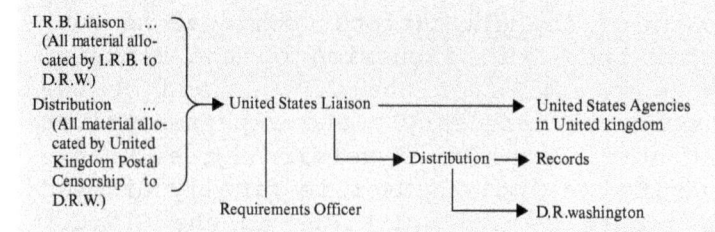

```
I.R.B. Liaison    ⎫
(All material allo-|
cated by I.R.B. to |
D.R.W.)            |
                   ├─→ United States Liaison ────────→ United States Agencies
Distribution    ...|                                    in United kingdom
(All material allo-|                  └──→ Distribution ──→ Records
cated by United    |
Kingdom Postal     |
Censorship to      |
D.R.W.)            ⎭  Requirements Officer        └──→ D.R.washington
```

I.R.B. Liaison sends all the material allocated by them to D.R.W. — telegrams, telephone intercepts, overseas submissions and reports — direct to U.S. Liaison, whilst Distribution sends all the U.K. submissions allocated to D.R.W. The U.S. Liaison Officers screen this material, send copies direct to the U.S. Agencies in the U.K., e.g., O.S.S. and O.W.I., whilst the master copies go to D.R.W., Washington, via Distribution. For D.R.W. Requirements, the U.S. Liaison Officer concerned contacts the Requirements Officer I.R.B. and an agreed version is issued by H.Q., I.R.B., as in Diagram IV above.

VIII.—*Control Section.*

Control Section, whose function is to examine objectively, statistically and critically all censorship material, is sited in I.R.B. because it can examine the material at any point in its flow: as it reaches Distribution; as it arrives at or leaves Cable Section or Liaison Section; as it lies in Records. It can thus work on current material, allocated or unallocated, or on past material allocated or unallocated. It is divided into four sub-sections: U.K.; Western Hemisphere; Eastern Hemisphere; Foreign Censorship. Each sub-section looks after and analyses from time to time the quality and quantity of the material produced in its own area, in the case of Foreign Censorship, collates its special material.

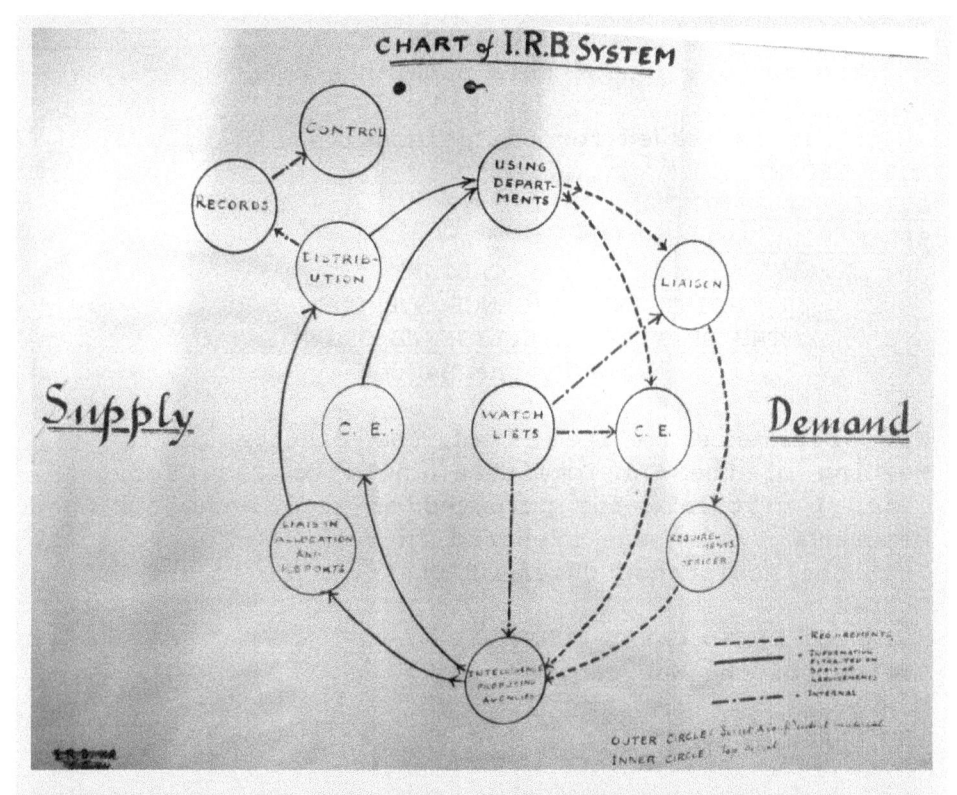

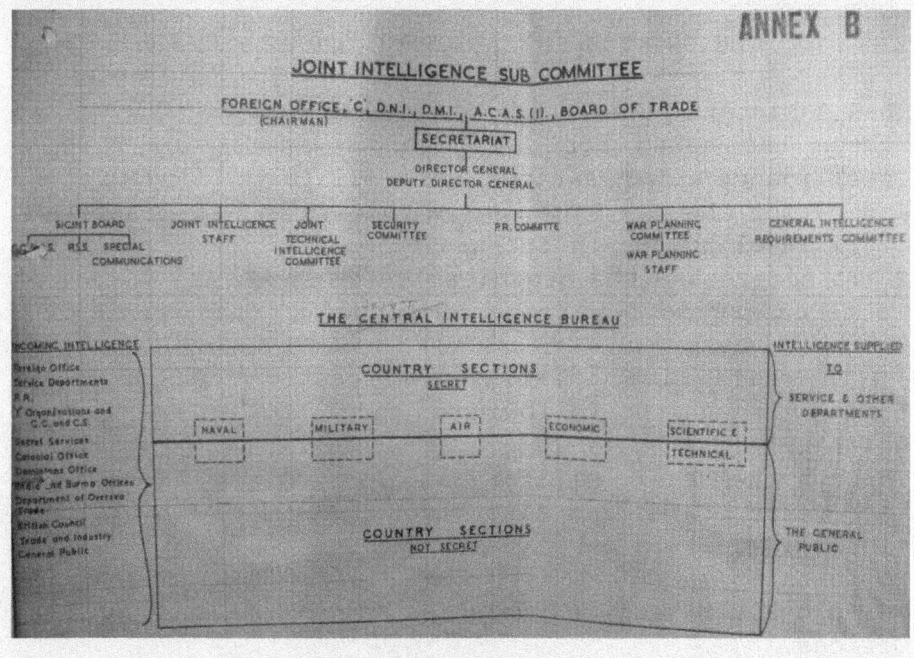

A POST-WAR INTELLIGENCE MACHINERY

```
                         JIC(44)86
     The circulation of this paper has been strictly
                          limited.
       It is issued for the personal use of file
MOST SECRET.                                     Copy No. 14
J.I.C.(44)86(O)
3RD MARCH, 1944
```

WAR CABINET
JOINT INTELLIGENCE SUB-COMMITTEE
THE BRITISH INTELLIGENCE ORGANISATION
Note by the Secretary

With reference to item 9 of the minutes of the 8th Meeting of the Sub-Committee, held on 22nd February, 1944, I circulate for purposes of record the attached memorandum which was prepared in response to a request from the Assistance Chief of Staff, G-2, in the United States.
(Signed) DENIS CAPEL-DUNN
Officer of the War Cabinet,
S.W.1.
3RD MARCH, 1944.

MOST SECRET
THE BRITISH INTELLIGENCE ORGANISATION

The Assistant Chief of Staff, G-2, in the United States has asked for a memorandum describing British Intelligence organisations both military and civil and indicating the way in which in this country military and civil intelligence is integrated.
2. To understand the organisation as it exists to-day it is necessary to have some knowledge of the roots from which it has grown.
3. In peace time intelligence reached the centre in London through the following channels.
<u>Military</u>
Through the Naval, Military and Air Attaches accredited to Foreign States and also through Naval staff officers (Intelligence) in certain ports.
<u>Political</u>
Through His Majesty's Embassies, Legations and Consular Offices.

Commercial and Industrial
Through Commercial - Diplomatic and Consular officers.
The Secret Service
The Security Service

4. While the task of Service attaches was primarily to report on military affairs and developments in the countries in which they resided, they of course reported to their departments also on other matters. Many of them, particularly in Eastern countries acquired a profound knowledge of the language, topography and people on matters other than strictly military. The same applies to the other channels through which intelligence reached London. The frontiers between political, military and economic intelligence are ill defined. The reports coming through these different service, diplomatic and other channels were collated in the departments at which the channels ended. While until a few years before the war there was little in the way of fixed machinery for the interchange of foreign intelligence between the different departments, in practice the more important telegrams and despatches were generally circulated to all interested departments so that each could make a cross check on the information reaching it direct.

5. In 1936 the Committee of Imperial Defence established the Joint Intelligence Committee. The Committee in those days had the task of preparing for the Committee of Imperial Defence long term appreciations on the trends of the policy, strategy and military preparedness of foreign countries. It was composed of representatives of the intelligence divisions of the three Service Departments and, latterly of the Foreign Office. Experts were called in from other interested departments and organisations such as the Industrial Intelligence Centre, the forerunner of the Enemy Branch of the Ministry of Economic Warfare.

6. It is unnecessary in this memorandum to give an account of the stages through which the Joint Intelligence Committee acquired its present responsibilities, but it is desirable at the outset to mention the Committee since it has developed in wartime into the focal point at which all intelligence, military and civil is discussed and the final deductions from it are made.

7. In wartime many of the peace time channels through which intelligence flows dry up, but new ones are opened.

The conquest and domination of a large part of Europe by Germany and of much of the Far East by Japan has closed very many of the diplomatic and consular sources of information which were previously available to us. On the other hand the activities of the Secret Service are in wartime greatly intensified. The establishment of the Special Operations Executive, though not itself a body responsible for the collection of intelligence, does provide a valuable contribution as will be seen below. Fighting the war itself provides our armed forces with many means of obtaining information about the enemy. Prisoners of War are captured and interrogated. Our own Prisoners of War who manage to make their escape from enemy hands have often much of value to relate. Refugees from occupied territory have their story to tell. A source of intelligence of the greatest value is available to us in wartime which is denied to us in peace time, that of photographic aerial reconnaissance. In addition we have in wartime the great benefit of receiving intelligence from our Allies and of discussion of it with them. Another source only available in wartime is provided by the censorship organisation which is administered by our Ministry of Information. Connected with the Ministry of Information also are the Monitoring services of the British Broadcasting Corporation and the Press Reading Bureaux that we have established for watching the enemy and neutral press.

8. There are two organisations whose function is primarily operational but which in carrying out their functions are enabled to collect a certain amount of useful intelligence. They are the Special Operations Executive and the Political Warfare Executive. The Special Operations Executive is charged, under the general direction of the Chiefs of Staff, with fostering, directing and helping resistance and subversive movements in enemy and enemy occupied territory, and in organising and carrying out direct sabotage of plant, communications etc., of value to the enemy. Some of the agents of this organisation are in a position to obtain information of value to us. Since, however, the primary function of these agents is not the collection of intelligence, intelligence received through them is not sent direct to the service departments and other "consumers" of intelligence but is sent to the "consumer" through the Secret Intelligence

Service. This is in order to ensure that all intelligence is canalised and the danger of crossing agents' lines is thus avoided or reduced. Reports from S.O.E. agents can under this arrangement be checked against other intelligence received through Secret means and the proper value placed upon it. In localities where organised guerrilla warfare is taking place missions under British liaison officers are sent, and their operational information is passed direct to the nearest Allied Commander in the field.

9. The Political Warfare Executive, as its name implies, is charged with assisting the war effort by propaganda, and the dissemination of information along lines of policy laid down by His Majesty's Government to fit in with the general military policy in force. The agents of the Political Warfare Executive abroad are also in a position to acquire useful information. This also, when it reaches London, is checked against the information reaching here by other means.

10. The co-ordination of the intelligence received through all these different channels is effected in two ways. In the first place there is a horizontal link between the diiferent collectors. Telegrams and reports received are circulated by collectors including the Service Departments, the Foreign Office, the Secret Service, and the Security Service to all customers who may be interested – primarily the Foreign Office, the Service Departments and the Ministry of Economic Warfare.

11. Secondly there is a vertical link between the collectors direct and also between the customers and the central organisation which in wartime advises the Chiefs of Staff and through them His Majesty's Government on the intentions of the enemy and on enemy activities throughout the world. That central organisation is the Joint Intelligence Committee which today consists of representatives of the three Service Departments, the Foreign Office, who provide the chairman, the Secret Intelligence Service, the Security Service and the Ministry of Economic Warfare. The Joint Intelligence Committee is served by a whole time staff (the "Joint Intelligence Staff") which did not exist in peace, and whose function it is to help in the drafting of J.I.C. strategic appreciations and memoranda and to

co-ordinate the views of the departments represented in the Committee.

12. It has been found that some bodies organised on an inter-service basis are required to fulfil certain special intelligence functions. These inter-service organisations staffed by experts from all the services and from other interested departments are controlled as to policy by the Joint Intelligence Committee itself direct. Such organisations are:-

(a) The Inter-Service Topographical Department whose function It is to prepare long terrn reports on the topography, communications, airfields, docks, beaches, industries, economic resources etc., of areas which may become of military interest.

(b) The organisation which deals both with the collection of information from enemy Prisoners of War in our hands and from British Prisoners of War in the hands of the enemy.

(c) The organisation responsible for the collation and interpretation of the product of aerial photographic reconnaissance.

(d) The Intelligence Section (Operations). This is a clearing house for _factual_ intelligence required by Force Commanders and the Planning Staffs. This organisation does not evaluate intelligence or make appreciations. It is designed to prevent the sections in the Service and other Departments having to answer questions on the same subject from different enquirers.

13. The complement of a good intelligence organisation is a strong counter-intelligence system to prevent enemy penetration and to make it as difficult as possible for the enemy to collect intelligence. Security measures often require full co-operation from many Government Departments and in order to achieve this such matters are discussed by a permanent Committee known as the Security Executive. As has been stated above the Security Service is represented on the Joint Intelligence Committee. Thus intelligence obtained by that organisation is made available to the Committee as a whole.

14. The Joint Intelligence Committee works under directions from the Chiefs of Staff Committee and in close and constant collaboration with the Joint Planning Staffs. It is thus enabled to direct the spot-light of intelligence upon those areas in which the operational staffs are most

interested. A continuous process of revision goes on of the priorities of intelligence work. It is perhaps worth mentioning that the Chiefs of Staff Committee, the Joint Intelligence Committee and the Joint Planning Staff all meet in the same building and are served by a common Secretariat.

15. The Joint Intelligence Committee in addition to its responsibility for co-ordinating the product of the various collectors of intelligence into the form of agreed advice on enemy intentions, has the additional responsibility of watching, directing and to some extent controlling the British Intelligence organisation throughout the world, so as to ensure that intelligence is received at the most economical cost in time, effort and manpower, and so as to prevent overlapping. During the course of the war subordinate Joint Intelligence Committees have been established in many parts of the world. In commands abroad these committees are of course under the direct control of the local commanders. In some theatres, however, such as the Middle East where there exists a committee or organisation responsible for co-ordinating political and military affairs, the local Joint Intelligence Committee with full representation of the services, the Foreign Office and other interested authorities reports to that committee. All these local Joint Intelligence Committees, however, maintain constant touch with the London Committee. Acting under the direct control of the Joint Intelligence Committee in London is a British Joint Intelligence Committee in Washington which works in with a similarly organised United States Committee and together with it forms the "Combined Intelligence Committee". Reports produced by the "Commbined Intelligence Committee" to the Combined Chiefs of Staff represent the agreed Anglo-American view upon the subjects with which they deal.

16. To sum up the British intelligence organisation is a loose-knit system under which it has been possible to provide to a remarkably successful degree for the information required by any authority for its own purpose to reach it rapidly, and also for co-ordination at the centre, so that there is now little reason for mistakes of military policy to be caused by the failure of any authority to receive information which is available.

Notes

1. JIC(44)86(O), 'The British Intelligence Organisation', 3 March 1944, TNA: CAB 81/121.
2. 'The Intelligence Machine', 10 January 1945 (emphasis added), TNA: CAB 163/6. For a more detailed examination of this paper see Michael Herman, 'The Post-War Organization of Intelligence: The January 1945 Report to the Joint Intelligence Committee on "The Intelligence Machine"', in Robert Dover & Michael S. Goodman (eds), *Learning from the Secret Past: Cases in British Intelligence History* (Washington, DC: Georgetown University Press, 2011).
3. JIC(45)265(O)(Final), 'Post-War Organisation of Intelligence', 7 September 1945, TNA: CAB 81/130.
4. Misc/P(47)31, 'Review of Intelligence Organisations, 1947', 6 November 1947, TNA: CAB 163/7.
5. DO(48)21, 'Charter for the Joint Intelligence Committee', 24 February 1948, TNA: CAB 131/6.

5

ORIGINS OF THE SOVIET THREAT

ONE OF THE lessons the JIC had learnt from pre-war intelligence was the importance of careful planning. Halfway through the war, therefore, the committee engaged in nascent efforts to gauge the nature of the post-war world. In fact the JIC was not alone in Whitehall in doing this; both the Foreign Office and the military did likewise. There was consensus that the fate and role of the Soviet Union would be of paramount importance, yet there was little agreement about what this would entail. In many ways the questions were simple – whether the Soviet Union was likely to continue to be an ally of the West and whether coexistence would be possible – but the answers were anything but straightforward.

Within Whitehall a wealth of different organisations were created from 1943 onwards, designed to look towards the post-war world. The difficulty underpinning them was the polar positions occupied by the FO and the military: in simple terms the former did not appreciate the idea of making plans against a current ally, whilst the latter thought that the wartime rapprochement was a temporary aberration, and once war was over the alliance would crumble. As the strategic assessment body of His Majesty's Government, the JIC should have provided a voice into this maelstrom. Its involvement, however, was limited. Why this was so is, at a glance, odd; certainly the JIC's wartime Chairman and Secretary were aware of the opposing positions. Victor Cavendish-Bentinck, the able wartime Chairman, did attempt to smooth over the cracks between his FO and military colleagues, but the positions were too entrenched.

What did the JIC forecast? The paper reproduced below is from December 1944. It is an extraordinary paper, as is evident from its title: 'Russia's Strategic Interests and Intentions from the Point of View of Her Security'. Here was a unique attempt to consider how the world looked from the vantage point of the Kremlin. At the outset the JIC conceded that 'any study ... must be speculative as we have little evidence'. Despite this it was given an unusually high classification with a specially restricted circulation. The paper concluded that whilst

> Russia will not, in our opinion, follow an aggressive policy of territorial expansion, her suspicion of British and American policy will nevertheless continue to cause difficulty as will also her tactlessness in the handling of international affairs. Accordingly Russia's relations with the British Empire and the United States will depend very largely on the ability of each side to convince the other of the sincerity of its desire for collaboration.[1]

The report was also hugely detailed. It provided information on Russian economic production, fuel, power and industry; but also its intentions towards Scandinavian and Baltic states, Germany, Poland, Romania, Bulgaria, Yugoslavia and Greece, in addition to the Western powers, the Black Sea region, the Middle East and the Far East. Summarising the conclusions, the JIC stated that Russia's primary policy would be directed towards 'achieving the greatest possible measure of security'. To achieve this, 'Russia will ... draw the States lying along her borders, and particularly those in Europe, into her strategic system'. Overall the report was sensible and offered a balanced assessment, but it did little to help settle debate.

Within Whitehall the arguments were vicious and acrimonious but events, fortuitously, intervened. Concern over Russian troop movements towards the Caucasus in late 1945 and in Persia in early 1946, together with Frank Roberts's telegrams from the embassy in Moscow, convinced many that the FO view had been incorrect. An updated JIC paper at this time – March 1946 – repeated many of its wartime conclusions but emphasised the Russian fear of attack, the necessity to create a 'belt of satellite States with governments subservient to their policy' and, crucially, that Russian policy will be 'aggressive by all means short of war', and that consequently, 'attention should be drawn to the dangers inherent in Russian policy as we see it'.[2] The assessment was approved by both the FO and the Chiefs of Staff Committee and it was forwarded to the Prime Minister and Foreign Secretary. By the summer of 1946 there was widespread support, particularly in the FO, that the JIC was *the* place to prepare judgements on Russian actions.[3] Perspectives were certainly hardening and in the aftermath of the Persian crisis that spring, when Moscow refused to remove troops as had previously been agreed, the JIC wrote that 'the Soviet Union will take every opportunity to foment anti-British feeling and to reduce British influence throughout the Arab world, and will ultimately hope to supplant it'.[4]

In London the anti-Soviet faction was clearly in the ascendant. Even the most sceptical of FO advisers had become convinced of the need to coordinate policy against the Russians. Such views were supported by concern over the fate of Turkey and Greece – countries, it was believed, that were firmly in Moscow's sights. In the summer of 1947, following the announcement a few months earlier of the 'Truman Doctrine', the American pledge to support 'subjugated' people worldwide, the JIC set itself the task of producing a fresh assessment of Soviet actions. This time it would be based on two overarching questions: what was Russia trying to do and how far was she capable of doing it? The answer to the first question was clear: 'The Soviet leaders are inspired by the conviction that it is their long-term task to hasten the elimination of capitalism in all parts of the world.' This was not based on any hard intelligence, but rather on a reading of the 'published maxims of Lenin and Stalin'.

The issue then, as the JIC posed implicitly in its second question, was: how was this to be achieved? With a pressing need to reconstruct the Soviet economy, it was felt that Russian policy would strive towards dependence on its own natural resources, and that until this was achieved Stalin would attempt to avoid war whilst continuing to establish a 'protective belt' around his borders and through the 'continued aggressive promotion of communism'. Thus, taking everything into account, it was unlikely that war would occur before 1955–60.[5] The consequences of this assessment were long lived. Discussions in the JIC in late 1947, for instance, centred on what might propel the Soviet Union into war before this period.[6] The COS and the FO were both, by now, avid readers of these JIC assessments. Ultimately, however, it would be events, rather than the JIC's assessments, that brought about a change in governmental thinking.

THIS DOCUMENT IS THE PROPERTY OF HIS BRITANNIC MAJESTY'S GOVERMENT

Printed for the War Cabinet. December 1944.

The circulation of this paper has been strictly limited. It is issued for the personal use of

TOP SECRET   Copy No. 32

J.I.C.(44)467(O)(Final.) RESTRICTED CIRCULATION

18th December, 1944

Circulated for the consideration for the Chiefs of Staff

WAR CABINET.

Joint Intelligence Sub-Committee.

RUSSIA'S STRATEGIC INTERESTS AND INTENTIONS FROM THE POINT OF VIEW OF HER SECURITY.

REPORT BY THE JOINT INTELLIGENCE SUB-COMMITTEE.

IN this paper we consider Russia's strategic interests in the period after the unconditional surrender of Germany and Japan, from the point of view of her security. We also consider the policy that Russia may be intending to pursue in the post-war period in supporting her interests. We examine in detail, in an Annex, Russia's strategic interests and policy in various countries. We have assumed that the depth of defence needed for the adequate deployment of air defences will not be greatly different from what it is to-day. We do not take account of forms of warfare not at present in use.

2. We must emphasise that any study of Russia's strategic interests and policy must be speculative as we have little evidence to show what view Russia herself takes of her strategic interests or what policy she intends to pursue. Moreover, Russian policy at present depends very largely on the decisions of Marshal Stalin; he is over 65 and it is impossible to predict what changes in the internal and foreign policies of Russia might follow his removal from the scene. We report as follows:-

3. Russia after the war will present a phenomenon new in modern history, a land empire containing within its frontiers a large, youthful and rapidly expanding population, nearly all the raw materials essential for an adequate war economy, and an industry capable of supporting in the field armies substantially larger than those of any other Power in Europe. In addition to this Russia's immense size and the distribution of her natural resources give her great advantages in depth of defence and dispersal of economically important targets; the only exceptions are the Caucasus oilfields, the coal, iron and industries of the Ukraine and, of lesser economic importance, the industrial areas of Moscow and Leningrad. Even these areas are far less vulnerable to attack than the corresponding areas in any other country in Europe.

4. Russia has already shown that she can make good military use of these natural resources. Although her level of technical efficiency is still below that of the most advanced modern Powers, she has proved her capacity to deploy and maintain in the field very large forces and to defeat immensely powerful German armies. Russia's technical and military efficiency are likely to increase; it is probable that there will be an improvement in the general standard of education and that technical training will be further developed, which will tend to raise the level of technical efficiency; similarly, the growth of a military tradition based on the experience gained in the present war is likely to bring about an improvement in Russia's military efficiency.

5. If, as we expect, no violent political upheaval takes place in Russia after the war, the military and economic development of the country will continue without serious disturbance, not perhaps at the exceptional intensity

of the years before this war, but at least on an upward curve. Russia will contain within her own frontiers such military and economic resources as would enable her to face without serious defeat even a combination of the major European Powers. It is true that Russia will probably want to import considerable quantities of oil, but her object would be to conserve her own internal resources and to facilitate industrial expansion and the development of road transport. Since Russian oil production in 1950 may be as high as 50 million tons, these additional imports could, if necessary, be dispensed with in time of war.

6. Russia could, therefore, with much less risk than any other Power in Europe, pursue a policy of isolation and rely exclusively on her own military strength to protect her against aggression. For reasons of geography and communications a serious threat to Russia's security can only be mounted across Russia's western frontier between the Baltic and the Carpathians; in all other directions considerations of terrain or communications make it impossible to deploy sufficient forces to challenge the Russian armies or involve advances of many hundreds of miles before strategically or economically important areas can be reached. Russia can therefore concentrate her immense strength very largely on the defence of her Western frontier.

7. Russia's desire for absolute security will, however, be very great. There is little doubt that the Russian Government is determined to raise the standard of living of the Russian people to something approaching that of the Western Powers; the fact that by the end of this war a large number of Russian soldiers will have had personal experience of the greater comfort available to the countries of the West will give a great impetus to this determination. Much of the industry of European Russia has been devastated; if the desired improvement of the standard of living is to be achieved, not only will the devastated areas have to be restored, but also there will have to be a great deal of fresh industrial and agricultural development. A programme of this size will require a long period of peace, and it would be considerably speeded up if Russia could import industrial equipment from abroad and exact large reparations deliveries from Germany.

8. Russia, therefore, will not be prepared to take any chances, and however small may be the risk of aggression, particularly in the period immediately after the war, she will seek to build up a system of security outside her frontiers in order to make sure, so far as is humanly possible, that she is left in peace and that her development is never again imperilled by the appalling devastation and misery of wars such as she has twice experienced within a generation.

9. With this end in view Russia will at least experiment with a policy of collaboration with the British Empire and the United States. She will consider it natural that world affairs should be largely regulated by these three Powers and she will tend to took on any world security organisation as a from of Grand Alliance through which this triumvirate will be able to settle the disputes of the lesser Powers. She will not regard a world security organisation as a suitable body to settle serious disputes between the three great Powers themselves, since she will argue that if they fall out the foundation of world security will have been destroyed.

10. While Russia will be prepared to join a world security organisation, if its aims are in line with her conception of its proper functions, she will insure against the failure of such an organisation by building up along her frontiers a system of buffer States closely linked with her and by destroying for the longest possible period the power of aggression of Germany and Japan. Thus in Europe, Russia will regard Finland, Poland, Czechoslovakia, Hungary, Roumania, Bulgaria and to a lesser extent Yugoslavia as forming her protective screen. She will, however, probably regard Norway and Greece as being outside her sphere so long as she is satisfied with British collaboration. She will wish to dominate the Black Sea and to be able effectively to control the passage of warships through the Straits. In the Middle East she will want to control North Persia. In the Far East, apart from the acquisition of Japanese Sakhalin and the Kuriles, she will try to get some form of control over Manchuria before 1904, which gave her control of Dairen and Port Arthur and of the lines of communication running to them.

11. Russia will tend to regard these territories as falling naturally within her special sphere of interest and

will not admit that there could be any conflict between such a national security system and a world security organisation. Russia will hope that the creation of such a protective screen will ensure that if at any time a combination of hostile Powers should seek to challenge her, the first shock of aggression would be taken so far as possible outside Russia's borders. Such a system would also add depth to Russia's defences, give greater time for mobilisation, increase the chance that the fighting would not take place on Russian soil and deny to the enemy the support of neighbouring States. She will wish to import oil from Roumania and possibly coal from Poland. She will also wish to prevent Germany from making use of the heavy industries of Silesia or importing oil from Roumania. Russia's relations with the States concerned will be affected by the practical possibility of exercising control over them, by their strategic importance and by the extent to which Russia feels that she can rely on the sincere collaboration of the local government and on the sympathy of the people as a whole. Generally speaking, Russia will wish to occupy in the strategically important countries along her frontiers a position rather similar to that of Great Britain in Egypt; that is to say, Russia will allow these countries independence so long as she is in a position to ensure that they pursue a policy that tends to protect her strategic interests.

12. Outside this bastion of associated Powers Russia will do her utmost to make certain that Germany and Japan are for longest possible time rendered incapable of aggression. As stated above, a serious threat to the security of Russia as a whole can in practice only be mounted across her western frontier between the Baltic and the Carpathians. This would involve the use of German territory and for this reason it will be the keystone of Russia's post-war policy to ensure that Germany is kept weak. Russia will favour the military and economic disarmament of Germany and perhaps her political dismemberment; she will attach importance to blasting the economic bases of Germany's military power. As part of the policy of dominating Germany, Russia will look to the Western Powers and particularly to Great Britain and France to act as the other side of the ring round Germany and she will regard as the acid tests of the sincerity

of their collaboration their determination to make and keep Germany weak. Russia would regard as a potential menace to her security any trend towards a reconciliation between the Western Powers and Germany. If events took such a turn, Russia might seek to outbid the Western Powers and thereby win Germany over to her side; alternatively, if Russia feared that Germany was joining a potentially hostile combination against her, she might launch a preventive war on Germany.

13. Though Japan could not be so serious a menace to Russia as Germany, Russia will nevertheless wish to make sure that if she was to fight a war in Europe, she will be able to do so without the threat of Japanese aggression in her rear. She will therefore favour the strict demilitarisation of Japan and control over her economy. Russia will hope that the control she will secure over the resources of Manchuria and Korea will not only enable her to develop her Far Eastern territories and so greatly increase her military strength there, but also make it difficult for Japan, cut off from these resources, to build up an adequate war economy.

Conclusion.

14. In the period after the war Russia's policy will be directed primarily towards achieving the greatest possible measure of security. She will not regard as sufficient even the security inherent in her vast size and great resources in men and materials, but will wish to take every possible precaution against being again invaded, however small the risk may seem to be. Russia has a further reason for seeking security: she will wish to raise the standard of living of her people to something more nearly approaching that of the Western Powers. To achieve this she will need a prolonged period of peace in which to restore the devastated areas and, in addition, to develop her industry and agriculture. Particularly in the years immediately after the war this programme of internal development would be greatly faciliated if Russia could import industrial equipment.

15. In order to achieve the greatest possible security Russia will wish to improve her strategic frontiers and to draw the States lying along her borders, and

particularly those in Europe, into her strategic system. Provided that the other Great Powers are prepared to accept Russia's predominance in these border States and provided that they follow a policy designed to prevent any revival of German and Japanese military power, Russia will have achieved the greatest possible measure of security and could not hope to increase it by further territorial expansion. Nor is it easy to see what else Russia could under such conditions hope to gain from a policy of aggression.

16. As a further measure of insurance Russia will at least experiment with collaboration with Great Britain and America in the interest of world security and particularly in removing the danger of German or Japanese aggression. If Russia came to believe that Great Britain and America were not sincerely collaborating along these lines, she would probably push her military frontiers forward into the border States in Europe, try by political intrigue to stir up trouble in Greece, the whole of the Middle East and India, and exploit her influence over the Communist parties in the countries concerned to stimulate opposition to an anti-Russian policy. If war appeared imminent Russia might strike first at the oil resources of the Middle East.

17. While, therefore, Russia will not, in our opinion, follow an aggressive policy of territorial expansion, her suspicion of British and American policy will nevertheless continue to cause difficulty as will also her tactlessness in the handling of international affairs. Accordingly Russia's relations with the British Empire and the United States will depend very largely on the ability of each side to convince the other of the sincerity of its desire for collaboration.

(Signed)

V. CAVENDISH-BENTINCK.
E. G. N. RUSHBROOKE.
J. A. SINCLAIR.
F. INGLIS.
C. G. VICKERS.

Offices of the War Cabinet, S.W.1.
18th December, 1944.

ANNEX.

Economic Background.

Man-power.
1. Owing to the high natural increase in the Russian birthrate and despite the permanent casualties from the present war, military man-power should be greater in five to ten years than it was on the outbreak of the Russo-German war. Even if land operations in any future war were on the scale of the present Russian commitment, shortage of man-power would not prove a limiting factor. The number of men in Russia between the ages of 15 and 34 which is estimated to have numbered about 30 million in 1940, will probably increase to about 37 million in 1955. German man-power between these ages was about 11 million and will slightly decline over the period.
2. In 1940 there were in Russia about 49 million men between the ages of 15 and 64. In 1955 the number will probably increase to about 67 million. Education, both elementary and technical, has made considerable progress during the last few years. Thus, not only is the labour force increasing numerically but individual productive capacity should also increase.
3. The above numerical estimates take no account of the effects of the present war on which statistical information is lacking. We do not think, however, that these will alter the broad trends of population.

Internal Resources of Raw Materials.
4. Russia possesses large resources of foodstuffs and raw materials which should in the long run render her self-supporting in time of war, though some imports of tin, copper, natural rubber and wool are at present necessary. Her resources are widely dispersed and are in the main at a considerable distance from her frontiers. Two exceptions are first the Ukraine, an important source of foodstuffs, iron and manganese ore and coal; and second, the Caucasus, from which Russia gets about 75 per cent of her petroleum supplies.

Fuel and Power.
5. In 1945, production of coal in the U.S.S.R. will approach the 1940 level, that of oil may be as much as 25 per cent above and that of electric power about 10 per

cent above. During the next five years a steady expansion of all three (and particularly coal, as the Donbass is restored) may be expected at rates which may amount to 5-10 per cent per annum.

6. It is, however, very difficult to forecast how far these supplies of fuel and power will be adequate to meet requirements. Before the war, the consumption of coal and particularly of power was relatively small by western standards having regard to Russia's size and population. In coal and oil and possibly in power as well, there was a tendency for production to lag behind plans — pointing to a fuel and power bottleneck. Development of hydro-electric power stations may help to fill the gap but will take a long time.

7. Russia's post-war fuel and power requirements will naturally depend on the kind of industrial expansion which she plans. If the long term objective is the kind of standard of living enjoyed before the war say in the United Kingdom or Germany, an enormous programme of capital expansion will be required, and this will require large fuel supplies.

8. Coal production may prove to be a brake on industrial expansion unless supplemented by the use of oil in industry on a considerable scale; and much the same consideration applies to power. The oil needs of an expanded road transport plan are unpredictable but may be very large.

9. Russia may therefore wish to import Polish coal at least until the productive capacity of the Donbass is fully restored.

10. Russia's oil production in 1940 was about 32 million tons and may have risen to about 40 million tons in 1944. About three quarters of this comes from the Caucasus. By 1950 production might be as high as 50 million tons. Such suppiles will probably be sufficient not to constitute a serious limiting factor on Russia's military and industrial effort in time of war. In peace time it would be sufficient to enable great advances to be made in industrial development and in the standards of life. Further supplies might facilitate more progress in industrial expansion, and would enable a yet higher standard of living to be attained through the development of road traffic. In time of war it would ease the Russian task.

11. The output of the Caucasus oilfields will probably increase somewhat during the next ten years, and will

probably continue to be a major source of oil for Russia during the foreseeable future. At present the Caucasus is believed to account for nearly three-quarters of the proved reserves of oil in Russia. There are believed to be considerable reserves in other parts of Russia, and as these are developed the reserves in the Caucasus will represent a smaller proportion of the total than is the case now. While the Russians can hardly fear that there is early danger of reserves being exhausted, it is possible that, with the large prospective increase in her requirements, Russia may consider it desirable to conserve some of her own supplies and to secure a share in supplies elsewhere. This line of throught has arisen in the United States which has much larger proved reserves than Russia.

12. We, therefore, think that Russia will wish to import oil from Roumania and possibly elsewhere and to develop oilfields in North Persia.

Industrial Areas.
13. Russia's long-dated industrial plans have been based on defence and strategic considerations. Industry has in consequence been developed as much as possible in areas remote from her frontiers, especially in the Volga-Urals and Kuzbas (Western Siberia) industrial regions. Important exceptions are, of course, the Moscow-Leningrad industrial region and that of the Ukraine.

14. Broadly speaking, within a period of say 10-15 years, Russia's industrial capacity should suffice to enable her in time of war to be independent of imports, and this capacity will naturally increase with the reconstruction of Ukrainian industry and with the completion of long-term projects for the development of communications and industrialisation of outlying areas such as the South Caucasus, Central Asia and the Far East. Russia east of Lake Baikal, however, lacks the population and resources required to make this area independent of imports from the rest of Russia or overseas. There is accordingly a need to add to the economic resources of Russia's Far Eastern territories.

Mercantile Marine.
15. To carry the imports needed for the rapid completion of her programme of reconstruction and development,

Russia may greatly expand her mercantile marine. It would be in keeping with her general policy to use her own ships so far as possible rather than to rely on foreign vessels. After the period of reconstruction foreign trade will not be so necessary for Russian economy, but it is probable she will continue to trade wherever she thinks it to her advantage to do so. We think, however, that she will so plan her economy that the continuance of her foreign trade for the maintenance of her economy in time of war will not be essential.

16. It is against this general background that we examine below in greater detail Russia's economic situation and her strategic interests and policy in Europe, the Middle East and the Far East.

Russia's Strategic Interests in Certain Areas.

Norway, Sweden and the Far North.
17. Russia's principal interests in this area requiring protection will be the mines of Petsamo, which will be an important source of nickel, the ports on the Murman coast and the sea route round the North Cape; this is the shortest route for supplies from Western Europe and America, if the Baltic and Black Sea routes are closed, as they have been in this war.

18. All the above and her Northern sea route to the Far East are vulnerable to attack by any Power with naval and air forces based on North Norway. Russia's security would therefore be increased if she were in occupation of North Norway or had bases there; but we do not think that this need dictate a Russian occupation of this area in time of peace, as it could so easily be occupied when the need arose. It would, however, be in Russia's strategic interest that Norway and Sweden should at least not fall under the exclusive influence of any potentially hostile Power or group of Powers.

19. So far as concerns Russia's policy in this area, present evidence suggests that she would regard it as natural that Norway should be closely associated with Great Britain. The Russian Government, indeed, stated in December 1941 that they would be prepared to support arrangements whereby Great Britain would have the right to maintain naval bases in Norway. We therefore think that, so long as Russia is satisfied with the

collaboration she is receiving from Great Britain, she will see no need herself to secure bases in Norway. Russia is likely, however, to consider the maintenance of an ocean-going fleet in Far Northern waters desirable for the protection of her interests.

20. In the immediate post-war period Russia is not likely to be well disposed towards Sweden, and she will be particularly suspicious of Sweden's relations with Finland. If there is any sign that Sweden is intriguing with the anti-Russian parties in Finland, Russia will bring pressure to bear to put an end to this. Russia will similarly try to prevent Swedish collaboration with Germany. Russia would also view with suspicion signs that Sweden was aligning herself politically with Great Britain.

Finland and the Baltic.

21. Russia's principal strategic interests in the Baltic are the defence of the industrial area of Leningrad, of her coast-line in the Eastern Baltic and sea communications in the Baltic.

22. The defence of Leningrad would be greatly improved by the occupation of South Finland; but so long as Finland follows a policy friendly towards Russia and is not closely associated with any potentially hostile Power or group of Powers the defence of Leningrad would be adequately assured by Russia's possesion of the Baltic States and by the base at Porkkalla which she has obtained in the armistice with Finland.

23. Since, as stated above, the maintenance of overseas trade is not likely to be of major importance for the maintenance of Russia's economy in time of war, it will not be essential for the protection of Russian security to undertake the large commitments involved in an attempt to control the sea routes out of the Baltic. It will, however, be strategically advantageous for her to control sea communications in the Eastern Baltic, which would enable Russia to deny to Germany a large proportion of her supplies of iron ore from Sweden. In this connexion it would be to her advantage to occupy the Aland Islands, but she has hitherto showed no signs of wishing to do so.

24. Russia's policy in defence of these interests may be as follows. It is just possible that the Russians may after the war try to stage a plebiscite in Finland such

as would lead to a Finnish application for incorporation in the Soviet Union. On the whole we think such a move unlikely, since it would not be easy to fake a plebiscite in Finland unless the whole country was under Russian occupation and possibly not even then. It seems more probable that Russia will be content with the degree of military control allowed her under the armistice terms. In addition, she will require that the Government in power in Finland should follow a policy of friendship and close collaboration with Russia. If any Finnish Government showed signs of breaking away from this policy the Russians would either seek to overthrow it by intriguing with the opposition parties in Finland or in the last resort would use force to secure the overthrow of the Government.

25. Russia would wish to annex Königsberg and probably also Tilsit in order to increase her security in the Eastern Baltic. Königsberg would also be an additional port for Lithuania and White Russia.

26. Russia will probably insist on some form of international control over the Kiel Canal, even though she will be aware that no international agreement is likely to keep the Canal or, for that matter the exit from the Baltic, open for the passage of Russian ships in time of war. Russia is unlikely to have any particular political interest in Denmark and, indeed, she stated in December 1941 that she would agree to the establishment of British naval bases there.

RUSSIA'S WESTERN FRONTIER.

27. For reasons of geography and communications a serious threat to the security of Russia as a whole can only be mounted across her Western frontier between the Baltic and the Carpathians. In this area Russia's frontier is geographically ill-defined and has no strong natural defences. Russia therefore requires considerable depth of defence to ensure that the enemy cannot by surprise-attack overrun Moscow and the industrial areas and sources of raw materials in the Ukraine. Russia also needs depth for the deployment of her air defences of these centres.

28. South of the Carpathians the poor communications of South-East Europe would make it very difficult to mount a major-attack on the Ukraine.

29. Russia's western frontier can in practice only be seriously threatened by Germany or by other Powers acting in concert with Germany. A threat might in theory develop from a combination of Poland with other Powers, but to be a serious menace this would also require the use of German territory. Accordingly the security of Russia's western frontier will depend above all else on the solution of the German problem.

30. In order to ensure that the menace of German aggression shall be eliminated for the longest possible period, Russia will wish, first to keep Germany weak, secondly to build up along her own frontiers a system of buffer States designed to take the first shock of aggression and to give added depth to her own defence, and thirdly to ensure that the Western Powers continue to act as the other side of the ring around Germany. We examine below the policy that Russia is likely to pursue towards the countries concerned in order to secure these objectives.

Germany

31. It is not possible to forecast the precise lines of Russian policy towards Germany. Stalin appears to favour the breaking up of Germany into a number of independent states; on the other hand, the Russian representative on the European Advisory Commission has strongly advocated the retention or creation of a central German Government. Though these proposals are not mutually exclusive, they suggest that Russian views on territorial questions have not yet crystallised. In general, however, Russia's main preoccupation in her policy towards Germany will be to ensure as far as possible that she does not again threaten Russian security. In the economic field it seems likely from her armistice terms with the satellites, that she will make heavy demands for reparation and satisfy the claim by the wholesale removal of industrial plant and equipment, transport facilities and the raw material surpluses from her zone of occupation; and by the use of several million German prisoners of war in the rebuilding of her devastated areas. Further, Russia is likely to exercise her political influence over her Western neighbours in the direction of dissociating their economies from that of Germany and perhaps of depriving Germany even in peace time of imports of strategic

materials from these sources. Though Russia might not be prepared to submit her own trade in raw materials to any form of international control, even if it were designed primarily to control German imports of such materials, she would probably be willing to give her general support to such a system so long as it served to keep Germany weak. She would be likely to intensify the violence of her economic measures against Germany if she regarded Anglo-American policy as being coloured by the desire to conserve the industrial potential of Western Germany, none the less if it were advocated in the interest of general European or world prosperity.

32. If Germany is kept dismembered, the complexion of the Governments of the resulting States would be a matter of secondary importance to Russia. No doubt she would support any Left-wing parties prepared to collaborate with her; but she would be equally ready to work with any other parties that were similarly disposed. If Germany were not dismembered, or having been dismembered were reunited, Russia would not necessarily welcome the development of a unified Communist Germany such as might become a dangerous rival to Communist Russia.

Poland.

33. While Poland by herself cannot be a menace to Russia, an attack between the Baltic and the Carpathians must come through Polish territory and it will therefore be in Russia's strategic interest to ensure that Poland's foreign policy is based on co-operation with Russia.

34. Russia considers that Poland's eastern frontier should run along the Curzon Line, leaving Vilna and Lvov in Russian hands. As compensation she is prepared to give Poland a large slice of Germany as far west as the Oder and East Prussia, with the exception of Königsberg and perhaps Tilsit. With East Prussia thus removed from German control, a frontier along the Curzon Line would, so long as Germany is kept weak and Poland is co-operative, adequately safeguard Russia's strategic interests between the Baltic and the Carpathians. The extent to which Russia will be prepared to allow Poland relative independence within these frontiers will largely be governed by how far she feels that she can rely on Poland's collaboration. For so long, however as Russia is not satisfied that Poland is willing to pursue

a policy of collaboration Polish independence is likely to be more nominal than real.

35. In the period immediately after the war Russian forces will be in occupation of eastern Germany and the Russians will certainly insist on maintaining troops and air bases on their lines of communication through Poland. How soon, if ever, these troops will be withdrawn will depend on Russia's appreciation of Polish readiness to collaborate, particularly in measures for common action to meet any threat to Russia's western frontier.

Balkans.
36. South of the Carpathians the best defensive line would run along the Carpathians to the Galatz Gap and thence along the Danube estuary. The threat from this direction is not, however, as great as north of the Carpathians. Russia will have a strategic interest in ensuring that Roumania shall not be hostile and thus a potential base for attack. Moreover, although it would be an advantage to Russia's economy to have the Roumanian oilfields, it would not be essential in time of war. On balance, we think that it will not be necessary for Russia, who will certainly exercise very great influence in all the Balkan countries except perhaps Greece, to hold a frontier further west than the 1940 frontier along the line of the Pruth.

37. *Roumania.*—Russia will probably be prepared to leave Roumania nominally independent, but will exercise close control over her. She will probably also maintain bases in Roumania and try to secure some form of control over the disposal of Roumanian oil. Having this control over Roumania, Russia will be satisfied with a frontier along the Pruth, leaving Bessarabia and Northern Bukovina in Russian hands. Russia will also favour the return to Roumania of at least the greater part of the territories ceded to Hungary under the Vienna award.

38. *Bulgaria.*—Russia will similarly control Bulgaria but here the control is likely to be more indirect, both because there is much less to be got out of Bulgaria economically and because the Russians can rely on the generally pro-Russian attitude of the Bulgarian people. Russia has so far refuted any Bulgarian claims to Greek Thrace.

39. *Yugoslavia.*—Russia's interest in Yugoslavia will be

less than her interest in Roumania and Bulgaria, but she will nevertheless wish to have considerable influence in Yugoslavia, particularly in view of the possible future relations between Yugoslavia and Bulgaria.

40. Greece.—Russia has stated that she regards Greece as being within the British sphere of interest. She did not occupy Salonika when she was in a position to do so and we see no reason why in the post-war years she should depart from this policy so long as she is satisfied with British collaboration. This statement of Russian policy suggests that she regards the Mediterranean as falling rather within the British sphere of influence, since if she herself aspired to play a leading role in the Mediterranean she would probably wish as a first step to get Greece and the Ægean Islands under her control, direct or indirect.

The Western Powers.

41. It will strategically be most important to Russia that the Western Powers should continue to act as the other side of the ring round Germany and pursue a policy designed to prevent any revival of German military power. So long as they do this, Russia is not likely to have any other special interest in Western Europe, though she would no doubt welcome the replacement of the Franco régime in Spain, and perhaps also the Salazar régime in Portugal, by a less anti-Russian Government. Russia will seek to maintain close relations with a resurgent France both because France will be the Western Power most closely concerned with the prevention of German aggression and also because Russia may not wish any Western *bloc* to fall too exclusively under British influence.

42. Russia would regard any trend towards a reconciliation between the Western Powers and Germany as a potential menace to her security. If Russia thought that the policy of the Western Powers was developing along such lines, she might seek to bring pressure to bear on them and particularly on Great Britain by indulging in political intrigue designed to stir up trouble in Greece, in the Middle East as a whole, and particularly in Persia, Iraq, Palestine and Egypt, in Afghanistan and in India. Russia might also seek to exploit to the full her political influence over the Communist parties in the countries of Western Europe and generally by

political intrigue to stimulate opposition on to anti-Russian policy. Russia might consider that her security required that she should at least have the right to maintain armed forces in Finland, Poland, Czecho-slovakia, Hungary and Roumania, in order to gain depth of defence and more times of military and economic mobilisation. If Russia believed that attack by the Western Powers was imminent, it is possible that she might seek to forestall it by a campaign in Persia and Iraq designed to deny to the Western Powers the oil resources of this area and to increase her security against air attack on her own oil resources in the Caucasus.

43. If Russia thought that Germany was likely to join the Western *bloc* forming against her, she might launch a preventive war against Germany. Alternatively, it is possible that she might seek to outbid the Western Powers and so win Germany over to her side, though fear of thus allowing Germany dangerously to increase her military power might decide Russia against this course.

BLACK SEA AND THE STRAITS.

44. Russia's strategic interest in the Black Sea will be the defence of her coast line against amphibious assault and also to protect her shipping there.

45. Russia will not have a major strategic interest in controlling the sea routes in and through the Mediterranean which, in any case, could not be secured without assuming very large commitments. We therefore think that Russia's strategic interest will only require that she should dominate the Black Sea, for which purpose she will require, as far as possible, to control the Straits. Full control of movement through the Straits could only be assured by occupations of a considerable stretch of territory on either side of them and of bases dominating the sea routes through the Ægean. We do not, however, think it would be essential to Russia's security to extend her territory so far; it would be sufficient for Russia's strategic interests if she had air and naval supremacy in the Black Sea and if Turkey was not closely associated with any potentially hostile Power or group of Powers.

46. As regards the Straits, Russia has already indicated that the Montreux Convention governing the passage of warships must be revised. She is likely to insist that

she shall have the right of passage for her warships as she thinks fit and the last word in deciding whether or not warships of other Powers should pass through the Straits. Russia will maintain an impressive fleet in the Black Sea. Since a serious threat to Russian control of the Straits would, in practice, depend on the establishment, by some major Power, of bases in Turkish territory, Russia is likely to desire that Turkey should remain independent and not allied to any major Power. Russia is therefore likely to work for the termination of the Anglo-Turkish Alliance and may try to win Turkey over to her side. It is also possible that Russia may demand from Turkey the return of the province of Kars, which passed into Turkish hands at the end of the last war.

MIDDLE EAST.
47. Russia's principal strategic need in the Middle East is to ensure adequate defence for the South Caucasus oilfields, which are essential for the maintenance of her war economy. These oil-bearing areas are protected against land attacks by very strong natural defences, and by the great distance from any adequate base from which a land attack against them could be mounted. The communications in the areas bordering on South Caucasus would require much development before they would be capable of maintaining land armies sufficient to constitute any serious menace to the armies that Russia could deploy in defence of the oilfields. We therefore do not consider that there can be any serious land threat to the oilfields.
48. There remains the threat of air attack. Oilfields, as such, are not particularly vulnerable to any form of air attack at present in use; but the Russians will have seen, at Ploesti, the damage that can be done to oil refineries and transport facilities by intensive air attack from comparatively distant bases. One method of increasing the defence of Russia's oil industry would be to locate the refineries at a considerable distance from the frontiers and build protected pipelines to them. Provided Russia takes this precaution, the protection of her oil supplies from the South Caucasus could be adequately secured within her present frontiers. It would not be essential for Russia's war economy to possess oilfields in Northern Persia, but for reasons given it

would be of considerable advantage to develop supplies there both for peace and war.

49. In the event of a threat of hostilities with Great Britain and the United States and possibly even if there was a threat of operations in the Middle East by the United States alone, Russia would have a strategic interest in being able to deny them the oil resources of the Middle East.

50. Since about 75 per cent of Russia's oil supplies come from the Caucasus she will be sensitive to any potential threat to them however remote. She will therefore wish to increase her security in this area and present indications are that, although her strategic interests may not demand it, she is determined to obtain some degree of control over Northern Persia. The control of Azerbaijan would give Russia certain military advantages. She would have greater space for the quick deployment of her forces which would otherwise be hemmed in to the mountains on the Persian frontier; the maintenance of forces in Persia would be greatly eased by the possession of Persian ports on the Caspian Sea; and she would be in a better position rapidly to seize the key communication centre and airfields at Tehran if any hostile Power threatened to establish forces in Persia. She would, moreover, be well placed quickly to develop a threat against the airfields of the Middle East.

51. While, as stated above, this probably is not essential to Russia's security, she may regard it as an added measure of insurance. Moreover, she may think that the British oil interests in Southern Persia will give Great Britain a considerable measure of control in that area; she may, therefore, wish, by controlling North Persia, to ensure that the whole country does not fall too much under the influence of Great Britain backed by the United States. Provided that Russia gets what she wants in Northern Persia, she will probably acquiesce in the status quo in Iraq, though she would probably prefer that Great Britain should cease to enjoy there the special position that she now has.

52. In general, Russia wishes to stand on an equal footing with other great Powers in the Middle East. She would prefer, as far as possible, to see in the Middle East a group of independent States with no special ties with any great Power. She is therefore likely to oppose Arab union

if it appears to be under British inspiration, and also French claims to a predominant position in the Levant. Russia may prefer that Palestine should become independent of British control.

FAR EAST.

53. From Sinkiang to Manchuria Russia has an enormous land frontier with China; but China is militarily weak and will remain so for very many years to come. Even if China emerges from this war orderly and united, she could not be a menace to Russia until she had developed into a first-class military Power or unless she entered into a close association with the United States. In any case geographical considerations rule out a major attack on Russia across the frontier from Sinkiang to Manchuria.

54. The Power in the Far East with whose aggressive ambitions Russia has to reckon is Japan, who, like Germany, dreams of world domination and who, also like Germany, has in the past fought a successful war against Russia. Moreover, Japan has long desired to drive Russia from the dangerous proximity of the Maritime Provinces. Accordingly, Russia's strategic interests in the Far East in relation to her security will be concerned primarily with the defence of the Trans-Siberian Railway east of Lake Baikal and the Maritime Provinces, particularly Vladivostok, from attack by Japan either direct or through Manchuria or Korea. Japan, however, can never be so serious a menace as Germany, because even a successful attack from this direction, though it would be a serious blow to Russia's prestige, would scarcely menace her security as a whole, in view of the enormous distances the attack would have to cover before it reached areas strategically or economically vital to her.

55. Accordingly, the first requisite for Russia's strategic security in the Far East is that Japan's power of aggression should be eliminated for the longest possible period. So long as Japan is weak, the only other Power capable of threatening Russia's security in the Far East would be the United States, either alone or in concert with the British Empire, and therefore, provided these Powers followed a policy of collaboration with Russia, it would not be essential for her to alter her present frontiers in the Far East.

56. As in other areas, however, Russia will wish to insure against aggression to a greater degree than the essential minimum. The security of the Maritime Provinces from attack from overseas would be increased if Russia held Japanese Sakhalin and the Kuriles; this would also reduce any threat to the airfields of Russian Sakhalin. Security from attack overland would be greatly increased by control over Manchuria and Korea, which would give much greater depth to the defence of the Maritime Provinces and cover the lines of communication with the rest of Russia. At present the main line is the Trans-Siberian Railway, which is very vulnerable to attack from Manchuria; but the Russians are believed to be building another line further north, branching off from the Trans-Siberian Railway west of Lake Baikal.

57. Economically also control over Manchuria and Korea would greatly increase Russia's security in the Far East. At present the Russian population east of Lake Baikal is only some 5 to 6 million. This area is deficient in food and is incapable of supporting an armament industry sufficient to maintain large armed forces. Manchuria and Korea have a population of 65 million, and are rich sources of raw materials. Supplies of food are such as would make the whole area self-supporting. There are industrial areas capable over a long period of substantial development; but coking coal from North China might be necessary if full use is to be made of all the resources.

58. Russia's security in the Far East would also be materially increased if she controlled the South Manchurian ports of Dairen and Port Arthur as naval bases, whose use could not easily be denied her by Japan. It would also be of some advantage to her to have the North-East Korean warm-water ports of Rashin and Seishin as potential bases within the Japan Sea.

59. Thus, with Manchuria and Korea, the whole of Sakhalin and the Kuriles, Russia's Far Eastern possessions would form a powerful military and economic bloc, self-sufficient in food and capable of maintaining large armed forces without much support from the rest of Russia. Moreover, Russia would be in a position to ensure that Japan could not draw from Manchuria and Korea the resources that are essential to her economy and war industry.

60. We have scarcely any evidence to guide us as to Russian intentions in the Far East and it is therefore difficult to estimate to what extent Russia will try to secure these strategic advantages or to go beyond them. We think it almost certain that she will demand Japanese Sakhalin and the Kuriles. She will probably also wish in one way or another effectively to control Korea and Manchuria, including particularly the ports of Dairen and Port Arthur. We cannot at present say how Russia will seek to achieve such a control and probably much will depend on the course of events in China after the war. It is true that Stalin's statements at the Teheran Conference indicated that Russia accepted the Cairo Declaration that Manchuria should be returned to China and Korea made independent; but if Russia comes into the war, it is probable that at the time of Japan's final defeat Russian forces will be in occupation of at least a part and probably the whole of Manchuria. If China showed signs of relapsing into chaos and civil war Russia would not find it difficult, while nominally respecting China's sovereignty over Manchuria, to secure a special position rather on the lines of the pre-1904 arrangement. Russia then had a lease of the Liaotung Peninsular with its two ports of Dairen and Port Arthur, the right to run the railway leading to it and also the right to maintain troops to guard the railway. The Czarist government were able to build up these railway guard troops to a force of 100,000 men and the present Russian Government could probably improve on this. Russia's desiderata in Korea might be secured by a treaty on similar lines with a nominally independent Korean Government. We do not think that Russia would rely on the support of the Chinese Communists to give her such far-reaching concessions in Manchuria and Korea. Such arrangements could probably be stretched to cover the stationing of air forces in Manchuria and Korea and effective economic control. This would adequately safeguard Russia's strategic interests.
61. The only disadvantage might be the opposition of the 65 million people of Manchuria and Korea. Initially this would probably not be a serious problem as these people have in the past shown little power of resistance to foreign domination; but the development of Chinese nationalism is likely to continue and the existence of a nationalist China just across the border might in time

stimulate resistance in Manchuria and perhaps Korea as well, and so present the Russians with a considerable security problem. It is, however, unlikely that such considerations would deter Russia from seeking to control Manchuria and Korea.

62. Russia will no doubt continue to hold her present positon in Chinese Mongolia and might possibly even annex it. Sinkiang is not of great importance to her and she will probably be prepared to leave it under Chinese control so long as that is reasonably effective; if Chinese control broke down Russia might resume the position she acquired there during the disturbances of 1932 and held up to 1942, with the object of suppressing disorder so close to her frontiers.

63. There is no evidence at present to show that Russia is likely to display any major interest in the rest of the Far East.

Russia's Post-War Naval Policy.

64. Before the present war Russia was developing her Navy and was building a considerable ocean-going fleet, including battleships and heavy cruisers, at Leningrad and Nikolaev. This building programme was virtually abandoned in 1941. Her eagerness to secure additions to her Navy from the resources of her Allies and enemies indicates her intention to continue the development of her fleet after the war. The Russians are sufficiently realist to appreciate that during a war against a major naval Power there would be little chance of redisposing heavy warships between the various coastlines in the Arctic, Baltic and Black Sea, and that it would only be possible to move ships to the Far East by the difficult and limited Northern Sea route. Consequently, the Russian fleets on their various stations will have to be more or less self-contained.

65. An ocean-going fleet would probably be maintained in Northern Waters. The Baltic Sea defence will be provided mainly by submarines and light surface craft, supported by Naval aircraft. In the Black Sea, Russia will raise her own prestige and impress the Balkans and Near East by a display of surface warships, but light craft and submarines will predominate in the defence of her frontiers there.

Far Eastern Waters.
66. The benefits to be derived from seaborne trade, both with her Western territories and in the Pacific, are likely to result in the building up of her mercantile fleet.
67. For the purposes of her economy in war, however, the maintenance of ocean trade routes will not be essential. It is, therefore, unlikely that Russia will station a powerful ocean-going fleet in the Pacific even if she acquires bases in South Manchuria; the development of the necessary facilities for building and maintaining heavy warships in the Far East would in any case take a long time. It seems more likely that Russia will maintain powerful land-based air forces to protect the sea approaches to her Far Eastern territories.

Notes

1. JIC(44)467(0)(Final), 'Russia's Strategic Interests and Intentions from the Point of View of Her Security', 18 December 1944, TNA: CAB 81/126.
2. JIC(46)1(0)(Final)(Revise), 'Russia's Strategic Interests and Intentions', 1 March 1946, TNA: CAB 81/132.
3. N4157/97/38. Notes by T. Brimelow, 29 March 1946 and C. F. A. Warner, 5 April 1946, TNA: FO 371/56763.
4. JIC(46)38(0)(Final)(Revise), 'Russia's Strategic Interests and Intentions in the Middle East', 14 June 1946, TNA: CAB 81/132.
5. JIC(47)7(Final), 'Soviet Interests, Intentions and Capabilities', 6 August 1947, TNA: CAB 158/1.
6. JIC(47) 85th Meeting, 3 December 1947, TNA: CAB 159/2.

6

SIGINT TARGETING

For at least the first two decades of the Cold War, the Joint Intelligence Committee served partly as a manager of the British intelligence community. It helped to review and reform structures whilst also assisting in the setting of targets and priorities. In the immediate post-war period the central machinery for the strategic management of the British intelligence community was underdeveloped. The year 1948 saw the emergence of the Permanent Under-Secretary's Department in the Foreign Office, absorbing the Services Liaison Department, which had previously been home to the chair of the JIC. This brought with it stronger liaison and intelligence coordination functions. But perhaps the most important step forward occurred in 1950, when Clement Attlee requested a thorough review of the intelligence and security services by Norman Brook. At this point no-one knew what Britain was spending on intelligence – still less whether there was any way of measuring efficiency and effectiveness. The following year, Brook's recommendations led to the creation of the Permanent Secretaries Committee on the Intelligence Services (PSIS), which took a lead on relating resources to priorities and targets.[1] In 1968, this system was enhanced with the creation of a Cabinet Office Intelligence Coordinator, who assisted PSIS with priorities and budgets.[2]

Perhaps the most demanding management task was overseeing Britain's largest intelligence agency, Government Communications Headquarters (GCHQ), located at Eastcote on the outskirts of London. This organisation had only recently moved from Bletchley Park and 'GCHQ' was the new title for an organisation of code breakers that had hitherto been owned by MI6 and was only just emerging as an intelligence service in its own right.[3] Indeed, in 1948 the Director of GCHQ, Edward Travis, did not sit on the JIC.[4]

For the JIC the spring of 1948 constituted an unsettled period dominated by accelerating East–West tensions in Europe, the Middle East and Asia. The previous year had produced the Truman Doctrine and the Marshall Plan, to which the uncompromising Soviet response had been the formation of the Cominform. March 1948 brought the Soviet coup in Czechoslovakia and Soviet pressure upon Scandinavia, events which spurred the completion of the Brussels Treaty and also led to highly secret negotiations at the Pentagon in Washington between British, American and Canadian officials seeking to explore a framework for a future North Atlantic alliance. By early April 1948 the West had begun to experience its first serious difficulties with rail transport to its sectors in Berlin, prefiguring a major confrontation over that city that would result in the Berlin Airlift and the despatch of American B-29 bombers to Britain during the autumn of the same year. In the Middle East and Asia, Britain had cause for concern about the situation in Palestine, Indochina, China and Korea, although in Malaya the outbreak of the 'Emergency' was still some months away.[5]

It was against this background that the JIC sought to prioritise Britain's signals intelligence requirements for 1948, identifying some forty-seven general target areas for the country's sigint effort and dividing them into five different levels of priority. In doing this the JIC was working within the definition of its duties as laid down by the recently redrafted JIC charter of 27 February 1948, under which it was supposed to give 'higher direction to operations of defence intelligence and security'.[6] Despite its clear remit, in reality the JIC was tussling with several other Whitehall bodies that directed the British sigint effort, including the London Signals Intelligence Board (LSIB) and the London Signals Intelligence Committee.[7] Over the next twenty years, the function of some of these powerful additional bodies that included the sigint elements of the armed forces overlapped with the work of the JIC, resulting in bureaucratic confrontations. Indeed, in 1951 the Brook Report had raised the option of abolishing the LSIB altogether and giving its functions to the JIC.[8] In the end it was left to the Chiefs of Staff to work out the exact relationship between these bodies in what Patrick Reilly, the JIC Chairman, described as 'a very tricky field'.[9]

The JIC gave the top sigint priority to four areas of Soviet activity related to strategic air attack and defence. These were the development of Soviet atomic, chemical or biological weapons; other new Soviet weapons; the Soviet air force; and guided weapons. This emphasis was a reflection of the intense concern which had been displayed by the Chiefs of Staff from as early as 1944 at the likely post-war disparity between the strength of Western military forces in western Europe compared with those of the Soviet Union.[10] This concern had been exacerbated during June 1945 and again in July 1946 by two highly classified studies that emphasised the radical scientific and technical developments that had recently taken place in the field of 'weapons of mass destruction' and in associated methods of strategic delivery, particularly the guided rocket. These reports noted that in contrast to the wide dispersal of population and infrastructure enjoyed by the United States and the Soviet Union, Britain was relatively crowded and hence seemed rather vulnerable to these new weapons.[11]

Consequently, it was the view of the COS that for as long as methods of attack remained far ahead of those of defence, the only credible British strategy appeared to be deterrence in peace, and an immediate pre-emptive air strike against the Soviet Union's own strategic capabilities in war. Consequently, Soviet fighter defences constituted an important British signals intelligence target. The central place of the strategic air offensive in British post-war defence planning certainly explains the high priority accorded in this document to the acquisition of signals intelligence on subjects such as the Soviet metropolitan fighter defence force.

In comparison with Soviet strategic offensive and defensive capabilities everything else was considered less urgent. Typically, despite the problems posed by aggressive Soviet espionage, underlined by the Igor Gouzenku affair and the subsequent arrest of Alan Nunn May, sigint relating to the 'organisation and activities of Soviet espionage and counter-espionage services' was accorded only a secondary level of priority, along with such significant political issues as the 'question of succession to Stalin'. More surprisingly, although Britain encountered serious difficulties in the Middle East during the late 1940s, subjects such as 'Arab nationalism' and the 'Zionist movement including its intelligence services' were accorded only fourth and fifth levels of priority.

What was actually achieved as a result of the high level of priority allocated by the JIC to signals intelligence on Soviet strategic weapons? As historians have now shown, the rate of intelligence success against Stalin's bomb project was not high.[12] Indeed, JIC papers repeatedly make the assertion that 'our intelligence about Soviet development of atomic weapons is very scanty'.[13] By contrast, JIC papers for the 1940s appear to display detailed knowledge in other areas such as the capabilities of the Soviet air force and Soviet troop movements in south east Europe. These two areas were partly indicative of a new kind of intelligence gathering that focused on non-communications intercepts such as radar and telemetry. Over the duration of the Cold War this new field, known as 'elint', would be of growing importance as GCHQ struggled to achieve success against high-grade Soviet communications traffic.[14]

```
              TOP SECRET
              Copy No. 40
           LIMITED CIRCULATION.

   J.I.C. (48)19(0) (2nd Revised Draft)

              11th May 1948

       JOINT INTELLIGENCE COMMITTEE

    SIGINT INTELLIGENCE REQUIREMENTS-1948

  Draft Report by the Joint Intelligence Committee
```

We have examined our intelligence requirements for Defence purposes from Sigint sources in order to guide the Sigint Board in allocating its resources.
2. We have consulted the Colonial Office and the Commonwealth Relations Office (India Department).
3. We have listed subjects of defence interest and have grouped them into five priority classes. These are attached at Annex. We realize however that technical factors will influence the final allocation of priorities.
4. Any further requirements that the departments may pass to L.S.I.C. should in future be related to this list, by bearing an indication of priority.
5. We propose to review these requirements in a year's time.

Ministry of Defence S.W.1.

11th May 1948

ANNEX

PRIORITY LIST

(No attempt has been made to arrange subjects in order of importance within each priority class)

PRIORITY I
1. Development in the Soviet Union of atomic, biological and chemical methods of warfare (together with associated raw materials).
2. Development in the Soviet Union of scientific principles and inventions leading to new weapons, equipment or methods of warfare.
3. Strategic and tactical doctrines, state of training, armament and aircraft of:-
(a) Soviet long-range bomber force.
(b) Soviet metropolitan fighter defence force (including P.V.O.).
4. Development in the Soviet Union of guided weapons.

PRIORITY II
5. Manpower, call-up and mobilisation of Soviet armed forces.
6. Strategical and tactical doctrines, state of construction and training and construction programme (especially new types) of:-
(a) Soviet submarines.
(b) Soviet air forces, including armaments (other than in Priority I).
(c) Soviet airborne forces.
7. Strategic industries (e.g. armaments, aircraft, fuels, steel, chemicals, power) in the Soviet Union.
8. Strategic stock-piling in the Soviet Union.
9. Railways in the Soviet Union.
10. Soviet economic successes or reverses (such as the drought of 1946) likely to have an effect on foreign policy.
11. Organisation and activities of Soviet espionage and counter-espionage services.
12. Significant internal political development in Soviet Union (especially question of succession to Stalin).
13. Soviet reactions to associations (actual or proposed) between powers outside the Soviet sphere of influence.
14. Soviet intentions in Germany and Austria, including Soviet employment of German Service and other personnel.
15. Organisation of, and foreign assistance to, Greek rebels (including any international brigade activities).

PRIORITY III
16. Strategic and tactical doctrines, training and morale of Soviet armed forces (except as already detailed in I and II).
17. Organisation of Soviet armed forces, including high command and M.V.D. troops.
18. Unit and formation identifications, locations, and movements of Soviet armed forces, including M.V.D. troops.
19. Present and future warship construction (with details of performance and armament) in the Soviet Union.
20. Weapons and equipment in the Soviet army (technical details).
21. Airfields in the Soviet Union, and areas under Soviet influence.
22. Location, organisation and activities of defence

research and development establishments in the Soviet Union.
23. Movements and activities of the leading personalities concerned with scientific research and development in the Soviet bloc and the Soviet occupied countries.
24. Scientific and technical education in the Soviet Union.
25. Movements of Soviet officials or service personnel to disturbed areas on the borders of the Soviet spheres of influence, such as Germany, Albania, India, Pakistan and the Far East.
26. Relations of India, Pakistan and neighbouring countries with foreign countries, particularly the Soviet Union, and with each other.
27. Soviet relations with the Jews in Palestine (particularly extent of Soviet and satellite assistance of emigration).
28. Organisation and activities of national communist parties and communist-inspired movements (including Cominform).
29. Indications of establishments in foreign countries in place of Soviet agencies designed to assist the Soviet Union in war.

PRIORITY IV
30. Soviet assistance to satellite armed forces.
31. Developments of bases, harbours and strategic waterways in the Soviet Union and satellite countries.
32. Soviet administrative network with particular reference to its vulnerability in war.
33. Arctic developments by Soviet Union, particularly extension of meteorological research and aircraft patrols.
34. Relations of satellite countries with neighbours outside Soviet Union.
35. Arab nationalism and relations of Arab states with U.K. and U.S.A.
36. Attitude of Soviet Union, France, Italy and Arab states towards future of ex-Italian colonies, especially Libya.
37. Organisation and activities of satellite espionage and counter-espionage.
38. Soviet intentions in India, Pakistan and Moslem countries.

PRIORITY V
39. Unit identification of Yugoslav armed forces.
40. Static defence system of the Soviet Union and satellite countries (other than P.V.O.).
41. Any marked increase of telecommunications facilities in frontier areas of the Soviet Union and satellite countries, notably Caucasus, Balkans, White Russia.
42. Contributions by the satellite countries to Soviet industrial potential.
43. Deliveries of grain from the Soviet Union to other countries.
44. Relations between satellite countries.
45. Soviet intentions in China and Korea.
46. Organisations and activities of Chinese penetrations of non-Chinese territories in the Far East, particularly their intelligence services.
47. Organisations and activities of:-
(a) Zionist movement including its intelligence services.
(b) Clandestine right wing French and Italian movements.
(c) Right wing movements in the satellite countries.

Notes

1. Richard J. Aldrich, 'Counting the Cost of Intelligence: The Treasury, National Service and GCHQ', *English Historical Review* 128/532 (2013), pp. 596-627.
2. J. W. Young, 'The Wilson Government's Reform of Intelligence Co-Ordination, 1967-68', *Intelligence and National Security* 16/2 (2001), pp. 133-51.
3. The first book to discuss GCHQ extensively was James Bamford, *The Puzzle Palace: America's National Security Agency and Its Special Relationship with Britain's GCHQ* (London: Sidgwick and Jackson, 1982), pp. 313-14.
4. Memo by Cliffe to Bridges, 'Committee on Sir Norman Brook's Report on Intelligence Services; Monday 30th July 1951 at 4.30 p.m.', TNA: CAB 301/18.
5. Alan Bullock, *Ernest Bevin, Foreign Secretary 1945-1951* (London: Heinemann, 1983); Ritchie Ovendale, *The English-Speaking Alliance: Britain, the United States, the Dominions and the Cold War, 1945-51* (London: George Allen and Unwin, 1985); Anne Deighton, *The Impossible Peace: Britain, the Division of Germany, and the Origins of the Cold War* (Oxford: Clarendon Press, 1993); Raymond Smith, 'A Climate of Opinion: British Officials and the Development of British Soviet Policy, 1945-7', *International Affairs* 64/4 (1988), pp. 631-47.
6. JIC(48)21, 'Charter for the Joint Intelligence Committee', 27 February 1948, f.2, L/WS/1/1051, IOLR.
7. 'The Signals intelligence Organisation', Top Secret Cream, Appendix A, approved at COS(46) 182nd meeting, 13 December 1946. TNA: FO 1093/478.
8. Memo by Cliffe to Bridges, 'Admiral Brooking's Report on Noise Listening', July 1951, TNA: CAB 301/18.
9. Reilly to Brook, 16 February 1951, ibid.

10. Julian Lewis, *Changing Direction: British Military Planning for Post-War Strategic Defence, 1942-1947* (London: Sherwood Press, 1988), pp. 55-178.
11. COS(45)402(0), 'Future Developments in Weapons and Methods of War', 16 June 1945, TNA: f.1A, AIR 2/12027; TWC(46)15(Revise), 'Future Developments in Weapons and Methods of War', 1 July 1946, TNA: DEFE 2/1252.
12. Michael S. Goodman, 'British Intelligence and the Soviet Atomic Bomb, 1945-1950', *Journal of Strategic Studies* 26/2 (2003), pp. 120-51.
13. JIC(47)65(0) Final, 'Summary of the Principal External Factors Affecting Commonwealth Security', 29 October 1947, attached to JP(47)139(Final) 30 October 1947, f.115, L/WS/1/986, IOLR.
14. JIC (45)10(0), 'Potentialities of the Soviet Air Force', 26 November 1945, TNA: N16448/16448/38, FO 371/48005.

7

THE BERLIN BLOCKADE

UP UNTIL 1947 there had been debate within His Majesty's Government as to the Soviet Union's future actions: would they remain friendly or would there be a return of the pre-war caution and hostility? Ultimately Russian actions would provide an answer. A succession of scares, crises and misperceptions served to highlight the belief that Stalin could not be trusted. The JIC predicted that he would avert war at all costs, but it was certainly thought that he would resort to subterfuge and underhanded tactics to undermine the West's position.

The 1948 JIC was in a far superior position compared to its earlier incarnations. It had emerged from the war victorious, having proved its value, and this had been recognised in an increased stature, a new charter and a more senior chairman. Yet despite this, the committee failed to predict the Berlin Blockade, the first real major confrontation of the Cold War.

Germany, and particularly Berlin, was seen as a window into the Soviet Union. In the JIC's words, Germany was a critical arena because it 'stands out as the most important single prize in the political and ideological struggle now in progress between the Soviet Union and the West'.[1] Here not only was there evidence of Russian intent, but also the opportunities for espionage were greatly increased. Berlin was thus to become, in the words of several American and Russian individuals based there, a 'battleground'.[2] Part of the explanation lay in the way that Marshall Aid had created an ever-expanding gap between the prosperity of the West and that of the East. In Berlin, perhaps more than anywhere else, the difference was glaring. The decision to create 'Bizonia', a merged Anglo-American zone in 1947 (France joined in 1949), was too much for Stalin. From early 1948 those crossing into Berlin were increasingly harassed.

One implication of the JIC's view that war with the Soviet Union was unlikely before 1955 was that an evolving list of 'indicators' was prepared. The idea was that the compartmentalisation of Soviet policymaking, in addition to the immense difficulties it posed as an intelligence target, meant that intelligence forewarning was unlikely. Indicators were therefore necessary to suggest that hostilities were imminent, that a decision to go to war had been taken. An American report in mid-1948 had provided a list of 112 factors that might be taken to imply the Russians were heading towards war. The JIC, in its version – which is included in the appended assessment – narrowed this list down to a mere 81 indicators. These included not just military signs, but economic and political ones too. They were divided into two aspects: 'preliminary preparations for an offensive' and 'immediate preparations for an offensive'.

The JIC's assessment, on 18 June 1948, judged that 'we believe the Russian armed forces to be in a high state of mobilisation and therefore able to undertake a limited offensive with little warning'.[3] Just a few days later the Russians cut transport links (road, rail, and river) between the western sectors of Berlin and western Germany. Thus the classic situation existed: evidence that something was about to happen but no information on the specifics of when, where, what etc. Consequently, the JIC produced no advance warning of the blockade.

The Berlin Blockade lasted from June 1948 to May 1949. The first reference to it by the JIC was some two weeks after it began. William Hayter, the Chairman, introduced events in Berlin by stating that the 'general situation demanded constant vigilance', and therefore proposed the introduction of a short periodical report on 'Russian preparations for war'. This sort of tactical assessment had served the JIC well during the Second World War.[4] Within a fortnight, and despite deteriorating relations in Berlin, the JIC concluded that there was no evidence that the Soviet Union was preparing to launch hostilities. The situation clearly remained fluid, though, and it was decided that the committee should revisit the topic every week.[5]

Just as with the fall of Norway in 1940, the Blockade of Berlin and the failure of the JIC to give any warning seem to have been something of a wake-up call for intelligence consumers. The Chiefs of Staff Committee requested a report on what might be done to avoid the Russians launching a surprise attack. This coincided with debates within Whitehall on measures to improve intelligence and, more precisely, on the gaps in coverage. The subsequent JIC report – which is included below – did little to allay fears. 'Preparations for war on a larger scale might . . . become apparent, despite all attempts at concealment'.[6]

The first substantial attempt to place the Berlin Blockade within wider Soviet intentions was completed in early 1949. Despite Soviet sabre rattling, events in Berlin revealed much to the JIC about the Russian psyche. It was still judged that Stalin would wish to avoid war before the mid-1950s and that, if anything, the successful Berlin Airlift had revealed the limits of Soviet policy, for despite their 'protests and threats' over the Western response, 'there has been no serious attempt to prevent it'.[7]

For the JIC there were two aspects to the blockade: the failure to predict it, and the ability, once it was underway, to provide a series of useful assessments. This pattern would be repeated often. What does this reveal about the JIC system? Firstly, it shows that it was able to adapt, relatively quickly, to developing situations. It also exposes something of the problems in identifying and reading Russian intentions: a feeling that something was about to happen but no detailed information as to the specifics. Finally, it also underlines the steadying tone of balanced JIC forecasts. It is clear that the Foreign Secretary, Ernest Bevin, appreciated the JIC's views as William Hayter, the Chairman, was tasked with personally briefing him on a weekly basis.[8] This was important, and the significance of Berlin should not be underestimated.

```
                           ANNEX.
                    (J.I.C.(48)42(0)Final)
                       (18th June, 1948.)
                   CHIEFS OF STAFF COMMITTEE
                  JOINT INTELLIGENCE COMMITTEE
            INDICATIONS OF RUSSIAN PREPAREDNESS FOR WAR.
            Report by the Joint Intelligence Committee.

We have examined the indications which might appear if
the Russians were preparing to launch an offensive. We
believe the Russian armed forces to be in a high state of
mobilisation and therefore able to undertake a limited
offensive with little warning. Preparations for war on
a larger scale might, however, become apparent, despite
all attempts at concealment. We have listed at Annex
those indications which we consider might be observed
by the British representatives in the Soviet Union, in
the Soviet Zones of Germany and Austria, or in countries
within or adjacent to the Soviet orbit. We have taken
note of the suggestions made by the British and American
Service Attaches in Prague* and of a paper prepared by
J.I.C. Germany.†
2. Certain precautions are normally undertaken by any State
in its own defence; e.g. training of the armed forces and
organisation of a skeleton civil defence. To these may be
added improvements, on purely economic grounds, in com-
munications and productive facilities. Since there is no
reason to deduce hostile intentions from such measures,
we have not detailed them in this report.
3. We have divided the list of indications of hostile
intentions into two main classes:-
(a) preliminary preparations for an offensive
(b) immediate preparations for an offensive.

─────────────────
* AAP/15/Air and AAP/15/5/Air
† J.I.C. Germany 48 (24) (Revised)
```

4. We recommend that copies of this report be forwarded to British Representatives in countries listed in the attached Appendix, and to the Joint Intelligence Committees abroad. They should not regard it as superseding in any way the more detailed questionnaires prepared by Departments or by the Joint Intelligence Committee, London, but as a framework for the reports requested in paragraph 6, below.

5. Posts in each country should arrange for Service Attaches, in consultation where possible with their American colleagues, to co-ordinate the coverage of their areas.

6. Items in the Annex which are marked with an asterisk are considered to be those which are bound to precede an offensive and, as such, should be the subject of a report by telegram as soon as they are detected. The remaining items should be reported by routine methods, as they are observed.

7. While it is not considered necessary to furnish periodic reports, it is recommended that the lists at Annex be reviewed monthly by Service Attaches in order to ensure that the examination of any possible indication is not overlooked.

8. The lists set out in the Annex should in no way be regarded as exhaustive, and any other indication which is considered to have a bearing on Russian preparations for war should be made the subject of a report.

(Signed) W.G. HAYTER
E.W.L. LONGLEY COOK
C.D. PACKARD
L.F. PENDRED
K.W.D. STRONG.

MINISTRY OF DEFENCE, S.W.1.
18th June, 1948.

ANNEX

PRELIMINARY PREPARATIONS FOR AN OFFENSIVE
These include: an abnormal intensification of defensive measures; any undue increase in the armed forces; the conversion of Industry towards a war footing; and a marked increase in Communist political activity. We give below a list of indications of this type; although it

includes both long-term and short-term preparations, the fact that many of the indications may appear at any time up to the outbreak of war renders further sub-division of the list impracticable.

Military.
1. Marked increase in the tempo of training in the army, particularly in field training of higher formations, or of specialist formations such as airborne troops.
*2. Reinforcement of army units to war establishment.
3. The re-equipping of units, and replacement of static guards with older men.
4. The supplying of arms to Communist parties in the countries associated with the West.
5. Increased activity of Communist para-military organisations.
6. Appearance of numbers of ex-Paulus and Seydlitz personnel in the Western Zone of Germany.
*7. Sabotage of installations, centres of communication etc. of strategic importance.
*8. Marked increase in the number of airfields and aircraft dispersal points, improvement in present airfields, and assembly of airfield construction equipment.
9. A strengthening of the Soviet Air Force; redeployment of air support units.
10. The replacement of flying training units by first line units.
11. A marked increase in armament practice and night flying in the Air Force.
12. Aircraft and searchlight co-operation exercises.
13. Provision of accommodation e.g. large scale building or requisitioning troops and aircrews.
14. Construction of sites for guided missiles.
*15. Efforts towards dispersal of military formations, installations and dumps.
*16. Provision of camouflage for airfields, installations, buildings and ships.
17. Increased attention to passive defence against air, chemical, and biological attack, including:-
(a) The construction of underground factories and stores.
*(b) erection of shelters, including submarine pens.
*(c) blackout arrangements.
*(d) issue of respirators.
*(e) training of civilians.

18. A speed up in refitting programmes at shipyards.
19. Combined operations training on a large scale.
20. Build-up of stocks of fuel, ammunition and stores at a number of ports simultaneously.
21. The requisitioning of auxiliary craft and fishing vessels.
22. Stricter control of sea traffic and fishing vessels in approaches to Russian and satellite ports.
*23. The collection of large numbers of barges, and the clearing, widening and deepening of canals and locks.
*24. Unusual movements of minelaying and minesweeping craft.
25. The installation of anti-submarine nets and boom defences.
26. Removal into Russia of Walther submarine components under construction in Germany.
27. A marked increase in the complements of Russian merchant ships.
28. The appearance of Russian Naval personnel in unimportant ports.
29. The building of large numbers of landing craft.

Economic.
30. Signs of conversion and re-tooling of plants for production of war materials.
31. An increase in the number of plants producing war materials.
32. An increase in the number of factories on which strongest security measures are imposed, an unusual measure of industrial dispersal, and camouflage of plants.
33. A reduction of effort in non-military production.
34. Evidence of production of unusual equipment, such as parachutes and civil defence equipment, by non-military factories.
35. An increase in the production of canned goods.
36. Stockpiling of essential commodities such as food, oil and rubber.
37. Unexplained alterations in the Ministerial control of industries.
38. Changes in the budget structure, which may indicate a hidden increase in the expenditure on the armed forces.
39. Large scale withdrawals from foreign countries of Russian controlled funds.

40. Synchronisation of times for the completion of contracts at various factories and yards.
41. An increase in the number of German technicians removed to the Soviet Union.
42. A large increase in the number of women employed in industry.
43. The improvement of rail systems, including the strengthening of bridges, laying of extra tracks, and construction of new sidings and marshalling yards.
44. The extension of the Russian broad gauge lines to the West, or of standard gauge lines to the East.
*45. The collection of large quantities of locomotives and rolling stock, including railway "flats".
*46. The assumption of the operational control of railways by the Soviet military authorities.
47. Improvement or extension of roads, the strengthening of bridges, and provision of alternative bridges or fords, with approaches; an increase in the production of bridging equipment.
48. Requisitioning of civil transport, accommodation or foodstuffs.
49. The appearance of increased numbers of water tankers (rail or road).
*50. Reduction in the number of civil telephone lines available to the public, with consequent abnormal delays.

Political.
51. An intensification of the normal propaganda campaign, designed to convince the Soviet and satellite peoples that they are about to be the victims of capitalist aggression.
52. An intensification of the normal propaganda campaign suggesting that the Anglo-American Powers are establishing bases with offensive intent.
53. Strike action by Communist parties on the grounds that the workers should not help preparations for an "imperialist" war against the Soviet Union.
54. Increase in staff of Russian Embassies or introduction of Russian military training missions.

IMMEDIATE PREPARATION FOR AN OFFENSIVE.
In selecting the indications listed below we have taken into account current appreciations of Russian capabilities and intentions.

Military.
*55. The appearance outside the Soviet Union of large quantities of MT, particularly of Soviet manufacture.
*56. The appearance of tank transporters in large numbers.
57. Abnormal laying of field lines near frontiers.
58. The identification of any new higher headquarters, or evidence of regrouping.
59. Changes in the position of Army units with reference to the frontier or to the likely lines of advance.
60. Call up of reservists, and comb-out of industrial workers.
61. Evidence that troops are moving to concentration areas.
*62. Abnormal officer reconnaissance near frontiers.
63. Transfer eastward, disbandment, or large-scale replacement by Soviet personnel of units of satellite armed forces.
*64. Stockpiling, particularly near frontiers, main communication centres, or airfields.
65. Medical preparations - Hospitals, hospital trains, etc.
*66. Appearance of large quantities of bridging and road mending materials.
67. Sudden increase in number of defections.
*68. Additional security measures including:-
(a) Intensification of frontier controls and river patrols.
(b) Increase in the number of areas closed to civilian movement.
(c) Increase in the use of cipher and closed telephone lines.
*69. Cessation of flying rights to foreign civil aircraft over certain countries.
*70. Deployment of A.A. guns, searchlights, barrage balloons and radar, particularly round airfields, stockpiles and centres of communication.
71. The preparation of emergency airstrips and a marked increase in the number of satellite landing grounds.
72. The development of dispersal areas.
*73. A marked increase in the volume of high grade cypher traffic, including Naval W/T traffic.
*74. Call up of that portion of the male population of North Germany which has had seafaring experience. (These have all been registered already).

*75. Concentration of landing craft in south Baltic ports.
*76. Concentration of merchant shipping, especially in the south Baltic.
*77. Fitting of warheads to torpedoes; ammunitioning of ships; landing of practice ammunition.
*78. A simultaneous exodus of warships from a number of ports.
*79. Laying of mines in the south Baltic.
*80. Arming of merchant ships.
81. A general withdrawal of Russian controlled merchant shipping from foreign waters.

Political.
82. Intensification of strike action (see Item 53 above).

APPENDIX

Finland
Germany
Austria
Czechoslovakia
Poland
Yugoslavia
Greece
Hungary
Bulgaria
Roumania
Soviet Union
Turkey
Persia
France
Belgium
Holland
Luxembourg
Norway
Sweden
Denmark
Italy
Afghanistan
Palestine
Syria
Lebanon

Transjordan
Iraq
Pakistan
India
Burma
China
Egypt.

* * *

J.I.C. (48) 78 (0)　　　　　　　　　LIMITED CIRCULATION.
　　　　　　　16th July, 1948.
Circulated for the consideration of the Chiefs of staff
CHIEFS OF STAFF COMMITTEE JOINT INTELLIGENCE COMMITTEE

MEASURES TO PREVENT THE RUSSIANS OBTAINING
STRATEGIC SURPRISE.
Report by the Joint Intelligence Committee.

We have been instructed*⁺ to examine what further arrangements are necessary to prevent the Russians obtaining strategic surprise, including any further steps that might need to be taken to accelerate the passage of tactical information on Russian activities across the Zonal frontiers.

2. We believe that the Soviet Armed Forces in Germany are sufficiently strong and sufficiently prepared to be able to undertake, with little or no warning, a limited offensive against likely opposition. Their formations are so disposed that this could be done with little preliminary movement.

3. Nevertheless, the fighter defences of Russia itself, and the Russian strategic long range bomber force, have not yet reached the standard of efficiency which we would expect if they are to play a major part in any immediate war. Furthermore, there is no evidence of the necessary administrative or industrial preparations having been made, or of general mobilisation having taken place. We do not, therefore, consider that the Russians are at present contemplating a major war.

4. Subject to the difficulties stated in paragraph 2 above, we have already taken certain action which may provide warning of preparations for war, as follows:-

---
* C.O.S. (48) 92nd Meeting Item 1. Confidential Annex.

Action to prevent the Russians Obtaining Strategic Surprise.

5. We have prepared and circulated to British representatives in the Soviet Union, in the Soviet Zones of Germany and Austria, and in the countries within or adjacent to the Soviet orbit, as well as to the joint intelligence authorities concerned, a report examining the indications which might appear if the Russians were preparing to launch an offensive. This report, of which a copy is annexed*[2], lists indications of hostile intentions and emphasises those which are considered to be bound to precede an offensive and which must therefore be reported by telegram at once.

Tactical intelligence concerning Soviet Military Activities

6. We have taken the necessary action to institute an organisation to obtain tactical intelligence concerning Soviet Military activities up to a depth of fifty miles in the Soviet Zone. The ultimate aim of the organisation is to obtain this intelligence by covering twelve targets within the fifty mile belt. This should ensure that no major Soviet Military move could take place within that belt without the responsible agency getting early knowledge of it and passing information back possibly within twenty four hours. Four of the most important targets are already covered and urgent consideration is being given to include a fifth, Rostock. Clandestine W/T communications are not at present provided for this network but the problem of providing this method of communication is under consideration with Germany.

Photographic reconnaissance.

7. We are having prepared lists of air photographic targets which are considered most desirable and worthwhile to complete in the near future, and also a comprehensive list of targets for clandestine air reconnaissance in Satellite countries. Consultations are in progress with the authorities in Germany on the feasibility of supplementing intelligence from ground sources by those means.

---

* J.I.C. (48) 42 (0) Final

Future Reports.
8. We intend to prepare periodical reviews of the short term indications of Russian preparedness for war drawing attention to any evidence that might indicate an alteration in Soviet intentions. Should significant intelligence of immediate importance arise, this will, of course, at once be brought to the notice of the Chiefs of Staff.

Recommendations.
9. We therefore recommend that the Chiefs of Staff:-
Take note of the arrangements made to prevent the Russians from obtaining strategic surprise and to obtain tactical intelligence concerning Soviet military activities across the Zonal frontiers.

(Signed) W.G. HAYTER
E.W.L. LONGLEY-COOK
C.D. PACKARD
L.F. FEMDRAD
K.W.D. STRONG.
Ministry of Defence, S.W.1
16th July 1948.

Notes

1. JIC(48)121(Revised Final), 'Possibility of War Before the End of 1956', 27 January 1949, TNA: CAB 159/5.
2. David E. Murphy, Sergei A. Kondrashev and George Bailey, *Battleground Berlin: CIA vs KGB in the Cold War* (London: Yale University Press, 1997).
3. The American and British papers are both in JIC(48)42(0)Final, 'Indications of Russian Preparedness for War', 18 June 1948, TNA: CAB 158/3.
4. JIC(48) 67th Meeting (0), 2 July 1948, TNA: CAB 159/4. The first such report is JIC(48)70(0)Final, 'Short Term Indications of Soviet Preparedness for War', 1 October 1948, TNA: CAB 159/3.
5. JIC(48) 73rd Meeting (0), 16 July 1948, TNA: CAB 159/4.
6. JIC(48)78(0), 'Measures to Prevent the Russians Obtaining Strategic Surprise', 16 July 1948, TNA: CAB 159/3.
7. JIC(48)121(Revised Final), 'Possibility of War before the End of 1956', 27 January 1949, TNA: CAB 159/5.
8. JIC(48) 80th Meeting (0), 30 July 1948, TNA: CAB 159/4.

8

CHINESE INTERVENTION IN THE KOREAN WAR

Much like Germany, Korea was split amongst the victors in the aftermath of the Second World War. North Korea became a Soviet proxy and the South an American one. The leaders of both halves of Korea were united in wanting to unify Korea in their own image but, inevitably, there could be no hope of both emerging victorious. On paper, then, this was a potentially explosive issue but the JIC did not specifically focus on it prior to the outbreak of war in in 1950 for one simple reason: it was perceived as an American concern. Thus, British intelligence collection was accorded the lower priority in the region.

In June 1950, in what is widely cited as one of the classic examples of intelligence failure, the North Koreans, without warning, invaded South Korea. Although the JIC did not focus specifically on Korea prior to this point, there had been a number of papers on the Far East, particularly following the success of the communists the previous year in the Chinese Civil War. The JIC had discussed the idea that the North Koreans could, potentially, launch a large military offensive, but it was discounted because it was thought small incursions would be favoured over the prospect of war. Consequently, with priorities for collection low, the assumption that the US were responsible and the belief that the North Koreans would avoid war, the invasion came as something of a surprise. The JIC conceded that it had been surprised and that no forewarning had been available.[1]

The North Korean attack was instantly assumed to be the work of Moscow and it prompted a swift rebuke in the United Nations. Writing a few weeks later, the JIC concluded that Stalin would have been surprised by the strength of the Western reaction and that events in Korea were not the start of a larger communist-inspired world war. Britain committed troops as part of the UN effort to repel the North Korean forces but in London the Chief of Staffs Committee remained hugely concerned at the scale and pace of events.[2] It was not clear to them, for instance, quite what the objective of the UN commanders was: would they stop at the border between North and South Korea or push beyond it? Related to this was angst about not provoking the Russian or Chinese into intervening militarily.[3]

To make matters worse, there was (rightly) great fear and trepidation about the intentions of General Douglas MacArthur, the American military commander in Korea. The JIC, which was instructed to watch out for any sign of Chinese intervention, asked the Joint Intelligence Staff to assess whether the Chinese would intervene if the UN forces crossed the border.[4] On 7 October the COS fears were confirmed when MacArthur's army advanced into North Korea. The JIC's initial reaction – included in the appended paper – was that the Chinese would not 'embark upon operations'.[5] Despite what, in hindsight, was an overly optimistic assessment, the JIC's report was subsequently accepted by the COS, who used it as a briefing document for discussions with the American Joint Chiefs of Staff.[6]

The JIC's assessment was not based on intelligence. Instead it relied upon a reading of the character of the Chinese leadership. The committee concluded that China would not risk war with the UN because this would, inevitably, lead to a major war with the West. And, according to the JIC, this was something the Chinese would want to avoid. The great difficulty was that there was simply no high-level, reliable intelligence to count on. Indeed, the JIC conceded that it was 'seriously concerned about the inadequacy of intelligence'. A JIC assessment in November 1950 stated that intelligence on the Chinese army was considered 'negligible', on the air force it was 'almost totally lacking', and 'very little' was known about the navy.[7] Perhaps naively, certainly in retrospect, the JIC's Assistant Secretary confidently reported that 'the war in Korea has developed even more rapidly than expected and it looks as if the real fighting will be over very shortly'.[8] Almost simultaneously, however, messages began to be received indicating a large concentration of Chinese troops, yet nothing was known about their intent.

On 1 November 1950 the People's Liberation Army advanced in huge numbers, pushing the UN's troops back to the border. The initial JIC reaction was one of uncertainty: it was not known whether this Chinese military involvement was officially sanctioned, whether it was merely an intensification of Chinese effort, or whether it was the start of something altogether new.[9] Furthermore, would China actually declare war in its support of the North Korean effort? Or would its assistance remain relatively covert?[10] Within a few weeks the situation had clarified. The JIC's earlier predictions had been proved incorrect and, for the first time, the intentions of the Chinese leadership became apparent: 'The scale of Chinese intervention in Korea leaves no doubt that the Chinese Communist Government is intent on defeating the main aim of the United Nations forces.' More alarming was what this move signified:

> This intention may be interpreted as a desire to drive back these forces beyond the 38th Parallel or even out of Korea altogether, but we must now face the possibility that China is prepared, with Soviet support and

approval, to accept the increase of existing risks of open war in an attempt to drive the United Nations forces from Korea.[11]

The JIC's efforts on the Korean War, particularly concerning Chinese intervention, highlight several important aspects: they emphasise the immense difficulties in producing analyses based on areas where there is negligible intelligence coverage and where priorities for collection are low; they also highlight the difficulties of using assumptions in the absence of intelligence and, particularly, the dangers of mirror-imaging. These would be hard lessons and ones that were not always heeded in future years.

```
                       JIC(50)88
        THIS DOCUMENT IS THE PROPERTY OF HIS BRITANNIC
                      MAJESTY'S GOVERNMENT
        The circulation of this paper has been strictly
                           limited.
             It is issued for the personal use of

              TOP SECRET       Copy No. 89

      Circulated for the consideration of the Chiefs of Staff

              J.I.C. (50) 88 (Final - Revise)
                     11th October, 1950.
                   CHIEFS OF STAFF COMMITTEE
                 JOINT INTELLIGENCE COMMITTEE
            CHINESE COMMUNIST INTENTIONS AND CAPABILITIES -
      1950/51. Report by the Joint Intelligence Committee.
```

As instructed*+ we have re-examined in the light of the latest political intelligence from China the Chinese Communists' military intentions and capabilities against Korea, Indo-China, Burma, Siam, Formosa, Macao, and Tibet in the period 1950/51. Our report is at Annex.
2. Conclusions. We conclude that:-
(a) Chinese Communist policy in the Far East and South-East Asia is dominated by the desire to secure the withdrawal of the Western Powers and the elimination of the Chinese Nationalists.
(b) In pursuing this aim they are likely to concentrate in the initial stages on political infiltration and

---
*+ C.O.S. (50) 160th Meeting, Minute 3.

subversion, combined, where appropriate, with military advice and assistance.
(c) They might, however, resort to overt aggression if they judged that the conflict could be localised and that aggression would therefore be in their own interest.
(d) They are unlikely to be pushed into overt aggression by the Soviet Union unless they judge that condition (c) above is fulfilled.
(e) Sufficient forces are available to undertake overt aggression against any of the territories under review. The possibility of such action cannot therefore be excluded.
(f) The likelihood of such action in each case is estimated to be as follows:-
(i) Korea. We do not think the Chinese Communists will embark upon operations in Korea as this would involve a risk of war with the United Nations. But the possibility cannot be excluded that they may enter Korea and occupy a defence line covering the Manchurian frontier and as far forward as possible without engaging in hostilities with United Nations forces, unless attacked by them.
(ii) Indo-China. We consider that the Chinese Communists are likely to give all possible support to Viet Minh short of armed intervention. The threat of armed intervention would, however, be increased in the event of Chinese armed intervention in Korea.
(iii) Burma and Siam. We have no evidence that overt aggression is amongst the short term objectives of Communist China.
(iv) Formosa. While the Chinese aim to gain control of Formosa, they are unlikely in face of American intervention to undertake an invasion at present. Indeed current indications are that the invasion has been postponed although the ability to invade remains and at present constitutes a dangerous threat. In the event of Chinese armed intervention in Korea the Chinese Communists would have to abandon all hope for the present of a successful invasion of Formosa.
(v) Macao. We believe the Chinese Communists will prefer to render the Portuguese position untenable in the Colony by means other than the use of force.
(vi) Tibet. We have no reason to doubt that the Chinese Communists intend to enforce their claims to sovereignty

over Tibet and that they will resort to force if negotiations break down.

3. The Chinese Communists' intentions with regard to Hong Kong have already been covered elsewhere*[2] and in this paper we have confined our examination to the repercussions on the Colony in the event of Chinese intervention in Korea. We conclude that in this event the risk of action against Hong Kong taking place would be much greater than at present.

Recommendation
4. We recommend the Chiefs of Staff endorse this report as an expression of their views.

(Signed) D.P. REILLY.
N.C. OGILVIE-FORBES.
P. SILLITOE.
B.K. BLOUNT.
A.J. BAKER-CRESSWELL (for D.N.I.)
R.F. JOHNSTONE (for D.M.I.).
M.Y. WATSON (for Director, J.I.B.).

Ministry of Defence, S.W.1.
11th October, 1950.

ANNEX

CHINESE COMMUNIST INTENTIONS AND CAPABILITIES - 1950/51
REVIEW OF CHINESE COMMUNIST INTENTIONS
The declared primary aim of Chinese Communist policy is to consolidate the revolution and to bring the whole of the national territory, including Formosa, under control of the Peking Government. It is also the avowed intention of the Chinese Communists to secure the withdrawal of the Western Powers from the Far East and South East Asia. These two aims can be pursued simultaneously but the Chinese Government must inevitably consider in every case whether a particular course of action, designed to further the second aim, will also contribute to the achievement of the first and they may be expected to

---
* J.I.C.(50) 15 (Final), J.I.C.(50) 1 Series, J.I.C.(50) 54 (Final), J.P.(50) 82 (Final).

refrain from any action which will in fact have the contrary effect.
2. Although the Chinese Government have a treaty of alliance with the Soviet Government and although they will take cognisance of Soviet policy, there is no evidence that they are amenable to Soviet dictation. Indeed any suggestion that they were acting as the tool of Moscow would weaken their claim to leadership over the whole Chinese people, and is consequently likely to be resisted. While therefore the Soviet Government and the Chinese Government are at one in desiring to see the withdrawal of the Western Powers from the Far East and South East Asia, and while the Soviet leaders would welcome a situation in which China was involved in conflict with the Western Powers, it may be assumed that the Chinese Government will not resort to overt aggression against any neighbouring foreign territory unless they are convinced and can demonstrate to the public at large that this action is dictated by China's own interests.
3. They may judge that this condition is fulfilled if the weakness of the Western Powers is so apparent as to make the prospects of success irresistibly attractive. This would most probably be the case if the Western Powers were already involved in a global war. They will correspondingly be deterred from action if it is clear to them that action will lead to general war with the Western Powers on several fronts. Except in the case of Formosa where at present only military action can bring the island under the rule of Peking, the Chinese Government will in our opinion concentrate in the initial stages on weakening the neighbouring territories by political infiltration and subversion combined, where appropriate, with military advice and assistance. They will prefer this policy to overt aggression as a means of eliminating Western influence since they will judge the risk of its provoking counter action by the Western Powers to be negligible.
4. The overall military intentions of the Chinese Communists throughout the period under review must be subject to constant variation depending on such factors as the outcome of the war in Korea, the future relation of China with the United Nations, a Japanese peace treaty and internal economic problems. These intentions

are covered in our monthly reports*⁺ on the Chinese Communist threat. In general we consider that the Chinese Communists will not attempt any independent external aggression unless they think the effects can be localised. We estimate below their current intentions towards Korea, Indo-China, Burma, Siam, Formosa, Macao and Tibet, and in each case examine the Forces likely to be used should circumstances prompt them to embark on a policy of aggression.

ECONOMIC FACTORS
5. China's economy, always backward, has been severely impaired by years of war and even though the Communists are pursuing a vigorous rehabilitation policy, Mao Tse-tung has said they can expect it to be at least three years before the economic situation improves.
6. The country as a whole produces about 90% of its requirements in foodstuffs; this 90% cannot be evenly distributed because of transport difficulties. Famines are therefore endemic. China's natural resources are rich, but only a fraction has been tapped, and industrially the country is poorly developed.
7. There is an almost complete lack of liquid fuel production in China. Electric power is inadequate and the engineering and armament industries produce only a small volume of inferior quality items. Communications are generally poor and in this, combined with China's heavy dependence on foreign oil, lies her great strategic weakness.
8. It is considered that rehabilitation and development of industry will not have progressed very far during the period under review. Development of communications will be comparatively slow. China, including Manchuria and its other territories, would not be able to supply and maintain a force in the field which would be capable of a large scale offensive against well-balanced Western forces of a comparable size. This does not, of course, preclude the possibility of their success against smaller Western forces through sheer weight of numbers.
9. The acquiring of the rice supplies of Burma and

---
* + J.I.C. (50) 1 Series.

Siam must constitute a standing temptation to the Chinese Communists since it would enable them to secure themselves against the dangers of a famine, always provided it could be effectively distributed. Any Chinese Communist action in these areas would have very grave effects on the rice supplies of South East Asia as a whole and be most damaging to allied interests there, particularly in Malaya. Overt action in this direction would, however, inevitably provoke strong reaction on the part of India and Ceylon. At present there is no evidence that the Chinese Communists will consider that the balance of advantage lies with overt action against Burma and Siam in the period under review.

MILITARY FACTORS
Army
10. The Chinese Communist Army (C.C.A) at present consists of 2,500,000 men, organised in 80 armies, with a militia of 1 million. It is estimated that in addition some 3 million men with war experience will be available for mobilisation but the total number mobilised will be limited only by the equipment available.
11. If adequate Soviet assistance is forthcoming, the standard of tactical and technical training will improve continually and present shortages of heavy equipment in the Chinese Communist Army are likely to be made good. The best of the Chinese fighting men will possibly be equal to their Soviet counterpart, but the army as a whole will be considerably inferior to any army of the Western Powers. Its discipline and morale will be of a high order and its training thorough. There will, however, be serious deficiencies in specialists and technicians. Its commanders and staffs will have little or no experience in handling armour and artillery on a large scale and will have little knowledge of air support or co-operation with other Services. They will also lack experience in modern war. From the point of view of operations in South East Asia and the Far East, the army will lack experience of jungle warfare.
12. In spite of these limitations, the Chinese Army should not be under-estimated, as it will be incomparably stronger than any of the other indigenous armies of the Far East and South East Asia or the forces of

Air Force

13. We believe that the Chinese Communist Air Force (C.C.A.F) now consists of four air regiments organised primarily as a tactical support force, and an independent communications unit.

14. The present strength is estimated to be as follows:-
(a) Fighters
53 Japanese types
110 Soviet LA-5, LA-7, and LA-9
22 Mustangs
(b) Bombers
80 Soviet TU-2 and IL-10
1 U.S. B-24
1 Mosquito
(c) Reconnaissance   10 Japanese types
(d) Transports   10 U.S. C-46 and C-47.

In addition there are believed to be about 50 Transport aircraft, probably C-47, in the Chinese Communist Civil Aviation. It is unlikely that any degree of emphasis will be placed on strategic bombing and there is no present information that a strategic bomber force is planned.

15. The personnel strength of the C.C.A.F. has recently been estimated to be about 35,000, of which some 1,000 are aircrew, including approximately 400 pilots. It is also estimated that 3,500-4,500 students are in training at the eleven flying and technical schools. We believe that a large number of students undergo advanced flying training in the Soviet Union, but no assessment of the number can be made.

16. The Soviet Union under the reported secret terms of the Sino-Soviet Treaty (the veracity of which has never been confirmed) undertook to provide the Chinese with an operational air force in the shortest possible time. It was, we believe, decided to place Soviet personnel in key positions throughout the organisation. As the Chinese become more efficient, Soviet personnel will probably be withdrawn from all lower formations, but will probably be retained in key positions in order to ensure that the C.C.A.F. is in a position to further Soviet policy in the Far East.

17. The C.C.A.F. is expanding rapidly and under the reported terms of the Sino-Soviet Treaty the Soviet

Union is to provide 300 fighters, 140 ground attack aircraft, 100 light bombers and 260 transport and reconnaissance aircraft. It is possible that these aircraft may be handed over by the end of 1951. We believe that the C.C.A.F. is being developed along Soviet lines to function as a fighter defence and army support force. We consider that, even with Soviet help, the C.C.A.F. ground organisation is likely to be inefficient by Western standards and this, coupled with lack of combat experience, will be reflected in a low standard of operating proficiency.

Navy

18. The Communists have acquired some 50 warships, including 5 destroyer escorts and six gunboats, together with a number of Nationalist personnel who are reported to be largely undergoing instruction in Communist indoctrination schools. The Communists could probably only muster in a weak operational state the number of ships shown BELOW. By the end of the year they may have crews that can man and operate them sufficiently well to attempt to tackle a Nationalist Force of similar size.

(a) First Line
3 Escort Vessels
1 Minesweeper

(b) Second Line
25 Gunboats, improvised Gunboats, armed launches and control boats.

(c) Landing Craft
About 60 landing craft of U.S. origin including some commandeered from commercial firms.

19. The Soviet Union is, however, providing considerable assistance in training and has probably given some material help. This is likely to continue, and as a result the Communist Navy will probably by the end of 1951 have considerably increased in efficiency although it will be a long way below Western standards.

20. Should the whole of the Nationalist Navy or any part of it become available to the Communists, either by defection or capture, it will increase the potential naval strength of the latter, but the Nationalists lack ammunition spares and equipment and their efficiency is low judged by Western standards. Therefore, although the addition of 120 Warships of all types, including 7 destroyers, 21 destroyer escorts, 22 gun-boats and 21

patrol craft, including minesweepers would be a great incREASE in potential for the Communists, their efficiency would remain low. Even, therefore, if the Chinese Communists acquire the entire Nationalist Navy before they embark on a major war, we do not consider that their force would constitute more than a minor threat provided the Western Allies maintain adequate forces in the area.
21. The Communists will have very considerable numbers of coastal craft, junks, sampans etc., available for use in landing operations. They have also acquired a large number of miscellaneous merchant vessels, some of the Liberty type, but mainly of small tonnage.

ASSUMPTIONS.
22. We have assumed that:-
(a) Although the Chinese Communists have over-whelming forces in comparison with neighbouring non-communist countries they are unlikely to use a ground force of greater superiority than five to one in any one campaign.
(b) That the governments of the anti-communist countries in South East Asia will remain anti-communist or neutral during the period under review.
(c) That the Soviet Union will limit its aid to China to military and technical advice and to the supply of material including arms, equipment and oil.

POSSIBLE CAMPAIGNS
23. We estimate below current Chinese Communist intentions and capabilities in relation to Korea, Indo-China, Burma, Siam, Formosa, Macao and Tibet.
24. While we are unable to assess with confidence the exact logistical requirements of the Chinese Communist forces we consider that the land communications available in South East Asia would be sufficient to maintain the forces whose employment there is envisaged in the following paragraphs.

KOREA
Present Situation
25. It is clear that the rapid success of the United Nations forces in South Korea and the increasing prospect that the North Korean Forces and Government will soon be eliminated are causing serious anxiety to the

Chinese Communists, who may regard the elimination of the North Korean buffer state as a direct threat to the security of China. During the past few weeks Chinese propaganda against the United States has become increasingly violent and has harped on the theme that the Americans intend to extend their aggressive designs not only against North Korea but against China. This propaganda has also attempted to discredit the United Nations (particularly over their action in Korea) as being no more than a cloak for United States aggression and to make it clear that in the absence of Chinese (Peking) representation in the United Nations all the decisions of that body must be considered illegal. At a large meeting of government officials on September 30th Chou En Lai stated that in no circumstances could the Chinese people tolerate or ignore reckless aggression against their neighbours by the imperialists. Two days later he summoned the Indian Ambassador and gave him to understand that if the United States Army crossed the 38th Parallel China would be forced to take "immediate steps". He added that such a crossing of the boundary would make it clear that the United States authorities had elected for war and that China would be forced to act "accordingly"; and a few days later he again confirmed this intention. These statements are in themselves somewhat unspecific, although clearly threatening, and the Chinese Government have not irrevocably committed themselves in writing to send troops into North Korea in the event of a crossing of the 38th Parallel, but they have deliberately made the Indian Ambassador believe that such is their intention.

Topography

26. Most of the country on both sides of the North Korean frontier is rugged and mountainous. Movement away from established routes is difficult (especially in an east-west direction) because of the steep slopes and dense forests. The areas around the western and eastern ends of the frontier are lower and less difficult than the centre; the west coastal areas and lover Amnok (Yalu) valley resemble the west coast lowlands further south; the east coast and Tomen valley have narrow areas of a lowland. Along most of its length the frontier is formed by the Amnok (Yalu) and Tomen rivers, which are the two largest rivers in Korea. The Amnok is normally not

fordable over long stretches, but the Tomen is shallow except when in spate. River levels are low from November to March; they are high after snowmelt in April and after summer rains in July and August. The rivers are normally frozen from mid-December to mid-March, when the ice is used for cart traffic.

Climate

27. The wet season is from April to September. In Winter appreciable depths of snow accumulate in the mountains which are normally snow-covered from December to March.

Communications (See Map)

28. There are two main routes of entry into Korea from the north: via Antung at the west end of the frontier; and along the narrow corridor down the east coast. The Antung route is served by a single track railway from Mukden (the focal point of the south Manchurian railways); after entering Korea the railway follows the west coast more or less closely via Pyongyang to Seoul. The east coast route is served by a railway (also single track) from central Manchuria; this railway, after meeting two lines from the Soviet territory to the east, enters Korea at Tomen and then follows the east coast, ending at Samchok. The only lateral railways connecting the two routes are those from Kowen to Pyongyang and from Wonsan to Seoul. The basic pattern of the roads system follows that of the railways, with the addition that there is a direct road from Dairen to Antung. In Korea a fair secondary road close to the frontier connects the two main entry routes, and there are lateral roads from Wonsan (east coast) to Pyongyang, Pyonsan and Seoul. A few minor roads cross the frontier, but before reaching a line from Wonsan to Pyongyang they all lead to either the west or the east coasts.

29. We lack the   information notably that concerning the effect of United Nations air attacks, necessary for a calculation of the size of the forces which the two main entry routes could support. As a very tentative estimate, we believe that each route could probably support Chinese Communist forces of the order of 250,000 men.

Chinese Armed Forces likely to be employed and their capabilities.

30. Land Forces. Our intelligence cover in Manchuria is almost non-existent. It is therefore impossible to check

information concerning the strength, organisation or equipment of the ChiNESE Army believed to be concentrated in Manchuria.

31. We believe the strength of the Chinese Army in Manchuria to be about 13 armies, comprising some 400,000 men; however, their strength could quite well be below or in excess of this figure. We also believe that formations of this force are not only being re-equipped with Soviet weapons including tanks, but have probably reached the combat efficiency described in para 11. It is difficult however to assess what proportion of the quantities of equipment arriving in Manchuria from the Soviet Union has gone to the Chinese Army, or how much has gone to Korea to replace losses in battle. Furthermore, although re-organisation of the Chinese army in Manchuria has taken place, we do not know whether the formations have merely received new equipment or whether they are emerging as Russian type divisions. We estimate that the Soviet Union had available sufficient equipment to equip the Chinese armies in Manchuria at least to the scale of the North Korean Divisions at the beginning of hostilities.

32. We consider therefore that the Chinese Army available for intervention in Korea must be assessed in terms of the best case and the worst case. We give these below:-

(a) The best case
A force of 400,000 men with artillery support of some 690 guns, but lacking in armour.

(b) The worst case
A balanced force of 400,000 men organised on the Russian pattern with adequate artillery support and including at least two armoured divisions.

33. In addition to the forces already believed to be in Manchuria, a Field Army of about 300,000 men is concentrated in the Hankow area of Central China. It is believed this formation is also being re-organised and re-equipped with Soviet weapons. This Field Army is therefore conveniently located as a strategic reserve and could quickly reinforce Manchuria if required.

34. Air Forces. The details given in paras 14 and 15 show that the first line strength of the C.C.A.F. amounts to some 300 aircraft. There have been several reports of aircraft (amounting to 300) on airfields in Manchuria.

These are in all probability Soviet aircraft which were intended as reinforcements for either the North Koreans or the C.C.A.F. It is reasonable to assume that if the Chinese intervened in the Korean War these aircraft would be made available to them. This would double the strength of the C.C.A.F. in aircraft, but the problem of air crews and maintenance personnel would still remain. Moreover, it is unlikely that the C.C.A.F. could afford to move all its aircraft away from their present duties. A figure of around 275 first line aircraft would, it is considered, be the maximum number which could be made available for operations in Korea.

35. <u>Naval Forces</u>. The Chinese Communist Navy located North of Shanghai at present consists of a few small craft whose operational value is likely to be negligible except for minelaying purposes. Consistent unconfirmed reports have been received, however, to the effect that Soviet advice and training have been given to the Chinese Communist Navy in Manchuria and North China, and that a small number of ex-Japanese craft and some submarines have been supplied. Even if these reports are true the operational value of the submarines is likely to be negligible and that of the other craft extremely limited without substantial Soviet support in trained personnel.

36. In the face of U.N. sea and air opposition we consider it unlikely that in the event of China becoming directly involved units of the Chinese Communist Navy could be moved from Shanghai or from South China into the Yellow Sea.

37. The Chinese Communist Navy is therefore likely to confine itself to mine laying and defensive patrols of the Manchurian and Chinese Yellow Sea coastline, but the possibility of the use of ex-Japanese craft, and of submarines with substantial covert assistance by Soviet personnel, cannot be entirely disregarded. In this event the maximum forces which could be employed would consist of six submarines based on Tsingtao or Dairen, 6 Destroyers, 17 Destroyer escorts and 22 miscellaneous craft including some Motor Torpedo Boats. Of these only 1 destroyer and 14 miscellaneous craft including MTBs are likely to be operational in the immediate future from purely Chinese resources.

United Nations Forces
38. <u>Ground Forces</u>. The total force at present numbers some 263,000 comprising six American Divisions (150,000), one Brigade of Commonwealth Troops (3,000) and six South Korean Divisions (100,000).
39. <u>Naval and Air Forces</u>. The exact strength of these forces is not known but the United Nations Naval and Air forces are overwhelmingly stronger than the maximum that could be employed by the Chinese Communists. United Nations sea and air supremacy will therefore continue.

Courses open to the Chinese Government
40. There are four courses open to the Chinese Government:
(a) To continue their political and propaganda campaign in the hope of deterring United States forces from entering North Korea and at the same time to encourage North Koreans to continue guerilla warfare in Korea.
(b) To enter Korea and occupy a defence line covering the Manchurian frontier, and as far forward as possible but not to engage in hostilities with United Nations forces unless attacked by them.
(c) To make their forces available to the North Koreans in the form of a "volunteer" army, but not to become committed nationally.
(d) To invade North Korea with the object of driving back any United Nations forces who had advanced North of the 38th parallel.
41. The main advantage in adopting course (a) would be that there would be no risk of China becoming involved in a major war with the West. In addition Chinese propaganda could effectively exploit their "moderation" and might appreciably increase their chances of obtaining membership of the United Nations and a say in the United Nations' settlement in Korea.
42. The Chinese Government may decide that they are now so committed that they must take some military action in the event of a crossing of the 38th parallel in order to save face and maintain national morale. The adoption of course (b) might in their view be the minimum military action feasible to demonstrate clearly their intention to defend Manchuria and resist American aggression. They might also hope that it would not involve them in hostilities with the West; but they would probably realise that it would increase the risk of a clash between Chinese and U.S. forces.

43. Course (c) would avoid their becoming involved nationally, but we doubt whether they would risk putting their best forces under command of the defeated North Koreans.

44. Course (d) would be their only method of restoring the status quo of North and South Korea but this course would however involve them in hostilities with British Commonwealth and American forces. If this occurs we consider it unlikely the conflict could be localised and war with China, though not necessarily world war, would result.

45. We still consider the Chinese do not wish to become involved in a major war with the Western Powers, and that they may therefore consider the risks intailed by course (d) are too great, despite the advantages of maintaining North Korea as a buffer state. Furthermore, with the lesson of the recent campaign in South Korea before them, they will undoubtedly appreciate that their lines of communication would be rapidly dislocated by the over-whelming U.N. air power which would lead to the isolation and defeat of their forces at the front. Moreover, as we have stated in paragraph 2, we do not consider that the Chinese Government are so amenable to Soviet dictation that they would impair their own interest to the extent of adopting this course.

46. On balance we consider the Chinese leaders are likely to adopt course (a), but should they consider themselves forced to pursue a policy of military intervention, we consider they would adopt course (b).

Implications of Chinese Communist Intervention in Korea.

47. If the Chinese do intervene, they will realise that the prospects of localising the conflict are poor, but they will, we think, try to do so at any rate at first. They are therefore unlikely initially to attempt to divert U.N. resources from Korea by staging some act of aggression elsewhere, for example, against Hong Kong, or Indo-China.

48. On the other hand it is clear that however much the Chinese might represent the conflict as a war between themselves and American aggressors the conflict would have repercussions in other areas on the Chinese perimeter, since Britain and France would find themselves obliged to tighten up the economic blockade of China in support of their American allies and to institute other

measures which would increase tension between themselves and China. In their inflamed state of mind the Chinese might regard these measures as a prelude to aggression against the southern part of China from Indo-China or Hong Kong and decide to forestall this by ejecting the Western Powers from these places.

49. We examine more detail below the implications on the threat to Hong Kong, Indo-China and Formosa.

(a) Hong Kong. We consider that on balance even if hostilities could not be confined to Korea and general hostilities were to ensue between the United Nations and China, China would still in the initial stages probably want to limit the field of hostilities as much as possible and would not extend the conflict by an attack on Hong Kong unless she considered that measures taken by the United Kingdom to strengthen the position of the colony compelled her to do so. The risk of action against Hong Kong taking place would, however, be much greater than at present.

(b) Indo-China. If the war extends to China we consider that the Chinese might openly intervene on the side of Viet Minh.

(c) Formosa. In the event of open war between the West and the Chinese Communists, we consider the latter would be forced to give up all hope for the present of mounting an operation to recover Formosa.

50. We believe that the Chinese Communists have sufficient ground forces in central and south China to carry out attacks against Hong Kong and Indo-China.

INDO-CHINA
General consideration
51. In attempting an invasion of Indo-China, the C.C.A. would, for the first time, come up against sea, land and air forces of a Western standard. The French have however, many limitations. Although they have the infantry component of the four divisions they consider necessary to meet external aggression, they are very short of artillery and armour. Their forces are almost entirely deployed on internal security tasks, and although several infantry battalions are earmarked as reserves, they too are deployed on an internal security role; in addition no brigade or mobile H.Q. exists which is capable of assuming command functions in field operations. The

French have no intention of meeting Chinese aggression on the frontier and are likely to pull back to a defensive position in the Red River Delta area, but no defence works have been prepared in this area nor has any reconnaissance been carried out. Furthermore as late as 17th August, General Carpentier stated he had not yet made up his own mind on how he would meet an external threat. In short, therefore, the French have no long or short term plan to meet external aggression.

52. Elsewhere in Indo-China the French would be likely to retain their garrisons in the main area which they occupy, namely Central Annam and Cochin China. The practicability of using in Tongking considerable reinforcements from these areas would be dependent on the state of security in the south.

Present situation and likelihood of invasion

53. We have no reason to change our previous view*⁻ that the Chinese Communists are unlikely to attack Indo-China in the near future; they are likely however to continue to give the Viet Minh forces considerable morale and material support. There are further reports that arms are already being supplied and recently arrangements were made to transport overland from the Canton area to Tongking a substantial consignment, including artillery, A.A. guns and Bazookas, which the Viet Minh forces have hitherto particularly lacked. Heavier junk traffic from Hainan to the Viet Minh held coastal areas has been reported. The Chinese have at present seven armies and elements of three more, totalling some 200,000 men, in the French Indo-China frontier area. And although this force may not be organised on the scale envisaged in para. 34 they constitute a very real potential threat and could quickly cross the frontier if such a decision were taken. Militarily we cannot be sure of receiving any warning, should Chinese Communist forces be used in Tongking. It is possible however that some warning might be obtained from Chinese and Viet Minh propaganda.

Topography and Communications (See Map)

54. The terrain on the Sino-Indo-Chinese border is generally hilly or mountainous and covered with thick forest, scrub and grassland. The main strategic route Liuchow-Langson-Hanoi is destroyed along most of its length, but

---
*⁻ J.I.C. (50) 1/11 (Final)

the French have already started work on a loop which may well be completed before 1952. Secondary routes are:-
(a) Nanning-Moncay-Haiphong;
(b) Nanning-Langson-Tien-Yen-Haiphong. Each has a very limited capacity but may be developed.
Further possible routes are:-
(c) Kweiyang-Caobang-Hanoi which, even after considerable reconstruction, would have a smaller capacity than (a) or (b);
(d) The Viet Minh have constructed a road from the Sino-Tongking border to their northern redoubt, by-passing Caobang, which, with further development, might become an additional route;
(e) The bed of the Kunming-Laocay-Hanoi railway which, after reconstruction of tunnels and bridges, could be used as a small capacity supplementary route. In addition, there are some hill tracks crossing the Sino-Tongking border which an invading force could use, but it would havE to be supplied by one of the main routes. The only railway link serving the above routes is that of the low capacity Shanghai-Nanchang-Liuchow line, with connections to Hankow and Canton. This railway terminates about 200 miles short of the Indo-China border but is being completed.
55. With the capture of Tongking the subsequent advance of the C.C.A. could follow either or both of the direct roads across Annam and Laos into Siam (924 and 1146 miles respectively to Bangkok), or the longer coastal route to Cochin China, and thence to Siam (1,627 miles to Bangkok).
56. <u>The Annam-Laos route</u>. Two roads strike westwards to the Laotian-Siamese border from the coastal road at Ha Tinh and Quang Tri respectively. They converge at Ubon Ratchatani in Siam (approximately 360 miles from Hanoi) east of which the river Mekong has to be crossed by ferry.
57. <u>The coastal route</u>. The coastal route from Hanoi to Saigon (1,077 miles) consists of a road and railway. Both are disrupted where they run through Viet Minh occupied territory and very considerable rehabilitation would be necessary there to restore them to normal working. From Saigon to the Siamese frontier there is a secondary road and from Phnom Penh there is also a rail link into Siam.

58. <u>Airfields</u>. There are three operational airfields in Tongking and numerous landing grounds in North and Central Indo-China. The landing grounds have a limited capacity: during the wet season serviceability declines and often they become unusable. The difficulties of supplying both airfields and landing grounds would restrict their use by the enemy, although there would be a threat of attacks from Soviet type twin-engined bombers based in South China.

59. <u>Weather</u>. Weather is best for campaigning during the dry fine period of November and December. Persistent very low cloud and drizzle would hamper air operations from January to March. Rain is not heavy between April and mid-June or between mid-October and November, and would not seriously hamper operations. There is, however, very heavy rain during the rest of the year, and this would restrict movement to the roads. Further restriction of movement may occur in the rice-growing areas of Tongking and northern Annam; double cropping is practised and the paddy fields are flooded from July to October and from December to May.

<u>Chinese Armed Forces Likely to be Employed</u>

60. <u>Ground Forces</u>. The strength of the force invading Tongking is likely to be in the nature of one field army (250,000 men) together with up to two artillery divisions, each of 108 guns. We believe that the Chinese would consider such a force to be strong enough to defeat the French and to advance thereafter through Siam to the Malayan border. In any case the capacity of the routes, probable shortage of motor transport, and Allied operations would probably limit the strength of their force unless the French and their Allies had been unable to deny them the use of sea communications.

61. <u>Air Forces</u>. The C.C.A.F. would probably throw all its available resources into the air battle, but the number of AIRCRAFT MAY well be limited by the necessity for retaining aircraft in China as a defence against possible Nationalist attacks from Formosan bases. The possibility of the Soviet Union undertaking responsibility for the air defence of China is remote. The main targets for attack by Chinese aircraft would probably be airfields and lines of communication together with military objectives in the area of the Red River delta, but Chinese pilots have little or no battle experience

and could be expected to prove inferior to those of any Western air force.

62. Naval Forces. Although the easiest way for the C.C.A. to move into Indo-China and southwards would be by sea they could not do this on a large scale so long as the Allies maintained control of sea communications. We have assumed that this will be the case although the Chinese Communists would probably employ large numbers of junks and coastal craft to supplement their land communications and for the purpose of landing raiding parties and guerillas.

Viet Minh Forces

63. The Viet Minh forces comprise 86,000 regular troops together with a militia of 90,000. Its regular forces are organised into some 188 battalions and constitute a well organised, well trained and well disciplined guerilla army of high morale. It is relatively well equipped with small arms but is short of heavy weapons of all kinds. Most of the Viet Minh operations are carried out by its irregular forces employing terrorist tactics. We believe that the Viet Minh is now approaching the status of a regular army. It is possible that without waiting for the assistance of Chinese Forces it will embark on a full scale offensive (as opposed to guerilla operations) against the French as soon as it considers itself strong enough.

French Forces

64. Ground Forces. Although the approximate strength of the French Land Forces in Indo-China totals some 300,000, the regular French Forces number only about 104,000 and are widely dispersed. In Tongking the French forces comprise 53,500, but practically the whole of this force is engaged on internal security duties and though a reserve of 13 battalions is earmarked it cannot be made readily available to meet an external threat. We doubt whether any further reinforcements for the French and Colonial troops can be provided by France without severely curtailing her contribution to Western Union land forces and jeopardising the reconstruction of the French Metropolitan Army. Recruits could be found for the units raised locally but equipment from French sources would not be forthcoming. However, considerable aid is now being provided under the American Military Aid programme and this is likely to be effective by October. In

addition the French submitted a general request for aid to H.M. Government.

65. Air Forces. The French Air Force has available in Indo-China 80 fighters/bombers, 56 transports, 6 reconnaissance aircraft are 30 light communication or spotter aircraft. 40 fighter aircraft are due to be delivered by the U.S. some time this year. In the absence of air opposition the French Air Force has been reasonably efficient with the limited equipment at its disposal. In the event of an attack by the C.C.A.F. it is thought that the French should give a good account of themselves.

66. Naval Forces. French naval forces at present in the area consist of one cruiser, ten sloops, fourteen minesweepers and about 170 miscellaneous landing craft and supporting auxiliary vessels. The effectiveness of this force is likely to be greater than that of the combined Chinese Communist and Nationalist fleets.

Most Likely Communist Plan

67. If it were decided to invade Tongking the Chinese Communists' attack would be directed as follows in conjunction with Viet Minh forces:-

(a) Force A. Up to 250,000 men supported by an Artillery force of 576 guns and all available aircraft would make an all-out effort to capture Tongking.

(b) After the capture of Tongking operations against the remainder of Indo-China would be in two parts:-

(i) Force B. About 60-80,000 men with an artillery force of 100 guns and 30 fighter and 20 light bombers in 1950, and possibly 70-100 fighters or fighter-bombers and 30-40 light bombers during 1951, would advance from the Annamite coast to the Siamese border.

(ii) Force C. About 60,000 men supported by artillery comprising about 100 guns with 30 fighter and 20 light bombers in 1950 and possibly 70-100 fighters or fighter-bombers and 30-40 light bombers during 1951, would advance along the Annamite coast to Cochin China.

68. Force A. A.C.C.A. attack will coincide with an all-out Viet Minh offensive designed to stretch French resources to the utmost and prevent, by guerilla operations of all kinds, the concentration of their reserves. Initially the C.C.A. is likely to infiltrate into Tongking on a broad front in preference to an advance down the main road axis in view of its preponderance of infantry, its lack of mechanisation and its known susceptibility to

attacks on the lines of communication. Its primary aim will be to pierce the French defended area and link up with the Viet Minh. Once this has been achieved the C.C.A. must concentrate to defeat the French forces in Tongking and thus open the road between China and the Delta. We estimate that those operations will probably succeed by sheer weight of numbers within four months unless the French can be strongly supported in time by a balanced allied Force. Thereafter consolidation for about a month will be necessary before the C.C.A. and Viet Minh advance against opposition can continue. No defensive position exists in Annam and the French will be faced with the alternative of making a stand in Cochin China or evacuating the peninsula altogether.

69. After defeat of its garrison in Tongking the balance of the French forces, less well equipped, and with relatively weak artillery support, would be likely to concentrate in the Mekong delta area and in the coastal plain of South Annam. If the Viet Minh had previously been cleared from North Annam the French might fight a delaying action in the Vinh area. The small existing garrisons on the other parts of the Annamite coast and in Laos would be unlikely to offer serious resistance.

70. Force B. Apart, therefore, from the possibility of delay at Vinh any C.C.A. advance from the Annamite coast to the Siamese border via Laos would be practically unopposed and allowing for shortage of transport should be able to reach the Siamese border in the area of Ubon Ratchatani within one and half months of leaving Hanoi.

Force C.

71. The advance along the Annamite coast to Cochin China would be more difficult both on account of resistance by the French defence areas in central Annam, and of the inferior communications, which run close to the coast for long stretches and are therefore particularly vulnerable to attacks mounted from the sea. If the French have regained control of the communications in this area and have effected a considerable measure of repair, without having the time to offset this by subsequent demolition, the Chinese force might be increased by an additional army group. Nevertheless, the coastal route from Quang Tri to Cochin China is very vulnerable to attack by a power having command of the sea.

72. The main battle with the French would be likely to be fought between the Mekong delta and the Cochin Chinese-Annamite border and, once the necessary build-up by the C.C.A. had been achieved, to result in the defeat of the French.

73. A minimum period of seven months would be required from the time of leaving Hanoi to the defeat of the French Forces in Cochin China. This would comprise three months for the southward advance and four months for the build-up and operations. If French resistance had ceased after the battle of Tongking the C.C.A. could move from Tongking to the Siamese border via Saigon in three months. With the capture of Saigon a force of one or two armies (20-40,000) could advance to the Siamese border in the area of Sisophon, and could reach it in six weeks. The administrative problem of this force would be increased by the necessity for road and rail tranship-ment at Phnom Penh.

Naval Operations

74. The Chinese Communists would probably use coast-creeping tactics with junks, small cargo ships and numerous other small craft to land raiding parties and guerillas as well as to supplement their land communications. The difficulties in preventing this sort of traffic even when the Allies have full command of the sea and air are considerable.

BURMA

Topography and Communications (See Map)

75. The present capacity of the Burma road running from Kunming to Mandalay is limited by that of the Chinese sector but there is no reason why some repairs should not be effected even before the beginning of the period.

76. The secondary route, direct from Kunming to Kengtung, has a negligible capacity at the moment.

77. Weather. The rainy season of the south-west monsoon is from May to October. During this period there is exceptionally heavy rainfall along the coast and high ground of Tenasserim and the Arakan, and both land and air operations would in consequence be difficult. Elsewhere in Burma the rainfall during this period is moderately heavy and would restrict and impede movement of military forces. During the north-east monsoon

(November to April) conditions are fine and dry and apart from interference to flying caused by persistent thick haze over the Irrawaddy Valley, the weather offers no bar to major military operations.

Chinese Forces Likely to be Employed
78. Ground Forces. Owing to the limited capacity of the routes from Yuanan into Burma, together with the road distances involved, the heavy requirements of motor transport, the difficulties of fuel supply and the very considerable road maintenance and commitment, it is unlikely that a C.C.A. force invading Burma would exceed 60,000 men together with some artillery.
79. Air Forces. The C.C.A.F. would in all probability use only sufficient aircraft to give ground support to their troops, plus a few transports for supplies and some reconnaissance aircraft. Shortage of suitable airfields near the border area would also be a limiting factor. It is considered that not more than 30-40 fighter bombers, 15-20 transports and 10 reconnaissance aircraft would be likely to be employed. It is quite possible that aircraft would not be employed at all in an operation against Burma unless other powers came to her aid.
80. Naval Forces. The Chinese Communists are unlikely to attempt to employ any Naval forces other than coastal craft in this campaign since the Allies maintain control of sea communications.

Fifth Column
81. The Chinese population in Burma is comparatively small and by no means all pro-Communist. There are enough pro-Communist Chinese in Rangoon itself however to create serious trouble. The Burma Communist Party, although now weak and on the defensive, has already showed its willingness to ask for Chinese aid, and might well use its countrywide organisation to help the invader. The number of extreme left-wing supporters of the present Burmese government, particularly amongst the Trades Union Congress Burma, are likely appease any Chinese invaders who look like being successful.

Burmese Forces
82. Ground Forces. The Burmese Army consists of some 35,000 regulars together with up to 20,000 armed auxiliaries. It consists of units recruited from the Shans, Chins, Kachins and Burmans of which the former three

compose the better fighting elements. This small force suffers from racial dissension and lack of training, and during the period may be almost entirely occupied with internal security operations so that it would be dispersed in small units in the areas of the more important towns and communications. It cannot be expected to offer any effective resistance to external aggression, although weak delaying forces would be stationed on the main routes of entry into the country. Should the Burmese Government reach an accommodation with the Karens during the period, a comparatively large supply of trained and reliable man-power would in time become available for recruiting, but it would take some time before Karen units would be ready for operations. If the present scale of insurrection continues in Burma the government will be unable to make forces available to defend the Chinese frontier.

83. <u>Naval Forces</u>. The Burmese Navy is the best of the three services, but has suffered a severe setback owing to the country's internal disturbances and political intrigue. The sea-going fleet consists of one frigate and some twenty-six smaller craft. The Burmese Navy would be likely to operate river and coastal patrols with the object of preventing the movement of C.C.A. by local craft.

84. <u>Air Forces</u>. The very small Burmese Air Force consists of a handful of non-combat aircraft, some of which are being used operationally at the expense of much needed training. Some expansion is planned, and in particular a few Mosquitoes are being added, but development will be slow. We consider it improbable that the Burmese Air Force would be able to exert more than a temporary and local effect on the course of the major military operations envisaged.

<u>Most Likely Chinese Communist Plan</u>

85. If it were decided to invade Burma, it should be possible for the C.C.A. to capture Meiktila and Mandalay in about one month and thereafter to advance on Toungoo and Rangoon. The capture of Rangoon and the occupation of the main economic areas of the country should then be possible within a further two months.

86. Any attempt to subjugate more than the lowlying area between Mandalay and Rangoon and the Shan States could result in a major internal security problem owing to the

likely resistance from frontier communities and possibly also from the Karens.

SIAM
General Considerations
87. Even with a government as favourably disposed towards the Western Powers as the present one, Siam would be unable to do more than offer token resistance to a Chinese invasion.
Topography and Communications (See Map)
88. Eastern axis. From the terminal of the Annan-Laos route at Ubon Ratchatani a railway runs direct to Bangkok, (357 miles). This railroad is reached by a limited capacity ferry over the tributary of the Mekong. There is no direct road from Ubon to Bangkok and movement along the country and jungle tracks would be indirect and difficult. Nevertheless a road has been started and might be completed by the end of 1952. The initial use of the railway could be denied to the Chinese Communists by withdrawing rolling stock at Bangkok, although it would be unwise to count on this happening. The southern route from Cochin China crosses into Siam northwest of Sisophon and runs direct to Bangkok (200 miles).
89. Western axis. The main route in Burma from Mandalay to the Siamese border via Kengtung has a very low capacity. Where this route enters Siam a road runs to Lampang. From Lampang to Bangkok there is at present, no through road. A direct railway runs from Lampang to Bangkok. The capacity of the Lampang-Bangkok axis could be augmented by using river transport. We consider that it would not be possible for a force larger than about 20,000 without supporting artillery, to be maintained along this axis into Siam.
90. Weather. The latter part of the dry season from December to February is particularly favourable for military operations of all kinds. Rainfall during the south-west summer monsoon is generally less heavy than in Indo-China but nevertheless movement would be restricted to the roads during August and September when the rainfall is greatest. Weather conditions during the inter-monsoon periods of October and March to April are unlikely seriously to restrict operations, but there may be extensive flooding in the Manam Chao Phraya River plains in October and November.

Chinese Armed Forces Likely to be Employed
91. Ground Forces. From logistic considerations we estimate that the strength of the Chinese Communists would be limited to 80,000 men with supporting artillery.
92. Air Forces. Assuming no intervention by Western Powers it is considered that the C.C.A.F. would not use more then 40-60 fighter/bombers, 10-20 light bombers, 15-20 transports (this latter may be increased if paratroops are used) and 10-15 reconnaissance aircraft. This of course assumes that aerodromes in Indo-China are available to the C.C.A.F.
93. Naval Forces. The Chinese Communists are unlikely to attempt to employ any naval Forces other than coastal craft in this campaign since the Allies maintain control of sea communications.

Siamese Forces.
94. Ground Forces. The Siamese Army consists of some 34,000 men and might be increased to 80,000 on mobilisation. The standard of leadership, morale and training in the force is not high and military equipment, which includes artillery and armoured fighting vehicles, consists of a wide variety of obsolete and obsolescent types of foreign manufacture. It is not, therefore, capable of effectively waging unaided a defensive war against the Chinese Communists. Efforts are being made to reorganise the forces and by the end of 1951 they should be better able to defend the frontiers for a limited period but, even so, will be incapable of offering prolonged resistance.
95. Naval Forces. The Siamese Navy consists of 1 destroyer, 2 corvettes, 35 patrol craft, 21 landing craft and some auxiliary vessels many of which are obsolescent. It is unlikely to have much effect on the course of operations.
96. Air Forces. The small Siamese Air Force does not at present constitute an effective fighting element. It has a few obsolescent aircraft, most of which are trainers. It is, however, about to be equipped with the equivalent of two fighter squadrons (Spitfires) and the addition of a small number of jet fighters is possible within the next two years. It could therefore make some initial contribution to defence against attack, but would have neither the backing nor the experience to sustain operations for any long period, or be effective against

the C.C.A.F. at the strength which it is predicted the latter would be during the period.

Fifth Column

97. The Chinese minority in Siam amounts to about 14% of the population with a far higher proportion in Bangkok. The Siam Communist Party (S.C.P.) is composed almost wholly of Chinese and is Chinese-led. In the event of a Chinese invasion the Chinese minority would tend to come under complete control of the S.C.P. and would presumably function as a fifth column. It is doubtful however whether the S.C.P. would have at its disposal very many trained saboteurs or sabotage and guerilla units. But those which they had would tend to exert an influence out of all proportion to their numbers, and their activities would be assisted by the dis-affection of the whole Chinese community. There is also a body of Viet Minh adherents among Indo-Chinese residents in N.E. Siam. These are believed to be well organised politically and could no doubt cause considerable embarrassment to an Army trying to defend Siam. Fifth column activities are however not likely to be necessary in conjunction with an attack on Siam unless the Siamese army is supported by troops of the Western Allies. In such a case the fifth column danger in Siam would be no worse and perhaps a little better than that at present existing in Malaya.

Most Likely Communist Plan

98. General Consideration. Siam is a country without any natural defensive positions other than those provided by waterways. It is therefore concluded that the Siamese Army would defend the frontiers in the area of the points of entry of the trans-Laos route, that from Cochin China and the Northern route from Burma. It could not hold these for long, and would be unlikely to offer any further serious resistance, except that it might be able to defend the Bangkok area for a short time. The estimate assumes there would be no intervention by the Western Powers.

Direction and Phasing

99. Eastern Axis. The employment of up to one army group (60,000 men) and supporting artillery would be possible on either of the main routes from Indo-China into Siam, and such a force would be adequate to penetrate the frontier defences and to defeat the Siamese Army in the Bangkok area. Such operations would probably be

accompanied by considerable fifth column and guerilla activity. After a period of one month to build-up at Ubon Ratchatani and/or Sisophon this force should be able to approach and defeat the garrison of Bangkok within two months on the northern route and one month on the southern route.

100. <u>Western axis</u>. The number of troops which could be maintained along this axis would be limited by the present low capacity of the Meiktila-Kongtung-Siam border road upon which the Siamese Sector of this axis is entirely dependent. It seems likely therefore that unless improvements to this axis have been carried out, a C.C.A. force would be limited to about one army (20,000) without supporting artillery. We do not consider that such a force would be adequate to over-run Siam and defeat the Siamese Army in the Bangkok area. Nevertheless such a force would probably be used in support of a main advance into Siam along the eastern axis, and in any case could be used to mount an active threat on Siam's northern frontier.

101. With the capture of Bangkok any further organised resistance by the Siamese Army would be unlikely. The occupation of the north-west part of the country would then be undertaken by the force advancing southwards from the Kengtung area. Although the internal security problem would not be large once Bangkok had fallen, the maintenance of some security forces would be necessary throughout the country.

FORMOSA
<u>Present Situation and Likelihood of a Communist Invasion</u>
102. The Chinese Communists' build-up in Fukien against Formosa now totals some 200,000 troops. It is considered that they have sufficient shipping to lift the large numbers of troops required for an invasion. Owing to U.S. air and sea patrols and the Nationalists' retention of three well placed islands off the mainland coast, there is little likelihood of a surprise invasion being carried out. An attempted invasion of Formosa under existing circumstances would be a hazardous operation and the Chinese Communists are likely to appreciate that without considerable Soviet naval and air assistance it would be unlikely to succeed. On the other hand, full-scale Chinese Communist propaganda on the intention to recover

Formosa continues, but seems to be carefully avoiding any mention of dates. Although there are signs*+ that an invasion has been postponed indefinitely and at least until U.S. forces are withdrawn, an attempted invasion remains a possibility.

Topography and Communications

103. Landing Areas. There are two main possible landing areas on Formosa:-
(a) the Keelung-Taipei-Tamsui area in the north together with beaches west of this area along the north-west coast.
(b) the Tainan-Takao area in the south-west.
In both these areas beaches and ports suitable for landing heavy equipment are available. The west central Tai-Chung delta area provides a subsidiary beach landing zone.

104. The Fukien coast abounds in harbours and bays from which an assault could be mounted, although proper communications with the hinterland are only available at the main ports of Foochow, Amoy and Swatow, and the subsidiary port of Tsinkiang.

105. Distances from assembly points to likely objectives are:-

Time taken at 5 knots
(a) Foochow (mouth of Min river) to Tamsai - 110 nautical miles..
22 hours
(b) Amoy to Tainan - 135 nautical miles..
27 hours
(c) Amoy to Takao - 155 nautical miles..
31 hours
(d) Swatow to Takao - 195 nautical miles..
39 hours
(e) Tsinkiang to Tai Chung area - 95 nautical miles..
19 hours
(f) Amoy to Tai Chung area - 130 nautical miles..
26 hours

106. Communications. There are adequate North to South road and rail communications in the Western coastal plain of Formosa although they have deteriorated from their excellent pre-war standard.

107. Weather Conditions. As far as weather conditions in

---
* + J.I.C.(50) 1/13 (Final)

the Strait of Formosa are concerned, the best time for a crossing and for landings on the west, north-west and south-west coasts would be during the period April to September, inclusive, and more particularly from April to June in order to minimise the typhoon risk. This risk is greatest in July, August and September, but the risk of a typhoon occurring at any particular time cannot be considered great. (Only six typhoons affected the west coast from 1932 to 1938). The disturbed conditions caused by a typhoon might last for 3 to 4 days. From October to March (inclusive) the north-east monsoon blows strongly. It is estimated that in an average year wind strength is force 6 OR over for more than half the time. The winds raise considerable sea and swell, and surf on the beaches, although the south-west coast is to some extent sheltered. Winds are usually appreciably less strong in March than during the rest of the period. We consider that unless an attack were to take place by the middle of October 1950 at the latest, weather conditions would compel its postponement until the following Spring.

Communist Armed Forces Available for this Campaign

108. Ground Forces. In view of the problem of providing adequate sea and air lift across the Formosan straits, it is probable that the Communists would aim at a superiority of only two-to-one in manpower. Such a force might consist of up to 300,000 men, or 10 Armies, together with up to 660 guns and 100 armoured cars and light tanks. Of this force it is likely that A minimum of 50,000 men would be required for the initial assault.

109. For some time past there have been reports of paratroops training in Manchuria under Russian auspices, and the arrival in Fukien of a large number of Chinese Communist paratroops is now reliably reported; a figure as high as 10,000 has been mentioned. The state of training of these troops is, however, unknown. The transport aircraft at present in the possession of the Chinese Communist Air Force could, however, only lift some 1,000 lightly armed troops in a single operation but the possibility that the Soviet Union may provide additional transport aircraft, with aircrews, cannot be discounted. The possibility of airborne operations against Formosa cannot be neglected.

110. Naval Forces. The Chinese Communists are likely to employ all the operational vessels of their fleet in an

operation against Formosa. Although the numbers given in paragraph 18 may seem considerable, the efficiency of the Communist navy is at a low ebb and maintenance is known to be poor.

111. Sea Lift. The Chinese Communists are building up an ocean-going merchant fleet. Although exact figures are not known it is probable that they have acquired by defection or purchase about 40 merchant ships. A number of large landing ships and craft which were left in China by the China Merchants Steam Navigation Company when the Nationalists withdrew will also be available to the Chinese Communists. In addition to acquiring ocean going ships the Chinese Communists have been reported to be building motor and sailing junks and to be purchasing or requisitioning engines for fitting in the latter. The Communists are also reported to be building 250 tugs and to have placed an order for 300 small landing craft in Manilla.

112. We consider that the Chinese Communists at present have sufficient sea transport, including junks, for all the troops that would be required for an invasion of Formosa, and for the military equipment and stores. The number of specialised craft capable of landing tanks and equipment direct on to the beaches is, however, very small. Although troop landing craft may be acquired from Manilla, the Chinese Communists are unlikely to be able greatly to increase the number of tank landing craft and amphibians within the period of this report, and therefore they will be able to land only a limited number of guns, tanks etc., in the assault.

113. Air Forces. The C.C.A.F. would probably employ all its available resources in the air battle.

Nationalist Forces available for Defending Formosa

114. Ground Forces. Because of the arrival of defeated Nationalist troops in the island from the mainland the strength of the Nationalist garrison in Formosa is not known with any accuracy, but it is believed to number nearly 300,000 men, of which at least a half are combatant troops. This garrison is made up of men trained on the island who have never seen battle and remnants of the Nationalist armies evacuated from the mainland. Under the leadership of General Sun-Li-Jen the efficiency and the equipping of the garrison have been improved and the garrison has reached a rather better standard than

the Nationalists achieved earlier in the civil war. The size of this force is likely to be enlarged as a result of local conscription and the ultimate evacuation of some Nationalist troops from the Quemoy and Pescadores Islands.

115. There are five Nationalist field armies in the island, together with a light armoured force and garrison troops. Two of the field armies are in the Taipei area in the north, one in the west central plain and two in the south. Substantial reinforcements have recently been sent to the Nationalist forces on the mainland from this garrison, but the organisation and locations of the above field armies are not believed to have been altered materially.

116. There are large stockpiles of arms and ammunition in Formosa, since the bulk of U.S. military supplies to China have been diverted to the island since February 1949. Some of the Nationalist armament factories are reported to have been transferred there. The agricultural resources of the island are believed to be adequate to support the requirements of the garrison indefinitely but it is not known how long financial support will last.

117. <u>Naval Forces</u>. The strength of the Nationalist Naval forces which could be concentrated to counter a seaborne invasion is assessed as follows:-

(a) <u>First Line</u> (Sea going).
1 Destroyer.
12 Escort Vessels.
12 Minesweepers
(b) <u>Second Line</u> (Coastal Operations).
4 Gunboats.
24 Patrol Craft or Motor Gunboats
About 40 Landing Craft.
About 20 auxiliary Vessels.

118. The Nationalist Navy is led by an able and determined Commander-in-Chief (Admiral Kwei). Morale is an uncertain factor, though it has hitherto been high. Maintenance is not of a high standard.

119. It must therefore be assumed that the Nationalist navy could send a force of at least 25 sea going ships, and some 80 or more armed small craft, against an invasion fleet, but there is a serious shortage of ammunition. The Nationalist navy already possesses a base in the Pescadores islands, and its position out in the

Formosa Strait is likely to be an important advantage to the navy in its anti-invasion operations. It also holds advanced bases at Quemoy, Matsu and other small islands off the coast of the mainland.

120. The Air Force. Practically the whole of the Chinese Nationalist Air Force (C.N.A.F.) is based on Formosa and its operational strength is estimated to be 36 heavy bombers, 60 light bombers, 192 fighters, 102 transports and 14 reconnaissance aircraft. Although the efficiency and offensive value of the C.N.A.F. is considered to fall well short of Western standards, the morale of the aircrews is thought to be quite good. Their standard of training is believed to be fair though limited in scope. The maintenance and repair organisation lacks proper facilities on Formosa and is probably inefficient.

121. The C.N.A.F. is thought to possess substantial reserves of aircraft and considerable stocks of spares and fuel, it is estimated that existing stocks will allow it to be maintained at, or near its present level for at least a year, provided that there is no sharp increase in its rate of activities.

Nationalism and Communism

122. A body called the Formosa Autonomy Movement Committee, which is alleged to have the covert backing of Americans and is apparently non-communist, is said to be working in Hong Kong (it appears also to have branches in Japan and the Philippines) with the object of setting up a Formosa Autonomy Government. Two other similar bodies, both Communist sponsored, are also reported to be operating from Hong Kong with a view to setting up a Red regime in Formosa, using self-government and opposition to the National Government administration as a means to arouse public sympathy.

123. The C.C.P. is reported to be trying to build up an active organisation in the island but there is no evidence to show that its efforts, so far, have met with any appreciable success. A Formosan People's Democratic Self-Government League has been formed in North China under the auspices of the C.C.P., but it is devoting itself to propaganda rather than to building up an organisation inside the island. Communist influence among the people of Formosa is unlikely to grow rapidly and thus to constitute a threat to the existing regime, so long as the Nationalist armed forces remain loyal.

The Assault

124. Although a proportion of the craft could probably effect the passage of the Straits of Formosa within 24 hours, the majority would take longer and the destination of the assault force would soon become apparent. This would facilitate the concentration of Nationalist land forces in the threatened areas.

125. Provided their loyalty remains unweakened, the Nationalist Navy and Air Force, even with their past record and present standard of performance, could achieve the destruction of a proportion of the invasion force during its passage. In this event it is unlikely that the small proportion of the invading force which effected a landing would be able to maintain a foothold, owing to the numerical superiority of the Nationalist force which it would encounter.

126. From the military point of view, we consider that the Nationalists should be able to repel an assault against the island, and that its capture can result only from the collapse of the Nationalist will to fight. The fact that Formosa is their last refuge from which there can be no retreat, and the immediate presence of Chiang Kai Shek and the more forceful leaders, increase the chances of resistance. But past experience of the unexpected collapse of Nationalist forces, when, on military grounds, resistance could have been successful, make us think that a collapse may nevertheless occur.

MACAO

127. Recent evidence indicates that Macao is thoroughly penetrated by Communists and that the small garrison is unlikely to be able to deal with the internal situation let alone an external attack. It is most improbable that any support would be available from outside.

128. The garrison is poorly equipped by modern standards and comprises a squadron of armoured cars, 3 batteries of artillery and 9 companies of infantry having a total strength of about 4,000 (half of whom are colonial troops from Angola). There are two naval sloops at present based on the colony and no air force garrison.

TIBET

Present Situation and Likelihood of Invasion.

129. It now looks as if the Chinese Communists intend to

resolve the Tibetan question by negotiation rather than by force, and a Tibetan Delegation has arrived in New Delhi for this purpose. Chou En Lai has however insisted that final talks must be in Peking. We have no reason to doubt that the Chinese Communists intend to enforce their claims to sovereignty over Tibet and that they will resort to force if negotiations break down.

Opposing Forces.

130. Chinese Communist forces for an assault total some 90,000 men. This force is considered more than adequate to carry a successful invasion of which we do not expect to receive any warning. The Tibetan army comprises some 10,000 men who are badly equipped and are incapable of offering much resistance.

* * *

J.I.C./2162/50

COPY NO. 12
KOREA - SITUATION REPORT NUMBER 90.
Attached is the Daily Situation Report on Korea.
(Signed) I.S. STOGKWELL.
1st November, 1950.

DISTRIBUTION:
H.M. The King
The Prime Minister
The Minister of Defence
The Chiefs of Staff
Chief Staff Officer to the Minister of Defence.
Joint Intelligence Committee
Commonwealth Relations Office
Combined Operations Headquarters.

TOP SECRET
SITUATION REPORT NO.90: KOREA.
SITUATION AS KNOWN AT 0900, 1ST NOVEMBER, 1950.

Military Report Source
BOUCHIER REPORT and TOKYO SITREP.

1. Enemy resistance to the Commonwealth and American advance along the West Coast has been moderate to stiff,

and tanks, self-propelled guns and mortars are being used in considerable numbers. The Allied advance, however, has been methodical and steady.

2. Further inland more ground has been given as the result of the confusion into which the South Korean Divisions have been thrown by unexpectedly strong North Korean counter attacks. The regimental group, elements of which had reached the Manchurian border, is now cut off, and has orders to withdraw. Meanwhile the American 1st Cavalry Division is moving up to restore the situation.

3. On the East Coast, the enemy drive towards Hamhung has been checked. while in the far North East a further advance has been made against moderate opposition. 10,000 men of the 7th U.S. Division have been landed at Iwon.

4. There is insufficient information to assess either the nature or the extent of the Chinese intervention. It appears to be merely an intensification of the policy of unofficial support to North Korea, which the Chinese Government has been giving throughout the war. During the last few days a considerable number of tanks, self-propelled guns and mortars have been supplied; and information given by a few Chinese prisoners indicates that elements of three Chinese divisions have crossed the Manchurian border into Korea and are fighting with and giving fresh life to North Korean formations. The support is 'unofficial' and the Chinese who have been captured have been without shoulder straps or Chinese markings on their uniforms.

Notes

1. For more see Michael S Goodman, The Official History of the Joint Intelligence Committee: Volume I – From the Approach of the Second World War to the Suez Crisis (Abingdon: Routledge, forthcoming).
2. See Anthony Farrar-Hockley, *The Official History of the British Part in the Korean War, Vol. I: A Distant Obligation* (London; HMSO, 1990).
3. COS(50) 152nd Meeting, 20 September 1950, Confidential Annex, TNA: DEFE 4/33.
4. JIC(50) 105th Meeting, 4 October 1950, TNA: CAB 159/8.
5. JIC(50)88(Final – Revise), 'Chinese Communist Intentions and Capabilities – 1950/51', 11 October 1950, TNA: CAB 158/11.
6. COS(50) 169th Meeting, 16 October 1950, TNA: DEFE 4/36.
7. Cited in Goodman, *The Official History of the Joint Intelligence Committee*.
8. JIC/2095/50, 'SITREPS', 25 October 1950, TNA: DEFE 11/202.

9. JIC/2162/50, 'Korea – Situation Report Number 90', 1 November 1950, TNA: DEFE 11/202.
10. JIC(50) 117th Meeting, 1 November 1950, TNA: CAB 159/8.
11. JIC(50)1/17(Final), 'The Chinese Communist Threat in the Far East and South-East Asia on 29th November 1950', 30 November 1950, TNA: CAB 158/9.

9

ESTIMATING SOVIET CAPABILITIES

ONE OF THE few wartime secrets to which the JIC had not been privy was the existence of the atomic bomb. The decision to withhold this information had been made by the Chiefs of Staff Committee. Yet by the end of the war, the JIC was at the centre of intelligence assessments of Soviet capabilities. This included everything from the disposition, size, quality of training and morale of conventional forces, through to highly scientific analyses of Soviet nuclear progress. These papers were often long and extremely detailed and were intended for a variety of audiences, from the technical consumers in the services to the policy planners in the Ministry of Defence.

At the centre was an estimation of the 'threat': a combination of assessing Soviet 'intent' and 'capabilities'. The JIC consistently asserted its view that the Soviet Union would not dare risk starting a nuclear war until it had stockpiled a sufficient number of nuclear weapons. Bombs, of course, were not the sole requirement: they had to be delivered somehow and in the pre-missile era there was a discrepancy between the relative proximity of the Soviet Union's targets in the UK and the much greater distances to those in the US. As the years progressed and the Soviets manufactured increasingly advanced weaponry and delivery systems, alongside a greater number of bombs, the JIC's assertion became something of a mantra. Given this assumption, JIC forecasts of Russian capabilities became crucial to post-war military planning.

Initial forecasts of atomic progress, beginning in 1945, foresaw that the Soviet Union would not be in a position to launch a nuclear offensive until 1957. This date was maintained throughout estimates produced in the 1940s. Even the premature detonation of the first Soviet bomb – Joe-1 – in August 1949, coming two or three years before expected, did not alter strategic estimates.[1] This discrepancy was easily explained away because the JIC believed it to be a test, and not the first bomb off the production line.[2]

The JIC maintained the belief that any conflict would involve the United States. As the 1950s wore on, and with Anglo-American relations growing closer, this assumption had more credibility. By 1957 it was assessed, for the first time, that the Soviet Union had now reached 'nuclear sufficiency' – defined by the JIC as being 'when the USSR has sufficient nuclear warheads and delivery systems to allocate to the targets which she would wish to destroy in nuclear war'.[3] The implications were disastrous, especially as only a matter of months later the Soviet Union launched Sputnik, thereby increasing the implied threat to the American heartland.

From the late 1940s onwards, there appeared a series of discrepancies between JIC and COS statements. The JIC paper below, from 1948, is a clear example of this. Here was a classic instance of a disagreement between intelligence producers and policy consumers. From the COS perspective, these were exhibited as doubts about JIC estimates. Such a critique was eloquently summed up in a note by Air Marshal Sir John Slessor, Chief of the Air Staff: 'I have long thought that there are serious dangers and disadvantages in accepting for planning purposes the JIC estimates of Russian capabilities.'[4] But despite such reservations, from the mid-1950s JIC and COS ideas began to converge again. The reason for this seems clear – the growing relationship with the Americans – which revealed COS anxieties about dealing with a Soviet attack alone.[5]

Relations with the US intelligence community were close but not without their problems. A fascinating insight into the bomber gap myth was offered by the JIC in 1952, when it was recorded that

> for some years the United States Air Force have been keenly concerned with obtaining the funds and authority to expand ... DDI [Deputy Director for Intelligence, RAF] who three years ago was in the USA recollects numerous occasions on which the USAF were at pains to establish the existence of the air threat to justify this expansion in the face of opposition from the Navy in particular. The USAF have worked hard on this, and the idea of this threat [of an 'aerial Pearl Harbor'] has gained wide acceptance. It is likely that this idea has now become so deeply embedded in American and in particular USAF thinking that collated intelligence upon the subject is often subjective to it; it is noteworthy that the intelligence organisation of the USAF lends itself to this sort of distortion ... there probably [are] powerful 'vested interests' at work to ensure that the 'intelligence threat' against the USA is not reduced.[6]

Comparing the estimates for different types of Soviet capability in the first decade of the post-war period is revealing. There were certainly some successes: intelligence on the Soviet air force was particularly good, with accurate assessments produced on the increasingly long-range bombers throughout the 1950s. British estimates of Soviet missile capabilities were more conservative than American ones. This was a deliberate move, for as the JIC had warned in 1954, the UK should be 'wary' of US forecasts, particularly given their tendency to overemphasise the Soviet threat.[7] In fact, estimates of Soviet progress in both missile and atomic programmes were based on similar, underlying factors: good intelligence on developments was lacking and so a number of assumptions were employed (including the incorrect belief that the Russians were technologically inferior and would not discover any new ways to develop weapons); by contrast, when either weapon was actually tested, remarkably accurate intelligence could be obtained.

By 1957 the JIC correctly concluded that the atomic and missile programmes had been merged, to the extent that it was inconceivable that any future missile would not be nuclear armed.[8] More scarce was intelligence on Soviet development of chemical and biological weapons. It was assumed that both were being worked on, but little evidence was forthcoming. Conventional forces, by contrast, offered a far more mainstream target for the JIC: regular assessments were produced on the Soviet capability and capacity to wage war, including estimates of the scale, nature and effectiveness of the Soviet military. Underlying all these sorts of forecasts was yet another assumption: as one 1947 JIC paper stated, whilst 'the Soviet land forces ... are sufficiently strong ... to achieve rapid and far-reaching successes against any likely combination of opposing land forces', it was unlikely that the Soviet leadership would choose to initiate hostilities in this way.[9]

Taken together, although it was by no means straightforward, the elements of military capability were easier to identify. The JIC faced a tremendously difficult task: to achieve a balance in its understanding of the scale, location and capabilities of the Soviet war machine, including producing forecasts of the circumstances in which it might be used and how. In the absence of access to what the Soviet leadership was planning to do, intelligence gaps could only be filled by analytical judgements and assumptions. Despite the ups and downs of intelligence forecasts, throughout the immediate post-war period the view of the JIC was that, although the Soviet Union undoubtedly had the capability to attack the UK, at no point did it intend to do so.

```
   THIS DOCUMENT IS THE PROPERTY OF HIS BRITANNIC
                  MAJESTY'S GOVERNMENT
   The circulation of this paper has been strictly
                        limited.
     It is issued for the personal use of _____ .
 TOP SECRET                                   Copy No. 75
              J.I.C. (48) 104. (Final)
                  8th November, 1948.
               CHIEFS OF STAFF COMMITTEE.
             JOINT INTELLIGENCE COMMITTEE.
  SOVIET INTENTIONS AND CAPABILITIES 1949 AND 1956/57.
     Report by the Joint Intelligence Committee.
```

The U.K. Joint Intelligence Committee and the U.S. Joint Intelligence Committee have jointly prepared an agreed U.K./U.S. Intelligence estimate* on Soviet Intentions and Capabilities. Agreement between the two Intelligence Committees has been obtained on all but five points in the estimate, and only two of these, the Soviet campaign in Turkey and the Soviet submarine potential, are important. Where the differences occur, the views of both Joint Intelligence Committees have been included in the estimate. A list of the paragraphs in which these appear is at Appendix to this report.

2. The appreciation is in two parts. Part I[†] covers the period between now and the end of 1949. Part II deals with the period 1956/57. In discussing Part II, it became evident that the U.S. Intelligence Team were principally concerned with the period between now and the end of 1949 and not fully briefed to discuss the period 1956/57. Part II has, therefore, been produced in a more abbreviated form than Part I.

3. The main conclusions in this paper on the strategic intentions of the Soviet Union are in line with those in our paper[‡] "Strategic Intentions of the Soviet Union", which were not acceptable to the Chiefs of Staff. The Chiefs of Staff held that it would not be within the capacity of the Soviet Government to conduct so many simultaneous campaigns. Although in drafting this section of the paper the views of the Chiefs of Staff on this point were borne in mind throughout, we found ourselves unable to modify our previous views, and we also found that the American Intelligence Team was in agreement with them.

4. It may be that some of our differences are due to faulty presentation of our original paper. We then listed some eight campaigns which we considered likely to be carried out simultaneously. In point of fact there

---

* J.I.C. (48) 100 (Final)
† Note: The Appendix B, which is referred to in Part I, contains an expansion of some of the arguments and certain additional data dealing with the period between now and the end of 1949. This is not being tabled as a part of the agreed U.K./U.S. appreciation.
  This Appendix B was agreed on a working level at the request of the U.S. Intelligence Team for use mainly for detailed studies by U.S. intelligence and planning staffs.
‡ J.I.C. (48) 26 (0)

are only two major campaigns, Western Europe and the Middle East.

It is possible that the Soviet leaders might wish to carry out these two campaigns in succession. They would appreciate, however, that to attack one area first would enable the Anglo-American powers to attack the heart of the Soviet Union from the other. The inescapable conclusion is that in the event of war the Soviet Union would decide to attack both areas simultaneously.

This would also make the best use of the overwhelming superiority of the Soviet Union in land and tactical air forces in the early stages of the war, and would enable her to retain the initiative.

5. If this argument is accepted, the differences between the Joint Intelligence Committee and the Chiefs of Staff would be resolved. The other six simultaneous campaigns are subsidiary or supporting operations employing resources which our intelligence shows are available without interfering with the two main operations.

6. In dealing with our previous papers* "Strategic Intentions of the Soviet Union" and "Forecast of World Situation in 1957", the Chiefs of Staff based their disagreement on the four following arguments:-

(a) Sufficient heed had not been paid to Russian psychology;

(b) All experience went to show that the Soviet Union, unless she was invaded, would limit her strategic objectives;

(c) Russian possibilities were greatly over-estimated and it was doubtful whether 155 Divisions and 1,500 heavy bombers with 20,000 other aircraft in peace time were within the economic capabilities of the Soviet Union, having regard to the immense number of skilled uniformed technicians who would be required to support modern forces of this order;

(d) The Russian command would not be capable of handling several large campaigns at once.

7. Of these arguments, (b) has been considered in paragraphs 3 to 5 above. As regards (a), (c) and (d) our comments are as follows:-

(a) <u>Psychology.</u> We understand that the Chiefs of Staff

---

* J.I.C. (48) 26 (0)
  J.I.C. (47) 42 (0)

mean by this criticism that the Russian mind is likely to be reluctant to fight an offensive war on many fronts outside the territory of the Soviet Union because Russian history shows few examples of such a policy. Present Soviet-foreign policy shows that, at least as regards the "Cold War" the attitude of the Soviet Leaders is different. Furthermore, we believe that, if they become convinced that their aims can only be achieved more rapidly by war, they would provoke it and would hope, by forcing the Anglo-American powers to initiate operations, to persuade the Russian people that they were fighting a defensive war against Capitalist aggression.

(b) Size of the Soviet Air Forces and the Shortage of Skilled Technicians. The figure 20,000 other aircraft quoted in para 6(c) not only includes the 1,500 heavy bombers already mentioned, but also some 3,000 aircraft of the Civil Air Transport Fleet which, it was thought, might be made available for military duties. We have now agreed with the American Joint Intelligence Committee that the Soviet Air Force contains some 15,000 - 17,000 aircraft, of all types, in operational units and that the establishment of the Civil Air Transport Fleet is of the order of 1,000 - 1,500 medium and 2,000 light transport aircraft. Thus the Soviet Air Force has to provide maintenance backing for some 15,000 - 17,000 front-line aircraft of all types, and not 21,500 as suggested in para 6(c). Further, we believe that the Soviet Union has in its armed forces a relatively smaller number of skilled technicians than the Anglo-American powers. Although the Russians have fewer enlisted technicians than the Anglo-American powers and do not therefore carry out such major repairs within units, their standard of maintenance is adequate. A senior German tank officer has for example reported that in World War II Soviet tank maintenance was good, although bigger repairs were not carried out so fast as in the German Army. The Red Army had plenty of well-trained mechanics and the German Army increasingly employed Russian prisoners of war in their own tank maintenance companies. It is therefore dangerous to assume that lack of mechanical skill would be a source of weakness in their armed forces.

(c) Capabilities of the Russian Command. During World War II the Russian Command showed considerable ability in handling a number of different operations simultaneously along a front which stretched at one time from the Baltic to the Caucasus. They accomplished this by a system of decentralisation, by grouping armies and supporting air units in "fronts", and allotting special command teams for specific operations to co-ordinate the action of groups of "fronts". On the battlefield itself they developed considerable skill in manoeuvring large numbers of armoured formations. They were moreover skilful in moving formations from one area to another and in maintaining the impetus of the advance by ruthless energy in railway construction and operation right into the forward areas. After V.E. day they switched considerable resources to open up a new front in the Far East in accordance with a previously arranged time table. It would be dangerous to assume that the inefficiency resulting from party interference that has been observed in other branches of Soviet life, will also be present in the Army.

8. In reaching our agreed conclusions we have carefully examined the economic* and logistic† implications. We have concluded that, if the Soviet Union wished to go to war in 1949, economic considerations would not in themselves be enough to prevent her from doing so, if she felt confident of attaining her primary objectives rapidly. Since the biggest campaign, as planned, is not expected to last more than two months, and none more than six months, we consider that the needs of the Soviet forces for military equipment could be met largely from mobilisation reserves. The demands they would make on new production from Soviet industry would therefore not be great.

9. The forces allocated to the main campaigns in 1956/57 do not materially exceed those estimated for the same operations in 1949 except in the case of the attack on Western Europe. For this campaign it is considered that an additional 50 line divisions with supporting air regiments might be required‡. Since the total numbers engaged in all the campaigns would still be less than the present strength of the Soviet forces, it is considered that reserves of equipment for these additional 50 line

---

* J.I.C. (U.K) (48) 100 (0) Part I, Paras 25-30.
† J.I.C. (U.K) (48) 100 (0) Part I, Para. 109
‡ J.I.C. (U.K.) (48) 100 (0) Part II, para. 70.

divisions and supporting air regiments would continue to be available. Since the campaigns at the later date are not expected to last any longer than in 1949, the demands on new production would probably be even less than before owing to the additional reserves accumulated during the intervening period of low wastage. During the same period, moreover, a very great increase of production capacity should have taken place in accordance with the planned expansion of Soviet Industry.
10. The agreed view of the British and the U.S. Joint Intelligence Committees as to the intentions of the Soviet Union in a war starting between now and the end of 1949 may be summarised as follows:-
A campaign in Western Europe would be undertaken simultaneously with one designed to seize control of the Middle East (including Greece and Turkey and the Suez Canal area.)
11. It was agreed that these two major campaigns would be accompanied by:-
(a) An aerial bombardment against the British Isles.
(b) A sea and air offensive against Anglo-American sea communications.
(c) A campaign against China, and South Korea, and air and sea operations against Japan and U.S. bases in Alaska and the Pacific, in so far as the Soviet Union can support such operations without prejudice to those in other areas.
(d) Small scale one-way air attacks against the United States and Canada, and possibly small scale two-way air attacks against the Puget Sound area.
(e) Subversive activities and sabotage against Anglo-American interests in all parts of the world, and possibly also by a campaign against Scandinavia and air attacks on Pakistan.
12. It was also agreed that:-
(a) On the successful conclusion of the campaign in Western Europe (and possibly Scandinavia), a full scale sea and air offensive would be directed against the British Isles.
(b) The Soviet Union will have sufficient armed forces to undertake campaigns simultaneously in the theatres mentioned in paragraphs 10 and 11 above, and still have sufficient armed forces to form an adequate reserve.
13. It was also agreed that the Strategic Intentions of

the Soviet Union would be substantially the same in the event of war during the period 1956/57.

Recommendations
14. We recommend that the Chiefs of Staff approve this report as a background for further planning and intelligence studies.
15. We further recommend that the J.S.M. Washington should be instructed to seek the comments of the U.S. Joint Chiefs of Staff and to obtain their agreement to the following distribution of this report:-
(c) The Chiefs of Staff in Canada;
(ci) The Commanders-in-Chief, abroad.

(Signed) W.G. HAYTER
E.W.L. LONGLEY-COOK
C.D. PACKARD
L.F. PENDRED
K.W.D. STRONG
P. SILLITOE
D. BRUNT.
Ministry of Defence, S.W.1.
8th November, 1948

TOP SECRET APPENDIX TO
J.I.C. (48) 104
LIST OF PARAGRAPHS IN J.I.C. (48) 100
CONTAINING DIVERGENT VIEWS OF THE U.K. AND U.S. JOINT
INTELLIGENCE COMMITTEES

New Soviet Naval Units Expected to be Brought into Commission During 1949.
Part I, Appendix "A", paragraph 29 (e).
Size, Strength, Disposition and Development of Soviet Submarine Force.
Part I, Appendix "A", paragraphs 49, 118, 160 and 176.
Part II, paragraph 53.
Mobilisation Potential of Soviet Air Force.
Part I, Appendix "A", paragraph 54.
Soviet Radar Defences.
Part I, Appendix "A", paragraph 63.
Soviet Campaign in Turkey – Forces Required, Phasing and Timing.
Part I, Appendix "A", paragraphs 153 and 154.

* * *

To be circulated for the consideration of the Chiefs of Staff
J.I.C. (51) 6 (Final)
19th January, 1951.

CHIEFS OF STAFF COMMITTEE
JOINT INTELLIGENCE COMMITTEE
THE SOVIET THREAT
Report by the Joint Intelligence Committee

1. We state below the present military strength of the Soviet Union, the trend of current developments and conclude with our views on the need for rearmament.

MILITARY AND ECONOMIC STRENGTH OF THE SOVIET UNION
Soviet Army
2. The general distribution of Soviet Army formations is as follows:-

	Line Divs.	Tank Divs.	Arty. And A.A. Divs.	Total
E. Europe and W. Russia	34	13	16	63
Balkans and Black Sea	29	3	3	35
Central Russia	19	1	1	21
Caspian	29	-	6	35
North Russia	15	-	1	16
Siberia	6	-	-	6
Far East	26	3	10	39
Total divisions	158	20	37	215

Soviet Air Force
3.

	Fighter		Ground Attack	Bomber	Transport Recce & Others	Total
	Jet	Piston				
Tactical Air Force	1100	5100	2810	2680	1580	13,270
Naval Air Force		1400	130	910	500	2,940
Long Range Air Force		200		1220	180	1,600

Fighter Defence Force	600	1150				1,750
	1700	7850				
Total	9550		2940	4810	2260	19,560

Soviet Navy
4.

Army	Baltic & Arctic	Black Sea	Far East	Total
Old Battleships	1	2	-	3
Monitors	1	-	-	1
Cruisers	7	7	3	17
Destroyers	72	20	46	138
Submarines (Ocean)	100*	15	64	179*
Submarines (Coastal)	54	36	40	130
Midget Submarines and Coastal Craft	Large Numbers	Large Numbers	Large Numbers	Large Numbers

* This includes 25 obsolescent craft under long refits and ex-German submarines.

Atomic Weapons
5. A combined Anglo-U.S. atomic energy intelligence conference has just concluded that the most likely size of the Soviet atom bomb stockpile will be 50 in mid-1951. Production is continuing, and may be stepped up considerably in about two years' time.

Soviet Armament Production
6. Our estimate of current Soviet production of the principal armaments is as follows:-

	Monthly rate of production (units).
(a) Aircraft	
Jet fighters	400
Piston-engined fighters	20
Medium bombers	60
Long-range bombers	30

Transports	100
Trainers and others	240
Total Aircraft	850

Monthly rate of production (Units)
(b) Tanks   325 - 350
(c) Self-propelled guns   100 - 125
Annual rate of production (Units)
(d) Submarines (other than midgets) 50
(e) Fast coastal craft   100

Soviet Industry

7. The general level of basic industrial activity in the Soviet Union has since the war surpassed that of the United Kingdom (e.g. her steel production now exceeds the United Kingdom's by 70% and her electric power production by 55%) but is still greatly inferior to that of the U.S.A. That the Soviet Union has succeeded nevertheless in maintaining a rate of armament production greatly in excess of that of other countries, while proceeding simultaneously with the expansion of her industrial capacity, has been due to her readiness to sacrifice the standard of living of her people. For instance, only 9 per cent of her coal supplies and 13 per cent of her electric power supplies reach the domestic consumer compared with 25 per cent and 37 per cent in the United Kingdom. High as the current rates of Soviet armaments production are, and although they are increasing with the overall expansion of the economy, they could yet be raised to several times the present figures if the Soviet rulers decided to expand war production to the limits of the country's capacity.

8. The amount spent on defence in the Soviet Union in 1949 was 13.4 per cent of the estimated national income as compared with 7.7 per cent in this country, even though the Soviet Union's defence budget excludes a number of important defence items, among them research and development and strategic stockpiling.

PRESENT TRENDS

9. *Ground Forces*. Since September last the Soviet forces in Germany have been over peace establishment by 40,000 men. The demobilisation of the 1927 class which would bring the forces back to normal is now overdue. Since

October there has been a large increase in the strength of all of the East European Satellites, both in men and equipment. These facts coupled with recent signs of a redeployment of Soviet Occupation forces and an intensification of civil defence preparations, all indicate increased military preparedness.

10. <u>Air Forces</u>. While not increasing appreciably in total numbers the air forces are steadily increasing in efficiency, both technically and in training. The recent decision to standardise on a single type of jet fighter and the development of a ring of modern airfields in the West also increases military preparedness.

TOP SECRET

11. <u>Naval Forces</u>. The efficiency of the Soviet Navy is rising steadily and considerable effort is being devoted to the production of a high speed prototype ocean-going submarine, suitable for mass production on a scale of 150 submarines a year. Cruisers and destroyers are being built to the limit of capacity and 4 cruisers and 16 destroyers will be added to the fleet this year.

12. <u>Economic</u>. While continuing to expand its basic industries, the Soviet Union is now paying increased attention to developing the engineering and other manufacturing industries, and in particular to the electronics industry, to increasing industrial efficiency and to training skilled labour. These measures will all contribute to strengthening her economic war potential. Stockpiling, though not yet on a large scale, is diminishing the Soviet bloc's dependence on supplies of raw materials from non-Communist countries.

<u>THE CASE FOR REARMAMENT</u>

13. Except for the atomic bomb the Soviet Union has an immense superiority over the West in ground and air forces. It also has the largest submarine fleet in the world.

14. In the present state of the defences of the free world, there is a grave danger that, through aggression by proxy or subversion from within, the Soviet Union will gain control of the raw materials, especially tin and rubber, of South-East Asia: materials which not only earn dollars, but contribute to the independent defence effort of the United Kingdom. In the same way it might well secure the Middle East oil which is vital to the

economy of the United Kingdom in peace and without which the West could not sustain a prolonged war. In a global war the Soviet Union could very probably carry out at one and the same time campaigns which would win it not only these prizes but also the industrial heart of Western Europe.

15. The only way in which the West can be sure of preventing these developments is to provide itself, before it loses the benefit of the deterrent of the atomic bomb, with armed forces adequate to deter or defeat local aggression and to deter the Soviet Union from deliberately starting a global war.

16. Unless such a force is at the disposal of the Western Powers the Soviet Union holds the strategic initiative, and the West will remain powerless to stop continued encroachment by the Soviet Union over the territories of the free world, or, in the event of war, the over-running of Continental Europe. The survival of the United Kingdom would then be in jeopardy. At best we should be faced with a long war of recovery and reconquest backed only by the resources of the Western Hemisphere. In such circumstances we should be forced to comply with the wishes of the United States.

17. It is therefore imperative to deprive the Soviet Union of the power to use this initiative. We cannot tell when or even whether the Soviet Government will use it. But we do know that only the existing preponderance of the Soviet Army vis-a-vis the Western Powers made it possible for the Soviet Government to carry out its programme of expansion in Europe since the end of the war without direct resort to force. Either Soviet Communism or Russian Imperialism may be the main spring. In either case it is most unlikely that the expansionist programme is complete. The pronouncements of all Soviet Communist leaders proclaim their implacable hostility to all non-Communist Governments. Even today it is clear that the existence of Soviet forces on their present scale without any comparable force to set against them contributes to defeatism in France and in parts of Western Germany, and paves the way for further expansion.

18. The main purpose of Western rearmament is therefore to take the political initiative from the Soviet Union and to show that no easy conquests await it or its Satellites, either in isolated acts of military

aggression in the cold war, or in global war. There is no question of building a force designed for aggression. The Western defence effort must be sustained until it is made clear to the Soviet leaders that the strength of the West forbids any further advance and makes some sort of negotiation essential. In this we must negotiate from strength. We cannot estimate how soon this point will be reached. We must recognise that the Soviet leaders think and plan in terms of a very long struggle.

19. Meanwhile, however, we can expect the Soviet Government to make strenuous efforts to hamper Western rearmament. Their efforts are unlikely to be confined to abuse and denunciation of the West. As they see the West building up its strength they may well try to reinforce their own position by accelerating their expansionist programme. They are likely to look for further key economic and strategic points to seize. The success achieved in Korea will no doubt in any case tempt them to accelerate their programme; the massive intervention of China in Far Eastern affairs leaves the Soviet Government greater freedom to act earlier elsewhere.

20. Some further Soviet expansion may have to be accepted. Other moves must be opposed by the Western Powers if their position is not to be weakened beyond hope of repair. Unless we have the forces to oppose such moves whenever they occur, the Western world will continue to be beset by threats of military aggression in the cold war against a background of a grave threat of global war. These conditions must render abortive all Allied efforts in diplomacy and social and economic progress, and we may well have no alternative left (short of surrendering ourselves to Communism) but to make full atomic war on the Soviet Union itself. Atomic war is no longer likely to be one-sided. The prospect is so grim that we can no longer allow ourselves to rely on this means of defence alone. We must in fact provide ourselves with other arms as an insurance against being drawn irresistibly into another world war.

Recommendation

21. We recommend that the Chiefs of Staff approve this report and use it as an intelligence brief for discussions on increased defence expenditure.

(Signed)
D.P. REILLY.
E.W.L. LONGLEY-COOK.
A.C. SHORTT.
N.C. OGILVIE-FORBES.
K.W.D. STRONG.
B.K. BLOUNT.
Ministry of Defence, S.W.1.
19th January, 1951.

Notes

1. For more detail see Michael S. Goodman, *Spying on the Nuclear Bear: Anglo-American Intelligence and the Soviet Bomb* (Stanford, CA: Stanford University Press, 2007).
2. JIC/2124/49, 'Implications of Soviet Atomic Development', TNA: CAB 176/24.
3. 'Nuclear Sufficiency', note by Chief of the Air Staff, September 1958, TNA: AIR 8/1942.
4. Slessor to Vice-Chief of the Air Staff, 20 December 1949, TNA: AIR 75/92.
5. Ian Clark and Nicholas J. Wheeler. *The British Origins of Nuclear Strategy, 1945–1955* (Oxford: Clarendon Press, 1989), p. 137.
6. JIC/2150/52, 'Likelihood of War', 22 September 1952, TNA: CAB 176/38.
7. JIC(54) 104th Meeting, 18 November 1954, TNA: CAB 159/17.
8. JIC(57)41(Final)(Revise), 'Soviet Ground–Ground Guided Missiles Threat to the United Kingdom', 10 May 1957, TNA: CAB 158/26.
9. JIC(47)7/2 Final, 'Soviet Interests, Intentions and Capabilities – General', 6 August 1947, TNA: CAB 158/1.

10

COUNTERINSURGENCY

Since the Second World War the United Kingdom has been confronted by a continual stream of insurgencies. After 1945 colonial and Cold War concerns converged, since imperial real estate – and especially the bases that overseas territories provided – was seen as central to the process of containing the Soviet Union. Whilst the transfer of power in India in 1947 pointed the way unambiguously towards the future, Britain was in no hurry to leave and a constant stream of colonial crises pressed upon Whitehall's security concerns.[1] Meanwhile, as Britain's global power dwindled, a growing intellectual and cultural consensus emerged challenging traditional forms of imperialism. Nationalist unrest spanned the entire empire, from the Americas to Asia to Africa. In part, this explains why the hotter moments of the Cold War increasingly occurred in the Third World.[2]

This unrest exploded into a number of violent insurgencies. Zionist insurrection in the mandate of Palestine interrupted the celebrations at the end of the Second World War. Britain was ultimately forced to hand responsibility to the United Nations, which created the new state of Israel in 1948. In that same year, communist guerrillas launched an insurgency from the jungles of Malaya. Although Britain granted Malaya independence in 1957, the fighting continued for three more years. During the 1950s, British security forces were despatched to quell two more nationalist uprisings: Kenya (1952–6) and Cyprus (1955–9). Both colonies achieved independence. However, there was no let-up for British forces in the following decade. Prime Minister Harold Macmillan might have noticed the 'wind of change' blowing against imperialism, but Britain refused to relinquish the strategic colony of Aden without a fight. From 1963, security forces countered a brewing insurgency in the mountainous hinterland of southern Arabia and a vicious urban terrorism campaign inside Aden itself. Britain lost and was forced to evacuate in 1967, leaving behind the leftist state of South Yemen. By the early 1970s, when trouble was brewing in Northern Ireland and Oman, Whitehall had experienced a quarter of a century of almost unbroken counterinsurgency.[3]

The JIC was unprepared for insurgency and was therefore often taken by surprise. Since its origins, the committee had served the Chiefs of Staff. It therefore traditionally focused on narrow military issues relating to conventional security threats. Naturally, this revolved around watching the Soviet Union and the communist bloc. And yet the rampant spread of insurgency raised two major problems. Firstly, it tied down increasing numbers of British troops. Security forces engaged in colonial policing operations would have been unable to combat the Soviets had they marched across central Europe. Secondly, Whitehall increasingly saw the colonial territories as a front line in the Cold War. Not only were they hotbeds for communist subversion and intrigue during the uneasy peace, but the empire was perceived as an arc of vulnerability in a potential Third World War.

Insurgencies could no longer escape the JIC's attention. The Colonial Office reluctantly agreed to join the committee in October 1948. This was too late for the outbreak of violence in Malaya, and the JIC consistently misunderstood the insurgency as directly instigated by the Soviet Union. Meanwhile, the JIC began to expand its role to consider intelligence more broadly, as opposed merely to *defence* intelligence, and gradually evolved to challenge the military's narrow understanding of security and threats. Firstly, the committee slowly attempted to monitor and provide warning of colonial unrest. Secondly, it devoted more attention to assessing insurgencies and their implications for British strategic planning. Thirdly, it even sought (generally unsuccessfully) to oversee reforms to colonial intelligence structures.[4]

As Michael Herman has argued, immediately prior to Suez the JIC was firmly focused on traditional strategic issues. In the first six months of 1955, the JIC's weekly 'Survey of Intelligence' (later known as the Red Book) was focused on the Soviet Union and major Cold War confrontations such as the Taiwan Strait. There were some ninety items on the USSR and eastern Europe, fifty on China, fifty-seven on Indochina and eighty-two on the Middle East, focused mostly on Egypt. Few other subjects were mentioned. More than 75 per cent of the JIC's full papers in this period were on the Soviet Union.[5]

The government was aware of this lacuna in the British assessment system. In early 1955, a senior Cabinet committee asked General Gerald Templer to conduct a review into colonial security. Then Vice-Chief of the Imperial General Staff, Templer had recently returned from two years in Malaya where he had served as combined high commissioner and director of operations – earning himself the epithet 'Tiger of Malaya'. He valued intelligence highly and had wasted little time in revamping the Malayan Special Branch.

Templer sought the JIC's advice and commissioned an assessment on colonial intelligence and security. The JIC issued its report on 23 March 1955. The timing and context are important: the assessment came in the wake of failures to predict (and swiftly respond to) the insurgencies in Malaya and Kenya, whilst violence in Cyprus erupted just one week later. Things clearly needed to change.

The JIC made a number of recommendations to Templer, which are clearly stated in the document reproduced below. Overall, however, the JIC pushed for greater coordination between the colonies and London. The committee sought clearer channels of communication to ensure that intelligence reached consumers in Whitehall as swiftly as possible. It also recommended that the Colonial Office be better integrated with the central intelligence machinery as a whole. As things stood, the weekly intelligence reviews did not cover colonial territories, whilst colonial officials were not properly integrated into the intelligence-drafting process. As a result, the JIC was unable to adequately consider insurgencies. The uprisings in Malaya and Kenya went unpredicted, whilst policymakers received inaccurate intelligence about the nature and causes of the violence.

The JIC's assessment was highly influential in the policymaking sphere. Templer drew heavily on the committee's conclusions in his report to the Cabinet.[6] His survey was a bombshell and made impact at the highest levels of government. Indeed the Prime Minister, Anthony Eden, was warned by his private secretary, Philip de Zulueta, that the report was 'frightening'. Consequently, Eden requested that the Cabinet discuss the findings as urgently as possible.[7] Templer's report was so candid and critical that the government only released the full text in 2011 – a full fifty-six years after it was written.

Templer's influential report on colonial security was broader than the JIC's assessment. It spanned police training, issues of financing and potential trouble spots (although the latter drew heavily on another JIC paper). The JIC's assessment on colonial intelligence and security annexed here, however, strongly influenced Templer's discussion of intelligence organisation. Importantly, Templer's clout ensured that many of the JIC's initial recommendations would be met.

Broadly speaking, Templer used the JIC's conclusions as a foundation. Combining them with his experience in Malaya, he added his own irascible and straight-talking style to the report. For example, he built on the committee's musings about the difference between political and security intelligence. Arguing for interaction between the two, the JIC defined security intelligence as information required to protect a colony from subversion, sabotage and espionage. Political intelligence, by contrast, was all other information required for the effective governance of a colony. Building on this idea, Templer made a similar point – albeit more critically and in a far blunter style. Security intelligence, according to Templer, was neglected in the colonial context. It was 'regarded as a kind of spicy condiment added to the Secretariat hot-pot by a supernumerary and possibly superfluous cook, instead of being a carefully planned and expertly served dish of its own'.[8]

At the local level, Templer echoed JIC calls to strengthen local intelligence committees (LICs). Although all colonies had an LIC by 1955, their terms of reference differed greatly from territory to territory. The JIC hoped to issue greater guidance from London about the constitution and function of local committees. Templer agreed. Drawing on his own experiences in Malaya and on the JIC recommendations, he rated LICs as 'a very useful step in the right direction'.[9] He sought to raise the LICs' status, ensure access to the governor and improve coordination and output. Templer's (and the JIC's) recommendations were met. The Colonial Secretary sent fresh instructions to governors on the functioning of LICs in May 1956.[10]

At the Whitehall level, Templer developed JIC ideas about Colonial Office integration. Contrasting with the committee's polite calls for greater Colonial Office input into the intelligence machinery, Templer lamented the Colonial Office's lack of 'intelligence mindedness'. Moreover, he criticised it for being 'an information rather than an action addressee'. It is likely that JIC members were thinking the same thing but, unlike Templer, were unable to commit such strong terms to paper. Templer recommended reform. He pushed for (and achieved) the creation of an Intelligence and Security Department within the Colonial Office. This promoted a hitherto absent 'intelligence culture' and transformed the relationship between the Colonial Office and central intelligence, allowing the JIC to better consider insurgency.[11]

Directly building on the JIC's recommendations, Templer also strengthened links between the committee and the Colonial Office. He backed the JIC's request to reissue its charter under the authority of the Colonial Secretary (alongside the Foreign Secretary and Minister of Defence). Once more, this was successfully achieved. Templer also recommended greater Colonial Office involvement in the JIC's report-drafting process, exactly as the committee had requested. This, however, pushed the Colonial Office too far. Colonial officials vehemently opposed what they saw as JIC encroachment onto their jurisdiction. They argued that the committee misunderstood the complexities of colonial territories and overplayed the communist threat. Senior colonial officials even threatened a 'Whitehall showdown' in a long-running battle which lingered until after the JIC moved to the Cabinet Office in 1957.[12]

In other cases, Templer made criticisms where the JIC had not. The committee, for example, praised the role of MI5 (and the document below gives a useful overview of MI5's colonial role). Templer, however, sought to strengthen the system. He successfully pushed for deputies to aid the security intelligence adviser seconded to the Colonial Office from MI5, whilst unsuccessfully seeking to strengthen the role of MI5's security liaison officers posted in the colonies.[13]

Overall, Templer drew heavily on JIC conclusions in an influential review of colonial security. This led to important reforms which significantly aided the JIC's ability to consider insurgency. In turn, the committee's future assessments were then used by policy practitioners considering strategic planning. Insurgency had reached the intelligence agenda, and Whitehall was now better equipped to respond. Importantly, however, the JIC conclusions and Templer's report started an important debate between the committee and the Colonial Office. They caused a reappraisal of the nature of the Cold War threat and the type of intelligence required to counter it. The JIC could no longer rely purely on defence intelligence and on conceptualising security in narrow militaristic terms. The world was changing. This JIC report not only aided the committee's ability to assess insurgencies, but also formed part of the debate which ultimately preceded the JIC's transition to the Cabinet Office, where it could take a more holistic account of security. With the Colonial Office better integrated into the intelligence machinery, policymakers were offered more accurate appreciations of future insurgencies.

(THIS DOCUMENT IS THE PROPERTY OF HER BRITANNIC MAJESTY'S GOVERNMENT)

J.I.C. (55) 28   COPY NO. 5
23rd March, 1955.

CHIEFS OF STAFF COMMITTEE
JOINT INTELLIGENCE COMMITTEE
COLONIAL INTELLIGENCE AND SECURITY
Report by the Joint Intelligence Committee

At the request of General Templer we have examined certain points relating to Colonial Security and Intelligence. Our report is at Annex. Our conclusions are as follows.

CONCLUSIONS
2. Intelligence Reports from the Colonies
The value of the periodic reports now rendered would be greatly increased if all Colonial Governors added regularly their own appraisal or evaluation of facts contained in the report, including an indication of likely future developments (Part I, para. 2).
3. Local Intelligence Committees
The guidance given to Colonial Governors over a period of years regarding the composition and working of Local Intelligence committees should be reviewed and consideration should be given to consolidating and re-issuing it in a single document (Part I, Paragraph 5).
4. The Functions of the Security Service in Colonial Territories
The present arrangements seem to enable the Security Service to make their contribution without weakening the responsibility of local Administrations for their own Security (Part I, para. 12).
5. Methods of handling and destination of Intelligence reports from the Colonies
In addition to existing arrangements for the dissemination of intelligence reports received from the colonies

we consider that the JIC's "Weekly Review of Current Intelligence" should cover the Colonies. Arrangements should be made to enable the Colonial Office to take a full part in the drafting of the review by the Heads of Sections on Tuesday afternoons (Part I, paras. 15 and 17).

SECRET
U.K. EYES ONLY

6. <u>Colonial Office representation on the Joint Intelligence Staff</u>

Similar arrangements should be made to enable the Colonial Office to take a full part in the work of the Joint Intelligence Staff (Part I, para. 17).

7. <u>The J.I.C. Charter and Colonial Intelligence</u>

The J.I.C. Charter issued in 1948 by the Foreign Secretary and the Minister of Defence, needs no substantive amendment, but should, in order to regularise and facilitate close co-operation between the Colonial Office and J.I.C., be withdrawn and reissued jointly by the Foreign Secretary, the Minister of Defence and the Colonial Secretary (Part I, para. 26).

(Signed) P.H. DEAN
V. BOUCHER
W.H.L. McDONALD
J.A. SINCLAIR
D.G. WHITE
K.W.D. STRONG
C.Y. CARSTAIRS
C.E. KEYS (for D.N.I.)

Ministry of Defence, S.W.1.
23rd March, 1955.

ANNEX
COLONIAL SECURITY

PART I

<u>THE FORM WHICH INTELLIGENCE REPORTS FROM THE COLONIES SHOULD TAKE AND THE MATERIAL THEY SHOULD CONTAIN</u>

1. Security Intelligence Reports are for the most part prepared by the special branches of the various Colonial police forces. They are submitted to Colonial Governors

but are not normally forwarded to London. Governors, however, include relevant matter contained in local security intelligence reports in their monthly Intelligence Reports which are sent to the Colonial Office. For this reason it will be more useful to consider the requirement for intelligence reports generally, rather than the more restrictive requirements for security intelligence reports.

2. At the present time Colonial intelligence reports received in London are generally speaking factual documents; they do not usually attempt an evaluation of trends nor do they include any forecast of possible future developments. Their value would be greatly increased if all Colonial Governors added regularly a final section giving their own appraisal or evaluation of facts contained in the report, including an indication of likely future developments.

CONSIDERATIONS ABOUT THE CONSTITUTION OF LOCAL INTELLIGENCE COMMITTEES

3. Governors from time to time receive advice. Guidance from the Secretaries of State for the Colonies on the working of Local Intelligence Committees. These are also referred to in a Chiefs of Staff paper* "Procedure for Calling for Assistance from the Armed Forces to Support Foreign and Colonial Policy" The relevant section is as follows:-

"Local Intelligence Committees.

Local Intelligence Committees exist in certain Colonial territories and are organised partly for the purpose of co-ordinating all intelligence within a particular territory for the guidance of the Governor and the local Service Commanders, and partly to provide a properly constituted body with which the Joint Intelligence Committee can exchange views. These Committees when constituted are normally under the chairmanship of a senior officer of the Colonial Goverment and contain representatives of the Services and of any Departments of the Colonial Government (e.g. Police or Native Affairs) who by their knowledge and experience are in a special possition to assist the Committee. Local Intelligence Committees are not necessarily subordinate to Local Defence Committees

---

* C.O.S. (50) 289

but may be responsible directly to the Colonial Governor himself, whilst co-operating freely with the appropriate Joint Initelligence Committee."

4. The foregoing extract, which was circulated in 1950, did not take fully into account the constitutional responsibilities of either the Secretary of State for the Colonies or of Governors; consequently it has not been followed to the letter. Local Intelligence Committees now exist in all Colonies and are advisory, and responsible to the Governors whose Intelligence report to the Secretary of State they draft. There is, of course, every reason for them to be in close touch with the appropriate regional Joint Intelligence Committees (i.e. J.I.C. (F.E.) and J.I.C. (M.E.)) and this is the practice. There has been very little contact between the J.I.C. (London) and the Local Intelligence Committees nor indeed, in practice, has there been a requirement for this. Occasions may arise when, because an external threat to a Colony has developed or if a Colony is outside the area of responsibility of a regional J.I.C., direct contact will become desirable. It can then be arranged on an ad hoc basis.

5. Although Local Intelligence Committees exist in all Colonies and the appointments of the members of each committee are known, there is no standard constitution for these committees. The level at which the different committees are constituted varies from Colony to Colony. Experience indicates that if representation on such a committee is at too high a level its value as a working body tends to diminish. A standard constitution would clearly be impracticable, and it would probably be better in any case to avoid too rigid a set-up; but it is suggested that the guidance given over a period of years should be reviewed and if necessary collated and reissued to all Governors, laying down a broad pattern of the way in which Local Intelligence Committees should be constituted and given guidance on the functions they should perform. These should perhaps be defined broadly as the study and proper presentation of all relevant security and political intelligence at monthly (or more frequent) intervals; the preparation where appropriate of studies relevant to their work; the continuous consideration of the state of intelligence in the Colony, and the submission of proposals for measures to improve

it where appropriate; forecasts of likely future developments and perhaps also the preparation of periodic reviews of the general situation in the Colony from the intelligence point of view.

THE RELATIONSHIP BETWEEN POLITICAL INTELLIGENCE AND SECURITY INTELLIGENCE IN COLONIAL TERRITORIES. DEFINITIONS OF POLITICAL INTELLIGENCE AND SECURITY INTELLIGENCE

6. As indicated above political intelligence and security intelligence in Colonial Territories must both overlap and interact. It is, therefore, difficult clearly to define them. As a rough and ready guide, however, it might be said that security intelligence is any information which may be needed to protect a Colony from subversion, sabotage and espionage; political intelligence is any other information required for the effective government of a Colony. Security intelligence includes all aspects of Communist activity and extremist "nationalist" activities. The Special Branch should collect and collate all information affecting the security of a colony and present it in collated form to the Local Intelligence committee where it can be related to political intelligence and the significance of both assessed before submission to the Governor.

THE FUNCTIONS OF THE SECURITY SERVICE IN COLONIAL TERRITORIES

7. The Director General of the Security Service is charged in his charter "in consultation with the Colonial Office (to) assist and advise Colonial administrations......"

8. Assistance and advice is given both in London and in the Colonial territories. In London advice is given to the Colonial Office at all levels on security policy for the Colonies and methods of implementing it. In addition, British and international communist policy towards the Colonies is studied centrally, and case work within the U.K. is conducted on behalf of the Colonies.

9. The Security Service has seconded to the Colonial Office a Security Intelligence Adviser (S.I.A.) who advises the Secretary of State and Colonial Governors on the organisation of the Special Branch and related intelligence matters. His work has been supported in a number of ways and particularly by training officers,

who have already visited many Colonial areas to give training courses to members of Special Branches within their own Colonies. In addition, training courses to Colonial Special Branch Officers of the higher ranks are given periodically by the Security Service in London.

10. Security Service representation within Colonial areas is not always in the same form. In Gibraltar and Malta there are Defence Security Officers (D.S.Os). In most other Colonies the Security Service representative is called the Security Liaison Officer (S.L.O). In some instances the Security Service representative has been placed within the Special Branch either as an adviser to the Head of the Special Branch, or as a research officer within the Special Branch.

11. The Security Service representative in a Colony has the duty to inform the Governor, Service Commanders, the Commissioner of Police, and other appropriate local officials on matters affecting security. He is the normal channel for security business between the Special Branch and the Security Service Headquarters in London and other security organisations within the Commonwealth; and, through London, with the rest of the free world. He is so placed that he can give advice to the Special Branch, based on his own experience and backed by the authority and experience of the Security Service, and can bring matters to the attention of the Colonial Administration when he thinks it necessary. He can on occasion support this by getting the Security Service to intervene with the Colonial Office in London.

12. It is believed that the present arrangements enable the Security Service to make their contribution without weakening the responsibility of local Administrations for their own security.

METHODS OF HANDLING AND DESTINATION OF INTELLIGENCE REPORTS FROM THE COLONIES

13. As mentioned in paragraph 1 above, Special Branch reports as such are not generally received in London. Bearing in mind the difficulties of separating security from political intelligence, the present form in which security intelligence is collected, collated and disseminated in the Colonies, serves, in general, the purpose for which it is designed. The problem lies rather in ensuring that matters of security intelligence interest

of moment are included in Governors' regular monthly intelligence Reports. These normally reach London from all Colonies on or about the 20th of the following month and total collectively some 6-800 pages.

14. The Joint Intelligence Committee is kept informed of intelligence affecting colonial security in the following ways:-

   (a) The Colonial Office compiles from reports received from Governors a monthly "Colonial Office Political Intelligence Summary". These summaries are circulated to interested Departments on or about the twelfth of each month, and comprise some twenty pages of factual information, mainly on events that have occurred in each Colony during the last month but one, but also include more up to date information based on telegraphic reports.

   (b) In addition, the Colonial Office compiles specially for the J.I.C. a much shorter selection from the above summary, called the "Colonial Office Review of Current Intelligence". This, also, is brought up to date by the inclusion of additional items that have been reported since the Political Summary was compiled. It is circulated to the J.I.C. on or about the 24th of each month.

   (c) Copies of Colonial Office Prints are circulated when issued.

   (d) When disturbances are feared or take place in a Colony the Colonial Office circulate to Defence and other Departments copies of telegrams from Governors.

   (e) In present circumstances regular reports on the situation from the Governors of Hong Kong and Kenya and the High Commissioner for the Federation of Malaya are circulated automatically to Directors of Intelligence.

   (f) The War Office circulates a number of Military situation reports received from Cs.-in-C. in Colonies where active operations are in progress, e.g. Kenya.

   (g) From time to time the Colonial Office representative on the Joint Intelligence Committee produces at a J.I.C. Meeting under "Unforeseen Items" an item of "hot" current intelligence from a Colonial territory.

15. The Joint Intelligence Committee approves each Thursday morning a "Weekly Review of Current Intelligence" which (or a summary of which) is submitted for the information of Ministers and Chiefs of Staff. At present this does not cover the Colonies except incidentally (e.g. British Somaliland in references to the Haud). The "hot" reports from the Colonial Office representative (paragraph 14 (g) above) are not normally incorporated in the "Weekly Review of Current Intelligence" or its summary. Colonial Intelligence Reports through Joint Intelligence Committee channels are limited to the "Colonial Office Review of Current Intelligence" (paragraph 14 (b) above). It would seem desirable that the "Weekly Review of Current Intelligence" should cover important events and trends in the Colonies also and that arrangements should be made to enable the Colonial Office to take part in the drafting of the review by the Heads of Sections on Tuesday afternoons. It is understood that this would require regular telegraphic reports from named Colonies (such as those mentioned in paragraph 14 (g) above), and, in addition, telegraphic reports from any Colony where the situation demanded.

THE FUNCTIONS AND RELATION OF INTELLIGENCE STAFF IN THE COLONIAL OFFICE IN SO FAR AS THIS AFFECTS THE J.I.C. INCLUDING QUESTIONS OF COLONIAL OFFICE REPRESENTATIONS ON THE J.I.S.

16. The Colonial Office is represented on the Joint Intelligence Committee by the Under Secretary supervising its Defence Department. The same Department furnishes representation on the Joint Intelligence Staff when and as necessary calling in if required specialist advisors from the Geographical Department concerned.

17. The arrangements for representation on the Joint Intelligence Staff are satisfactory, subject to the condition in the last sentence of this paragraph. If the suggestions in paragraph 15 above are accepted and in order to make possible the rapid collation and presentation of intelligence from the Colonies in the Weekly Review and Summary, it will be neccessary for a Colonial Office representative to attend the weekly Heads of Sections meetings at the J.I.C. Both he and the Colonial Office representatives attending meetings of the Joint Intelligence Staff should be

able to discuss, and modify where appropriate, their contributions.

THE J.I.C. CHARTER AND COLONIAL INTELLIGENCE
History of Charter
18. The present Charter of the J.I.C. was issued early in 1948 (D.O. (48) 21). It reads as follows:-
"The Joint Intelligence Committee is given the following responsibilities:-
>   (i) Under the Chiefs of Staff to plan, and to give higher direction to, operations of defence intelligence and security, to keep them under review in all fields and to report progress.
>   (ii) To assemble and appreciate available intelligence for presentation as required to the Chiefs of staff and to initiate other reports as the Committee may deem necessary.
>   (iii) To keep under review the organisation of intelligence as a whole and in particular the relations of its component parts so as to ensure efficiency, economy and a rapid adaptation to changing requirements, and to advise the Chiefs of Staff on what changes are deemed necessary.
>   (iv) To co-ordinate the general policy of Joint Intelligence Committees under United Kingdom Commands over-seas and to maintain an exchange of intelligence with them, and to maintain liaison with appropriate Commonweallth intelligence agencies."

19. In none of the discussions connected with the charter was there any mention of Colonial Territories or the Colonial Office, which was not at that time represented on the J.I.C. The Charter was issued under the authority of the then Foreign Secretary and Minister of Defence who circulated it for the information of the Defence Committee.

Colonial Office Representation
20. In the autumn of 1948, largely at the instance of the then Foreign Secretary, the Prime Minister agreed to ask the Colonial Office to appoint a permanent representative on the J.I.C. Mr. Bevin's minute to the Prime Minister read as follows:
>   "As you know it is my belief that our Colonial territories are likely to be one of the principal objectives

of Communist attack in the near future. With this in mind it seems to me very important that we should do everything possible to ensure that we have the best possible intelligence about Comnunist activity in the Colonies, so that we may not be taken unawares.

As a first step towards this I suggest that the Colonial Office might consider appointing a permanent member of the J.I.C., so that the Colonial Office would remain in constant touch with the intelligence picture as a whole and with the development of communism throughout the world, in so far as it is known to our intelligence organisation. I am sure that such an appointment would be of great value not only to the Colonial Office but to the other departments represented on the J.I.C."

21. On September 23, 1948, General Hollis, Principal Staff Officer to the Minister of Defence, supported the Foreign Secretary's proposal in a minute to the Prime Minister as follows:

"My views on the Foreign Secretary's proposal that the Colonial Office should have a permanent member on the J.I.C. are as follows.

The object of this proposal is to ensure that we have the best possible intelligence about Communist activity in the Colonies so that we may not be taken unawares. The best way to achieve this is to strengthen and tune up our Colonial Police Forces. We must have good Intelligence services on the spot so that communist activities can be apprehended right from the start, and not after they have secured a firm foothold. Recent events on the Gold Coast and in Malaya demonstrate this need."

22. The Colonial Office accepted this invitation and after the Chiefs of Staff had given their approval a representative of the Colonial Office took his seat at the J.I.C. on October 8, 1948.

23. Since that date the Colonial Office have been represented at meetings of Directors and Deputy Directors but have had no regular representations of the J.I.C. or at Heads of Sections meetings.

Scope of charter

24. From the outset it has been assumed that the charter of the J.I.C. is wide enough to authorise them to deal

with operation of defence intelligence and security in colonial territories. This view seems correct and the reference in paragraph (iv) of the Charter to "appropriate Commonwealth intelligence agencies" is clearly to the intelligence agencies in the self-governing territories of the Commonwealth. No change therefore in the present terms of reference of the J.I.C. appears necessary from this point of view.

25. At the time that the Colonial Office joined the JIC no changes were made in the Charter or in the issuing authorities, who remained the Foreign Secretary and Minister of Defence only.

Conclusions

26. In these circumstances it is suggested that it would materially assist the Colonial Office to play a full part in the work of the J.I.C. and to give effect to the objects for which a representative of the Colonial Office was invited to join the J.I.C., if the present Charter of the J.I.C. were withdrawn and reissued under the authority of the Foreign Secretary, the Minister of Defence and the Colonial Secretary.

27. The advantages of this would be as follows:-

(a) to place the Colonial Secretary in the same position as the other two Ministers as regards calling on the J.I.C. to prepare intelligence estimates etc. within its terms of reference;

(b) to record formally that the J.I.C. has a responsibility under its charter for intelligence and security in the colonial territories;

(c) to enable the J.I.C. more easily to ask for information, advice and assistance from the Colonial Office in the same way as it at present does from the Foreign Office, the Ministry of Defence and the Service Departments;

(d) to encourage and facilitate closer association and exchanges in the fields covered by the terms of references between the Colonial Office and the colonial territories on the one hand and the other departments represented on the J.I.C. on the other;

(e) to enable the J.I.C. to present to the Chiefs of Staff and to Ministers proper intelligence appreciations on the colonial territories, both individually and within the general framework of the threats posed to them by Russian and Chinese imperialism, Communism, nationalism, racialism etc., and to perform as regards those territories the functions with which it is charged at present in respect of intelligence and security in other territories.

Notes

1. John Kent, *British Imperial Strategy and the Origins of the Cold War, 1944-49* (Leicester: Leicester University Press, 1993), pp. 9-33.
2. Odd Arne Westad, *The Global Cold War: Third World Interventions and the Making of Our Times* (Cambridge: Cambridge University Press, 2005).
3. David French, *The British Way in Counter-insurgency, 1945-1967* (Oxford: Oxford University Press, 2011), pp. 13-24.
4. Rory Cormac, *Confronting the Colonies: British Intelligence and Counterinsurgency* (London: Hurst, 2013), pp. 195-221.
5. Michael Herman, *Intelligence Services in the Information Age: Theory and Practice* (London: Frank Cass, 2001), pp. 113-15.
6. Gerald Templer, 'Report on Colonial Security', 23 April 1955. CAB 21/2925.
7. Note from de Zulueta to Eden, 13 May 1955, PREM 11/2247; note from Eden to Lord Chancellor, 5 June 1955, PREM 11/2247; Rory Cormac, 'Organizing Intelligence: An Introduction to the 1955 Report on Colonial Security', *Intelligence and National Security* 25/6 (2010), p. 803.
8. Templer, 'Report on Colonial Security', p. 14.
9. Ibid., p. 16.
10. Cormac, 'Organizing Intelligence', p. 808.
11. Templer, 'Report on Colonial Security', pp. 15, 18-19.
12. Cormac, *Confronting the Colonies*, p. 72.
13. Cormac, 'Organizing Intelligence', pp. 805-6.

11

THE SUEZ CRISIS

Whilst Europe might have been the primary Cold War battleground in the decade following the end of the Second World War, it was by no means the only one. Indeed, the success of the communists in the Chinese Civil War and the subsequent Korean War had embedded the Cold War in Asia. In the Middle East, with Britain's responsibilities reducing, there arose an increasing amount of hostility to the remnants of her colonial past. In every other theatre the hand of Moscow was perceived to be present, even if its scale and level of involvement varied. In the Middle East, by contrast, the JIC immediately equated nationalist uprisings with communist-inspired insurrections: it was simply unthinkable to have one without the other.

Trouble in Egypt, and in particular the Suez Canal Zone, began several years before it reached boiling point in 1956. The canal itself was an important trading route which reduced shipping times, cut costs and shortened voyages. A 1936 Anglo-Egyptian treaty had solidified matters, with the British promising, amongst other things, to supply the Egyptians with arms and training. The reasoning was not just economic: Egypt was perceived to be central to British defence planning in the Middle East. The status quo was thrown into chaos by several changes starting with the 1951 Egyptian renouncement of the treaty, introducing fears that communism was on the rise.

Despite concern in some parts of Whitehall, the JIC's initial assessments discounted the spread of communism. From 1951 the JIC regularly monitored events in Egypt. Indeed, there were a number of significant developments to understand, including the successful coup by military officers and the various governments that ensued. One of those closely involved was Colonel Gamal Nasser, who, initially at least, was welcomed in London as someone the British could deal with. Accordingly, preparations began for a new mutual defence agreement. Relations certainly seemed to be improving but, from 1955, they faltered and then completely disintegrated as both nations slipped towards war.

The abrogation of the 1936 treaty meant that the UK no longer provided arms to Egypt. As a result, the JIC was charged with monitoring Egyptian efforts to obtain arms.[1] At its meeting on 29 September 1955 the JIC discussed a startling new piece of intelligence: the report that an arms deal had been struck between Egypt and Czechoslovakia.[2] The instant reaction was that this was not simply a deal between two nations but a sign that Nasser, by now President, had welcomed the Russians into the region. Such sentiments were heightened by evidence in late 1955 to suggest that the Russians were offering to bankroll the construction of the Aswan Dam project. A key task for the JIC was to consider how far Nasser had been captured by these deals. Its assessments were remarkably measured, although it noted that eventually the Egyptians would reach the point of 'no return'.[3]

From the first weeks of 1956 plans began to be formalised in various parts of the government, designed to remove Nasser from power. The rationale was twofold: not only was he increasingly seen in some political quarters as irrevocably lost to the Soviet cause, but he was also affecting Britain's commercial interests through his control of the Suez Canal. The JIC took a sober and levelheaded view. The appended assessment from August 1956 provides evidence of the role that the JIC often played in unfolding events. Whilst the title of the report might seem narrow, its contents were anything but. The relatively brief assessment (for that period) offered a broad survey of the situation.[4]

The assessment was produced in the aftermath of Nasser's decision to nationalise the Suez Canal. According to the JIC, Nasser had two primary motives: to divert domestic attention (a move seen as a 'triumph') and to provide a means of striking back against the West. The assessment then considered Nasser's character (an emotional demagogue) and attempted to gauge the effect of the nationalisation on regional states. Next it moved into the prophetical by discussing 'possible future developments'. The JIC emphasised that the actions of the West would have a direct bearing on Soviet decision making but argued that there was still some independence in Egypt's position. Perhaps more importantly, certainly for what would transpire next, the report looked at different regions and examined the potential effect of either a protracted conflict or war with Egypt. It concluded:

> Although most, if not all, the Arab States would sympathise with Egypt [in the event of military conflict] we do not think that in the event they would come to her aid ... We also doubt whether the Soviet Union would take any action ... we do not believe she [the Soviet Union] would embark on global war on behalf of Egypt.

Apart from COS approval of the paper, there is no other evidence to suggest how it was greeted. Increasingly from August 1956 the JIC's products were received and used in different ways. Its tactical assessments were important and appreciated by the military, but its strategic assessments were marginalised and ignored by policymakers.[5] Between late September and mid-October papers were issued on: Nasser's possible future courses of action if the Suez dispute was settled on terms favourable to Egypt; the

Israeli attitude towards Arab states; and a larger study on the threats to UK interests worldwide.[6]

Whilst its Chairman, Patrick Dean, was involved in the signing of the Sèvres Protocol and other intimate details of the military plans concerning the Suez Canal, the JIC itself continued to meet, oblivious to the collusion being formed with Israel and France. In fact the JIC had more pressing matters to deal with: in mid-October events in Hungary took precedence over Suez. That changed on Monday, 29 October, when Israel attacked Egypt. The JIC was immediately called into action: it began the production of five daily outputs, it maintained an around-the-clock presence, and its military members met daily. Within a week military operations were halted, amidst widespread international condemnation. The JIC, marginalised and unheard, had nonetheless produced useful assessments. Its tactical reports were of huge value to the military and had its strategic assessments been read and digested, the folly of Suez might have been averted. Meanwhile, for the JIC, its unhappy marginalisation during Suez contributed to the decision to remove it from the machinery of the Chiefs of Staff and locate it more centrally within the Cabinet Office.[7]

```
CIRCULATED FOR THE CONSIDERATION OF THE CHIEFS OF STAFF

            J.I.C. (56) 80 (Final) (Revise)
                   3rd August, 1956
                CHIEFS OF STAFF COMMITTEE
                JOINT INTELLIGENCE COMMITTEE

    EGYPTIAN NATIONALISATION OF THE SUEZ CANAL COMPANY
         Report by the Joint Intelligence Committee

INTRODUCTION
Egyptian motives. The Egyptian nationalisation of the
Canal Company followed promptly upon the withdrawal of
the United Kingdom, United States and World Bank offers
to help finance the Aswan High Dam. Nasser's declared
motive was to obtain from the operation of the Canal
the funds he needed to build the Dam. We doubt however
whether this is the real reason for his action. There
have been a number of indications that he himself has
recently had doubts whether the High Dam is the best way
of solving his power and irrigation problems, and he must
have realised that the net annual profit likely to be
derived from the Canal is only a fraction of the Dam's
cost. The building of the Dam had, however, come to be
seen in the popular mind as the cure for all Egypt's ills
```

and Nasser's own position and prestige were staked upon its accomplishment. When the Western offer of financial aid was withdrawn, therefore, he urgently needed to distract public attention and at the same time find a new method to arouse their enthusiasm and to repair any damage which his stock might have suffered in other Arab countries. As a means to this end his nationalisation of the Canal has been a triumph; it has also served the subsidiary purpose of retaliation against the West for the withdrawal of the High Dam offer.

2. <u>The character of Colonel Nasser</u>. There is a considerable element of emotion in Nasser's actions. As a demagogue he is liable to be carried away by the violence of the passions he himself has whipped up. As a dictator, his actions over the past three years show subtlety and calculation and have so far all resulted in gain to Egypt. We should be prepared for any action that may enhance his prestige and maintain him in power.

3. <u>Effect on other Middle East States</u>. A clear distinction must be made between reactions of governments friendly to the U.K. and press and mob reactions. The Bagdad Pact powers and Nuri Pasha in particular would be delighted to see Nasser brought down but the press, even in Iraq (apart from the one government controlled paper), has welcomed Nasser's action. While President Chamoun would like to see strong action against Nasser the Lebanese in general support Nasser's move. Among the mob Nasser's action has won acclaim not only in Egypt but throughout the Middle East. King Hussein sent a congratulatory message (though he has tried to explain this away to our Ambassador); thanksgiving sermons are reported to have been preached in the mosques of Damascus; in the Sudan the step was welcomed by newspapers of all shades of opinion. King Saud has conveyed his unqualified support for Egyptian action to Nasser through the Saudi Ambassador in Cairo but this has received no publicity as yet in Saudi Arabia. Saud could hardly have done less. The B.B.C. correspondent in Karachi has similarly reported that the man in the street unanimously supported Egypt's action. Such is the hold built up by the Egyptian propaganda machine that the instinctive reaction of the Arab mind is that the seizure of the Suez Canal is an extension of the national liberation movement, a theme which has also been played up in the Soviet press.

4. <u>Egyptian counter-action to Western measures</u>. Egypt reacted quickly to the West's announcement of financial counter measures. She has said that she will contest at the International Court the freezing in the United Kingdom and France of the Company's assets. She has issued a statement alleging that the decision to submit to exchange control Egyptian current accounts in sterling, and financial transactions through the medium of sterling, contravenes the provisions of the United Kingdom-Egypt Monetary Agreement. She has now taken retaliatory exchange measures against U.K. and French accounts. So far no attempt has been made to refuse transit to ships if they have paid dues in cheques drawn upon British or French banks and on July 30 the Minister of Finance announced that this system would be allowed to continue. It appears that Egypt is now adopting a passive attitude of injured innocence towards Western economic measures in order to put the West in the wrong and she is anxious to prove that she can run the Canal without infringement of the Convention of 1688. All her present actions suggest that she wishes to ensure that if there is a breakdown, responsibility can be put on the West.

POSSIBLE FUTURE DEVELOPMENTS

5. <u>Prospects over the next few months</u>. Nasser's triumph has been spectacular, and such is his control of public emotion and opinion that he need not show any tangible return for his action, at any rate for the moment. There seems a reasonable prospect that, provided present staff stay at their posts, the canal's operation can be continued. Only about one third of the canal company's revenue, however, derives from money paid in cash in Egypt or in cheques negotiable in Egyptian banks. The remainder is paid to London or Paris. To finance the canal's operations, let alone make any profit from it, some attempts must be made to obtain the two thirds of its current income that are at present unavailable to Egypt. The Egyptian Government may therefore be forced to insist upon payments that will be available to themselves. They may also announce increased charges for transit. If this is done and if the shipping companies give way, Nasser will be able to proclaim a further triumph of the revolution. If they refuse he will be faced with the choice of letting defaulting vessels through or detaining them.

5. <u>Relations with the Soviet bloc</u>. Meanwhile it may gradually become apparent to the Egyptian public that nationalisation cannot provide the funds that are required for the Dam. If the shipping nations were to devise means to avoid using the canal the revenues would be greatly diminished. In these circumstances much would depend upon the actions the Soviet Union might take to supplement Egypt's sources of income. Nasser's regime has served the Soviet Government's interests well but, until the reactions of the Western Powers become clearer, the Soviet Government may well have some misgivings about his latest action. Their present interest is that Egypt's relations with the West should be as bad as possible without Egypt becoming so completely dependent on the Soviet Union that the concept of neutrality is discredited. The Soviet Government can be expected to pose as Egypt's and the Arabs' best friend and to continue to give Egypt economic aid of all sorts, but they probably do not wish to risk a direct clash with the West in support of Colonel Nasser's ambitions, and they may not wish to take on the whole burden of supporting Egypt financially and economically if Western countermeasures threaten the Egyptian economy with stagnation. Khrushchev has already spoken of the need of a peaceful settlement. The most satisfactory outcome from the Soviet point of view might be some sort of international discussions, preferably in the U.N., leading to an indecisive face-saving solution which would satisfy neither the West nor Egypt. The Soviet Government would then have Colonel Nasser very much at its mercy and would be able to continue penetration of Egypt systematically and at leisure. Nasser is due to visit Moscow in August. The Soviet Government will no doubt take advantage of his weak position but they may hesitate at this stage to make take-over bids.

6. <u>Other possibilities short of intervention by the West</u>. If the economic struggle continues along the lines outlined above, particularly if the financial powers taken by the U.K. and French Governments are applied stringently (or if next January the next instalment of the sterling balances is withheld), there are a number of other actions the Egyptian Government might take. She might:-

(a) Break off diplomatic relations with the British and the French Governments.
(b) Abrogate the Base Agreement of 1954.
(c) Withdraw air transit facilities.
(d) Nationalise all British and French undertakings in Egypt.
(e) Cancel the residence permits of all British and French subjects in Egypt.
(f) Persuade other Arab states to take anti-Western measures including the denial of military facilities.
(g) Incite feeling against British and French nationals in Egypt so as to make their position precarious.

We do not rule any of them out; but we think that it would need further Western "provocation" before Egypt would resort to them, since she evidently wishes to demonstrate her ability to take over the Canal peacefully.

8. Effects in other Arab states. If only financial action is taken by the West, other Arab states might feel able to take steps to weaken their ties with or dependence on Great Britain, France and the United States. These steps might include:
(a) Jordan may call for drastic revision of the Anglo-Jordan Treaty.
(b) Libya may denounce the Anglo-Libyan Treaty.
(c) The Tunisian and Moroccan Governments may adopt an even more intransigent attitude towards France.
(d) Syria and the Lebanon may stop or delay deliveries of oil from the Mediterranean terminals.
(e) Members of the Arab League may refuse transit, landing and refuelling facilities for British military aircraft.
(f) Saudi Arabia may step up demands for a greater share of the profits from oil.

In addition, other effects might be:-
(g) Our position may be weakened in Aden, Bahrein, Buraimi, Kuwait and Qatar.
(h) Sabotage of oil installations might occur in any of the Arab states.
(j) The effectiveness and cohesion of the Baghdad Pact might be undermined.
(k) Nuri might feel we had not gone far enough towards bringing Nasser down and his own position in Iraq would become doubtful.

(1) The position of the Oil Consortium in Iran would be greatly weakened.

WESTERN ACTION

9. Threat of armed intervention. We do not believe that threats of armed intervention or preliminary build up of forces would bring about the downfall of the Nasser regime or cause it to cancel the nationalisation of the canal. Anti-Nasser influences might be encouraged, but we believe the general effect would be to increase support for the Government and Nasser might proceed to take some or all of the measures listed in paragraph 7, if he had not already taken them. He could count on continued support from other Arab countries.

10. <u>Blockade</u>. If imports, particularly of oil, could be prevented from entering Egypt it would have severe effects on the Egyptian economy. A total stoppage of imports could only be effected by a blockade, in the exercise of a belligerent right. The international problems likely to follow, e.g. how to deal with Soviet Bloc vessels, are so complex that they should form the subject of a separate study.

11. <u>Armed intervention</u>. Armed intervention by the West to secure control of the Canal Zone would lead to a state of war with Egypt. Although most, if not all, the Arab States would sympathise with Egypt we do not think that in the event they would come to her aid. Iraq would certainly not help Egypt and might even be prevailed upon to stop Syria or Jordan doing anything in this direction. We also doubt whether the Soviet Union would take any action. She has no treaty of alliance with Egypt and as far as we know, no secret agreement. The support of Egypt in peacetime as a thorn in the side of the West accords with the policy of competitive co-existence, but we do not believe she would embark on global war on behalf of Egypt. The Soviet Government might send technicians and further arms to Egypt but we doubt whether, in the event of hostilities, these would greatly affect the issue. Language difficulties would hinder the operational effectiveness of the former; we have appreciated elsewhere that Egypt is unlikely to be proficient in her existing bloc armaments before the end of 1956. Although the morale of the Egyptian armed forces is at present likely to be high (see Appendix) we consider that the

temperament of the Egyptian people is such that were they themselves subject to immediate physical danger, their morale would probably collapse and the downfall of Nasser might result.

12. Effects of Western action on other Arab States.

(a) If steps taken by the West were to lead to an early change of Government in Egypt and a settlement satisfactory to the West, the other Arab States who have a natural admiration for strength, would probably swing in our favour and would in any case probably feel insufficiently strong to abrogate their respective treaties and agreements. Iraq would expect to reap the benefits of her pro-Western attitude and to be set up in Egypt's place as the leader of the Arab World.

(b) Should Western military action be insufficient to ensure early and decisive victory, the international consequences both in the Arab States and elsewhere might give rise to extreme embarrassment and cannot be forecast.

EFFECT ON THE ARAB/ISRAELI DISPUTE

13. Egypt. As stated above we believe that Egypt is likely to tread warily and to avoid giving the West cause to intervene against her. She would only make her position more difficult in the immediate future by aggression against Israel. If the dispute dragged on without positive action by the West the Egyptian public might come to realise the meagre benefits of nationalisation: should the Soviet Union decline to offer the economic aid that Egypt will need, Nasser might seek to divert attention by raising tension on the frontier with Israel and perhaps by further Fedayeen raids.

14. Israel. Whatever steps the West take there will be a strong incentive to Israel to take military action against Egypt, in the belief that the West will now no longer wish to prevent a blow at Nasser. While there is doubt about the West's intentions to use force however it is probable that Israel will act with caution and await developments. In the event of Western military action Israel might well take action also on her own account, unless considerable pressure particularly by the United States were brought to bear on her to stay out of the dispute.

15. Other Arab States. Were Israel to attack Egypt while the West were merely applying some form of sanctions the

other Arab States would probably be forced by public opinion to go to Egypt's aid. If Israel attacked when Western forces were engaged with the Egyptians action by the other Arabs would depend on whom she attacked. If Israel attacked only Egypt the other Arab States would probably not join in, but great resentment would undoubtedly be created by what would be interpreted as a plot between Israel and the West.

RECOMMENDATION
16. We recommend that the Chiefs of Staff approve our report, and submit it to Ministers as an expression of their views.

(Signed) P.H. DEAN
J.G.T. INGLIS
C.R. PRICE
C.S. MOORE (for W.M.L. MacDONALD)
M.Y. WATSON (for K.W.D. STRONG)
Ministry of Defence.
3rd August, 1956.

Appendix to J.I.C. (56) 80

General.
1. We have appreciated elsewhere that the Egyptian Armed Forces will not be fully proficient with the new Soviet weapons before the end of 1956. Nevertheless, morale in the Armed Forces must for the moment be high. The political situation and Nasser's coup against the Suez Canal can only have stifled criticism and united the Army behind him.

Army.
2. Technical efficiency. This is taking its expected course. As each month passes, it is inevitable that the Egyptian Army will become more efficient and better trained although they will remain dependent for some considerable time on foreign technicians.
3. General efficiency. Training in, and absorption of, the new equipment can only lead to increased morale and a higher standard of efficiency. This will be particularly apparent in the armoured corps, who pride themselves on being the elite of the Egyptian Army.
4. Command. The failure of the Egyptian Army against the

Israelis in 1948 was largely due, not to the lack of fighting ability of the Egyptian troops, but to the inadequacy of the higher command. The fat, dissolute senior commanders of the Farouk era have now been replaced by younger professional soldiers, who, while lacking in experience, cannot but be better than their predecessors.

5. To sum up, although it has been customary to decry the efficiency of the Egyptian soldier in the past, we feel that for the reasons stated above it would be dangerous at this time to underestimate the capability of the Army, which, although untested under fire since 1948, has developed and improved during the past few years.

Air Force and Navy.

6. Present indications are that the Egyptian Air Force and Navy will not be efficient with their new aircraft and ships, even by Egyptian standards, until towards the end of this year.

7. It is considered, that any increase in efficiency in the Navy may be counterbalanced by deterioration of material and machinery due to poor maintenance during the period. In the Air Force, technical and logistical problems associated with the absorption of relatively large numbers of new aircraft may well delay the attaining of operational efficiency by as much as 6 months. The solutions of these problems are almost entirely dependent on Soviet bloc assistance and supply arrangements.

Notes

1. JIC(54)57, 'Egyptian Arms Imports', 19 June 1954, TNA: CAB 158/17.
2. JIC(55) 79th Meeting, 29 September 1955, TNA: CAB 159/21.
3. Keith Kyle, Britain's pre-eminent historian on Suez, has praised the JIC for its even-handed assessments during 1956; see Keith Kyle, *Suez: Britain's End of Empire in the Middle East*, rev. ed. (London: I. B. Tauris, 2011), pp. 552–3.
4. JIC(56)80(Final)(Revise), 'Egyptian Nationalisation of the Suez Canal Company', 3 August 1956, TNA: CAB 158/25.
5. For instance, the minutes of the COS meetings for this period are full of references to JIC papers. See TNA: DEFE 4/90 and TNA: DEFE 4/91.
6. JIC(56)97(Final), 'Probable Actions by Nasser in Certain Circumstances', 11 October 1956, TNA: CAB 158/25; JIC(56)102, 'Israel Attitude towards Arab States in the Context of the Suez Canal Crisis', 28 September 1956, TNA: CAB 158/26; JIC(56)104(Final), 'The Threat to United Kingdom Interests Overseas', 18 October 1956, TNA: CAB 158/26.
7. Philip Davies, *Intelligence and Government in Britain and the United States: A Comparative Perspective, Vol. 2: Evolution of the UK Intelligence Community* (Santa Barbara, CA: Praeger, 2012), pp. 163–8.

12

THE CUBAN MISSILE CRISIS

THE CUBAN MISSILE Crisis highlighted the importance of both the tactical and the strategic intelligence assessment roles of the JIC. Since the early 1950s it had produced two parallel series of reports: the 'Weekly Review of Current Intelligence' or the Grey Book, after the colour of its cover, and the 'Weekly Survey of Intelligence' or the Red Book. The Grey Book in this period produced four relevant reports whilst the Red Book included seven. Taken together they reveal something of the JIC's views and awareness of what was happening 4,650 miles away.

The JIC has to be given credit for anticipating the nature of the Cuban Missile Crisis. Much of the JIC's work during the Cold War was connected to issues of alerts, warning and nuclear crisis. As early as 1957, the JIC envisaged a situation in which the Soviet Union might send weapons and volunteers overseas to a friendly country. They envisaged that the struggle for prestige might lead to escalating support for proxies and this might include the supply of nuclear weapons.[1]

The first indication of what would become the Cuban Missile Crisis was a notice on 23 August 1962, some two months before the crisis erupted. It warned that since July there had been a steady arrival of Soviet merchant ships into Cuba. Intelligence also reported that more ships were en route. For the JIC, this influx could be explained in two ways. Either it could be military personnel returning from training in the Soviet Union; or, more plausibly, it was for economic purposes: the delivery of equipment and economic aid under various recent trade agreements.[2] Both interpretations were supported by a Soviet communiqué of 2 September that announced that the USSR was 'sending arms and military experts to Cuba and is giving her extensive economic aid'.[3]

On 4 September the JIC aired the 'possibility' that the Russians were installing surface-to-air missiles on behalf of the Cuban air defence system.[4] A fortnight later this assessment was strengthened as new intelligence was received. Taken together, the JIC concluded, the evidence 'suggests that Soviet policy at present is to give military assistance to strengthen the defensive capabilities of the Castro regime without giving it an independent offensive capability'.[5] The crucial language here is 'offensive' and 'defensive'. Thus, over a month before the crisis, evidence of a new level of Soviet support was being put before ministers.

On 1 October, in its first detailed assessment since Soviet supplies to Cuba were identified, the JIC considered the likely developments of Soviet defence policy. Its paper concluded that Khrushchev would maintain his desire to avoid war, a position that the JIC had consistently argued. This desire, the paper continued, was underlined by the fact that the US had an overwhelming advantage in its 'attack capability'. Furthermore, this had 'probably caused the Russians some concern about the credibility of their deterrent'.[6] Yet in arguing this, the JIC failed to appreciate the lessons of Pearl Harbor and other instances of asymmetric warfare when one side perceives itself to be backed into a corner and resorts to seemingly suicidal tactics.

On 25 October, the JIC referred to developments as the 'Cuba Crisis' for the first time.[7] It is possible to make several observations about the period up to 25 October: the JIC was relatively well informed on developments and tried to assess Soviet intentions in light of what was known but also in respect to public statements and disclosed trade agreements; more important, perhaps, was the assumption that the Soviet military deployment was a defensive move, designed to bolster Cuban defences. Yet at no point did the JIC consider why this was happening.

Through the Grey and Red Books the JIC was able to produce short, weekly analytical observations on developments. In addition, though, the committee played a tactical role in the production of a daily assessment of what was happening. Related to the JIS were the 'heads of sections' meetings, involving the relevant people from across Whitehall responsible for different geographical locations. From 23 October onwards, the date by which access to US photographic reconnaissance evidence had been obtained and the crisis was underway, the heads of the Western and Latin American sections went onto two hours' notice to prepare assessments, which they began to do on a daily basis.[8]

The increase in tempo and concern was based largely, although not entirely, on the photographic reconnaissance images provided by the United States. In discussion both intelligence communities agreed on their meaning.[9] The JIC concluded there 'was no question but that a strategic offensive missile threat existed in Cuba'. The key here is the word *offensive*, and it therefore signalled a reversal of the committee's earlier conclusion.[10] The first JIC assessment of what the Soviets were up to was issued on 26 October. It did not question grander Soviet motives but examined, more closely, the reaction to the US quarantine of Cuba and concluded that the Soviet response would be threefold:

1. to stall whilst the construction of the missile sites continued;
2. to use its position in Cuba as a bargaining chip with the Americans over Berlin;

3. and to mobilise world opinion by 'representing themselves as moderate and peace-loving'.[11]

In response to the grave danger presented by the situation, JIC members agreed to 'hold themselves at two hours' notice for an emergency meeting'.[12] To ensure that ministers and officials were given the best possible information, the JIC met on both Saturday, 27 and Sunday, 28 October. In addition the heads of sections continued to issue daily reports, providing an update on Soviet military developments worldwide and the progress of the missile construction on Cuba itself. From 29 October, once it had been reported that Khrushchev had agreed to dismantle the offensive missile sites in Cuba, the frequency of the heads of sections' report on other worldwide events declined.

By 8 November, the JIC concluded that unless there were any 'unexpected developments', the heads of sections could reduce their meetings to twice weekly,[13] and by 13 November, the date of the last heads of sections' report, it was stated that Soviet missile sites were being dismantled and heavily laden ships were returning to the Soviet Union.[14] The Cuban Missile Crisis, in the JIC's view, was over. Unsurprisingly, though, this was not the end of the JIC's interest in Cuba. In fact the JIC's most telling and valuable contribution was in the aftermath of the crisis, when it tried to explain Soviet motives.

Immediately following the cessation of the crisis the JIC approved an assessment, four months in preparation, entitled 'Escalation'. It began with the hypothetical premise that a hostile act had been committed by either the Soviet Union or the West and had been opposed by the other. Building upon how the crisis had developed, it concluded that 'it is now the fear of global war arising through a process of escalation which constitutes the deterrent to limited aggression, rather than the fear of immediate, massive retaliation'.[15] There was a real danger in misunderstanding the opponent's motives or misreading his intentions. A subsequent JIC paper, disseminated in early December, concluded that the Soviet Union would wish to avoid deliberate war; therefore, 'apart from an accident, and assuming the Soviet leaders act rationally, we only envisage global or limited war between the Soviet Union and the West coming about as a result of a process of miscalculation'.[16]

However, the most important assessment was a further paper also disseminated in early December. It was the first, substantial attempt by the JIC to consider what the Soviet motives had been in placing missiles in Cuba. The report re-examined the JIC's earlier judgements on Soviet defence policy in light of what had happened in Cuba, concluding that its previous assessments were still valid. The Soviet Union's concern about its strategic vulnerabilities vis-à-vis the United States was thought to be central to its actions, and this was reflected in the desire to strengthen Cuban defences against a future US invasion, but also to place offensive Soviet missiles as close to the US mainland as possible. As a by-product, the Soviets could have used their new-found position to strengthen their hand in dealings about Berlin.

Khrushchev was, of course, the pivotal character, as the second of the documents reproduced below suggests. The JIC assumed that he knew that the Americans would not resort to all-out war and so he would have planned to use the political defusing of the crisis to enhance his own position as the leader of world communism. The nature of the termination of the crisis meant that Khrushchev had not been entirely successful. Yet, the JIC warned, the Soviet retreat in Cuba should not be taken as a sign that similar retreats should be expected elsewhere.[17] In a sense, therefore very little had changed.

THIS DOCUMENT IS THE PROPERTY OF HER BRITANNIC MAJESTY'S GOVERNMENT

The circulation of this paper has been strictly limited. It is issued for the personal use of _____.

TOP SECRET   Copy No 113
J.I.C. (62) 99   UK EYES ONLY
27th October, 1962.

CABINET

JOINT INTELLIGENCE COMMITTEE

POSSIBLE SOVIET RESPONSE TO A U.S. DECISION TO BOMB OR INVADE CUBA

1. We have considered the above in the light of information given to H.M. Ambassador by the U.S. Government on the evening of 26th October that the U.S. must obtain within 48 hours three objectives:
(i) The cessation of the shipping of offensive weapons;
(ii) The cessation of construction work on the sites, and
(iii) The "de-fusing" of the weapons already in Cuba.

2. Once these objectives had been obtained, the U.S. would then be prepared to negotiate over two to three weeks the removal of the weapons from the island. All these arrangements would have to include satisfactory verification of compliance, and the U.S. could not suspend their quarantine arrangements until there was a satisfactory substitute including such verification. If there was a flat refusal to permit any inspection or control, the U.S. would have to pursue "other courses". They would have to consider destroying the sites by bombing.

3. We assume that the U.S. would not launch an attack on Cuba before they had received a refusal to permit inspection or control. If, however, the U.S. did launch an attack before a Russian reply had been received, the Russians might conclude that it was no good talking to

the U.S. and their reactions would be unpredictable because the element of irrationality might enter in.

4. The extent to which the Soviet Government are committed to defend Cuba is covered by the statement on 12th September, 1962.

5. We have said and we repeat, that if war is unleashed, if the aggressor makes an attack on one state or another and this state asks for assistance, the Soviet Union is capable of rendering assistance from its own territory to any peace-loving state and not only to Cuba. And let no one doubt that the Soviet Union will render such assistance, just as it was ready in 1956 to render military assistance to Egypt at the time of the Anglo-French-Israeli aggression in the Suez Canal region. But, at a time when the U.S.A. is taking steps to mobilise its armed forces and is preparing aggression against Cuba and other peace-loving states, the Soviet Government wishes to draw attention to the fact that it is now impossible to attack Cuba and consider that the aggressor will be free from punishment for this attack. If this attack is made it will be the beginning of the unleashing of war.

6. We have taken notice of the fact that the Soviet response so far to U.S. action over Cuba following the President's statement of 22nd October has been relatively moderate. They have clearly attached importance to playing for time during which they hoped to complete the offensive sites, though President Kennedy gave clear warning of his determination to prevent this happening. The Soviet Government have given no observable sign so far of an intention to respond by force to a U.S. bombing attack or invasion. We do not think that they have any intention of carrying out a pre-emptive strike against the U.S.A. although they have taken precautions to put their forces at a high state of readiness.

7. It is conceivable that the initial Soviet response either to a U.S. ultimatum of a bombing attack on Cuba or to an actual attack would be to avoid immediate resort to arms. They might confine their riposte to appeals to world opinion and to the U.N., seeking to win world wide support for the Soviet Union as a model peace-loving power compared with a belligerent U.S... They are not bound to Cuba by a defence treaty such as they have with all other bloc countries. They must recognise that any

military action they might take in response to a U.S. move would be bound to carry a grave risk of escalation into nuclear war. We believe too that they are conscious at the present time of an overall strategic inferiority vis-a-vis the US. This inferiority, which may have been a major factor in the build-up in Cuba, would militate against creating a showdown with the U.S. at the present stage. The response the Soviet Government have already made to the U.S. blockade amounts to a considerable climb-down on their part and to a loss of face. They are clearly at the moment playing for time and bidding for support as a peace-loving country and it is possible that they would continue to adopt this line as the lesser of two evils even in the event of a direct U.S. resort to force in Cuba.

8. Any minor response would undermine any attempt they might be making to represent themselves as a completely pacific party to the dispute, whereas it would do nothing to demonstrate their ability and determination to support Cuba nor would it avoid great impairment to their image as a great power comparable to the U.S.A.

9. We think it likely that, should the Russians decide that they must retaliate by some form of action, such action would be significant and would not be confined for instance to minor harassment to western access to Berlin.

9. We think that if therefore the Russians resort to arms it will be an effective military response, and we suggest that the most likely blow will be a tit-for-tat as nearly parallel as possible to the U.S. action. It seems unlikely therefore that they will attack directly either U.S. territory or the territory of any of the NATO powers. The closest parallel would appear to be a U.S. base in some third country or an attack on some major U.S. naval vessel. They might also attack Guantanamo though they must expect that this would invite a full-scale U.S. invasion of the islands.

10. We have considered the possibility of large-scale military action against Berlin but suggest that this is unlikely in view of the clear warning from the U.S. that this would bring about a full confrontation. Indeed central to Soviet thinking in deciding upon their reply will be their fear of doing anything that might escalate into general nuclear war. Their overriding concern

therefore is likely to be to limit their reply to the least dangerous possible place. Should the Russians make an attack such as we have suggested they would probably follow it up with clear indications that this went as far as they intended to go at the present stage. Their aim indeed would be to carry out an exact tit-for-tat and no more.

11. It seems unlikely that the Russians will use nuclear weapons in reply to such a U.S. attack as may be envisaged.

(Signed) HUGH STEPHENSON
Chairman,
on behalf of the Joint Intelligence Committee.

Cabinet Office, S.W.1.
27th October, 1962

* * *

THIS DOCUMENT IS THE PROPERTY OF HER BRITANNIC MAJESTY'S GOVERNMENT
The circulation of this paper has been strictly limited.
It is issued for the personal use of.................................
TOP SECRET   Copy No........
J.I.C. (62) 101 (Final)
6th December, 1962.

CABINET
JOINT INTELLIGENCE COMMITTEE
SOVIET MOTIVES IN CUBA
Report by the Joint Intelligence Committee

The object of this paper is to determine, in the light of events to date, the motives underlying recent Soviet actions in Cuba. In order to do this we first review briefly the evidence available as to the pattern and timing of the build-up of Soviet arms. We are not able to assess how far the Russians may have been planning to increase it later. We then relate these activities to what we believe to be the principles governing Soviet defence policy. Finally, we discuss Khrushchev's reasons for agreeing to withdraw the offensive weapons.

THE BUILD-UP OF SOVIET ARMS

2. The build-up of Army, Naval and defensive Air equipment is set out at Appendix.

Bomber Aircraft

3. On 5th October, United States reconnaissance discovered ten large crates on the deck of a Russian freighter unloading in Cuba. These crates were identical to those used for shipment of IL28 (BEAGLE) bombers to Egypt. Between 5th and 14th October, air reconnaissance revealed crated BEAGLE bombers and subsequently more than forty BEAGLES were identified. These aircraft are capable of carrying nuclear weapons.

Surface-to-Surface Missiles

4. On 5th September there was some indication that missile sites which were not SAM sites might be under construction. On 14th October aerial photography showed a possible MRBM site. Subsequent photography was carried out over the whole of Cuba. On 22nd October, sixteen MRBM pads appeared to be operational, and by 26th October a further eight, making twenty-four in all. Four IRBM sites each of four launches seen under construction were assessed as likely to be operational by early December. There was no indication of work starting on further sites. Buildings were seen of the type needed for storing nuclear warheads.

5. It is thought that the MRBMs were probably taken to Cuba in the Soviet Missile Carrier ship Poltava, which had made two sailings, arriving on 3rd August and 14th September respectively. The ship would have been due again on 29th October.

6. The United States assessment of what would have existed in Cuba if all offensive sites had become operational is as follows:-

(a) Six sites each of four launchers for 1100 n.m. missiles, i.e. a total first salvo of twenty-four missiles of this range (MRBM).

(b) Four sites each of four launchers for 2200 n.m. missiles, i.e. a total salvo of sixteen missiles of this range (IRBM).

7. The launching of these missiles could immediately be detected by United States radar on the Florida coast; the average time of flight of Soviet MRBMs, which varies little with range, is of the order of thirteen minutes. BMEWS at present should give about sixteen minutes warning

of ICBMs launched from the Soviet Union. The warning time of attack by submarine launched missiles could not possibly be more than seven minutes, the flight time of the missile, and is likely to be much less. As regards warning time, therefore, missiles in Cuba would have given the Russians at the best only a marginal advantage.

Soviet Personnel

8. It is believed that at the height of the crisis there were some 16,000 military and 3,000 civilian Soviet personnel in Cuba. It is estimated that about 9,000 military personnel would have been needed to operate all missile systems of types set up in Cuba, including the dismantled surface-to-surface missiles. In addition, there are an unknown number of Soviet military personnel in various command, communications and other support installations in Cuba, serving as advisers and technicians with the Cuban forces.

Timing

9. It is apparent that after the beginning of August there was a significant change in the character and volume of the Soviet build up of arms. Offensive weapons and more modern types of defensive weapons began then to be introduced, SAM sites, radar and Mach 2 fighters were deployed, missile firing patrol boats arrived and the numbers of tanks and field guns greatly increased. We do not know when the decision to send the missiles was made. For technical and logistic reasons it could not possibly have been made later than the beginning of July; we believe it must have been made earlier.

KHRUSHCHEV'S MOTIVES

Soviet Defence Policy

10. We have described elsewhere the objectives of Soviet defence policy as follows:-

"Khrushchev's conviction about the 'non-inevitability of war', a doctrine not held by previous Soviet leaders, implies not only that the Soviet Government do not regard war as an expedient means of pursuing their ends but that the non-Communist world can be prevented from making war in pursuit of theirs. The only exceptions to this belief are:-

(a) the Soviet fear that the non-Communist countries may indulge in 'local' wars, confident that the balance of nuclear terror rules out the risk of escalation; and

(b) the Soviet conviction that it is the duty of Communists to support 'wars of liberation' everywhere, though cautiously, so as to avoid the risk of escalation into general war.

Nevertheless, their history and convictions about capitalist intentions must prevent the Soviet leaders from feeling complacent. The Soviet Union must be made as invulnerable as possible against the possibility of capitalist attack in any form. Apart from direct military needs, a ceaseless effort is required to alter the correlation of forces in the world in favour of Communism. The greater the strength of Soviet armed forces vis-a-vis the capitalist world, the greater the impulse behind political expansion and subversion".

11. We continued:

"Within this general framework the Soviet Union see their armed forces as necessary for the following specific requirements:-

(a) to secure the Soviet Union and Communist bloc from external attacks by the possession of a credible deterrent;

(b) to defend the Soviet Union and bloc and secure the most favourable outcome to hostilities if the deterrent fails;

(c) to provide support for national liberation wars and the necessary counter to imperialist local wars;

(d) to provide a backing of impressive military strength for Soviet foreign policy;

(e) to assist in maintaining internal security and to frustrate any attempt to overthrow Communist regimes anywhere in the bloc."

12. We further stated:

"Soviet policy is likely to be guided by the following principles, at least until such time as the Russian leaders are entirely confident about the relative balance of military power:

(a) great caution in foreign policy so as to avoid the risk of war or of having to back down because of this risk; nevertheless,

(b) a reluctance to negotiate from weakness on major issues."

13. We now discuss how far Khrushchev's actions over Cuba were consistent with the above.

Defence of the Soviet Union

14. The increased confidence of the Americans in their strategic capability, coupled with their evident determination to increase their strength yet further, appear to have caused the Russians some concern about the credibility of their deterrent. They therefore embarked in the second half of 1961 on a major expansion of their defence programme. The main Soviet effort in this respect must clearly be directed to those weapon systems, such as hardened ICBM sites and submarines, which could survive an initial surprise attack. The missiles in Cuba would have been very vulnerable to surprise or preemptive attack. Nevertheless, the additional nuclear potential which they would have provided would have significantly increased the overall Soviet nuclear capability. Moreover, as the word itself implies, the "credibility" of a deterrent is determined not only by numbers, quality and invulnerability of weapons but also by such considerations (which might perhaps be called psychological) as their nearness to the target country and the degree of control over their use likely to be exercised by the other side. Seen in this light, the Soviet nuclear strength in Cuba, despite its vulnerability, would have contributed in some measure to the requirement at paragraph 11(a) above.

Defence of Cuba

15. Since the Bay of Pigs attack in 1961 the Russians may well have had a genuine fear that sooner or later the United States might consider it necessary to attack Cuba. By supplying the Cubans with large quantities of conventional arms over the last two years they showed the Americans that an invasion of Cuba could only be conducted as a major and costly operation. The establishment in Cuba of surface-to-surface missiles and BEAGLE aircraft with a nuclear capability, even though under Soviet control, would have added to this deterrent. If they had wished to invade Cuba under these conditions the Americans would have had either to accept the risk of grave damage to their homeland or to guard against it by neutralising the weapons at the outset. Complete success in the latter could probably not be guaranteed by conventional attacks. The establishment of Soviet offensive nuclear power in Cuba would therefore have contributed considerably to requirements at paragraph 11(c) above.

Backing of Strength for Soviet Foreign Policy
16. The establishment of an offensive nuclear capability so close to the United States clearly posed an additional and substantial threat of Soviet attack on America. The Russians could have expected that this would have reduced the confidence with which the United States approached future critical confrontations with the Soviet Union and significantly increase the pressure which the latter could safely bring to bear in seeking to force Western acceptance of Soviet demands, for example in Berlin. The Russians had given the strong impression that they were planning such pressures towards the end of the year when the missile sites would have been completed.
17. Such a spectacular achievement would also have:-
(a) encouraged Communists throughout the world and particularly in Latin America;
(b) impressed the Chinese, whose accusations that Khrushchev has not been pursuing the communist cause with all the revolutionary vigour, would have been debunked;
(c) boosted Castro's regime;
(d) appeased such elements, if any, in the Soviet hierarchy as may have been dissatisfied with Khrushchev's policy of moderation.
18. All this would have been a significant contribution towards the requirements at paragraph 11(d) above.

Khrushchev's Assessment
19. It is clear from the foregoing arguments that Khrushchev saw several important gains in the establishment of a nuclear capability in Cuba. He probably believed that in the last resort the Americans would not risk global war over this issue. He must have realised that to withdraw once he had begun the operation would result in a weakening of his authority within the Communist Bloc and perhaps also his personal position; it would give added substance to the Chinese claims that he was ineffective as the leader of world Communism against imperialism; and it would detract substantially from the credibility of Soviet threats to back up encroachment on Western interests by the use of military power.
20. Khrushchev's calculation was therefore probably that the Americans would not go beyond political action, particularly if the Russians moved quickly enough to face them with a _fait accompli_. He may well have believed that there was a reasonable chance of success if he acted

fast enough. He may well have been persuaded that the infrequency of the routine United States surveillance of Cuba, the public knowledge that SAM sites were being built there, the lull in political activity presented by his undertaking not to raise the Berlin issue until after the Congressional elections, and the Russians' misleading statements, would enable the Soviet nuclear strength to become at any rate partly established in Cuba before discovery. He may well also have appreciated that the Americans on discovering it, would lose time by going first to the United Nations, where Khrushchev could count on the support of the neutral and uncommitted nations, so that he would then have further time in which to consolidate the build-up. Furthermore, he may have thought that once the force was fully operational, he would have been in a stronger position to deal with United States reactions. The Americans would not then have had the option of imposing a blockade on incoming weapons.

21. Against this Khrushchev must have considered the risk of U.S. discovery of his project before its completion. Furthermore he must have appreciated that discovery would inflame American opinion and that in these circumstances the Administration would be under considerable pressure to neutralise the Soviet move. Admittedly he had done his best through public and private warnings to browbeat President Kennedy into believing that any forceful action, including blockade, would mean war and to deter him from the use of force. He had also strongly hinted that if the Americans acted against Cuba he would act where he had local tactical superiority, e.g. Berlin. He could not, however, completely have ignored the possibility that the Americans would use force and in this event he would be obliged to withdraw.

22. We believe that to have taken the risks involved Khrushchev was not simply actuated by the desire to seize the opportunity of turning a local situation to great advantage, but must have had specific and compelling motives for the action that he took. These may well have arisen from a concern that little Soviet progress had recently been made in the Cold War and that there had been no weakening in the West's determination to maintain the status quo in Berlin. We believe that Khrushchev probably considered it very important, both

for the Communist cause and his personal position, to try to obtain some lever against the West at this particular moment in the world's history. He may have concluded that by placing missiles with nuclear warheads "in their own backyard", he could jolt the Americans out of what he considered an exaggerated confidence in their superior nuclear strike capability, and wake them up to the realities of the present nuclear confrontation.

23. We believe that Khrushchev must have been influenced more by the politico-military advantages discussed in paragraphs 16, 17 and 22 above than by fine calculations of numbers of missiles and warning periods.

Khrushchev's Withdrawal

24. The speed and decisiveness of the United States reaction coupled with the substantial support of the O.A.S. and the NATO governments, appears to have completely surprised the Russians. Khrushchev's actions then were entirely consistent with his character and with our appraisal of Soviet defence policy at paragraphs 10 and 12 above. Finding his major assumption about United States reactions invalid, his paramount concern was to avoid the risk of global war through a head-on collision with the United States, even to the extent of accepting a major political setback to achieve this. He must also have attached considerable importance to safeguarding the communist position in Cuba.

25. Khrushchev has in the past shown a talent for making the best of such situations. He is making the best of this situation by representing himself as the man of peace who has saved the world from thermo-nuclear war; and he can claim that he has achieved his aim of obtaining a clear United States commitment not to attack Cuba. It is certainly his intention that Cuba should remain a Communist outpost of the western hemisphere. He is likely to feel that he cannot now accept any further set-back, and in this he may be influenced by the strong Chinese criticism of the Soviet climb down in Cuba. The Soviet retreat in an exposed area such as Cuba should not therefore be taken to imply an equal willingness to retreat on other issues where the Russians are in a stronger tactical position and where a retreat would more seriously affect their national interests.

(Signed) HUGH STEPHENSON

Chairman, on behalf of The Joint Intelligence Committee.
Cabinet Office, S.W.1.
6th December, 1962

Appendix to J.I.C. (62) 101 (Final)
BUILD-UP OF ARMY, NAVAL AND DEFENSIVE AIR EQUIPMENTS IN CUBA

Army

1. For the last two years at least the Russians have provided a continuous flow of military equipment to the Cuban Army, and have been helping to train it by a military mission in Cuba and by courses for individuals in the U.S.S.R. Equipment received up to November this year included the following major items:-
920 Pieces of artillery
300 Anti-tank guns
810 Conventional A.A. weapons
75 SU 100 self-propelled 100 mm guns (currently in the Soviet Army).
185-210 T.34/85 medium tanks (no longer in the Soviet Army but used to equip Satellites).
100-140 T.54/100 medium tanks (current Soviet medium tank)
40 JS-2 heavy tanks (no longer in the Soviet Army but used to equip Satellites).
600 82 mm mortars
180 120 mm mortars.
Five FROG free flight rockets (launched from a tank chassis) have been sighted, and about 20 SNAPPER anti-tank missiles have been identified.

2. More than half of the tanks and field artillery pieces listed above were delivered after the beginning of August, 1962.

Navy

3. Between January and June 1962 six anti-submarine coastal escorts of the Kronstadt class and twelve P-6 class torpedo boats were supplied to Cuba. During August and September these were augmented by twelve Komar class patrol boats and another four P-6 torpedo boats. The Komar class are P-6 torpedo boats converted to carry two 10-15 mile surface-to-surface missiles instead of torpedos.

4. There is evidence that there are Soviet technical

personnel in the Komars; otherwise these ships are believed to be manned by the Cubans. There are also indications that the Russians may have intended to base submarines in Cuba.

Radar

5. Since early August over 100 modern radars were sited.

SAM Systems

6. Between 29th August and 5th September, air reconnaissance revealed the strengthening of Cuban defences by the introduction of SAM. By 5th October, twenty-four sites each with a range of approximately 25 n.m., were being installed and were operational before the end of the month, giving almost complete coverage of Cuba.

Fighter Aircraft

7. Sixty-one MIG15 (FAGOT), MIG17 (FRESCO) and MIG19 (FARMER) fighters have been identified on Cuban airfields. In addition, by 5th September, thirty-nine MIG21 (FISHBED) supersonic fighters have been detected by aerial reconnaissance.

Notes

1. Peter Hennessy, *The Secret State: Whitehall and the Cold War* (London: Allen Lane, 2002), pp. 37–41.
2. For more see Michael S. Goodman, 'The Joint Intelligence Committee and the Cuban Missile Crisis', in David Gioe, Len Scott and Christopher Andrew (eds), *An International History of the Cuban Missile Crisis: A 50-Year Retrospective* (Abingdon: Routledge, forthcoming).
3. WRCI (4 September 1962), TNA: CAB 179/9.
4. Ibid.
5. Cited in Goodman, 'The Joint Intelligence Committee and the Cuban Missile Crisis'.
6. JIC(62)81(Final), 'Likely Development of Soviet Defence Policy in the Next Five Years and Its Bearing on Soviet Foreign Policy', 1 October 1962, TNA: CAB 158/47.
7. WCRI (25 October 1962), TNA: CAB 179/9.
8. JIC(62) 50th Meeting, 23 October 1962, TNA: CAB 159/38.
9. JIC(62)93(Final), 'The Threat Posed by Soviet Missiles in Cuba', 26 October 1962, TNA: CAB 158/47.
10. JIC(62) 51st Meeting, 25 October 1962, TNA: CAB 159/38.
11. JIC(62)97, 'First Soviet Reactions to US Action and Intentions Concerning Cuba', 26 October 1962, TNA: CAB 158/47.
12. JIC(62) 52nd Meeting, 26 October 1962, TNA: CAB 159/38.
13. JIC(62) 57th Meeting, 8 November 1962, TNA: CAB 159/38.
14. Cited in Goodman, 'The Joint Intelligence Committee and the Cuban Missile Crisis'.
15. JIC(62)70(Final), 'Escalation', 2 November 1962, TNA: CAB 158/47.
16. JIC(62)77(Final), 'Likelihood of War with the Soviet Union up to 1967', 6 December 1962, TNA: CAB 158/47.
17. JIC(62)101(Final), 'Soviet Motives in Cuba', 6 December 1962, TNA: CAB 158/47.

13

VIETNAM

AMERICA'S PROLONGED CONFLICT in Vietnam asked difficult questions of the British government. It strained the transatlantic relationship and challenged the UK's understandings of its role east of Suez. Asia was an area of notable Anglo-American friction during the Cold War, dating back to the disagreements over Clement Attlee's decision to recognise Communist China in 1950. Indeed, the JIC had long held a more realistic assessment of communism in the region than Washington, which was more determined to resist its spread at all costs. Whitehall had more limited aims.[1]

Because they were preoccupied with the Malaysian confrontation, British Conservative governments generally supported American policy over Vietnam. Harold Macmillan and Alec Douglas-Home sought to demonstrate solidarity with the Americans during the Cold War. Indeed, the Conservatives publicly supported American action as defensive. They had even sent a five-man advisory mission to Saigon in 1961, in an attempt to demonstrate to Washington that Britain was willing to take its share of the Cold War burden in the region.[2] The British genuinely thought their advice would be helpful, whilst they also sought to use the opportunity to gather useful information about the situation in Vietnam. By contrast, however, certain historians, such as Nigel Ashton, have dismissed the mission as merely 'a sop to try to make up for [Britain's] reluctance to become engaged in Laos',[3] where Britain had long refused to offer military support to prevent a French defeat in Indo-China in the 1950s.

Whitehall's attitude was somewhat torn. On the one hand, Britain had co-chaired the 1954 Geneva Conference alongside the Soviet Union, which led to French withdrawal from Indochina and the creation of a ceasefire line between North and South Vietnam. Accordingly, Britain had developed by the early 1960s what it considered to be a monitoring role. The government was therefore apparently keen to uphold this settlement where possible. On the other hand, Douglas-Home when Foreign Secretary privately stated that Britain was 'prepared to turn a blind eye' to American intervention (that violated the Geneva Accords).[4]

Under pressure from Washington but also dealing with its own problems, Whitehall needed to be aware of American activity in Vietnam. Moreover, policymakers had to understand the consequences of deeper intervention. The JIC was instructed to assess American actions. By the early 1960s, the committee had become far more adept at monitoring and understanding insurgencies. Drawing on experiences from Malaya and other colonial conflicts, the JIC learnt that military and political security had become increasingly blurred in the Cold War world. It was well aware that military solutions alone would not end insurgencies. In 1962, the committee conducted an important assessment on Vietnam. It was not to be shared with the Americans. Although the JIC underestimated the number of troops needed to secure South Vietnam, it made some prescient observations. For example, it correctly predicted that the war would be long and inconclusive. It also warned, accurately, that the Vietcong could not be defeated through military means alone. Interestingly, the committee predicted that increased US involvement would create discomfort within Whitehall. Awkward questions would be asked by Washington.[5]

Interestingly, the JIC's assessments of Soviet and Chinese intentions were echoed in Foreign Office planning documents just weeks later. The committee accurately forecast that the Soviets would seek to avoid direct involvement in the conflict. Meanwhile, it argued that the Chinese were unlikely to intervene should American activity be limited to South Vietnam, but perhaps overestimated the Chinese threat should the Americans interfere in North Vietnam. The assessment drew on MI6 and Foreign Office analysis, where it was argued that although China would take advantage of troubles in any adjacent area, Peking would be unlikely to intervene decisively. Shortly afterwards, diplomats in the Foreign Office repeated the JIC's view when planning policy. They wrote that 'the Russians do not welcome a war in Indo China and we do not believe that the Chinese would intervene unless they felt the security of North Vietnam was directly threatened'.[6]

The JIC returned to the issue in February 1964. The Chiefs of Staff requested an intelligence assessment of the consequences of deeper American involvement in Vietnam and of American withdrawal from South Vietnam. Despite the JIC's transition into the Cabinet Office in 1957, the Chiefs of Staff continued to request all-source intelligence assessments on military matters. They remained keen consumers. Regarding Vietnam, however, the Foreign Office also sought information. Diplomats therefore supported the military's request. Indeed, Douglas-Home's government as a whole was concerned about Soviet or Chinese intervention in the conflict should it escalate. This would have turned the conflict into a major, and potentially devastating, Cold War confrontation. Douglas-Home's successor, Harold Wilson, shared these concerns.[7] The JIC's assessment was issued around two weeks later, on 12 March. Marked 'Top Secret' and 'UK Eyes Only', it is reproduced below.

The assessment was similar to that of 1962. Echoing its earlier concern, the JIC warned about the disastrous consequences of withdrawal. It must be remembered that the UK's primary focus at this point was the confrontation between Indonesia and Malaysia. An American retreat from Vietnam would have had disastrous effects on the British position in Malaysia. Indeed, Douglas-Home was busy discussing these various scenarios with Washington in early 1964 whilst the JIC assessment was being prepared. Britain sought to link the two conflicts in the hope of being able to influence American policy in the region.[8]

Meanwhile, the committee remained realistic that a military victory would be long and difficult. In fact, the JIC judged that deeper US intervention might not lead to victory at all. This was an important assessment given the context of imminent American escalation. Once more the JIC predicted embarrassment. The British government was torn between its Cold War and 'special relationship' commitments on the one hand, and fears, on the other, that deeper military engagement was not working.[9] Indeed, the JIC concluded that conflict inside Vietnam would place severe strains on SEATO.

This proved to be prophetic. As the report was being prepared, Douglas-Home reported to the House of Commons that he had recently met with President Lyndon Johnson and that his government supported American policy, which was intended to 'help the Republic of South Vietnam to protect its people and to preserve its independence'.[10] Shortly after the report was disseminated, Foreign Secretary Rab Butler told US National Security Advisor McGeorge Bundy that 'an incursion into North Vietnamese territory would ... create difficulties for us'. Echoing JIC conclusions, he feared that US plans would 'probably provoke the Soviet Union and China into action'.[11] And yet the following August, the US Congress authorised Johnson to engage in military activity against North Vietnam. This essentially allowed a dramatic escalation of the Vietnam War. Johnson's advisers stressed to him that America would win if more pressure was applied and, from February 1965, bombing of North Vietnamese targets began. Increased military action served only to intensify the British government's dilemma. Moreover, the election of Harold Wilson in October 1964 complicated matters further. Unlike his predecessor, Wilson not only had to balance American pressures but had to factor in the left-wing views of the Labour Party.[12]

In contrast to its American equivalent, the JIC had acquired around twenty years' experience of assessing counterinsurgency by the time of Vietnam. Unlike the United States, the UK maintained a consulate in Hanoi with MI6 representation for most of the Vietnam War, which was a continued source of excellent reporting for both London and Washington.[13] Although the JIC learnt its lessons slowly, it was well equipped to issue realistic appreciations of the situation in the 1960s. As a result, its conclusions were highly relevant to government policy deliberations.

SECRET

(THIS DOCUMENT IS THE PROPERTY OF HER BRITANNIC
MAJESTY'S GOVERNMENT)

J.I.C. (64) 26 (Terms of Reference)   COPY NO. 26

27th February, 1964   IMMEDIATE
U.K. EYES ONLY

CABINET

JOINT INTELLIGENCE COMMITTEE

THE CONSEQUENCES OF DEEPER UNITED STATES INVOLVEMENT IN VIETNAM OR UNITED STATES WITHDRAWAL FROM SOUTH VIETNAM

Note by the Secretary

The Chiefs of Staff (C.O.S. 17th Meeting/64 Item 9) have invited the J.I.C. to examine the consequences of deeper United States involvement in Vietnam and of United States withdrawal from South Vietnam. An up to date report on this subject is also required urgently by the Foreign Office, and Departments mainly concerned have been asked to send contributions by 10 a.m. on MONDAY, 2nd MARCH to the J.I.S. (2nd Team) who will prepare a Preliminary Draft for early circulation.

2. The report will be based on relevant material in J.I.C. (64) 22 (Final) and J.I.C. (62) 12 (Final), and an examination of the various forms which United States action might possibly take. A list of these is attached at Annex.

(Signed) J.M.C. VIVIAN

for Secretary,
Joint Intelligence Committee

Cabinet Office, S.W.1.

27th February, 1964.

SECRET - U.K. EYES ONLY

ANNEX TO
J..I.C. (64) 26 (Terms of Reference)

POSSIBLE FORMS OF UNITED STATES ACTION

South Vietnam
(a) Stationing of United States forces in Saigon or other population centres.
(b) Participation of United States combat forces in the fighting either individually or in support of South Vietnam forces.
(c) Direct air attacks on Viet Cong targets.
(d) In connection with (b) use of tactical nuclear weapons in the fighting.
(e) Air surveillance of the land and sea frontiers to prevent infiltration by the Viet Cong.
(f) Implementation of SEATO plan 7 (counter insurgency in Vietnam) thereby involving other SEATO countries in the fighting.

North Vietnam
(a) Invasion by United States combat troops.
(b) Support for invasion by South Vietnam combat units.
(c) Support for the establishment of South Vietnamese guerrilla operations including covert sabotage and terrorist activities.
(d) Air attacks on lines of communication or installations used for supplying the Viet Cong.
(e) Bombing of military and population centres with aim of weakening the economy.
(f) Naval blockade or harrassing [sic] by light naval forces.
(g) Bombing of targets in China close to North Vietnam border.
(h) Use of selective nuclear bombing.

THIS DOCUMENT IS THE PROPERTY OF HER BRITANNIC MAJESTY'S GOVERNMENT
The circulation of this paper has been strictly limited.
It is issued for the personal use of……………….

TOP SECRET

Copy No. 10

J.I.C. (64) 26 (Final)
12 March, 1964   U.K. EYES ONLY

                              CABINET

                  JOINT INTELLIGENCE COMMITTEE

THE CONSEQUENCES OF DEEPER UNITED STATES INVOLVEMENT IN
VIETNAM OR UNITED STATES WITHDRAWAL FROM SOUTH VIETNAM

              Report by the Joint Intelligence Committee

                SUMMARY OF THE REPORT AND CONCLUSIONS

In Part I of our report at Annex we examine the implications of deeper United States involvement in Vietnam in the form of either a heavier commitment, including combat troops, in South Vietnam or of action against North Vietnam. In Part II we examine the likely consequences of United States withdrawal from South Vietnam.
2. Since 1962 the United States has provided massive military assistance to South Vietnam. Over the same period the rapid expansion of the South Vietnamese forces has inevitably resulted in a number of weaknesses which have been aggravated by the recent coups and the consequent confusion in the military and civil administration. Since January, 1964 Viet Cong military and subversive activities have increased throughout the country. Prospects of any significant improvement in the military situation in the immediate future are not good.
3. We conclude that:-

                              PART I
(a) Whatever the form of United States action and whatever the degree of South Vietnamese Government/United States military success against the Viet Cong thereby achieved, decisive and final defeat of the Viet Cong cannot be achieved by military means alone. The fundamental task remains that of inducing the South Vietnamese authorities to undertake and persist in a programme of the necessary administrative, social and economic measures, and to winning popular confidence in, and support for such a programme;
(b) a heavier United States military commitment in South Vietnam in the form of the garrisoning of key towns

and/or the introduction and use of combat units, might halt the present deterioration in the military situation and give the South Vietnamese Government a breathing space to get new measures under way, but it would raise difficult problems and might in the longer run be counter-productive;

(c) even full-scale intervention would not lead to a lasting solution for a very long time, if at all;

(d) the cutting off of North Vietnamese assistance to the Viet Cong would not ensure a speedy end to the insurrection in South Vietnam;

(e) if the United States took military action confined to South Vietnam the North Vietnamese would probably increase their covert support to the Viet Cong and appeal to the Soviet Union and China for increased material support, the Chinese would give them full diplomatic and propaganda support and probably step up military supplies. The communist countries generally would probably mount a world-wide campaign, in particular demanding the reconvening of Geneva Conference in the interests of maintaining peace;

(f) there is some scope for covert support for guerrilla activity among the tribes of north-west North Vietnam and this if successful could lead to localised disturbances and perhaps to revolts elsewhere in the countryside, the news of which could have some effect on Viet Cong morale, and encourage Government forces in South Vietnam;

(g) if the United States took military action against North Vietnam the Chinese would give direct military support, including "volunteers" and air cover to the North Vietnamese. They might give overt support to the Pathet Lao in Laos, and would step up their subversive effort elsewhere in the area. Unless they expected general war, they would not take military or other decisive action against Hong Kong;

(h) the first Soviet objective would be to avoid the issue if at all possible by seeking to deter the United States from action against North Vietnam. The Soviet Union might also put pressure on North Vietnam to make some temporary concessions, if they thought this would work. If the United States went ahead with action against North Vietnam the Soviet Union would probably supply the North Vietnamese with some arms and ammunition and might well reconsider the possibility of arms supply to China to the same end. Nevertheless the Russians would wish to keep their involvement to a minimum, and in any case would stop short of any action which might lead to their involvement in nuclear war;

(i) it would be difficult for the United States to obtain much support internationally for direct military action against North Vietnam, or to avoid condemnation in the United Nations;

(j) a limited non-nuclear war in Vietnam would probably be protracted and indecisive; it would not spread outside mainland South East Asia and it could lead to severe strains within SEATO;

PART II

(k) if, as the eventual result of United States withdrawal, South Vietnam were to fall under complete or partial communist control, the West would suffer a severe blow in the context of the world-wide struggle against communism; the United States and SEATO would be discredited and the latter would probably disintegrate; communist influence in South East Asia would increase; and the whole Western position in the area would be seriously damaged.

(Signed) BERNARD BURROWS
of [sic] behalf of the
Joint Intelligence Committee

Cabinet Office, S.W.1.

12th March, 1964

ANNEX TO
J.I.C. (64) 26 (Final)

THE CONSEQUENCES OF DEEPER UNITED STATES INVOLVEMENT IN VIETNAM OR UNITED STATES WITHDRAWAL FROM SOUTH VIETNAM

In this report we examine in Part I the consequences of deeper United States involvement in Vietnam and in Part II the consequences of United States withdrawal from South Vietnam. We set out an introduction to both parts of the paper in a single section immediately below.

INTRODUCTION

The Viet Cong

2. We believe that the strength of the Viet Cong regular forces has now risen to about 25,000 men. In addition there is a large reservoir of at least 100,000 partly armed and trained supporters in South Vietnam, the number may even be as high as 200,000. The population of South Vietnam is about 15 million and that of North Vietnam about 18 million.

3. The Government of North Vietnam exercises general direction over the Viet Cong. Some equipment, mainly small arms and light support weapons and medical items, from North Vietnam reaches the Viet Cong in the hands of the infiltrators, who numbered about 3,000 in 1963. But in the main the guerillas [sic] rely on obtaining weapons, about 6,000 in 1963, by capture from South Vietnamese Government forces, and recruits by local "recruiting". The hard core of the Viet Cong are by now so well indoctrinated and trained that even if it were possible to cut off their ties with North Vietnam this would probably have little or no immediate effect on their ability to continue their operations, although it might have some effect on their morale and it would force them to rely entirely on local sources for expansion. It would not significantly reduce the problem of defeating the Viet Cong for a very considerable time.

4. Although it might be possible to seal off the frontier between North and South Vietnam, large stretches of the South Vietnamese frontier with Laos and Cambodia are controlled by the Viet Cong, and the terrain is such that interdiction of supply routes across it would be virtually impossible. Furthermore the long coastline offers considerable scope for the smuggling of arms by sea.

5. Civil Administrative Activities. The broad Viet Cong aim has been to weaken and ultimately supplant the Government by controlling as much countryside as possible and isolating the urban centres remaining under Government control. Starting in relatively inaccessible areas the Viet Cong's plan was to establish zones whose original main purpose was to train and re-group military cadres, serve as a launching area for attacks, and to provide reception centres for infiltrators and arms. These areas have been progressively increased. Certain

of them have become completely communist-controlled and strong enough to resist attack by government forces. In these areas the Viet Cong levy and collect taxes, finance and direct agricultural programmes, engage in multifarious economic and commercial enterprises, conscript cadres and indoctrinate the populace. Though coercion and extortion are used in many cases, the Viet Cong are under strict orders to respect the peasant and his property. All this presupposes some sort of administrative machinery. Whilst the broad co-ordination of policy appears to be carried out by the Liberation Front presumably in Hanoi, the Viet Cong war zones and organisations in South Vietnam appear to have a very large measure of local autonomy probably with overt party organisations in the controlled areas, and also provisional local government units similar to those established in the war against the French. If it is true, as reported recently, that civil administrative specialists are infiltrating from North Vietnam and dispersing to various areas in the communist-held south, this could mark an important stage in the consolidation of the Viet Cong foothold.

The United States, and South Vietnamese Forces

6. Following the United States decision to increase military aid to South Vietnam, a United States Military Assistance Command M.A.C.(V) was set up in Saigon in January, 1962 and was completely formed by May, 1962. This Command replaced the United States M.A.A.G. which had operated in South Vietnam for some years, and which remains in the country, subordinate to M.A.C.(V). The clear determination on the part of the Americans to give massive aid overtly to the South Vietnamese had an immediate result. At practically all levels of the official South Vietnamese civil and military hierarchy, morale began to rise and the defeatist sentiment, which had been widespread in 1961, began to dissipate. However, any hopes that there might have been for a quick solution to the problem have been dissolved by the drawn out and bitter 1962/1963 campaigns.

7. The United States build-up was impressive. In late 1961 barely a thousand United States servicemen were stationed in South Vietnam. There are now about 15,000 in the country. These do not include combat troops but in practice American supporting units are frequently closely involved in actual operations.

8. The present strength of the South Vietnamese army is about 196,000. In addition there are para-military forces of about 200,000 mainly in the Civil Guard and Self Defence Corps. The rapid expansion of the Government forces has inevitably resulted in a number of weaknesses which have been aggravated by the recent coups and the consequent confusion and bewilderment thrown up by the fresh wave of changes in the High Command, corps and divisional commanders and provincial chiefs (who are also military sector commanders). Uncertainty about what is going on and fear of further changes and further dismissals have induced a form of paralysis and a reluctance to display initiative or to take offensive action.

The Military Situation

9. There is not much time left before the arrival of the south-west monsoon in May/June. The rains and the resultant flooding in the Delta area have generally had the effect of restricting the activities of the Security Forces and of the Viet Cong but in the mountains the Viet Cong are less affected than the Security Forces. The situation continues quietly to deteriorate. The capability of the Viet Cong is increasing. They are successfully penetrating more and more hamlets and villages and it is possible that they could now over-run some of the chief towns of districts (but not of provinces) before Government reinforcements could intervene. Prospects of any significant improvement in the military situation in the immediate future are not good. If some confidence in the military leadership can be restored, however, and if action can displace the current inaction, further deterioration could be checked. The Government will need to use the monsoon period to organise the administration, to bring continuity to senior military appointments, to perfect a comprehensive pacification plan (which we would expect to include a fresh approach to the strategic hamlets programme) and win popular support, if they are to be in a position at the beginning of the next dry season, October/November, to make positive progress. Pacification has always been a long-term project. Recent events have made it even longer.

TOP SECRET - U.K. EYES ONLY

PART I

THE CONSEQUENCES OF DEEPER UNITED STATES INVOLVEMENT IN VIETNAM ACTION CONFINED TO SOUTH VIETNAM

Types of Action
10. Possible forms of United States action confined to South Vietnam include the following:-
(a) maintenance of aid more or less at present levels but with increased pressure on the South Vietnamese to get on with the job themselves;
(b) stationing of United States forces in Saigon or other population centres;
(c) participation of United States combat forces in the fighting either independently or in support of South Vietnam forces;
(d) the transfer of offensive elements of the U.S.A.F. to bases in South Vietnam for combat missions against Viet Cong targets;
(e) implementation of SEATO plan 7 (counter-insurgency in Vietnam) thereby involving other SEATO countries in the fighting.

Effectiveness of such action and problems involved
11. Whatever the form of United States action and whatever the degree of South Vietnamese Government/United States military success against the Viet Cong thereby achieved, decisive and final defeat of the Viet Cong cannot be achieved by military means alone. The fundamental task remains that of inducing the South Vietnamese authorities to undertake and persist in a programme of the necessary administrative, social and economic measures, and to winning popular confidence in, and support for such a programme. If the South Vietnamese can be induced to go ahead on these lines there might then be a reasonable chance of ultimate success against the Viet Cong. In the meantime, however, in order to halt the present deterioration in the military situation and to give the South Vietnamese Government a breathing space to get new measures under way, there is clearly a requirement for some greater military effort mainly by the South Vietnamese forces but perhaps also by United States forces. We therefore examine the probable effectiveness of various forms of United States action under

the criterion of achieving a temporary stabilisation of the situation rather than of aiming at any more radical solution such as complete annihilation of the Viet Cong.

12. The problems facing the United States Forces brought into South Vietnam would vary in direct proportion to the scale of intervention. If it were limited to garrisoning key towns only, their difficulties would be localised and could be largely resolved with the assistance of the South Vietnamese administration. The arrival of United States forces for garrison duties could initially provide a substantial boost to the morale of the South Vietnamese Government forces. The long term value of this operation would depend largely on the effectiveness of the Government forces thus released for action against the Viet Cong. There would also be a risk that any improvement would eventually be counterbalanced by increased assistance to the Viet Cong by the North Vietnamese (see paragraph 19 below).

13. Limited operations in the interior with United States combat units, either initially or as a second step if the garrisoning of key towns did not produce adequate results, could also have a useful effect on the morale of Government forces and would be effective in rapid clearing of small selected areas. They would, however, involve formidable difficulties and inevitably the use of tough methods. The identification of friendly Vietnamese from the Viet Cong could only be resolved with the wholehearted co-operation of the South Vietnamese authorities and the setting up of a form of military control in the areas of operations. Appreciating this difficulty, the Viet Cong would probably rely entirely on guerilla [sic] tactics and, judging from British experience in Malaya, it would probably be necessary for United States and South Vietnamese forces to outnumber guerrillas [sic] many times over. There would be even greater risk of increased North Vietnamese support.

14. We believe that full-scale intervention, which would require 100,000 or more United States combat troops, would involve proportionately greater difficulties for the United States in South Vietnam. In addition to the military problems of setting up a major base area and communications zone, they would have to establish in effect a military government, with or without the co-operation of the civil power, and probably in the face of

increasing xenophobia on the part of the general population. They would have to induce the indigenous forces to accept a subordinate role in the prosecution of the war and in the maintenance of law and order throughout the country. In view of South Vietnam's limited road and rail communications, its difficult terrain and few tactically sited airfields, the supply problem would be complex and difficult. Air support would be essential for such operations to be effective and the congested state of the limited number of airfields indicate that some construction of new airfields would have to be undertaken. While the Viet Cong would certainly be held in check, the United States commitment could not be substantially reduced without leading to a resurgence of present problems, unless and until considerable progress had been made in establishing a desirable system of internal security which could be run by a non-communist South Vietnamese government. This would almost certainly take a very long time.

15. The likelihood of successful interdiction by conventional air attacks of the Viet Cong supply lines and bases is remote.

16. The SEATO Council resolved in March 1961 that it would not acquiesce in a communist takeover of Vietnam. The practical military aid which individual members of SEATO could give would depend on circumstances at the time but it seems unlikely that France and possibly Pakistan would wish to become involved. In any case the problems involved in intervention by SEATO forces would not be less than those described in paragraphs 11 to 15 above.

CONSEQUENCES

17. United States intervention by means of the introduction of garrison or combat troops would create a major international crisis. The communists would seek to secure condemnation of the United States action in the Security Council and the passage of resolutions calling for the immediate withdrawal of their forces. A full-scale propaganda campaign would probably be accompanied by threats of military counter-action. Communist propaganda, emphasising the reactionary nature of the Republican regime in South Vietnam, and the indigenous

nature of the revolutionary struggle and drawing a comparison between United States action in South Vietnam and their support for other "corrupt dictatorial" regimes (e.g. Korea, Formosa) might have some success in blurring the real issues involved, and would undoubtedly appeal to the anti-colonialist powers.

18. <u>Effects in Laos.</u> It is difficult to conceive that the situation in Laos would remain unchanged. If no settlement to the Laotian problems had been achieved, the North Vietnamese forces would probably make greater use of Laotian territory for infiltration in South Vietnam. This in turn might induce the United States to extend military operations to Southern Laos in order to prevent communist reinforcements from reaching South Vietnam. It would be in Souvanna Phouma's interest to isolate Laos from the struggle to the south east. It is doubtful, however, whether his weak administration would be able to stop a large increase in infiltration through Laotian territory. Again there would be grave danger of the Phoumi and Pathet Lao factions seizing the opportunity to extend the fighting in Laos.

North Vietnam

19. The first reaction of North Vietnam would be to increase her covert support to the Viet Cong. North Vietnam has already threatened, in a communication to the International Control Commission, to match United States intervention "man for man and gun for gun". She would also probably appeal to the Soviet Union and China for increased material support, and, depending on her immediate assessment of the scale of intervention, might feel bound to ask them to be ready to assist in the defence of North Vietnam. Doubtless the North Vietnamese would appreciate that open aggression across her southern frontier would invite a sharp reaction from the United States and very probably cause an increase in the scale of United States intervention. Since this would increase the danger of eventual United States incursion into North Vietnam, it is doubtful if the North Vietnamese would take such a step without first assuring herself of the full and active support of the Soviet Union or China. We believe that no such assurance would be given by the Soviet Union and that the Chinese would only give this support if it appeared to them that the United States intended invading North Vietnam. It seems

probable, therefore, that North Vietnamese reactions would be confined to covert support.

China

20. China's suspicions of United States intentions could lead her to believe that any large scale United States intervention in South Vietnam was a direct threat to North Vietnam and consequently to China's strategic interests. The Chinese would probably hesitate to become directly involved but, should the North Vietnamese have become openly engaged in South Vietnam, they would be reluctant to see her defeated.

China

21. Chinese reactions would depend on the type and success of United States intervention and on assessment of its aim. If the United States forces were to fail to achieve any substantial success against the Viet Cong at least outside the southern half of South Vietnam, there is no reason to suppose that the Chinese would do more than they have so far. They would use every bit of bluster and political pressure to hamper the United States effort and would give the North Vietnamese all the help in the way of equipment and advice that the North Vietnamese requested, in order to prevent the suppression of the insurgency and to keep the United States bogged down. It is doubtful whether the Chinese would feel compelled to intervene themselves, even to the extent of putting token forces into North Vietnam. They might concentrate forces on the border and set up some sort of joint military command, but in the last resort they would probably resign themselves to a temporary setback.

22. If on the other hand the United States appeared to be on the way to complete success and to establishing a strong military presence on the frontier of North Vietnam, it must be assumed that China would react more sharply. If they considered North Vietnam to be threatened, or if they believed, perhaps erroneously, that the United States had the intention of crossing the 17th Parallel or making some other incursion into North Vietnamese territory (for example air attack on tactical targets), there is little doubt that they would do their utmost to ensure the security of North Vietnam, even to the extent of sending their own forces in and of intervening in the fighting themselves. China could not afford to let the Americans have a completely unopposed

military success on her own doorstep and the possibility of the development of a Korean type war in Indo-China could not therefore be excluded.

The Soviet Union

24. United States intervention would place the Soviet Union in a dilemma, aggravated by her providing the Co-Chairman of the 1954 Geneva Conference. On the one hand, if the Russians failed to support the North Vietnamese, Chinese influence in Hanoi would inevitably become preponderant. On the other hand, they would certainly reject any policy which involved them in armed conflict with the United States in Indo-China. Above all, such a conflict would entail the risk of nuclear escalation. Soviet influence in Indo-China has since 1954 tended to be on the side of moderation and restraint. Indo-China is not of the first importance to Russia strategically, and although the Soviet Government have come out in support of the insurgency in South Vietnam as a "just" revolutionary struggle, we believe that the Soviet Union would wish to avoid actions by the communist powers which could invite an enlargement of the conflict. Their private advice would be in this vein but their public attitude would be to make the greatest possible fuss.

ACTION AGAINST NORTH VIETNAM

Types of Action

24. The type of action that the United States could carry out against North Vietnam could vary in extent from the relatively indirect measures of naval blockade and the support of South Vietnamese infiltration of North Vietnam to full-scale invasion with nuclear or conventional bombing. In the choice of the measures to be taken the ensurances of a speedy and effective result would be a major consideration. The possible forms of intervention considered are as follows:-

Indirect Support

(a) Support for the South Vietnamese in -
  (i) Ranger type operations;
  (ii) Covert support for insurgency in North Vietnam;
  (iii) Limited war operations across the 17th parallel;
(b) naval blockade of North Vietnam;
(c) support for Right wing and Neutralist forces in Laos

against the Pathet Lao and D.R.V. forces which could extend United States/Lao operations into North Vietnam.

Direct Support
(d) invasion of North Vietnam by United States and South Vietnamese forces from the air and sea;
(e) the bombing or bombardment of military targets and population centres in North Vietnam;
(f) the extension of bombing targets to include parts of Southern China.

Problems and Effectiveness of Type of Action
25. Indirect Support
(a) Ranger type operations. There is a lack of worthwhile targets for short penetration operations. Deeper penetration targets are likely to be more rewarding but introduce problems of supply and require a higher standard of training. No quick or decisive results could be expected by this method because South Vietnamese forces have shown little aptitude for this type of operation against the Viet Cong. There have been raids into communist territory since mid-1961. These have been conducted in secrecy so far as the South Vietnamese were concerned but trials of captured guerrillas by the North Vietnamese have been public. These operations appear to have had little success;
(b) Covert support for insurgency. There are large areas in the north west of North Vietnam where the mountain tribes are not subject to day-to-day government control and there are indications that resentment of government authority exists among these tribes. There is therefore some scope for the fostering of guerrilla activity in this area. The problems of covert supply would be difficult, but communications are such that these problems are probably surmountable. North Vietnam is at present going through political and economic crises and there is discontent among the Vietnamese peasants as well as among the tribes. Guerilla [sic] activity by the tribes could lead to localised disturbances and perhaps to revolts elsewhere in the countryside. As news of these reached South Vietnam, this could lower the morale of the Viet Cong and correspondingly raise that of the Government forces. It would obviously be essential if the risk of international repercussions were to be kept to a minimum, that the support operations should be so

conducted that the United States would be able to deny direct responsibility.

(c) <u>Limited war operations</u>. The South Vietnamese Army has now been trained in counter insurgency operations, it would therefore take some time to revive an effective force for limited war operations across the frontier; nor is the terrain south of the Red River delta suitable for operations by conventionally equipped forces.

(d) <u>Naval blockade</u>. It would be extremely difficult to make a naval blockade effective against coastal junk traffic within the Gulf of Tonking. Even a successful blockade would have but little effect on the jungle war.

(e) <u>Operations in Laos</u>. If the Viet Cong supply routes could be cut by military action in Laos some advantage would be obtained but only in the long term. Politically, this course would be most difficult because of the "neutralist solution" for Laos.

26. Direct Support

(a) <u>Invasion of North Vietnam</u>. Direct invasion would, by the diversion of North Vietnamese resources to meet it, be likely to have an immediate effect upon supply of personnel and arms to the Viet Cong, though this would not diminish the Viet Cong resistance for some time because they can live on their fat. The nearer the invasion point to the Hanoi-Haiphong (Red River delta) area the more decisive the result could be though equally, the sharper the reaction from North Vietnam and the Chinese. We consider that if invasion was undertaken in -

(i) the Dong Hoi area, an important centre controlling operations in South Vietnam and the supply route across the 17th parallel would be eliminated. Opposition would initially be confined to little more than one North Vietnamese Division. However, such an operation would not cut the supply line to the South through Laos nor bring a speedy <u>end to Viet Cong resistance;</u>

(ii) the Vinh area. The normal supply routes to South Vietnam across the 17th parallel and through Laos could be cut. Opposition would <u>initially be confined to one North Vietnamese Division</u> though reinforcements from the Delta <u>area could more easily be brought up. Direct</u> Chinese military support for the North Vietnamese would be probable;

(iii) the Red River delta area. This would strike directly at the heart of the country. The landing would quickly be opposed by about five divisions. An initial advantage might be obtained but direct Chinese military involvement would be certain which would lead to a long drawn out "Korean" type war.

(b) <u>Bombing of Viet Cong supply routes in North Vietnam</u>. Identification of targets on the Viet Cong supply routes would be so difficult as to make tactical interdiction ineffective and uneconomical.

(c) <u>Other air attacks</u>. Conventional bombing of population centres in North Vietnam or targets in South China although conceivably effective as punitive measures would not be decisive in bringing the Viet Cong under control. The use of nuclear weapons raises issues which go beyond the scope of this report.

CONSEQUENCES

<u>North Vietnam</u>
27. In the face of a threat of United States action against North Vietnam, or even in the initial stages of such action, the North Vietnamese would have to consider whether they were prepared to allow matters to go to the point where the devastation of North Vietnam might become inevitable. We cannot confidently predict the psychological attitude of the North Vietnamese leaders, but it may be an indication of the dependence of their attitude on the Chinese reaction that they have officially announced that if the United States intervene they will have to reckon with "China or eventually the Socialist camp as a whole."

<u>China</u>
28. (a) If the United States took military action against North Vietnam by means of air strikes; the Chinese would:-
  (i) say that the situation in South Vietnam was not the result of North Vietnamese or Chinese action; give North Vietnam maximum diplomatic and propaganda support and mount a worldwide campaign for the reconvening of the Geneva Conference in the interests of maintaining peace;
  (ii) provide what air cover they could for North Vietnam using their own planes and pilots, and

airfields in China if those in North Vietnam were untenable, and supplying A.A. artillery where necessary. The terms of the Geneva Agreement would make it difficult for them to maintain the fiction that the pilots were volunteers in the North Vietnamese air force or that the planes were North Vietnamese. Nevertheless they might be expected to adopt what devices were possible in order to maintain the fiction that China was not directly involved. They would do this partly for propaganda purposes, and partly to minimise the chances of United States retaliation against targets in China;

(iii) threaten to bomb similar targets in South Vietnam. An air defence system would need to be created to meet this threat.

(b) If the United States took military action against North Vietnam using ground forces; the Chinese would:-

(i) act as in sub-paragraph (a) (i) above;

(ii) take ground and air action as in the case of North Korea and occupy North Vietnam with regular Chinese units, which they would probably describe as volunteers for the reasons in (a) (ii). If once involved in such an operation their objective would probably be confined to the ejection of American forces from North Vietnam and the elimination of the threat they would represent to the Chinese frontier, although we would expect a very significant increase in Viet Cong activities as South Vietnamese and American forces were deployed to cover the Northern frontier. In the event of action by land against North Vietnam, in addition to sending units into North Vietnam, the Chinese might well give overt support to the Pathet Lao in Laos and step up their subversive efforts elsewhere in the area.

(c) If United States naval forces were used in air or other attacks against North Vietnam, the possibility of light coastal forces being used in North Vietnamese waters or their immediate vicinity cannot be excluded. As the Chinese would wish to localise the conflict to Indo-China they would not be used except in the Gulf of Tonking. If United States naval forces were used to blockade North Vietnam, it is unlikely that Chinese naval forces would intervene.

29. The Chinese actions would be dictated primarily

by the threat to South China that United States military action in Northern Indo-China would represent. In these circumstances, the Chinese would be unlikely to be influenced by Russian advice, or action unless the Russians were to take the two extreme steps, both equally unlikely, of –

(a) engaging themselves to give the Chinese full military support, and cover against the United States retaliation against the Chinese mainland;
or
(b) serving notice on the Chinese that if they did not avoid a clash and force the North Vietnamese to do so, they would cut off P.O.L. and other vital deliveries.

30. The possibility of war in the Far East inevitably represents some threat to Hong Kong but in all the circumstances described above the Chinese would wish to confine action to Indo-China and unless they became convinced that intervention in Vietnam would be quickly followed by general war, they would not take military or other decisive action against Hong Kong. They would, however, be likely to put some pressure on the Colony both in order to discourage the United Kingdom from supporting the Americans and to interest the United Kingdom in ending United States intervention.

The Soviet Union

31. Both as the major communist power and as a co-chairman of the Geneva Agreement the Soviet Union would be immediately involved. The Russians have already reacted to the press reports from the United States in a TASS statement issued on 25th February which says that "the Soviet people cannot remain indifferent to such developments (i.e. the extension by the United States of the war in South Vietnam) and will render the necessary assistance and support to this struggle" (i.e. the liberation struggle of the South Vietnamese). The attitude implied in this statement would not necessarily preclude the possibility that at the same time as warning off the United States the Soviet Union might urge caution on the North Vietnamese to avoid any action which might place the Soviet Union in an excessively awkward dilemma.

32. A United States threat of direct military action against North Vietnam would face the Russians with a decision which they have never been called upon to face before. If the Americans added a warning concerning

action against Chinese territory the Russian dilemma would be intensified. They would obviously wish to do their utmost to avoid getting involved militarily in a clash with the United States. At the very least such a clash would negate their present policy of trying to maintain reasonable relations with the United States. They would recognise that at the worst such a clash even in North Vietnam would risk escalation to nuclear war.

33. At the same time to counsel negotiation or "surrender" by North Vietnam would be to accept that the Americans could similarly threaten other states allied to the Soviet Union if they continue to support "national liberation movements". The possibility of some future action against Cuba would be obvious. Faced with this issue and with the possibility that the Chinese might support the North Vietnamese in defiance of the United States, it would be very difficult indeed for the Russians not to back the North Vietnamese at least in public. The first Soviet objective would therefore be to avoid the issue if at all possible by seeking to deter the United States from proceeding against North Vietnam by threat of incalculable consequences, and if this failed by mobilising international pressure against the United States. If the United States nevertheless persisted the Russians would probably supply the North Vietnamese with some arms and ammunition and might well reconsider the possibility of arms supply to China to the same end. In the last resort it seems likely that the Soviet Union would choose not to risk escalation of the conflict by direct military intervention and would probably maintain their attitude even in the face of United States air action against South China. Beyond this point it becomes increasingly hazardous to predict Soviet reactions.

International Reactions

34. Outside the communist world, the international reaction to overt United States action against North Vietnam would probably be to regard it as aggression. Although many Asian and African countries are increasingly suspicious of Chinese support for revolutionary and subversive movements, old habits die hard and their attitude for example, in the United Nations, towards United States action would certainly be hostile. France would certainly disapprove strongly, and we see little prospect of spontaneous positive support from any other

major country in the present state of opinion about South East Asian affairs; although the United States might persuade some of her allies to abstain. Therefore if the Soviet Union appealed to the United Nations, the United States might well have to resort to use of the veto in the Security Council on a motion of condemnation. The communist countries might be reluctant to appeal to the General Assembly because of their liability to loss of voting rights through being in arrears with their contributions. Nevertheless the United States would probably be unable to prevent an emergency session from passing a motion of condemnation. At the same time the North Vietnamese Government would probably appeal to the United Kingdom and the Soviet Union as Geneva co-chairman [sic] to call an international conference to discuss the problem, and to call on the United States to desist from further action in the meantime.

OTHER IMPLICATIONS

35. A limited non-nuclear war, whether confined to Vietnam or extended to other countries in South East Asia, would probably be protracted and indecisive. If it spread, there would be severe strains within SEATO, arising in particular from France's favouring a neutralist solution for South Vietnam, and possibly Pakistan's new attitude to China. With the United States preoccupied in Vietnam and United Kingdom and Commonwealth forces earmarked for possible action under existing commitments in mainland South East Asia, anti-Western elements elsewhere might exploit the opportunities so offered.

PART II

A UNITED STATES WITHDRAWAL FROM SOUTH VIETNAM

36. If the United States decided to withdraw from South Vietnam, and therefore a negotiated settlement had to be sought, the communists would be unlikely to agree to any arrangement potentially less damaging to the other side than that arrived at in Laos. There would thus be a very real prospect of South Vietnam eventually falling wholly or partially under communist control.

37. The loss to the West of South Vietnam would be a

major blow to the West in the world-wide struggle against communism. It would cause an immediate crisis of confidence in the relations of the United States with her Asian allies, some at least of whom might seek accommodation with China. The United States and SEATO would be discredited and the latter would probably disintegrate. Neutralist pressure would develop in Thailand, which the present right-wing regime would be unable to resist even if it managed to obtain a specific guarantee of United States protection. Non-communist neutrals would lose confidence in the West; Cambodia's traditional policy of neutrality might be maintained on paper, but in practice she would lean heavily towards China and Burma might well increase her efforts to stay on good terms with China. Indonesia and India might become even more suspicious of China's intentions than they are at present, but would be unlikely to make any radical changes in their foreign policy. Communist influence amongst the overseas Chinese communities in South East Asia would increase, and communist and pro-communist parties throughout the region would gain in confidence. The economic consequences for the West would probably be confined initially to losses of trade and investment in South Vietnam itself. The French have a particularly big stake which they might however be able to retain. The long term economic effects are difficult to predict but in our view would not necessarily be significant.

38. The general western position in South East Asia would be seriously damaged; the strategic position would be impaired directly by the increased subversive and military threat and indirectly through loss of political prestige. It is impossible, for example, to say whether Malaysia would lose confidence in the West as guarantors of her defence against the threat from China or decide that the increased threat to her safety required still closer ties.

CONCLUSIONS

39. We conclude that:-

PART I
(a) whatever the form of United States action and whatever the degree of South Vietnamese Government/United

States military success against the Viet Cong thereby achieved, decisive and final defeat of the Viet Cong cannot be achieved by military means alone. The fundamental task remains that of inducing the South Vietnamese authorities to undertake and persist in a programme of the necessary administrative, social and economic measures, and to winning popular confidence in, and support for such a programme;

(b) a heavier United States military commitment in South Vietnam in the form of the garrisoning of key towns and/or the introduction and use of combat units, might halt the present deterioration in the military situation and give the South Vietnamese Government a breathing space to get new measures under way, but it would raise difficult problems and might in the longer run be counter-productive;

(c) even full scale intervention would not lead to a lasting solution for a very long time, if at all;

(d) the cutting off of North Vietnamese assistance to the Viet Cong would not ensure a speedy end to the insurrection in South Vietnam;

(e) if the United States took military action confined to South Vietnam the North Vietnamese would probably increase their covert support to the Viet Cong and appeal to the Soviet Union and China for increased material support, the Chinese would give them full diplomatic and propaganda support and probably step up military supplies. The communist countries generally would probably mount a world-wide campaign, in particular demanding the reconvening of Geneva Conference in the interests of maintaining peace;

(f) there is some scope for covert support for guerilla [sic] activity among the tribes of north-west North Vietnam and this if successful could lead to localised disturbances and perhaps to revolts elsewhere in the countryside, the news of which could have some effect on Viet Cong morale, and encourage Government forces in South Vietnam;

(g) if the United States took military action against North Vietnam the Chinese would give direct military support, including "volunteers" and air cover to the North Vietnamese. They might give overt support to the Pathet Lao in Laos, and would step up their subversive effort elsewhere in the area. Unless they expected general war, they would not take military or other decisive action against Hong Kong;

(h) the first Soviet objective would be to avoid the issue if at all possible by seeking to deter the United States from action against North Vietnam. The Soviet Union might also put pressure on North Vietnam to make some temporary concessions, if they thought this would work. If the United States went ahead with action against North Vietnam the Soviet Union would probably supply the North Vietnamese with some arms and ammunition and might well reconsider the possibility of arms supply to China to the same end. Nevertheless the Russians would wish to keep their involvement to a minimum, and in any case would stop short of any action which might lead to their involvement in nuclear war;

(i) it would be difficult for the United States to obtain much support internationally for direct military action against North Vietnam, or to avoid condemnation in the United Nations;

(j) a limited non-nuclear war in Vietnam would probably be protracted and indecisive; it would not spread outside mainland South East Asia and it could lead to severe strains within SEATO;

PART II

(k) if, as the eventual result of United States withdrawal, South Vietnam were to fall under complete or partial communist control, the West would suffer a severe blow in the context of the world-wide struggle against communism; the United States and SEATO would be discredited and the latter would probably disintegrate; communist influence in South East Asia would increase; and the whole Western position in the area would be seriously damaged.

Notes

1. Percy Cradock, *Know Your Enemy: How the Joint Intelligence Committee Saw the World* (London: John Murray, 2002), pp. 192–3.
2. J. W. Young, 'Britain and "LBJ's War", 1964–68', *Cold War History* 2/3 (2002), p. 65; Rhiannon Vickers, 'Harold Wilson, the British Labour Party, and the War in Vietnam', *Journal of Cold War Studies* 10/2 (2008), p. 44; Peter Busch, 'Supporting the War: Britain's Decision to Send the Thompson Mission to Vietnam, 1960–61', *Cold War History* 2/1 (2001), pp. 69–94.
3. Nigel Ashton, 'Harold Macmillan and the "Golden Days" of Anglo-American Relations Revisited, 1957–63', *Diplomatic History* 29/4 (2005), p. 709, fn. 54.

4. Mark Curtis, *Unpeople: Britain's Secret Human Rights Abuses* (London: Vintage, 2004), p. 205.
5. Cradock, *Know Your Enemy*, p. 197.
6. Ibid., p. 198; 'Vietnam Background', FO draft 13 June 1962, FO 371/166705, quoted in Curtis, *Unpeople*, p. 202.
7. Vickers, 'Harold Wilson, the British Labour Party, and the War in Vietnam', p. 45.
8. Peter Busch, *All the Way with JFK? Britain, the US, and the Vietnam War* (Oxford: Oxford University Press, 2003), pp. 188–92.
9. See Cradock, *Know Your Enemy*, p. 199.
10. Curtis, *Unpeople*, p. 205.
11. Rab Butler, May 1964, quoted in Stephen Dorril, *MI6: 50 Years of Special Operations* (London: Fourth Estate, 2000), p. 716.
12. Vickers, 'Harold Wilson, the British Labour Party, and the War in Vietnam', p. 44; Cradock, *Know Your Enemy*, p. 196; Ashton, 'Harold Macmillan and the "Golden Days" of Anglo-American Relations Revisited', pp. 691, 694.
13. State Department to Saigon, 9 September 1964, File POL 27-14, Box 2922, CFPF, RG 59, NARA. John Colvin, *Twice Around the World* (London: Leo Cooper, 1991), pp. 96–117.

14

THE SOVIET INVASION OF CZECHOSLOVAKIA, 1968

NINETEEN SIXTY-EIGHT WAS a significant year in the history of the JIC. The committee was split into two: JIC(A) and JIC(B). A continuation of the traditional body, the former remained concerned with political, military and defence intelligence. The latter assessed economic, commercial and non-military scientific intelligence. It proved to be a short-lived experiment, however, and the JIC was reunited in 1974. The year 1968 also saw a strengthening of the report-drafting process. A new Assessments Staff was created inside the Cabinet Office to replace the long-serving Joint Intelligence Staff. More independent than its predecessor, the Assessments Staff brought together around twenty members from different departments across Whitehall. Its chief became an influential position in its own right, whilst other members chaired the JIC's Current Intelligence Groups. Finally, a new Intelligence Co-ordinator was appointed in 1968 to oversee the central intelligence process and machinery. The post was initially filled by Dick White, formerly head of both MI5 and MI6.[1]

Events during the summer of 1968 seriously tested the new system. On 20 August, Warsaw Pact forces, led by the Russians, invaded Czechoslovakia in an attempt to counter reformist trends developing in Prague. Since its incorporation into the Soviet bloc via a communist coup in 1948, Czechoslovakia had caused few concerns for the leadership in Moscow. That changed, however, when Alexander Dubček became head of the Czechoslovakian Communist Party in January 1968. Despite claiming to work within the ideological boundaries of Marxism-Leninism, Dubček began to introduce liberal reforms. For example, he made widespread personnel changes inside the party, eased censorship to allow more open debate about government policy, and even talked about opening the economy to the world market. Recalling the ill-fated Hungarian uprising of 1956, anxious about losing influence in Prague, and fearing the spread of liberalisation across eastern Europe, Moscow grew increasingly concerned. Although the leadership was divided and Leonid Brezhnev wavered, the Soviets decided to intervene militarily. It is unclear exactly when this decision was taken, but Kremlin hawks were pressing for military action as early as April

1968.² The operation was a military success. Czechoslovakian forces did not resist and the Warsaw Pact troops swiftly occupied Prague. Although the invasion proved more problematic politically, Dubček was ultimately replaced by a more amenable candidate the following year. As Percy Cradock, a former JIC Chairman and Chief of the Assessments Staff, put it, '"socialism with a human face" was effectively snuffed out'.³

The JIC failed to provide warning. Despite monitoring Soviet military exercises near the Czechoslovakian borders in the months before August, the committee endorsed the Foreign Office view that an invasion was unlikely. Policymakers were therefore taken by surprise – although the more senior amongst them had previously acknowledged that should the JIC be wrong Western reprisals would have been impractical anyway.⁴ Despite being caught off guard, Cabinet members insisted to each other that 'we had been aware that forces were being concentrated on the borders of Czechoslovakia and were not therefore taken by surprise'.⁵ The first half of this statement is true; the second is not.

The JIC struggled to believe that the Soviets would find the use of force politically acceptable. Guilty of mirror-imaging, in transferring British values and constraints onto Soviet thinking, the committee overestimated the value placed by Moscow on world opinion. This view was strongly held by the JIC Chairman, Denis Greenhill, underlining the important role that a consumer department can sometimes play in shaping assessments. An in-house post-mortem of JIC intelligence failures conducted in 1981 concluded that 'in March to August 1968 the JIC consistently took the view that the USSR was unlikely to invade Czechoslovakia because of the effect a move would have on world opinion (not least in the world communist movement) and on détente'.⁶

This was not the only cognitive error of which the JIC was found guilty. Committee members decided 'very early' on that the Soviets would not invade Czechoslovakia. Remaining committed to that view, the JIC refused to alter this assessment despite growing evidence to the contrary in the form of military manoeuvres. Warnings that Russia would be prepared to 'flout world opinion', such as that given by the British ambassador in Moscow, were overlooked in favour of the prevailing mindset. As a result, the JIC's Current Intelligence Group prepared a draft note for the Top Secret Red Book in late July, which suggested that the Soviet leaders would try to avoid military intervention if they could. Policymakers in the Foreign Office generally agreed that the Russian leaders would seek instead to increase pressure on the Czechs. The JIC therefore dismissed Soviet preparations as mere military exercises and bullying. This psychological flaw is known as 'perseveration', or belief in the virtue of consistency.⁷

The aftermath of the invasion raised serious questions for policymakers in the United Kingdom (and for NATO more broadly). It is some of these which are assessed in the document reproduced here. What impact did the surprise have on existing warning procedures? Where did the invasion leave East–West relations? In which other territories might the Soviet Union attempt something similar? How tight was the Soviet grip on eastern Europe? The JIC sought to consider the importance of eastern Europe to the Soviet Union economically, politically and militarily, and how Moscow would maintain control in the future. The paper was disseminated in early December 1968, just over three months after the invasion of Czechoslovakia.

A first point of note arising from the report was that the JIC had learnt the dangers of mirror-imaging the hard way. Now under a new Chairman, the diplomat Edward Peck, the assessment clearly stated that 'developments in Eastern Europe might make [Moscow] feel obliged to use force there again, even at the risk of provoking a reaction from NATO countries'.[8] The committee did not want to make the same mistake twice.

Secondly, despite acknowledging that the Soviet grip on eastern Europe had tightened, the JIC's conclusions were generally calm, prudent and non-inflammatory. The committee reassured policymakers that the invasion was a defensive action inside Warsaw Pact territory.[9] It did not render the Soviet Union any more likely to use force in a more volatile area of East–West confrontation, such as the Middle East. Moreover, there was no reason to believe that the strategic balance between East and West had changed. The JIC continued to espouse optimism. Despite acknowledging that he could be replaced by a more pliable leader, intelligence suggested that Dubček would implement only the minimum of Soviet requirements. As explained in detail in the document, the JIC also predicted that various internal forces, from nationalism to economics, would continue to put pressure on the Soviet Union. In short, policymakers had no cause for alarm. Echoing the Foreign Office's Northern Department, the JIC optimistically assessed that some reformist elements established under Dubček, especially in the economic sphere, would continue owing to weaknesses amongst the hardliners.[10] By March 1969, however, Dubček had been replaced by a hardliner – Gustáv Husák. The new pro-Soviet regime lasted until the Velvet Revolution of November 1989.[11]

The one area of uncertainty lay in Soviet attitudes to Romania and Yugoslavia. Bucharest and Belgrade had vigorously condemned the invasion of Czechoslovakia in August. If the same thing had happened in one of these other 'dissident' states, the leaders might have resisted, thereby causing serious conflict. Indeed, both strengthened their self-defence accordingly.[12] The JIC acknowledged that the events in Prague created uncertainty about the Soviet attitude towards the use of force – although Whitehall had learnt that fear of international condemnation would not serve as a deterrent. Possible action against Romania prompted a war scare during August 1969, triggering partial mobilisation.[13]

Nevertheless, during 1968, the JIC remained calm and senior British policymakers did not treat the events in Prague as a crisis. They received little Cabinet attention and had limited impact on Britain's trade and defence policies. Harold Wilson, the Prime Minister, remained focused on Soviet trade prospects and sought to return to business as usual, once the furore over the invasion had died down. The government refused to reverse cuts in military expenditure and opposed economic sanctions against the aggressor countries.[14] Three days after the JIC assessment was disseminated, and upon receiving a provocative note from the Soviets about the British response to Czechoslovakia, Wilson's Cabinet agreed that 'Britain should not over-react, and should maintain correct relations without indulging in petty pinpricks'.[15]

```
JIC (68) 54 (Final)

2nd December 1968
```

THE SOVIET GRIP ON EASTERN EUROPE

Report by the Joint Intelligence Committee (A)

SUMMARY AND CONCLUSIONS

1. The aim of the paper is to assess the importance to the Soviet Union of Eastern Europe, and the ways in which the Soviet government will seek to maintain its grip in the foreseeable future. The paper deals with the political, military and economic requirements of the Soviet Union in Eastern Europe and the implications of likely Soviet policies for the countries in the area, and for East-West relations. Likely trends are assessed against the background of the Soviet invasion of Czechoslovakia.

2. Since the end of the Second World War, successive Soviet governments have imposed political, military and economic requirements on the East European governments. Political requirements have included a monopoly of power for the Communist Party, and absolute obedience to the Soviet Union in all matters of substance. Military requirements have involved making the national territory of each country available to the Soviet Union when needed; accepting Soviet assessments in military affairs and Soviet domination of the country's armed forces and defence policy; and where necessary the stationing of Soviet forces on its territory. The threat of military force has always been implicit behind Soviet demands, and has been a significant factor in gaining their acceptance. Economic requirements have meant collaborating with the Soviet Union and other East European

countries in the work of the Council for Mutual Economic Aid (CMEA), and running the economy of each country in accordance with Communist practice in the Soviet Union. At the same time, the national interests of the countries of Eastern Europe often conflicted with Soviet requirements, and Soviet policy towards the countries of the area was never consistent or carefully planned.

3. However, in Soviet eyes, the most important of these requirements were called into question by the Czechoslovak reform programme and the results of the liberalising trends which stemmed from the election of the Dubcek leadership in January 1968. The official reform programme, which advocated separation of Party and government functions and an apparent withdrawal of Party control over aspects of security policy and the armed forces, as well as the end of censorship was regarded in Moscow as prejudicial to the maintenance of the leading role of the Communist Party in the country. The replacement of tried and experienced political, military and security officials by the Dubcek regime may have worried a Soviet leadership which traditionally laid great stress on the selection of key personnel in East European countries. The end of censorship and the licence to criticise Party thinking and to explore liberal ideas was regarded as dangerously "infectious" throughout the area and even in the Soviet Union itself. The Soviet military leaders probably feared that a serious gap in the Warsaw Pact defence structure might develop either by the defection of Czechoslovakia from the Pact, or through a decline in the efficiency of her armed forces. In economic affairs the Russians feared that the more radical economic ideas on the need for greater economic freedom and closer contacts with the West could have led to a weakening of the Party's power in economic matters and a growth of Western, especially West German, influence, with a corresponding loosening of Czechoslovak ties with their communist allies.

4. The Soviet military occupation of Czechoslovakia effectively destroyed the possibility, never very strong, that the present Soviet leader would tolerate the loss of orthodox communist party control in an active member of the Warsaw Pact. The effect of the invasion in Eastern Europe will, in the short term, be to strengthen the influence of the countries and personalities most loyal

to the Soviet Union, and to induce fear of Soviet military might and Soviet readiness to use it against actual or potential dissidents in the area of the Warsaw Pact. In the longer term, the invasion may strengthen currents of unrest in Eastern Europe which could cause concern to the East European governments. Thus, one important effect may be to focus Soviet attention inwards on to the problems of Eastern and Soviet relations with the countries of the area; for the Russians will be anxious to ensure that any future moves for change, e.g. economic reforms, do not develop in the kind of political atmosphere which appeared in Czechoslovakia in the first part of 1968.

5. In the short term, at least, the outlook for Czechoslovakia is bleak. A Soviet military presence in the shape of a group of Soviet forces will continue for some time, and Soviet forces will always be available in neighbouring countries to intervene again if necessary. The Dubcek regime will try to cushion the Czechoslovak people against the worst effects of the Soviet intervention, but what appears to be the gradual erosion of the regime's freedom of manoeuvre by Soviet policy may ultimately lessen and perhaps destroy the popularity which the leadership has so far enjoyed with the Czechoslovak people. However, some elements of the Dubcek reform programme, notably the economic proposals and the establishment of a federal structure for the State, will continue, and the fact that the Soviet Union agreed to the return to power of the legitimate government of the country under the Moscow protocol of 27th August suggests that the Russians still want to work within the terms of this arrangement.

6. The present leaders of East Germany, Poland and Bulgaria will be relieved that the danger of "infection" to their countries has been eliminated, at least temporarily, and their loyalty to the Soviet Union will have been strengthened. In Hungary, where much sympathy for the Czechoslovak reforms existed, the intervention was undoubtedly a personal blow to Kadar, who will probably have to proceed more cautiously. The Rumanians, while maintaining their criticism of the Soviet action, will aim at preserving the essence of their independent stand: their economic freedom of action and their independent foreign policy, on both of which the Rumanian

leaders' nationalist policy largely depends, at the expense, if necessary, of political gestures on international issues where Rumanian interests are not directly concerned. But Soviet economic and political pressures will continue with the long-term intention of subverting the present Rumanian leadership. Yugoslavia will continue her opposition to Soviet policy in Czechoslovakia; she is alarmed by recent Soviet talk of the overriding interests of the "Socialist Commonwealth" and the potential effect on national sovereignty. A prolonged period of cool relations with the Soviet Union is likely.

7. Militarily, the Czechoslovak occupation has eliminated the Soviet fear that the Czechoslovaks might defect from the Warsaw Pact. Thus the situation in which Czechoslovakia is regarded, in Soviet eyes, as a buffer zone between the West and the Soviet frontier, has been restored. However, the effective loss of the Czechoslovak armed forces in the potential offensive role means that Soviet operational plans will have to be re-assessed and their own military commitments extended. In addition, events leading up to the Soviet intervention in Czechoslovakia will make future proposed Warsaw Pact exercises extremely delicate political issues and may complicate, at least in the short term, plans for improving the structure of the alliance. The Soviet Union may aim to achieve even tighter control over the East European armies.

8. In the economic field, the occupation has restricted potential Czechoslovak moves towards closer economic and technical co-operation with West Germany and the West in general, but it has not altered the basic economic problems of Czechoslovakia or Eastern Europe, which remains dependent on the Soviet Union, particularly for supplies of raw materials (crude oil and iron) and also in some cases grain and electrical energy. The possibilities for strengthening CMEA may even have been improved in the post-invasion circumstances, for the Soviet Union will be anxious to correct CMEA's shortcomings, if only as a counterbalance to the political and military effects of the invasion, and a number of East European proposals are in existence which might be taken up at future meetings of the Council. There is also the continuing attraction for the East European countries of economic links with the West, and this is a trend of which the Soviet Union

will have to take account. Much depends therefore on the Soviet Union, but its leaders may decide in the longer term to take more account of national economic ambitions and existing economic differences between the members of CMEA.

9. The implications for East-West relations involve a set-back to hopes of the growth of a more liberal Eastern Europe which could play an important part in bringing about a comprehensive European settlement. While the evidence suggests that the Soviet action in Czechoslovakia was essentially to preserve an orthodox Communist regime, it has introduced new uncertainties about Soviet actions and the situations in which the Russians may be prepared to use armed force. It seems unlikely that because the Soviet Union used force in Czechoslovakia she will be more willing to do so henceforth in order to extend her influence in the Mediterranean or the Middle East. However developments in Eastern Europe might make her feel obliged to use force there again even at the risk of provoking a reaction from NATO countries. We believe that the strategic balance between the super-powers will not be affected, and Soviet-American contacts on political and defence matters will continue. Indeed, the Soviet Union has an interest in restoring a "business as usual" relation with the West, and is anxious that its actions in the Warsaw Pact area should not affect East-West relations elsewhere.

10. We therefore conclude:

(a) The Soviet Union has shown that it will use its armed forces within Eastern Europe to preserve a Communist regime which they consider vital to basic Soviet political, military and economic interests. Both the West and Eastern Europe must assume that Soviet readiness to use force for these purposes in the Warsaw Pact area will remain valid for the foreseeable future.

(b) The Soviet action in Czechoslovakia was, however, a defensive one inside the area covered by the Warsaw Pact. It has probably succeeded in removing both a political and a potentially serious military weakness in the central sector of the Pact's area of responsibility. We do not believe that because the Soviet Union used force in Czechoslovakia she will be more willing to use it in areas of East-West confrontation, such as the Mediterranean or the Middle East. But the Russians could use force again in Eastern Europe even if this provoked a reaction from NATO countries, and many areas of uncertainty in the Soviet attitude towards the use of force have emerged from this crisis. However, there is no reason to believe that the strategic balance between the East and the West has changed.

(c) In the short term, the Soviet grip on Eastern Europe has been tightened by the demonstration that Soviet leaders are prepared to use military force where their interests are threatened with erosion. This demonstration will be a discouragement to liberal movements inside and outside the ruling East European Communist Parties. It has buttressed the Old Guard regimes at the expense of widening the gap between the Party leaderships and the public, especially in Poland. In Hungary, Kadar's policy of reform and national reconciliation has been seriously threatened, and Rumania's freedom of manoeuvre has been limited by her need to emphasise her solidarity with the Warsaw Pact.

(d) In Czechoslovakia, the Soviet Union will seek to use its position of strength to reimpose acceptance of the full range of Soviet requirements by the Dubcek regime. The latter will try to fulfil the minimum Soviet demands while protecting the population from the full rigours of direct Soviet rule - although it may lose some of its popularity with the people in the process. But it must be recognised that the Soviet Union has the power to remove Dubcek at any time, and to replace him and his colleagues by more pliable leaders.

(e) The Soviet grip on Eastern Europe is so important to the Russians that it is unrealistic to expect major changes in Eastern Europe except in the context of some significant change in Soviet attitudes. There may be some spontaneous evolution in the Soviet Union and, in the longer run, pressures from Eastern Europe will begin to have an effect on the Soviet Union. Nationalism will be an increasingly powerful force. Among the young people of Eastern Europe a process of growing resentment against the existing order may appear which may ultimately be expressed by methods of protest already used by the younger generation in the West. Economic pressures, which in Czechoslovakia opened the way to the political and social reform movement, will continue to be exerted on Communist leaderships in the direction of greater efficiency, more freedom of action and individual responsibility including increased trade and contacts with the West. There will, therefore, be continuing pressure in Eastern Europe towards both economic and political liberalisation with which the Soviet Union will be confronted, and these pressures may in the long run find outlets which the Soviet Union will no longer use force to block.

(Signed) EDWARD PECK

Chairman, on behalf of the
Joint Intelligence Committee
(A)

Cabinet Office, S.W.1.

2nd December 1968

Annex to JIC(68) 54 (Final)

THE SOVIET GRIP ON EASTERN EUROPE

INTRODUCTION

1. The aim of the paper is to assess the importance to the Soviet Union of Eastern Europe, and the ways in which the Soviet Government will seek to maintain its grip in the relatively short term. The paper deals with the political, military and economic requirements of the Soviet Union in Eastern Europe, factors influencing their fulfilment and the implications of likely Soviet policies for the countries in the area and for East-West relations. Likely trends are assessed against the background of the Soviet invasion of Czechoslovakia.

GENERAL FACTORS

The Background to Soviet Policy in Eastern Europe
2. Since the end of the Second World War, when the Soviet Union came into military possession of Eastern Europe, successive Soviet governments have established a number of requirements in Eastern Europe corresponding to the

political, military and economic policies of the Soviet Union of the time. Each Soviet Government chose its requirements within the framework of the Soviet Union's right to "super-power" status, and of the ever present Soviet claim that Eastern Europe should be acknowledged as the Soviet Union's main "sphere of interest" - rather as the "Monroe Doctrine" has been applied by the United States in relation to the New World.

3. After eight years of Stalin's rule of Eastern Europe as an extension of the Soviet Union, with its emphasis on police methods and economic exploitation, Khrushchev spent much time and energy attempting to "rationalise" Soviet political domination of the area. By relaxing Stalinist rule, reorganising the military forces of the East European countries within a multi-national alliance, and by encouraging each state to remove the worst features of Stalin's economic system, Khrushchev appeared to be searching for a workable relationship between the Soviet Union and Eastern Europe which would guarantee absolute political loyalty to the Soviet Union without the need to hold down the area by brute force. Like Stalin's before it, however, the Khrushchev leadership had its failures, and in 1956 resorted to military invasion to keep Communism in power in Hungary.

Soviet Requirements in Eastern Europe under Brezhnev and Kosygin

4. Brezhnev and Kosygin and the collective leadership which they head have presided over some important changes in Soviet policy, including the development of capabilities aimed at effecting a Soviet presence overseas, but in East European affairs their approach appeared to differ little at first from that formulated by Khrushchev. Brezhnev and Kosygin began by accepting the East European leaderships inherited from Khrushchev, even though one of them, the Rumanian, was showing signs of deviation along nationalist lines in foreign and economic policy. As time went on, the Soviet leadership somewhat hardened its ideological line in Eastern Europe. Dismay at the decline of Communism as a doctrinal inspiration both inside the East European Parties and in the Parties of Western Europe became a feature of the Soviet outlook. Moreover, the increasing outspokenness of East European and Soviet intellectuals and the ideological apathy prevalent in West European Communist

Parties led the Soviet leaders to seek ways of injecting new life into the movement as a whole – a trend reflected in the Karlovy Vary conference of Communist Parties in 1967 and the theses prepared for the 50th anniversary of the Russian Revolution in November 1967.

5. Whatever the motives for this new emphasis on ideology, its relevance to Soviet requirements in Eastern Europe is undeniable, for it buttressed the Soviet Union's political needs. These requirements represent the Soviet view of their vital interests in Eastern Europe, and may be summarised as the retention in power in each East European country of a loyal Communist Party which should:

(a) exercise absolute control of all political power in the country, and, in conjunction with Soviet experts, dominate all security and intelligence activity;

(b) entrust all key Party and government posts to Party members enjoying the confidence of the Soviet Union;

(c) control education, the press, radio and television;

(d) maintain well-trained national armed forces of unquestioning loyalty to the Soviet Union, and accede to all Soviet requests for the use of national territory and resources for Soviet or Warsaw Pact military purposes, accepting, at all levels, Soviet military appreciations of Western intentions and Warsaw Pact capabilities;

(e) maintain an efficiently-run economy and external trade policy capable of supporting a rising standard of living, subject always to using methods in conformity with Soviet practice and interests; co-operate with the Soviet-sponsored Council for Mutual Economic Aid (CMEA);

(f) support the general line of Soviet foreign policy, particularly with reference to the German question, nuclear policy, and assistance to established Communist states involved in hostilities, e.g. North Vietnam;

(g) support the Soviet Union's position in intra-Bloc disputes;

(h) keep current trends towards intellectual freedom within bounds, retaining censorship to prevent the dissemination of non-Communist and "anti-Soviet" views.

6. The Soviet view of its military requirements in Eastern Europe is primarily concerned with the security of the Soviet Union's open Western frontier, but is also concerned with the deployment of Soviet forces in Europe in the most advantageous position to fight a European

campaign should hostilities break out. The Soviet Union requires in essence that the East European governments should do everything in their power to support the Soviet forces, and actively assist them in achieving their peacetime and wartime aims which may, in greater detail, be listed as follows:

(a) in peacetime:
   (i) to maintain the political status quo in Eastern Europe, providing a buffer zone between NATO and the Soviet Union.
   (ii) to continue the division of Germany on a permanent basis in order to safeguard the Soviet Union against the consequences of a re-emergence of German military power.
   (iii) to command and control the Warsaw Pact forces, and direct the co-ordination of their training and equipment.
   (iv) to control the air defence of the area.

(b) in wartime:
   (i) to defend the territory of the Soviet Union by ensuring that ground and air operations are conducted as far to the West as possible.
   (ii) to destroy NATO forces and occupy NATO territory.
   (iii) to protect Eastern Europe and the Soviet Union from air attack.

Complicating Factors in Soviet Policy towards Eastern Europe

7. Before the introduction of the Czechoslovak reform programme, most of the East European governments were by and large fulfilling these requirements. But the process was greatly complicated by pressures arising from the special interests and requirements of the East European countries, and their bilateral relations with the Soviet Union and with each other. The Russians did not consistently treat them all in the same way. Soviet objectives in Eastern Europe were also variable, as were the tactics they pursued: for example, there were periods when deviation from standard Soviet practice in individual East European countries led to harsh Soviet reactions, while on other occasions the Soviet leaders seemed to be prepared to acquiesce in nationalist or even liberal manifestations in certain countries, mainly in economic affairs.

8. The German problem is at the heart of Soviet policy towards Eastern Europe. It is a cardinal point of Soviet policy that the German population in Central Europe should remain divided, and the Russians therefore promote the claim of the East German regime to be a second German State. The continued existence of West Berlin as an outpost of the West under allied occupation is a source of strain between the Russians and the East Germans, who sometimes appear to be trying to manoeuvre the Russians into policies designed to make the Western position in the city untenable. The Russians are generally prepared to permit the East Germans to engage in minor harassment, and on occasion have themselves taken part in such activities. But although the Russians have in the past undertaken more serious measures against West Berlin and the access routes, there have been no recent signs that they want a major crisis over Berlin or a confrontation with the allies over allied rights in the city.

9. The Poles and the Czechoslovaks have deep and persistent fears of German militarism which created a genuine interest in the protective shield of the Warsaw Pact. But fear of German power has not been felt to the same extent in Hungary, Rumania and Bulgaria, and even in countries where such memories were bitter, the anti-German bogey has been used so intensively and indiscriminately in Soviet propaganda that some of its credibility may have been wearing thin - especially with the younger generation. This diminishing credibility may have added to the doubts which always existed about the degree to which the Soviet Union really feared a West Germany which had no access to nuclear weapons, was a full member of the NATO alliance, and had accepted the same limitations on its military policy as all the other members of the alliance.

10. Contradictions and uncertainties in Soviet policy in Eastern Europe also arose as a result of Rumania's successful defiance of Soviet rulings on relations with West Germany and Israel, on military liabilities under the Warsaw Pact, as well as on obligations towards CMEA. While Soviet relations with Poland, Hungary, Czechoslovakia and Bulgaria were more stable, there were in each case specific issues on which the Soviet leaders were obliged to pay attention to national peculiarities and interests which worked against a uniform application

of Soviet requirements in Eastern Europe. Some of these individual peculiarities were associated with potential struggles for power and succession problems in the leaderships of the Communist Parties, and others with the varying degrees and types of pressures brought to bear on these leaderships by their populations. In all these factors the force of nationalism in East European countries has played an important role.

11. Economic problems also brought their contradictions to the ruling Parties' attempts to fulfil Soviet requirements. Soviet insistence on the primacy of Soviet economic interests and models clashed to some extent with the kinds of economic reform which most of the East European countries realised were necessary, both for internal economic progress and for external trade. The lack of any authority in CMEA to enforce its decisions on member countries has enabled the Soviet Union - as the dominant partner - to derive maximum benefit from the organisation, particularly in the sphere of foreign trade. Apart from Rumania, whose dispute with CMEA was on important issues of principle, none of the other East European countries has sought - or indeed was in a position - to abandon CMEA or disrupt its arrangements. Their efforts were directed rather towards improving the existing machinery. Amongst the proposals put forward were more rational specialisation of production, improvement of foreign trade pricing and the system of payments settlement through some form of rouble convertibility, and a general tightening up of discipline with regard to intra-CMEA commitments and obligations.

12. Military requirements were of vital importance to the Soviet Union, but evidence of the period before the Czechoslovak crisis suggests that contradictions similar to those in the political and economic fields were less obvious. With the exception again of Rumania, which had no frontier with a NATO country, all the active members of the Warsaw Pact appeared to be fulfilling Soviet military requirements, and Soviet satisfaction with the military scene may be deduced from the fact that the last significant change in the number of Soviet forces in the area took place in 1958.

The Soviet View of the Czechoslovakia Reform Programme

13. The Czechoslovak liberalisation programme and the political, military and economic developments in the

country which stemmed from it can be summarised under three main headings:
(a) official acts of political, economic and social reform;
(b) personnel changes at the highest level in the Party, the government and the armed forces;
(c) semi-official and unofficial activity by liberal elements anxious to quicken the pace of reform in the country.

14. There seems little doubt that the Soviet leaders believed that elements of this programme threatened the monopoly of decision-making of the Czechoslovak Communist Party, and exposed a lack of will-power on the part of the Dubcek leadership to maintain orthodox Party rule in the country. The Russians' decision to go ahead with the military occupation of the country may have been directly connected with Soviet interpretations of Dubcek's intention to reorganise the whole structure of the Czechoslovak Communist Party at the September Party Congress, and the probability that this Congress would elect a liberalising Central Committee of the Party which would be its constitutional authority for at least two or three years. The Russians appeared to believe in any case, that the atmosphere in which the Dubcek reforms were being debated and put into effect (including the relaxation of censorship) was contributing to loss of control over the country by the Party, and made reforms which could be tolerated under Kadar's more orthodox and cautious leadership in Hungary, for example, difficult to support in Dubcek's Czechoslovakia. Some of Dubcek's actions may have suggested to the Russians that if they were carried to what the Soviet leaders saw as their logical conclusion, Czechoslovakia would cease to be a member of the Soviet bloc, cease to adhere to the basic tenets of Marxism-Leninism as interpreted in the Soviet Union, and would be either unable or unwilling to meet the full range of Soviet military requirements. In this connection, it is important to recognise that Soviet actions were as frequently based on their leaders' interpretation of the possible consequences of Dubcek's methods and intentions as with actual measures which his regime had put into effect.

The Future of Soviet Policy towards Eastern Europe

15. There is no doubt that the Soviet Union regards Eastern Europe as of vital importance to her and that

she will seek to maintain her grip there. As they look ahead and consider the growth of Chinese power, the Russians will see no reason to alter this assessment. The Soviet Union's future policy towards Eastern Europe in the light of the occupation of Czechoslovakia, both in the short and the longer term may conveniently be grouped under three headings: political, military and economic.

THE POLITICAL OUTLOOK

The Soviet Union

16. The most immediate effect of the Soviet invasion of Czechoslovakia was the removal of all doubts that the Soviet Union was and will be prepared to use its military forces to uphold its political and military requirements within the area covered by the Warsaw Pact. Despite a brave and ingenious display of non-military resistance by the Czechs and Slovaks, the Soviet military moves were swift and efficient, and put the Soviet government in a position from which it could exercise a decisive influence on events in Czechoslovakia.

17. One of the important factors in assessing the future course of events in Eastern Europe is the effect which the resort to force in Czechoslovakia will have on the Soviet leadership itself. It is impossible to tell whether or not the Soviet Politburo was divided on the issue, or if it was, which members of the leadership supported military action and which opposed it. While military factors described below in para. 45 ff. must have weighed heavily with the leadership, there is no evidence that the Politburo came under strong pressure from the Soviet military to intervene. We are inclined to the view that as the crisis developed and in Soviet eyes came increasingly to endanger the continuation of orthodox Communist rule in Czechoslovakia and of Soviet security arrangements in Eastern Europe, the Politburo probably closed ranks, and achieved unanimity at the moment of decision-making. Any divisions of opinion and hesitations within the Politburo were probably not over the desirability of putting an end to the development of liberal communism in Czechoslovakia, but over ways and means of doing so.

18. At the culmination of this crisis, at all events, the

Soviet collective leadership showed a capacity to act decisively, as it has done on other occasions, for example, the decision to extend military aid to North Vietnam in 1965. The fact that the Soviet leaders resorted to force in Czechoslovakia may encourage them more readily to use force or the threat of force again within the Warsaw Pact area in order to bring recalcitrant leaders to heel.

19. This general hardening of the line in Moscow appears to have been reflected in attitudes towards Communist doctrine and the rights and obligations of ruling Communist Parties. The article on this subject in "Pravda" of 26th September 1968 laid down that a Communist country has the right to self-determination only so far as this does not jeopardise the interests of other Communist states ("the Socialist Commonwealth"), that each Party is responsible to the other fraternal Parties as well as to its own people, and that the sovereignty of each country was not "abstract" but an expression of the class struggle, e.g. that the Soviet Union had the right to define each country's sovereignty.

20. While the Soviet leaders have tightened their direct control over events in Czechoslovakia, restated their political requirements for Warsaw Pact countries and demonstrated their readiness to use military means to enforce then, the Russians must also be aware of the miscalculations which they made in the political preparation of the occupation. It is very likely that they expected to find sufficient numbers of collaborators with whose help a pro-Soviet government could be formed as soon as the occupation became effective, and they were certainly taken aback by the unity and resourcefulness of the Czechoslovak people, and by the absence of political figures willing to serve in a Soviet-sponsored government. The Soviet Union's resumption of dealings with Dubcek and the legal Party and State leadership at the end of August 1968 suggests that the Russians abandoned their attempt to instal a regime of collaborators, and decided to compromise rather than make Czechoslovakia a military province, and to present their demands for the rectification of the political situation in Czechoslovakia to the regime which they had originally hoped to overthrow.

21. The reaction of the Soviet leadership to their occupation of Czechoslovakia may therefore be three-fold:-

(a) that their capability to use military means within the Warsaw Pact area in pursuit of political objectives has been supported by the will to act, and this demonstration, they may believe, will promote a greater sense of conformity with Soviet demands in Eastern Europe;
(b) that Soviet understanding of, and intelligence on, the East European countries, Party leaderships and national aspirations was faulty, and could lead in the future to further miscalculations;
(c) that nationalism is strong even within the friendliest Communist countries in Eastern Europe, and that it may not be worth insisting on complete compliance with Soviet wishes provided that the main Russian requirements are met.
The Russians may conclude that while their capability and determination to take firm action has been successfully demonstrated, their ability to take appropriate preventive action at the political level before the last resort is reached should be improved. The Soviet leaders may therefore decide to complete the restoration of orthodox Communist rule in Czechoslovakia, using, as long as possible, the legal Dubcek Party leadership to implement Soviet requirements. The Russians may complement their policies towards Czechoslovakia by a longer term overhaul of their relations with each East European country in the light particularly of the political miscalculations which emerged from their handling of the Czechoslovak crisis. But in the short term, we should be in no doubt that the Soviet loaders will insist that their requirements are met in Czechoslovakia.
22. It is beyond the scope of this paper to consider internal developments in the Soviet Union, but it is necessary to stress that the Soviet grip on Eastern Europe is so tight and so important to the Russians that it is unrealistic to expect any major change in Eastern Europe without the agreement or acquiescence of the Soviet Union. Since the status quo suits the Soviet Union well, the Russians are unlikely to agree to major changes unless there are moves for change inside Russia. Whatever evolution does take place spontaneously in the Soviet Union, other strong pressures are likely to come from the countries of Eastern Europe themselves. For Eastern Europe is very vulnerable to change: it is closer to the West and its countries lack the long-standing Soviet

traditions of Communist bureaucracy. The East European pressures for change which include nationalism, the drive for greater economic and administrative efficiency, and more freedom of action and individual responsibility are bound to have important long term effects in the Soviet Union. Among young people in Eastern Europe, a process of resentment against the existing order may appear which may ultimately be expressed by methods of protest already used by the younger generation in the West, and even this may spread to the Soviet Union. The Soviet leaders, we believe, will continue to fight change, but in the long run they may not be able or willing to do more than to slow down and delay the process.

Czechoslovakia

23. There is little hope that the Czechoslovak leadership under Dubcek can do more than fulfil the requirements of the Soviet Union, while trying, in increasingly adverse conditions, to retain the loyalty of the Czechoslovak people. Certainly the regime will hope to salvage something from the Action Programme and to soften the impact of the reintroduction of censorship, of Soviet personnel into key Ministries (if this should happen on any large scale) and of a prolonged military presence in the country under the terms of the treaty signed on 16th October 1968. Although the Russians have agreed to remove the bulk of their forces, leaving a "Group of Forces" behind on an indefinite stay, Dubcek and his colleagues must be aware that they cannot regain such independence as they enjoyed before the invasion. Indeed, the room for manoeuvre of the Czechoslovak regime (whether under Dubcek or a more amenable successor, or even Soviet military rule) has been diminishing steadily, and depends effectively on decisions taken in Moscow.

24. While the Russians hold nearly all the significant cards in Czechoslovakia, their policy since the Moscow agreement of 27th August 1968 has contained elements of hesitation and delay. Having achieved some of their immediate political aims, e.g. the abandonment of the 14th Party Congress originally scheduled for 9th September 1968, and the annulment of the Extraordinary Congress held in the week of the invasion, the Russians may have been content to take their time in achieving "normalisation". Provided he was willing to meet Soviet policy requirements, such an approach might help Dubcek

in his relations with the Czechoslovak people, and, in the longer term, it might provide a better atmosphere for the emergence of a pro-Soviet political group with whom, presumably, the Soviet leaders would prefer to work.

25. The future of the Czechoslovak armed forces is another problem which faces the Russians. Their loyalty to the Dubcek regime throughout the crisis renders them, in the Soviet eyes, of doubtful value as an ally of the Soviet Union. Disbandment of the Czechoslovak forces now seems to be out of the question. However, the Russians may consider it necessary to replace the more liberal minded officers and to make some organisational adjustments although not on the scale applied to the Hungarian forces after the 1956 uprising. The most likely solution is some reduction in size, consequent on the removal of the liberal elements, followed by a gradual resumption of their former role within the Warsaw Pact, under close Soviet supervision.

26. Among elements in the Czechoslovak reform programme which may survive will be some of the economic proposals. While any proposals believed by the Russians to be disruptive of CMEA will be banned, it seems possible that measures of internal flexibility such as those introduced at the beginning of 1967 and normal East-West trade will be approved. The Russians will be anxious not to impede a rise in the standard of living in Czechoslovakia or to veto methods of improving efficiency in industry and trade, so long as these do not threaten to disrupt established Soviet practices and commitments.

27. Nevertheless it is hard to see Czechoslovakia attaining any substantial measure of independence of Soviet policy. Liberalising currents are likely to continue, however and pressures will continue within the country for internal reforms.

East Germany

28. In many important respects the East German Party and Government has gained from the Soviet occupation of Czechoslovakia. This is partly due to the fact that Ulbricht's position has been strengthened by the tough Russian action, for no Soviet government would now be interested in replacing a man of Ulbricht's dedication to the Soviet cause, even though he may not last very long in power because of his age. East Germany has also gained because the invasion has halted, for some time at

least, possible expansion of Czechoslovakia's economic and political contacts with West Germany; although the West German trade mission is still in Prague, the East Germans probably believe that Czechoslovak-West German ties will dwindle, and that all chances that the Dubcek regime would respond favourably to Bonn's Ostpolitik have disappeared. Such a response was probably viewed in East Germany as the most pressing danger in the Czechoslovak crisis. The East German regime is also doubtless relieved that the process of liberalisation in Czechoslovakia has been stopped; the East German leaders showed signs of nervousness during the summer that their own population might become infected.

29. The relationship between Czechoslovakia and East Germany is a particularly delicate one: it is fragile for emotional and historical reasons, yet important to both in the economic field. To some extent the success of one works to the detriment of the other. East Germany may appear in Moscow to be a model of loyalty combined with efficiency. Its economy is strong, its relatively small numbers of known intellectual dissidents seem to be under control, and its armed forces appear to be disciplined and of high morale – all of which are important Soviet requirements.

30. On the other hand, East Germany still represents something of a liability to the Soviet Union. The country is still an artificial creation, born of the Soviet Union's refusal to permit the subordination of all Germans to one government, and the East Germans' preoccupation with German affairs cannot easily be reconciled with this long-term Soviet aim. Moreover, the East German press reaction to the Czech liberalisation programme was harsher than the Soviet, and there is evidence that Ulbricht consistently urged a tough line on Moscow. Yet when the invasion took place, East German popular reaction was hostile to the Soviet action: local and industrial Party organisations failed to produce the necessary resolutions of approval, demonstrations in support of Dubcek took place, and citizens called at the Czechoslovak Embassy in East Berlin with petitions opposing the occupation. The authorities have since taken strong measures to deal with opponents of the invasion. East Germany's development of its own nationhood and a more articulate public opinion, combined with

its economic stability, efficiency and rising standard of living, may in the longer run generate more tensions with the Soviet Union than its present ideological correctness and political loyalty to the Russians may suggest.

Poland

31. Reports from Poland before the occupation of Czechoslovakia suggested that the Polish leadership generally upheld Soviet criticism of the Czechoslovak reforms, and since 21st August have given full public support to the invasion and the official reasons for it. The latter have included military reasons, the alleged threat from West Germany and the danger of Western subversion inside Czechoslovakia, though no doubt the fear of infection in Poland had the Dubcek reforms been accepted by Moscow played an important part in securing Polish support for the occupation.

32. The reaction of Polish intellectuals, however, to the invasion was one of great hostility, of which the open letter by the Polish novelist Andrzejewski, expressing solidarity with the Czechoslovak writers, was one remarkable example. The majority of students, too, probably opposed the invasion, and the danger of unrest by the younger generation is probably assessed by the Polish authorities as still high. It may increase when Gomulka finally steps down especially if, in the course of a struggle for the succession, one or more contenders rely on the support of younger people or anti-Russian elements. Poland has a tradition of freedom and nationalism with which the Russians have always had to reckon, and their preoccupation with this factor may increase in the longer term.

33. At the top, however, the Soviet grip on Poland is not likely to be shaken in the short or medium term, and the present Polish regime will hardly query or evade Soviet political or military requirements. On the economic side, too, Poland is unlikely to cause the Russians undue concern. For its part, the Soviet Government will no doubt underline, in its dealings with Poland, the security which the Warsaw Pact offers to Poland, and the Russians' proved ability and intention to act firmly and quickly in defence of their requirements. In the longer term, when Gomulka is no longer in power, the future of the Soviet-Polish relationship may depend in part on

whether the Polish leadership falls under the modernising influence of Gierek, or the nationalist influence of General Moczar.

Hungary

34. During the development of the Soviet-Czechoslovak crisis the Hungarian party leader, Kadar, seemed to play a dual role, approving the Czechoslovak reform programme, which was relevant to the reform policies which he was implementing in Hungary in a more subdued and cautious atmosphere, and at the same time remaining loyal to the Soviet Union. Kadar was clearly anxious to avoid armed intervention, but in the last resort, when his mediation failed to produce a compromise acceptable to the Soviet leaders, he was obliged to side with the Russians and send Hungarian units into Czechoslovakia.

35. The invasion was a personal blow to Kadar's position both domestically and in his relations with the Soviet leaders. The Hungarian Press has maintained that Hungarian policies will be unaffected, but the Hungarians may now proceed rather more cautiously with their reforms, and the growth of economic ties with the West may be slowed down. It may even be that Kadar's own position as leader of the Hungarian Party could be in doubt. In general, however, the effect of the Soviet action is likely to be similar in Hungary to that in Poland: in both countries, which are by tradition anti-Russian, the current mood in Moscow will be carefully assessed, and existing censorship and security regulations will be even more rigorously enforced.

Bulgaria

36. Little requires to be said about Bulgaria whose unswerving loyalty to all Soviet Governments since Stalin's day has been one of the permanent features in Eastern Europe. The nominal Bulgarian Army contingent which participated in the occupation of Czechoslovakia was no doubt willingly provided on Soviet request, and there is every reason to believe that the Bulgarian Government viewed the Czechoslovak political reforms with hostility, although they themselves have approved a programme involving some reform of the economy of the country.

37. The loyalty of the Bulgarian leadership to Soviet policies and the primacy which the Soviet Union enjoys in Bulgarian decision-making are unlikely to be altered

by the Czechoslovak crisis. If anything, the Bulgarian Party leadership will be encouraged to take stronger action against their own dissident intellectuals (about one third of whom were reported to have been critical of the invasion) and students by the display of Soviet military power, and the long-term Soviet-Bulgarian relationship is likely to remain undisturbed.

Rumania

38. Rumania's recent opposition to Soviet policy, with its strong undercurrent of nationalism, began in 1962-63 in the economic field, and was later extended to intra-Bloc affairs (the Sino-Soviet dispute), foreign policy (relations with West Germany and Israel) and the country's military obligations to the Warsaw Pact. The Rumanian Government, which maintained a tight grip on the country's internal affairs and operated a strict censorship, was not favourably disposed towards the Czechoslovak liberalisation movement, but was excluded from the series of conferences called by the Soviet Union to deal with the problem – in Moscow, Dresden, Warsaw and Bratislava – because of the Rumanians' known opposition to interference in the affairs of other countries. The Rumanians criticised Soviet pressures on Czechoslovakia and condemned the military invasion. They ordered partial mobilisation and made clear their determination to resist an invasion of their own country. In spite of rumours of troop movements on their frontiers and fears of Soviet military intervention, the Rumanian leaders have upheld, though with diminishing intensity, their criticism of Soviet policy.

39. The Rumanian Communist Party, however, is not likely to relax its control over the country or weaken its monopoly of decision-making; and while this can be used to reduce Soviet influence in Rumania, it is difficult for the Russians to level accusations against the Rumanian leadership on this score. Nor is the Rumanian domestic model likely to prove attractive to other East European countries. But the Soviet Union will be sensitive to any sign that Rumanian foreign policy is attracting these countries, and will do her best to counteract any trends in this direction. Rumania's natural resources and her strategic position (with no common border with a NATO country), set her apart from her allies and make it unlikely that, even if they wished to, the other

East European states could follow Rumanian policies in practice.

40. Rumania's divergence, therefore, from Soviet requirements is neither dangerous to the Soviet Union nor, in the post-invasion atmosphere, particularly infectious. The Soviet Union will try to obtain the maximum benefit from its display of military power to intimidate the Rumanians and isolate them from their neighbours, with the long-term intention of subverting the present Rumanian leadership. The latter will concentrate on maintaining the ground already won in foreign and economic policy, while playing down points of disagreement with the Soviet Union on issues where Rumanian interests are not directly concerned. They may judge it wise to co-operate with their allies in holding Warsaw Pact exercises, and perhaps reforming CMEA, where this can be done without undermining the principles on which Rumania's independent stand is based.

Yugoslavia

41. Yugoslavia's reaction to the Soviet occupation of Czechoslovakia was one of violent hostility caused partly by the resurrection in Yugoslav eyes of Soviet demands for hegemony over Communist countries which precipitated the 1948 Soviet-Yugoslav split, partly by the feeling in Belgrade that Czechoslovakia was consciously following the Yugoslav model, and partly because the Soviet action confronted the Yugoslavs with a series of political, military and economic problems which they had successfully evaded for years.

42. There is no evidence that Soviet policy towards Eastern Europe involves military action against Yugoslavia in present circumstances. But it is now more difficult to say with any certainty what developments in Yugoslavia or in her relations with the West might be regarded by the Russians as provocative. Though neither side seems to want a complete break in relations, a prolonged period of mutual recrimination seems to be in prospect, possibly accompanied on the Yugoslav side by efforts to expand trade with the West. A reconciliation does not seem likely unless the Russians can satisfy the Yugoslavs that they are prepared to abandon the definition of sovereignty for Communist states laid down in the "Pravda" article of 26th September 1968.

43. It is unlikely that the Soviet Union would find any

reliable basis for internal pro-Soviet subversion in Yugoslavia as long as Tito is in power. If his death was followed by a struggle for power among contenders for the succession, the Soviet Union might try to exploit the situation to its own advantage.

Albania
44. Albania followed the Chinese lead in attacking the Soviet invasion of Czechoslovakia, while criticising the Dubcek regime as "capitulationist". Albania has announced her withdrawal from the Warsaw Pact, and has made tentative moves towards an improvement of relations with Yugoslavia. There is no reason to believe that Soviet policy towards Albania will change, or that Albania's pro-Chinese alignment will alter to the Soviet Union's advantage.

THE MILITARY OUTLOOK

Basic Concepts
45. Much of the material which the Soviet Union and its Warsaw Pact allies have published in their attempt to justify the invasion of Czechoslovakia has concentrated on the alleged military threat from NATO, particularly from West Germany. Before assessing the military outlook in Eastern Europe, in the wake of the invasion of Czechoslovakia, it may be useful to look at Soviet military and strategic concepts for war in Europe and at the organisation of the Warsaw Pact.
46. In the formal Soviet view, general European war would begin with a NATO attack on Eastern Europe, followed by a rapid counter-offensive westwards by Warsaw Pact forces. Whether or not the Russians seriously attribute aggressive intentions or capabilities to NATO, the important feature of their military doctrine is the seizure of the initiative at the earliest possible moment, retaining all options open on the level of the conflict and the types of weapons used, at least at the outset. The Warsaw Pact ground and air forces would engage NATO forces on a broad front, manoeuvring swiftly and boldly, considering speed and continuity of action as the main manoeuvre assets. It is probable that in the main these tactics would be used both in conventional and nuclear supported operations, and they imply the probability of thrust and counter-thrust in great depth, with a battle zone

extending over very large areas. If the fighting is not to intrude into Soviet territory, the initial deployment of forces must be well to the west of the Soviet frontier. Thus the right to deploy Soviet forces in peacetime on the territory of the East European countries is fundamental to Soviet defence policy.

<u>The Warsaw Pact</u>

47. Some of the Soviet preparations and measures to fulfil these military requirements are co-ordinated through the Warsaw Pact, while others, for example, in air defence, are the subject of even more direct Soviet command and control. For the first five or six years of its existence, from 1955 to 1960–61, the High Command of the Warsaw Pact existed only as a Directorate of the Soviet General Staff, and the Commander-in-Chief was at the same time the Soviet First Deputy Minister of Defence. The Secretary-General of the Organisation held three posts: Secretary-General, Chief of Staff of the Pact's forces and First Deputy Chief of the Soviet General Staff. During the reorganisation of the Soviet forces in 1960–61, the Main Staff of the Warsaw Pact was apparently separated administratively from the General Staff and established in effect as a "Chief Directorate" of the Soviet Ministry of Defence with responsibilities for liaison with the non-Soviet Warsaw Pact armies, for training and, since February 1966, for the co-ordination of the defence industries of the member-nations (see Appendix A for the contribution of the non-Soviet Warsaw Pact countries to armaments production for the Warsaw Pact).

48. Although the Defence Ministers of the non-Soviet Warsaw Pact countries are Deputy Commanders-in-Chief and liaison officers of each country are attached to the Main Staff in Moscow, these are largely titular appointments, and all key posts in the military structure are in Soviet hands. All important plans and policies are Soviet, and standardisation of equipment and material to Soviet specifications contributes towards the dominant influence of the Soviet Union. In wartime, given the present structure, the chain of command would almost certainly by-pass the Warsaw Pact organisation and run from the Soviet Supreme Headquarters through Soviet "Front" commanders to the commanders of the Soviet and non-Soviet Warsaw Pact armies in the fields.

The Czechoslovak Crisis and its Aftermath

49. The Soviet military leaders probably feared, as a result of the Czechoslovak reform programme, that a serious gap in the Warsaw Pact defence structure would develop, either through Czechoslovakia's defection from the Pact or a decline in the efficiency of her armed forces. In the first place, the Dubcek leadership removed a number of tried pro-Soviet military figures including the Minister of Defence, General Lomsky, two of his deputies, the Chief of the General Staff and the Head of the Political Directorate of the Armed Forces, and replaced them by officers whose military abilities and political reliability the Russians may have doubted. Secondly, the Soviet military authorities made specific criticisms of the performance of the Czechoslovak Army in the Warsaw Pact exercise "SUMAVA" in June 1968, and commented on the shortage of tank divisions within the force which the Czechoslovaks proposed to use for the defence of their frontier with West Germany in the event of war. There were reports that in the light of their doubts the Russians made – and the Czechoslovaks rejected – a request to station Soviet troops in Czechoslovakia. If these reports were true, the Czechoslovak refusal may have contributed to a growing Soviet belief that in spite of Czechoslovak assurances of complete loyalty to the Warsaw Pact, in the longer run Czechoslovak loyalty to and interest in the Warsaw Pact could not be taken for granted by the Soviet Union.

50. There has been a steady run-down of Soviet ground and air forces in Czechoslovakia, subsequent to the signing of the Status of Forces agreement on 16th October. The scale of reduction gives credence to Premier Cernik's statement concerning the agreement, that the Czechoslovak forces are to have responsibility for the defence of the Western frontier of their country returned to them.

51. Although the Czechoslovak forces would doubtless fight loyally in defence of their own country, the Soviet leadership must retain some reservations as to their effective potential for offensive operations and it is clear that the Russians intend to maintain at least substantial ground forces on Czechoslovak soil. Hence their operational plans will presumably have to be reassessed in the light of the extension of their own military

commitments and of any adjustments which NATO may decide to make in its plans or deployments.

52. In consequence of the Czechoslovak crisis future proposed Warsaw Pact exercises are likely to become extremely delicate political issues. However, in the longer term, the Soviet government is likely to seek ways of establishing a better structure for the Warsaw Pact than was formerly the case. Politically the Soviet government may offer concessions to the non-Soviet members of the Pact in the field of national representation and consultation. Militarily, however, the Soviet Union may insist upon even tighter Soviet control over the East European armies, including, perhaps, increased Soviet participation at the lower levels of command (e.g. Army Group and Army) which up to now have been wholly national.

THE ECONOMIC OUTLOOK

53. The effect of the Soviet invasion of Czechoslovakia on the economic outlook in Eastern Europe may best be assessed by looking first at CMEA's methods of operation and some of the criticisms which have been levelled against it within Eastern Europe, and then at the evidence relating to the interdependence in trade of the Soviet Union and the East European countries. The detailed figures supporting this evidence are in the Tables in Appendix B.

The Council for Mutual Economic Aid (CMEA)

54. The basic task of CMEA - once the concept of supra-national planning as put forward by Khrushchev in 1962 had been finally rejected - reverted to the co-ordination of the long-term economic plans of member countries. Specialised agencies are responsible for drawing up preliminary balance sheets of individual countries' estimated requirements for raw materials and basic equipment over a given period, and these are discussed first on a bilateral basis and then multilaterally prior to the formation of the national plans. In the course of these consultations agreement is reached in principle on the types and quantities of goods to be exchanged between member countries in order to cover their investment and other requirements. The work of co-ordination is thus a lengthy and complex process, involving the co-operation

of numerous national and international bodies. So far there are no indications of a break in the established pattern of this activity. Preparatory work has begun on the co-ordination of economic development plans for 1971-75 and at the meeting of the Executive Committee of CMEA in September 1968 (at which Czechoslovakia was represented as usual) preliminary estimates of the fuel and energy balance of member countries up to 1980 were submitted, and recommendations on various aspects of economic co-operation, including expansion of mutual goods exchanged over the 5-year period, were approved.

55. It may be that, in the post-invasion circumstances, the possibilities for making CMEA a more efficient organisation have been to some extent strengthened. Criticism of its workings had been widespread, although seldom openly voiced, for some time. Hungary, Czechoslovakia and Poland had all at various times criticised the lack of progress made in production specialisation within CMEA, the tendency being for each country to maintain a wide production range which was basically uneconomic. The divergence of views amongst CMEA members as regards specialisation spring [sic] from the differing stages of economic development of each country, and the consequent problems which they have to face. Thus, Czechoslovakia had long been pressing for a reduction in the wide range of engineering goods she produces to meet CMEA requirements, so that she could concentrate on a narrower range of highly specialised products. Poland, on the other hand, has been keen to expand her production range in order to be able to compete with the products of the more developed member countries such as Czechoslovakia and East Germany. So far a very great number of recommendations have been put forward covering production specialisation within CMEA in the fields of machinery and equipment and the chemical industry. How far these proposals have been implemented however, is difficult to assess. In general, it seems that little real specialisation has yet been achieved. Another problem which products a conflict of views within CMEA is that of pricing. Thus when an up-dated price base for goods exchanged in intra-bloc trade was introduced in 1965 the Soviet Union was severely critical of the new (lower) prices now obtaining for raw materials, claiming that the revised price-base worked in favour of exporters of machinery

and equipment whilst discriminating against raw materials suppliers (the USSR is the main such supplier within CMEA). The Soviet argument was that the high costs of producing raw materials are not compensated for by the prices received from the buyers. At the same time the Soviet Union claimed to be paying world market prices for most East European machinery and equipment which was not up to world standards. A further point of issue concerned the method of settling intra-bloc payments. Some member countries, notably Poland and Czechoslovakia, have in recent years accumulated large surpluses in transferable roubles in their trade with each other. The inability to convert these transferable rouble balances into other currencies, or even – because of the general shortage of acceptable goods within the area – to offset them with additional commodity deliveries from debtor countries has led to pressure from those countries most concerned for even partial conversion of the transferable rouble.

56. Against the background of all these problems, leading economists from some of the more industrially developed member countries of CMEA – notably Czechoslovakia, Poland and Hungary – have for some time been suggesting various ways to improve the working efficiency of CMEA. In the past, progress on joint capital projects had frequently been halted due to the exercise by one or other member states (most often, Rumania) of the right of veto of proposals for co-production or division of production. This was based on the principle of unanimity written into the Basic Charter of CMEA, according to which all decisions or recommendations of the Council, to be binding, must have the consent of all members, and any country has the right to disassociate itself from proposed projects which it considers are not in its national interest. However, gradually the view has been increasingly gaining ground that voluntary bilateral arrangements are proving more effective than multilateral co-operation agreements dictated by CMEA. Emphasis has recently been laid on the need for wider co-operation between member countries in informing each other in more detail of their respective investment programmes, so that the coordination of investment plans for the whole area can be carried out more effectively on a long-term basis.

57. The future development of CMEA will depend to a large

extent on how the Russians react to these views and trends. It seems unlikely that the Russians will agree to suggestions that the surpluses of "transferable roubles" should be made convertible. But the Soviet Union may decide that, in the longer term, the cohesiveness of the Bloc demands more attention to national economic ambitions and a more realistic appreciation of existing economic differences between the members of CMEA.

Trade Interdependence General

58. In 1967 the Eastern European countries accounted for some 56 per cent of the Soviet Union's total trade (58 per cent including Yugoslavia). The share of the Soviet Union in the total trade of each of the six East European countries varied from over 50 per cent for Bulgaria to 28 per cent for Rumania (12 per cent for Yugoslavia). Soviet deliveries cover one-third of Eastern Europe's import requirements for machinery and equipment, while the Soviet Union takes almost half of these countries' exports of machinery and equipment (mainly from East Germany and Czechoslovakia). Next to machinery the Soviet Union imports from Eastern Europe mainly consumer goods – chiefly footwear, clothing and furniture. As regards raw materials, East European dependence on the Soviet Union is shown by the fact that Soviet deliveries cover East European import requirements for crude oil and pig iron by nearly 100 per cent, for iron ore by about 85 per cent, for cotton on an average by about 60 per cent, and as regards grain by some two-thirds to three-quarters for East Germany and Poland respectively, whilst nearly all Czechoslovakia's grain imports come from the USSR (See Table V). Under the current (1966-70) 5-year trade agreements between the Soviet Union and the six East European countries, in all cases except for Rumania, the Soviet sector in these countries' trade is planned to increase at a higher rate than their total trade.

59. Apart from trade, the East European countries and the Soviet Union are linked by numerous joint investment projects, involving two or more countries. Under these agreements machinery and equipment are supplied on long-term credit, the recipient repaying through long-term deliveries of the finished products. A recent example of this type of joint project is the Soviet-Czechoslovak oil exploration agreement. Another example is the Soviet-Hungarian agreement on aluminium, under which Hungarian

alumina is delivered to the Soviet Union for processing, and then sold back to Hungary as aluminium.

Czechoslovakia

60. Over a third of Czechoslovakia's foreign trade in 1967 was with the Soviet Union and a further 36 per cent with other East European countries. The Soviet Union supplies by far the largest proportion of Czechoslovak imports of fuels, raw materials and foodstuffs, including practically all the country's oil requirements and about three-quarters of her wheat imports. Machinery and equipment imports from the Soviet Union include agricultural machinery, cars, diesel locomotives and aircraft.

61. Czechoslovak dependence on the Soviet Union for supplies of basic raw materials is likely to continue, and in the case of crude oil, will no doubt increase since, under an agreement of September 1966, Czechoslovakia is to deliver on long-term credit machinery and equipment for the exploitation of Soviet oilfields, with eventual repayment in oil deliveries over a long period. Czechoslovakia has also agreed to invest, on similar terms, in the Soviet gas and iron ore industries, and will receive supplies of natural gas and pelletised ores in repayment. A switch in source of supply for such raw materials would in any case not be feasible because of the need to recoup on investments already made.

62. As regards Czechoslovak exports, machinery and equipment form about half of the total; the largest single customer being the Soviet Union. Altogether, the communist countries take nearly 80 per cent of these exports of machinery and equipment. Czechoslovakia would like to expand her machinery exports to the West - at present they form only a small share of the total - but the general quality of such goods makes them in most cases uncompetitive in Western markets. Traditional Czechoslovak manufactures, such as glassware, jewellery and leather goods have a better chance of being accepted in the West, and it is the output and sale of such products, as well as light engineering goods, that Czechoslovakia plans to promote. For advanced technology, Czechoslovakia - like other East European countries and indeed the Soviet Union - will continue to look to the West. So far there is no evidence that the Soviet Union intends to disrupt the normal pattern of Czechoslovakia's trade with this area. It is indeed ultimately to the Soviet Union's advantage

that not only Czechoslovakia but all the East European countries should continue to import Western technology, since this will improve the quality of the goods these countries deliver to the Soviet Union.

Poland

63. About a third of Poland's trade is with the Soviet Union and a further third with other East European countries. Poland differs from her East European neighbours, Czechoslovakia and East Germany, in that the structure of her trade relations with the Soviet Union shows a greater diversity in both imports and exports. Not only does Poland export industrial and engineering products, especially ships, to the Soviet Union, but she is the Soviet Union's main external supplier of coal and coke. In exchange, the Soviet Union sends Poland vital raw materials such as oil, pig iron and iron ore and a variety of machinery and equipment. Like other East European countries, Poland would like to increase her trade with the West, but her ability to compete in Western markets is a limiting factor. About one third of her trade is with non-Communist countries (a considerably higher percentage than for Czechoslovakia); she became a full member of GATT in 1967, but it is too soon to assess the effects of her membership on her foreign trade.

East Germany

64. East Germany has the highest total trade turnover of all East European countries and conducts three-quarters of her trade with these countries. She is the Soviet Union's chief trade partner in East Europe. Complete industrial plants, especially chemical plants, are a major feature of East German exports to the Soviet Union and in exchange she receives raw materials, particularly crude oil and iron ore, and foodstuffs. The Soviet Union makes up most of her deficiencies in raw materials and foodstuffs, and these together with military supplies and small amounts of machinery and equipment, make up the greater part of Soviet deliveries to East Germany. There is no doubt that imports from the Soviet Union have provided the main basis for East Germany's recovery and growth. Czechoslovakia and Poland are her other main suppliers in East Europe; from Czechoslovakia she receives machinery, industrial consumer goods and certain industrial materials, while Poland sends large amounts of coal and some foodstuffs and machinery. East Germany has a

high level of trade with West Germany, particularly in the more specialised varieties of iron and steel products which are unavailable or scarce in East Europe.

Hungary

65. Hungary's economy is very dependent on foreign trade, since she has few resources of her own. Over two-thirds of this trade is with East European countries, of which the Soviet Union accounts for nearly half. In the current five-year period Soviet-Hungarian trade is planned to increase by some 50 per cent. Nearly all of Hungary's imports of crude oil, iron ore and crude phosphates come from the Soviet Union. She also receives the greater part of the machinery and equipment she needs from the Soviet Union and the other East European countries, though she has been notably increasing her purchases of Western equipment in recent years. Hungary's exports to the Soviet Union include machinery and engineering products, particularly chemical plants and telecommunications equipment, and large quantities of alumina which are processed in the Soviet Union and sold back to Hungary in the form of aluminium. Pharmaceuticals are also an important export to the Soviet Union.

Rumania

66. Of all East European countries, Rumania is least dependent on them in her foreign trade. Only about half of her total trade is with East European countries, of which the Soviet share is 28 per cent. Credits to Rumania from NATO countries are higher than those extended to any other East European countries except the Soviet Union. Imports from the Soviet Union are lower than for any other East European country; they include raw materials, especially coal, iron-ore, ferrous and non-ferrous metals, and machinery and equipment. Rumanian exports to the Soviet Union consist mainly of plant and drilling equipment for the Soviet oil industry. Within CMEA Rumanian participation is on the basis of national interest; e.g. Rumania does not belong to all the CMEA-sponsored agencies. If Soviet economic sanctions were applied to Rumania, the economy would certainly suffer in the short-term, particularly in the industrial field dependent on Soviet ferrous and non-ferrous metals and on Soviet machinery and equipment. In the long term, however, she would be able to buy these and other goods from the West, depending on her ability to expand exports to

the West; of the goods currently exported to the Soviet Union, agricultural products, wood and oil products could probably be easily marketed in the West, while machinery and equipment could be sold to the underdeveloped countries. The Soviet Union would also encounter difficulties if relations with Rumania were severed; in particular, oil-well drilling equipment, oil refinery equipment and steel pipes would be difficult to replace, at least from within Eastern Europe.

Bulgaria

67. In foreign trade, Bulgaria is extremely dependent upon the Soviet Union, both as an outlet for her exports (notably machinery and equipment, and light industrial goods) and as a supplier of capital equipment vital to the implementation of Bulgaria's economic plans. In addition, the Soviet Union is the main supplier of a number of key raw materials, and has granted Bulgaria very large credit facilities, mainly for the development of large-scale enterprises. Although Bulgaria's trade with the West has increased appreciably in recent years, she still has difficulty in making competitive any commodities but her foodstuffs.

THE IMPLICATIONS FOR EAST-WEST RELATIONS

68. The invasion of Czechoslovakia has increased the uncertainties about Soviet actions and the situations in which the Russians would be prepared to use force. On the whole the invasion was a move to maintain what they saw as a desirable status quo, but subsequent developments in Eastern Europe could lead them to use force again, perhaps in more dangerous circumstances, and for ostensibly the same motives. Soviet policy in other areas will be governed as before by other factors e.g. the circumstances of the situation, the Russians' own capabilities on the spot, and the likelihood of a direct confrontation with the United States.

69. There is no reason to believe that the Soviet action in Czechoslovakia has in any way diminished the Soviet leaders' determination to avoid nuclear war and a direct challenge to the United States or NATO. But the policies they may decide to follow could lead them into situations leading to a confrontation with NATO. This does not mean that the appearance of Soviet divisions where

Czechoslovak divisions were formerly deployed indicates an intention to initiate hostilities in the NATO area. Nevertheless a higher proportion of the Warsaw Pact forces available for rapid action against the West will be Soviet, and NATO forces may have to consider the purely military effect of this on their plans.

70. Negotiations with the United States on political and defence matters in which both sides have lasting interests, such as the Non-proliferation Treaty and the proposed discussions on limiting strategic offensive and defensive weapons, will probably proceed on a strictly practical basis. The Russians will also be anxious to pursue trade and other East-West contacts in a "business as usual" atmosphere, although thanks to the popularity won by the Czechoslovak reform movement in Western Europe and North America, and the wide radio and television coverage given to the Russian invasion and the Czechoslovaks' non-military resistance, the Russians may not be able to create this atmosphere in the short term as easily as they probably hoped.

71. In the main, however, the greatest upheaval caused by the Czechoslovak crisis is within the Soviet alliance itself, in the relations between the Soviet Union and Czechoslovakia and the other East European countries. It is probable, therefore, that Soviet attention will be focussed very largely on the internal problems of Eastern Europe in the foreseeable future with the intention of restoring orthodox Communist rule to Czechoslovakia and ensuring that economic reform programmes there and in other East European countries are not undertaken in the kind of political atmosphere which grew up in Prague in the first eight months of 1968. The problem of the nationalism of the East European countries will continue to create difficulties for the Soviet Union. At the same time, the Soviet Union will continue to act as a super-power and her policies in Eastern Europe will not necessarily affect her ability or intentions to pursue a policy designed to increase Soviet influence elsewhere in the world, e.g. the Mediterranean area or the Middle East. In practice, therefore, the Soviet Union will strive to isolate her East European policy from her actions in the rest of the world. There should be no doubt, however, that her aim in Eastern Europe is to maintain her grip on the area as long as she can.

APPENDIX A

The Contribution of the Non-Soviet Warsaw Pact Countries (NSWP) to Armaments Production for the Warsaw Pact

Naval
The only naval ships constructed in NSWP countries and supplied to the Soviet Union, are the landing ships built in Poland. The NSWP countries are more or less self-sufficient in the production of the smaller ships of their navies, e.g. minesweepers and landing craft. However, they rely on the Soviet Union for the supply of submarines, most of their escorts and all missile-armed Fast Patrol Boats.

Ground Forces
All of the NSWP countries can produce small arms and ammunition, and between then Czechoslovakia, Poland and Hungary are able to meet most of their needs for AFVs, artillery weapons and soft-skinned vehicles. They do not produce the full range of equipment at present, but they could make themselves self-sufficient without any major expansion of existing facilities. There is reliance on the USSR for some of the heavier kinds of equipment, including large calibre artillery, multi-round rocket launchers, engineer equipment and heavy transport.

Air Forces
The Czechoslovak and Polish aircraft industries are capable of producing combat and military support aircraft, and have in the past made them under licence from the USSR. They are not, however, producing currently any military aircraft. The aircraft industries of the other NSWP countries are negligible.

Missiles
There is no production of missile weapon systems in any NSWP country.

Conclusion
In general therefore the main contribution the NSWP countries make is to the equipment of their own sea and land forces; on the other hand they rely heavily on the USSR for many of their naval units, aircraft and missiles, for some ground forces equipment and for much ancillary electronic equipment. In view of the great preponderance of Soviet forces in the pact, the contribution of these

other countries to its armaments production as a whole is therefore very small.

APPENDIX B

TABLE I
Growth of Soviet Trade with East European Countries 1962-1967

Million Roubles
Source: Soviet Foreign Trade Yearbook

		1962	1963	1964	1965	1966	1967
Russia	Total	12137	12898	13878	14610	15078	16367
	Exports	6327	6545	6915	7357	7957	8684
	Imports	5810	6353	6963	7252	7122	7683
Bulgaria	Total	754	846	991	1084	1216	1382
	USSR Exports	403	446	511	530	627	686
	USSR Imports	351	400	480	554	589	696
Hungary	Total	720	780	877	955	915	1064
	USSR Exports	370	399	443	491	454	527
	USSR Imports	350	381	433	464	461	537
East Germany	Total	2202	2356	2442	2383	2380	2546
	USSR Exports	1235	1183	1247	1227	1266	1274
	USSR Imports	966	1173	1195	1156	1114	1271
Poland	Total	1043	1149	1240	1357	1383	1633
	USSR Exports	535	596	594	654	723	821
	USSR Imports	508	553	646	703	660	812
Rumania	Total	651	728	823	759	713	737
	USSR Exports	337	359	444	363	348	355
	USSR Imports	314	369	379	397	365	382
Czecho-slovakia	Total	1436	1620	1683	1765	1632	1755
	USSR Exports	694	764	811	833	805	871
	USSR Imports	742	856	372	932	828	884

TABLE II
Growth of USSR Foreign Trade

	% change 1961–65	% change 1966–67 (annual % increase)
USSR		
Total	+ 37.27	+ 8.55
Export	+ 36.3	+ 9.14
Import	+ 38.27	+ 7.74
Bulgaria/USSR		
Total	+ 76.54	+ 13.65
Export	+ 68.11	+ 9.41
Import	+ 89.0	+ 18.12
Hungary/USSR		
Total	+ 54.78	+ 16.26
Export	+ 52.0	+ 16.07
Import	+ 57.8	+ 16.48
E. Germany/USSR		
Total	+ 26.95	+ 6.98
Export	+ 12.78	+ 0.63
Import	+ 46.6	+ 14.09
Poland/USSR		
Total	+ 49.61	+ 18.08
Export	+ 36.8	+ 13.55
Import	+ 63.86	+ 23.03
Rumania/USSR		
Total	+ 33.39	+ 3.37
Export	+ 38.02	+ 2.01
Import	+ 29.31	+ 4.67
Czechoslovakia/USSR		
Total	+ 45.26	+ 7.54
Export	+ 41.90	+ 8.16
Import	+ 48.4	+ 6.76

Column I: represents the <u>actual</u> growth of USSR trade with partners over the period 1961-65.

Column II: represents the <u>actual</u> growth of USSR trade with partners over the single year 1966-67.

NB: Imports growing at a faster rate than exports in all countries except Czechoslovakia

TABLE III
Planned Increases in Foreign Trade in CMEA 1966-70

Country	Overall trade	Trade with USSR
Bulgaria	60-70%	70%
Czechoslovakia	32%	50%
East Germany	42%	43%
Hungary	46%	50%
Poland	40%	50%
Rumania	55%	30%

TABLE IV
CMEA Countries' Trade with USSR

Sources: 1st column – "Foreign Trade" June 1968
2nd column – Countries' own statistics for 1967 or for 1966*

	% of USSR's Trade	% of East European countries' Trade
USSR-Bulgaria Trade	8.4	51.2*
USSR-Czechoslovakia Trade	10.7	35.1
USSR-East Germany Trade	15.5	43.3
USSR-Hungary Trade	6.5	33.0*
USSR-Poland Trade	10.0	36.3
USSR-Rumania Trade	4.5	33.5*
USSR-Yugoslavia Trade	2.8	12.0
	58.4	

TABLE V
CMEA Countries: Imports of Important Commodities from USSR as % of Total Imports of That Commodity 1966

Country	Crude Oil	Iron Ore	Pig Iron	Cotton	Grain	Coal
Bulgaria	100%	84%	95%	72%	–	96%
Czechoslovakia	98%	82%	93%	54%	99%	51%
East Germany	96%	82%	80%	91%	64%	62.9%
Hungary	85%	95%	99%	49.1%	–	37%
					Wheat 1967	Small amount
Poland	100%	83%	96%	61%	75%	100% Poland exports coal to USSR
Rumania	–	85%	100%	39%	–	51%

TABLE VI
CMEA Countries' Exports to USSR – 1966
Important Commodities as % of total

Country	Total Exports to USSR million roubles	of which: Machinery and Equipment	of which: Ships	Clothing	Furniture
Bulgaria	589	29.2%	3.0%	12.5%	3.5%
Czechoslovakia	828	53.3%	3.1%	4.1%	2.1%
East Germany	1114	55.3%	8.6%	7.1%	4.2%
Hungary	461	47.7%	3.5%	9.3%	0.9%
Poland	656	35.6%	14.7%	6.8%	2.7%
Rumania	365	13.9%	3.0%	8.5%	10.2%

TABLE VII

CMEA Countries: Imports from USSR – 1966 –
Important Commodities as % of total imports from USSR

Country	Total Imports from USSR million roubles	of which: Machinery and Equipment	Crude Oil	Iron Ore	Pig Iron	Chemical Products	Raw Cotton	Grain	Coal	Rolled Ferrous Metals	Non-Ferrous Metals and Alloys
Bulgaria	627	46%	7%	1.5%	1.2%	1.0%	5.0%	–	(and anthracite) 6%	7%	0.8%
Czechoslovakia	805	17%	12%	9%	0.6%	1.3%	5.2%	9%	2%	5%	5%
East Germany	1,266	9%	7%	1.6%	2.0%	0.9%	4.5%	5%	6%	16%	7%
Hungary	454	24%	10%	5%	2.0%	2.7%	6.0%	–	2.4%	4.4%	2.4%
Poland	723	19%	6.5%	8.9%	4.2%	0.6%	8.3%	3.8%	2.0%	6.0%	2.2%
Rumania	343	27%	–	6.1%	4.2%	0.8%	5.9%	–	1.3%	25.9%	1.3%

TABLE VIII
Structure of Imports and Exports of some CMEA Countries
(as a % of total import and exports)

Country	Machinery and Equipment Exports	Machinery and Equipment Imports	Consumer Goods Exports	Consumer Goods Imports	Raw Materials and Fuel Exports	Raw Materials and Fuel Imports	Foodstuffs Exports	Foodstuffs Imports
Bulgaria	25	44	13	5	25	43	36	7
Czechoslovakia	49	30	17	5	30	48	4	16
East Germany	49	18	19	4	29	60	4	17
Hungary	33	29	21	5	24	55	22	10
Poland	34	33	12	7	35	47	18	13
Rumania	19	39	11	7	49	50	21	3
USSR	20	33	2	14	57	29	8	20

Notes

1. J. W. Young, 'The Wilson Government's Reform of Intelligence Co-Ordination, 1967–68', *Intelligence and National Security* 16/2 (2001), pp. 133–51.
2. See especially Günter Bischof, Stefan Karner and Peter Ruggenthaler, 'Introduction', in Günter Bischof, Stefan Karner and Peter Ruggenthaler (eds), *The Prague Spring and the Warsaw Pact Invasion of Czechoslovakia in 1968* (Lanham, MD: Lexington, 2009), pp. 3–15.
3. Percy Cradock, *Know Your Enemy: How the Joint Intelligence Committee Saw the World* (London: John Murray, 2002), pp. 240, 242.
4. Geraint Hughes, 'British Policy towards Eastern Europe and the Impact of the "Prague Spring", 1964–68', *Cold War History* 4/2 (2004), p. 125.
5. Cabinet minutes, 22 August 1968, CC(68) 38th Conclusions. TNA: CAB 128/43.
6. Doug Nicoll, 'The Joint Intelligence Committee and Warning of Aggression', November 1981, reproduced in Robert Dover and Michael S. Goodman (eds), *Learning from the Secret Past: Cases in British Intelligence History* (Washington, DC: Georgetown University Press, 2011) pp. 278–80.
7. Nicoll, 'The Joint Intelligence Committee and Warning of Aggression'; Cradock, *Know Your Enemy*, p. 253; Minute from 24 July 1968, FCO 28/48, quoted in Cradock, *Know Your Enemy*, p. 251.
8. 'The Soviet Grip on Eastern Europe', 2 December 1968, JIC(68)54. TNA: CAB 158/71.
9. Such action would later become known as the Brezhnev Doctrine.
10. Hughes, 'British Policy towards Eastern Europe and the Impact of the "Prague Spring"', p. 129.
11. Ibid.
12. Cradock, *Know Your Enemy*, p. 257; Hughes, 'British Policy towards Eastern Europe and the Impact of the "Prague Spring"', p. 127.
13. Richard J. Aldrich, *GCHQ: The Uncensored Story of Britain's Most Secret Intelligence Agency* (London: HarperPress, 2011), pp. 255–6.
14. Cradock, *Know Your Enemy*, p. 258; Hughes, 'British Policy towards Eastern Europe and the Impact of the "Prague Spring"', pp. 130, 133.
15. Cabinet minutes, 5 December 1968, CC(68) 49th Conclusions. TNA: CAB 128/43.

15

THE RISE OF INTERNATIONAL TERRORISM IN THE MIDDLE EAST

Terrorism currently features prominently in government defence and security discourse. Whitehall machinery, such as the Joint Terrorism Analysis Centre, is designed to counter the threat in a coordinated manner. This, however, was not always the case. Although the United Kingdom has endured a comparatively lengthy experience of modern terrorism, the JIC traditionally focused on the conventional Cold War. In the 1960s, most eyes looked towards Moscow at Soviet military activity. Any encounters the JIC had had with terrorism were predominantly of the anti-colonial variety. Even then, the committee was reluctant to characterise certain insurgents as 'terrorists'. Fearing that the term held connotations with British defeat in Palestine, the JIC warned against using the label to describe the Malayan insurgents. Despite this, nationalist attacks were sporadically described as terrorism throughout the era of decolonisation.

By the late 1960s, terrorism found a regular place on the JIC agenda. Security in Northern Ireland deteriorated dramatically from 1969 (as discussed in the following chapter). At around the same time, the threat of international terrorism in the Middle East escalated. The aftermath of Israeli victory in the 1967 war, which so unambiguously confirmed Israel's conventional military superiority over the Arab states, provided the opportunity for the emergence of Palestinian resistance movements as a political force. From among this disparate grouping, the Popular Front for the Liberation of Palestine (PFLP), led by George Habash, rose to gain notoriety. International terrorism, and specifically incidents of aviation hijacking, rose sharply between 1967 and 1976.

The year 1970 was particularly intense. The most notorious incident came in September when terrorists hijacked four planes, taking the passengers hostage in the Jordanian desert. The UK was not immune from the terrorist threat. In May 1970, for example, two Molotov cocktails were thrown at the US embassy in London. The following October, two parcels containing grenades addressed to the Israeli embassy and the Israeli airline El Al were found in the London office of the British Overseas Airways Corporation.[1]

Whitehall was unprepared. In 1968 Burke Trend, a Cabinet Secretary particularly interested in intelligence, established a working party to examine attacks on aviation. More, however, was needed. MI5 was still primarily a counterespionage service, hunting Soviet moles. Indeed, the JIC did not formally establish MI5's lead role in counterterrorism until late in 1972. Even then counterterrorism fell under the jurisdiction of MI5's countersubversion branch until the mid-to-late 1970s, when an independent department was established.[2] Meanwhile, GCHQ similarly focused on the Soviets. Although Britain's signals intelligence targets were more diverse than those of the American National Security Agency, Soviet military activity remained the highest priority in Cheltenham. Therefore whilst GCHQ had large-scale intelligence collection programmes operating in the Middle East, these were focused on Soviet activity or the likelihood of a conventional conflict between Israel and her neighbours.[3]

To complicate matters further, the rise of international terrorism muddled the intelligence community's operating procedures that had evolved alongside the Cold War. Terrorism crossed departmental boundaries and transcended national borders. It even eroded the state's monopoly on national security by involving private companies in activities such as transport and oil infrastructure. Accordingly, countering international terrorism involved diverse and myriad actors. On the one hand these included the intelligence agencies and the Foreign Office, which were well accustomed to the workings of the secret world. On the other hand, counterterrorism involved actors such as the Department of Trade and Industry and the Department of Transport, which were far less experienced in handling intelligence. Various Cabinet committees were also formed to deal with different aspects of the 'threat'.

The document reproduced below focuses on a specific but highly instructive case.[4] In 1970, set against the background of accelerating international terrorism, rumours of impending maritime terrorist attacks circulated around Whitehall. Officials feared that terrorist tactics were evolving. As governments grew increasingly wise to the dangers of aviation hijacking, the PFLP would apparently switch its attention to the sea. Fragmented and flawed intelligence was disseminated in a haphazard and contradictory manner. Speculation created unfounded panic not only amongst certain government officials, but also within private oil and shipping companies operating in the Mediterranean. Corporations, as well as British military forces in the region, were left confused and frustrated.

A coordinated, all-source intelligence assessment was vital. According to the Foreign Office, the JIC desperately needed to compose an assessment which would 'pull the threads of existing and future reports together and provide us with a better evaluation on which to base our own countermeasures and to advise the commercial interests involved'.[5] The document reproduced here fulfilled this function. It was issued at the end of October 1970, roughly six weeks after the first rumours were received in Whitehall and the confusion had begun. This particular document is also interesting as it is a rare example of a declassified Current Intelligence Group (CIG) report. The vast majority of JIC current intelligence has not yet been released, primarily owing to its sensitivity and the difficulty in camouflaging sources derived from both signals and human intelligence. Created from the Heads of Sections in 1964, CIGs were, and remain, composed of the relevant specialists from Whitehall's intelligence agencies and government departments. Organised functionally or geographically, each CIG was usually chaired by a Deputy Chief of the Assessments Staff (the JIC's report-drafting body). This particular report was drafted by the Middle East CIG. In short, CIGs were expert groups which drafted current intelligence reports for the main committee.[6]

CIGs reflected the organisation of both MI6 and GCHQ. Originating as JIC sub-committees, they proliferated during the 1970s and 1980s with groups on Africa, Latin America, the Middle East, the Far East/south-east Asia, Europe, Northern Ireland, the Soviet Union and terrorism. The creation of new CIGs reflected areas of major concern: typically in the early 1990s a Balkans CIG was created to address the multiple wars in the former Yugoslavia. Meeting weekly, their business was not unlike a university seminar and could be combative. Sir Michael Butler, who looked after the CIGs in the mid-1960s, recalls that they were constituted from appropriate departments in the Foreign Office, the Defence Intelligence Staff, MI5, MI6 and GCHQ, with participating observers from the CIA and other 'Five Eyes' services. They met every Tuesday to prepare drafts for submission to the JIC on Thursday, reviewing what had come in during the week in their area. But during a crisis in their region they might be in almost permanent session. CIGs constituted a core component of the Joint Intelligence Organisation.[7]

Sir Robin Hooper, the Chair of the Working Party on Acts of Violence against Civil Aircraft, requested this JIC paper. Like the Foreign Office, he sought a thorough and interdepartmentally agreed assessment, from which action could be recommended.[8] Moreover, Hooper argued that the report was necessary because it was 'reasonable to expect that the terrorists would seek new targets now that Arab Governments had announced themselves hostile to aircraft hijacking and security at airports had improved'.[9]

The report was an important development. It brought together all available intelligence to assess not only whether a terrorist attack was possible, but, crucially, whether it was likely. It added intentions to capabilities – vital for accurate assessments. The CIG also inserted qualifications regarding the quantity and reliability of intelligence, whilst discrediting some of the earlier rumours. The report is therefore an excellent example of the JIC reviewing the available evidence and attempting to issue an authoritative threat assessment. The committee was able to provide a fresh perspective on the problem and escape the earlier incremental analysis and perseveration by examining the body of evidence as a whole and in a detached manner. All-source analysis utilised in a coordinated and interdepartmental approach helped restore a sense of realism and counter the forces of threat exaggeration.

Hooper's working party discussed the JIC's intelligence the following week. Hooper was grateful for the intelligence and summed up the conclusions for his colleagues. The JIC had found that whilst a risk of sabotage existed, hijacking proved a lesser danger and there was very little evidence of any attacks planned against passenger ships. Moreover, the JIC had discredited the rumours which had alarmed the oil companies. Interestingly, however, Hooper was cautious about one particular JIC conclusion. The intelligence report asserted that 'it does seem that the PFLP – the largest and most important extremist group – is now less interested in the hijacking of aircraft and the same may be true of the other extremist groups'. Hooper and his colleagues were wary of lowering the threat level in accordance with this assessment. The working party claimed that whilst the JIC assessment could be taken as 'one indication that the risk of aircraft hijacking had diminished [...] for practical purposes, it was best to treat the risk to aircraft as continuing the same'.[10] Today, it is still politically more difficult for governments to decrease threat levels than to raise them.

The JIC's report and the working party's discussion were useful in countering confusion. The assessment 'had the virtue of highlighting the risk to shipping and showing the need for interdepartmental co-operation'.[11] Indeed, interdepartmental coordination in dealing with the international terrorist threat was swiftly enhanced. Departmental responsibilities and channels of communication were strengthened to ensure that a similar incident of threat exaggeration was less likely in the future. The first six months of 1971 saw practical improvements in terms of sharing intelligence and the use of JIC machinery. Similarly, the declassified files demonstrate increasing examples of departments commenting on other departments' reports before they were formally issued.

SECRET
(THIS DOCUMENT IS THE PROPERTY OF HER BRITANNIC MAJESTY'S GOVERNMENT)

GEN 9(70) 22   COPY NO 38

30 October 1970

CABINET
WORKING PARTY ON ACTS OF VIOLENCE AGAINST CIVIL AIRCRAFT

THE ARAB TERRORIST THREAT TO SHIPPING AND OIL INSTALLATIONS

Note by the Secretaries
...

At the request of the Chairman of the Working Party the attached assessment has been produced by JIC(A). It will be considered at a meeting of the Working Party on Monday 2 November at 4 pm in Conference Room A, Cabinet Office.

(Signed) T D O'LEARY
B M WEBSTER

Cabinet Office, SW 1
30 October 1970

SECRET

ARAB TERRORIST THREAT TO WESTERN INTERESTS (DELICATE SOURCE)

...

The Middle East Current Intelligence group met at 2.30 pm on THURSDAY 29 OCTOBER 1970 to consider the Arab Terrorist threat to Western Interests. The following is their report.

...

1. In this assessment, which has been requested by the GEN 9 Working Party on Acts of Violence against Civil Aircraft, we consider the potential threat to shipping and to oil installations from the Arab terrorist groups. We consider the potential threat to Western interests and particularly oil installations both in the Middle East and elsewhere in the world. The evidence on terrorist intentions so far available is slight but we hope to obtain some useful information based on captured fedayeen documents in the near future.

The Evidence

2. Earlier this month there were 2 reports suggesting that the terrorists were considering operations against oil tankers and oil installations. The first report, derived from CALTEX in New York, indicated that a 5-man commando team had left the Lebanon on 9 October for the Persian Gulf with the intention of destroying a major oil installation and of hijacking an oil tanker. The second report, from a Director of Mobil in London, was to the effect

that Palestine guerrilla activities were likely to be extended to ocean tankers in the Eastern Mediterranean, and that guerrillas had "probably obtained" 2 torpedo boats, together with fast craft, with the aim of taking over a tanker, emptying some of its oil into the sea, and exploding it. The captains of Mobil tankers had on 13 October been advised to be on their guard. However, in neither case has the threat in fact materialised and we understand that the Mobil report was based on speculation within the company. At about this time we also had a report from an apparently good source indicating that the PFLP were feeling disillusioned about the hijacking of aircraft, in view particularly of the very adverse reaction of Arab governments, and were now thinking more in terms of sabotage operations.

3. We have now just received a further report, obtained from the Jordanians, about the morale and plans of the PFLP. This reflects the result of questioning by the Jordanian security services of captured members of the organisation. According to this report the hijacking of aircraft has been "dropped as a technique" in view of the hostility of Arab governments. It was also observed that the Chinese government had warned Habbash (the leader of PFLP) during his visit to Peking that hijacking was likely to damage fedayeen relations with Arab governments. The Jordanians expected the PFLP to move on to sabotage and kidnapping. They had evidence that a sabotage plan exists but did not know the details. They believed that the Americans would be a priority target but that attacks might also be attempted against British interests. Gulf oil installations were thought to be a likely prime target, but there might also be "terrorising small time bomb attacks" in the UK and in the Lebanon. (Lebanon was considered the most likely place for this type of activity in the Arab world, as other Arab states would, in the Jordanian view, react too violently for the PFLP to be willing to take the risk). We have also had other indications that members of the PFLP have plans for kidnapping. The Jordanian view that the PFLP would drop hijackings is supported by a reported recent conversation between Mr Anthony Nutting and Yasin Arafat, in which the latter stated that he had received a written undertaking from Habbash not to engage in further hijackings (meaning presumably of aircraft).

4. We next attempt to define more precisely the possible targets for the terrorist groups.

Sabotage Operations

5. Although theoretically the most attractive target for the PFLP and the other terrorist groups who have gone in for sabotage would be oil installations inside Israel or the occupied territories, they are well aware of the formidable difficulties this would involve. Israeli oil terminal facilities in the port of Eilat could be attacked by fedayeen operating from the opposite Jordanian port of Aqaba. However, this would be no easy task given the close surveillance which the Israelis exercise and in any event the Jordanian authorities have for long taken measure to prevent such fedayeen activities in the knowledge that any Arab attack on Eilat are [sic] likely to be followed by harsher Israeli retaliation against Aqaba. In view of these considerations we think that the extremist fedayeen will go for American targets in the first instance, followed by other Western interests which can be identified with Israel. Pipelines represent a relatively easy target, but they can be repaired fairly quickly, and sabotage operations against those other than Israeli pipelines are open to the charge that they harm Arab interests as much or more than Western interests (as in the case of the PFLP's sabotage of Tapline last year). All types of US, and to a lesser extent British and other Western European oil installations in all parts of the Middle East must be reckoned to be at some risk. However, it seems likely that the terrorists will be tempted to concentrate their efforts in areas where they would hope that police counter-measures would be the least effective. In this respect US and to a lesser extent other Western oil installations in the Gulf area may seem a particularly inviting target. Kuwait may be a partial exception to this rule as the PFLP and other extremist fedayeen groups would stand to lose if, as a result of their actions in Kuwait, their substantial financial support from Kuwaiti sources were placed in jeopardy. Although we believe that the American and British oil companies operating in the Gulf have adopted fairly elaborate precautionary measures, the large Arab labour forces employed by the oil companies

give the terrorists obvious scope for this kind of activity.

6. It certainly cannot be excluded that terrorist groups may contemplate sabotage operations against oil installations outside the Middle East, although there is at the present moment no evidence of such planning. They might be attracted by the consideration that security precautions in some countries are likely to be much less stringent than in the Middle East, where they know that the companies are to some extent alerted to the risks. However, they would face greater practical difficulties in organising sabotage and making a success of it.

7. We believe that the reports of terrorist plans to carry out acts of sabotage against oil tankers deserve to be taken seriously. In the Mediterranean and in Europe the most likely target might be Israeli tankers or other ships carrying oil from, or trading with, Israel. However, in the case of Israeli ships the terrorists will be aware of the far-reaching security precautions the Israelis are believed to have instituted. In the Persian Gulf the terrorists may be interested in US, British and other Western European-controlled ships, particularly tankers, even though these are not trading directly with Israel. One particularly inviting target would be the tankers, most of which are registered in Panama but belong to American companies, which carry oil to Eilat.

8. Sabotage attempts can be expected to take place while ships are in harbour or at anchorage. The terrorists could either attempt to plant explosives after insinuating themselves onto a ship or to blow them up by placing limpet mines.

Hijacking

9. If Arab terrorists wished to attempt to hijack a tanker or other ship it is possible that they might seek to do this by acquiring high-speed vessels on which they might place armaments. They might also, in the Gulf, use distressed dows as a way of getting hijackers aboard a vessel. We have however no evidence, other than the tenuous Mobil speculation that they might be planning this. Another possibility is that they might seek to board vessels while in port and to take them over by holding

hostages. This would be the obvious method if a passenger vessel was involved. In such an operation the terrorists' object might be either to blow the ship up as a demonstration or to demand ransom in the form of ransom of fedayeen prisoners held in Europe or in Israel. We are inclined to think that the likelihood of such hijacking operations, which are open to some of the same political objections as the hijacking of aircraft, is less than that of sabotage. However, it cannot be altogether discounted.

Kidnappings and other activities

10. While the evidence is scanty, we continue to believe that there is a significant risk that the extremist groups may attempt kidnappings of Israelis and prominent Jews associated with Israel anywhere in the world, and of prominent American, British and other European individuals such as diplomats in the Middle East or elsewhere. The groups may also continue small scale bomb attacks against Israeli property such as the attack on the El Al office in London last year. In the Middle East itself, it is probably correct that, as the Jordanian authorities are suggesting, the fedayeen groups would now find it less easy than previously to stage such activities and would to some extent be deterred by the thought of counter-measures. Even in the Lebanon, where they enjoy the greatest freedom of action at present, the latter prospect could have this effect.

Conclusion

11. The evidence available to us does not permit us to draw any firm conclusions about the order of priority of the terrorist groups. However it does seem that the PFLP - the largest and most important extremist group - is now less interested in the hijacking of aircraft and the same may be true of the other extremist groups. This appears to be largely the result of the increasing hostility of Arab governments, whose attitude may make it somewhat harder for these groups to carry out other kinds of terrorist activities in most Arab states. However, the terrorists may reckon that circumstances in the Gulf area have not greatly changed and that US and to a lesser

extent British oil installations present an attractive target for sabotage. The evidence suggests that terrorist groups may have particular plans for sabotage of oil installations including tankers. While politically Israeli oil installations or tankers would be the best target, these are known to be well guarded, and tankers or other ships belonging to US or British controlled companies may seem a more practicable proposition. Tankers of any nationality carrying oil to or from Israel would be a particularly inviting target. The terrorists are, in our view, more likely to contemplate sabotage than the hijacking of ships, though the latter possibility cannot be discounted. The threats of sabotage/hijacking of ships are by no means confined to the Middle East, though the Gulf may be seen as offering the greatest scope for successful operations at the present time. At the same time we would expect the extremist groups to continue to show interest in other types of terrorist activity, including particularly kidnappings, which will similarly not be limited to the Middle East.

Signed W N ASH
for Secretary,
Joint Intelligence Committees

Cabinet Office, SW1
30 October 1970

Notes

1. Gérard Chaliand and Arnaud Blin, 'From 1968 to Radical Islam', in Gérard Chaliand and Arnaud Blin (eds), *The History of Terrorism: From Antiquity to Al Qaeda* (Berkeley: University of California Press, 2007), pp. 225–41; Ariel Merari, 'Attacks on Civil Aviation: Trends and Lessons', *Terrorism and Political Violence* 10/3 (1998), p. 10; Incident Detail, RAND Database of Worldwide Terrorist Incidents, http://smapp.rand.org/rwtid/incident_detail.php?id=704 (last accessed 31 October 2013).
2. Christopher Andrew, *The Defence of the Realm: The Authorized History of MI5* (London: Allen Lane, 2009), pp. 600, 614.
3. Richard Aldrich, *GCHQ: The Uncensored Story of Britain's Most Secret Intelligence Agency* (London: HarperPress, 2011), p. 299.
4. For more information on this case study see Rory Cormac, 'Much Ado about Nothing: Terrorism, Intelligence, and the Mechanics of Threat Exaggeration', *Terrorism and Political Violence* 25/3 (2013), pp. 476–93.
5. Dudgeon (Marine and Transport Dept FCO) to Ritchie (Permanent Under-Secretary's Department), 'Guerrilla Threat to Shipping: Intelligence Aspects', 16th October 1970. TNA: FCO 76/18.

6. Philip Davies, *Intelligence and Government in Britain and the United States: A Comparative Perspective, Vol. 2: Evolution of the UK Intelligence Community* (Santa Barbara, CA: Praeger, 2012), pp. 40–1.
7. Sir Michael Dacres Butler, interview, 1 October 1997, Churchill Archives, Cambridge.
8. Hooper to Trend, 'Guerrilla Threats to Shipping', 23 October 1970; handwritten note from Summerscale (Assessments Staff) to Thomson, 'Guerrilla Threat to Shipping', 26 October 1970. TNA: CAB 163/196.
9. Working Party on Acts of Violence Against Civil Aircraft minutes, 2 November 1970, GEN 9(70) 10th Meeting. TNA: CAB 130/475.
10. Ibid.
11. Ibid.

16

NORTHERN IRELAND: DIRECT RULE

SINCE ITS CREATION in 1936, the JIC has overwhelmingly focused on developments overseas. From eastern Europe to the Middle East to Malaysia, the committee has scoured the globe for threats to British security and interests. From the late 1960s, however, the JIC was also forced to concentrate on issues closer to home. An escalation of intercommunal violence in Northern Ireland brought about the lengthy period known as the Troubles. As was often the case regarding irregular and non-Cold War threats, however, the JIC was slow off the mark.

The JIC began to consider Ireland in the months leading up to April 1966, when officials grew concerned about security during the fiftieth anniversary of the Easter Rising. As the historian Eunan O'Halpin has revealed, however, the JIC then proceeded to ignore the deteriorating political and security conditions in Northern Ireland over the following couple of years. The JIC did not revisit the situation until 1968 in the aftermath of unrest following the civil rights marches. At this point, the committee established an Ulster Working Group. Although the JIC was initially surprised by the extent of the unfolding crisis, Northern Ireland featured fairly regularly on the JIC agenda by the summer of 1969.[1]

Demonstrating interesting similarities with the committee's response to earlier unrest in the British colonies, the JIC's role was twofold. Firstly, it sought to improve the intelligence system in Northern Ireland. Given the initial flaws in the machinery, this proved to be an important function. Indeed, the Prime Minister himself, Edward Heath, read and annotated the JIC Secretary's valedictory thoughts on the topic in 1972, and in fact called for action to implement some of the points made.[2] The committee's input into the intelligence and security machinery raises interesting questions about its role in setting the parameters of intelligence operations, from internment to sanctioning the infamous five interrogation techniques (including stress positions and sleep deprivation). Secondly, the JIC maintained its traditional role of intelligence assessment to aid policy formulation. This chapter focuses on the latter role.

As the Troubles became a regular fixture on the JIC agenda, the committee began to update policymakers on the security situation as well as the strength and intentions of the paramilitary groups.[3] Perhaps owing to the complexity, sensitivity and proximity of the violence, the JIC felt compelled to issue both a warning and a reminder to its consumers in 1971. The assessment opened by stating that 'the summary below only highlights some of the major points in the paper and cannot by its very nature convey the nuances of the Irish situation'. Such a statement is highly unusual and perhaps represents JIC caution given the contentious issues involved. The committee was apparently more conscious of political misuse of its intelligence with regard to Ireland than to other irregular threats in more far-flung places. The same report also included a reminder to the government of the importance of policy in shaping the landscape of the conflict, including that such matters lay beyond the jurisdiction of the JIC. The committee, of course, does not recommend policy but it seems strange that, again when it came to Ireland, a reminder was necessary.[4]

JIC intelligence assessments did, however, influence policy debates. The imposition of direct rule in March 1972 instructively demonstrates the interaction between the JIC and the policy community. Military planners and the most senior policymakers needed intelligence to inform contingency planning. Heath's strategy was based on the assumption that in circumstances of direct rule 'we could continue to rely on the loyalty of the Royal Ulster Constabulary (RUC) and the public service in Northern Ireland'. But the Prime Minister had concerns. He asked his Home Secretary, Reginald Maudling: 'Suppose that that assumption proved to be invalid. Have we alternative plans ready?'[5] Maudling reassured Heath that there was no reason to assume that 'the vast majority [of NI civil service] would not remain basically loyal'. He believed that the RUC would remain faithful but would be 'likely to need a good deal of stiffening'. Maudling informed Heath that JIC reports on intelligence requirements remained valid but that the issue was being looked at again.[6]

New evidence began to question this optimistic outlook. Lord Carrington, the Defence Secretary, had recently visited Northern Ireland and warned of a real risk of mass withdrawal of labour from all public services, including not only the civil service but also the police. Summarising the new information, which also included other reports and a recent JIC paper, Burke Trend, the Cabinet Secretary, warned that 'direct rule would represent an even more appalling strain on our resources than we have hitherto been prepared to contemplate'. If Carrington was correct, according to Trend, ministers needed to abandon the concept of direct rule as had hitherto been conceived, and instead be prepared to consider 'something like military government and martial law administration'.[7]

Ministers needed a fresh intelligence assessment of the implications of direct rule. So too did the military. Indeed, the Chiefs of Staff emphasised the 'urgent need' for an assessment upon which planning could be based. This was particularly the case given that word was beginning to reach the military that ministers now feared direct rule would have a much more serious effect on the police and civil service than had previously been assumed. Despite the urgency and to the frustration of the military, intelligence was not immediately forthcoming. The JIC had been provided with a list of questions to consider, but, for reasons that remain unclear, the committee had not actually started the assessment. The Chiefs of Staff were forced to ask the Permanent Under-Secretary at the MoD to pressure Trend to get the ball rolling.[8]

The JIC's report was eventually issued on 6 January 1972 and is reproduced below. Acknowledging the highly speculative nature of the assessment, the JIC broadly concluded that reactions to direct rule would depend principally on the circumstances of its introduction.[9] Trend later summarised the conclusions for the Prime Minister:

> A recent JIC assessment of reactions to direct rule suggests that the majority of the RUC and the Civil Service would remain loyal but that for the bulk of the Protestant population (and to some extent for the RUC) much would depend on the circumstances in which measures were taken, the way in which they were presented, and what they appeared to be leading to. Assurances regarding the border would be important; the reaction to the possibility of minor boundary adjustments is difficult to assess.[10]

Trend explicitly drew on the JIC's conclusions when briefing Heath on policy options. The Cabinet Secretary's advice, offered in January 1972, is worth quoting in full:

> We must accept that we have really reached the end of the road as regards solutions which do not carry a serious risk of direct rule as the inevitable outcome; and we can perhaps extract some comfort from the latest JIC assessment which, in assessing probable reactions to the introduction of direct rule, says that 'the Protestant reaction would probably be calmest if direct rule were introduced at a time when IRA violence had ceased but their capacity for violence remained unimpaired and there seemed a high risk of its resurgence in the not too distant future. In these circumstances the Protestants would probably be ready to wait and see what occurred.' We may not be far from the point at which these conditions could be said, broadly, to have been realised. If so, we are perhaps approaching the juncture at which the Home Secretary's plan could be launched with the least risk of provoking an uncontrollable situation.[11] If we let that moment pass, it may not recur – if only because attitudes will tend to harden once again as the Protestants believe that they have 'won' and the Catholics retreat into sullen opposition. This suggests that, in principle, we should perhaps be prepared to give the plan a run at the right moment, even if only *faute de mieux*.[12]

Trend's plan was overtaken by events. Bloody Sunday, the killing of fourteen unarmed civilians by the British army, occurred ten days later. The republican backlash clearly negated Trend's belief that the JIC's aforementioned criteria were close to being met. Despite this, something needed to be done. Violence had escalated too far.

Heath hesitated. The JIC had warned him that both sides would see direct rule as the first step towards reunification. However, the head of the army in Northern Ireland assured him that any Protestant backlash would develop slowly, allowing reinforcements to be sent.[13] Accordingly, direct rule was implemented in late March 1972. Interestingly, the civil service of Northern Ireland adapted to direct rule remarkably well. In line with JIC predictions, it remained loyal. Indeed, the civil service helped provide continuity and stability in the administration of key services.[14] Although seen as a temporary measure, direct rule would last until 1999.

```
                    U.K. EYES ONLY
                        SECRET


                      PERIMETER

THIS DOCUMEMT IS THE PROPERTY OF HER BRITANNIC MAJESTY'S
GOVERNMENT


JIC(A)(71) 54     COPY NO 152


6 January 1972    PERIMETER
                  UK EYES ONLY
                  NOT FOR INTEGRATED OR EXCHANGE POST
CABINET           OFFICERS


             JOINT INTELLIGENCE COMMITTEE (A)
                           ...
   THE PROBABLE REACTIONS TO THE INTRODUCTION OF DIRECT
                RULE IN NORTHERN IRELAND
                           ...
       Report by the Joint Intelligence Committee (A)


                    PART I - SUMMARY


1. Predictions can at this stage only be highly specula-
tive. Reactions to Direct Rule would depend principally
on the circumstances of its introduction, particularly in
relation to the security situation, and on what the two
Communities believed would follow it. The current belief
among both Catholics and Protestants is that Direct Rule
would be the first step towards reunification. Opinions
```

in Northern Ireland are changeable, particularly on the Protestant side and this paper will need to be kept under constant review.

2. There is a degree of general recognition among Protestants that it is now impossible to return to the system that has prevailed hitherto. They would, if Direct Rule were introduced, attach the highest importance to a pledge that the consent of the majority would be needed before reunification could take place, although it might be difficult to dispel doubts about Her Majesty's Government's ability or willingness to keep the pledge for any length of time. If such a pledge were not believed, they might oppose the measure with violence. But even in this case the violence would probably be of manageable proportions unless Protestants believed they were in danger of being handed over to the South at an early stage without their consent.

3. A majority of the Civil Services, Judiciary and RUC would be likely to co-operate. The attitude of the RUC would be critical for the continued flow of intelligence. The essential point for them would be their confidence in Her Majesty's Government's intentions on the border.

4. The Catholics would see the measure as ending the Unionist monopoly of power and expect it to be used to introduce radical changes. The Brady IRA would probably step up violence against the Army and RUC if they could, while the Gouldingites would be likely to concentrate on the Civil Disobedience campaign. Both would use intimidation where necessary. Direct Rule would be welcomed in the Republic if it seemed likely to be the prelude to radical change in the North.

5. Even if IRA violence were to be suppressed now, it could be expected to break out again before very long and Catholics would not acquiesce in permanent Unionist rule. Direct Rule would not by itself make much difference to the situation. Neither Community has full trust in Westminster. Most would see Direct Rule as providing at best a breathing space, perhaps a short one, in which Her Majesty's Government could introduce new policies. If early proposals for radical change were not made by Westminster, continued action against the IRA could persuade Catholics that Her Majesty's Government's purpose was to ensure Protestant domination.

Signed STEWART CRAWFORD Chairman, on
behalf of the Joint Intelligence
Committee (A)

Cabinet Office
6 January 1972

THE PROBABLE REACTIONS TO THE INTRODUCTION OF DIRECT RULE IN NORTHERN IRELAND

PART II: MAIN REPORT

INTRODUCTION

Predicting the effects of Direct Rule in Northern Ireland is highly speculative. It is important to bear this in mind from the outset, for in January 1972 the Committee cannot be sure of the circumstances in which the measure might be introduced, the immediate policies Her Majesty's Government might adopt, or even the long-term purpose of Direct Rule. Opinions in Northern Ireland are changeable, particularly on the Protestant side, and this paper will need to be kept under constant review.

2. We therefore begin this paper by setting out some of the major considerations which might govern the timing of the measure and the reasons for its introduction, together with some of the assumptions which seem likely to govern Her Majesty's Government's policy. With these points in mind we then describe probable first reactions to Direct Rule. The likely reactions of people in Northern Ireland to various constitutional arrangements which might be considered following the imposition of Direct Rule are discussed in the Annex.

CIRCUMSTANCES IN WHICH DIRECT RULE MIGHT BE INTRODUCED AND POLICY ASSUMPTIONS

3. Direct Rule might be introduced because it appeared to be the only way to stop the security or general political situation getting out of hand, or because Her Majesty's Government wished to introduce a particular policy in an effort to get round a political stalemate in Northern Ireland itself, or for a combination of both these reasons. The major purpose of Direct Rule would probably

be to prevent further deterioration in the overall position. If, however, the worst were over, and the security situation had become sufficiently stable for it to be generally recognised by both Protestants and Catholics that a major revival of IRA activity was unlikely in the immediate future, the main object of taking further power into Westminster's hands would be to introduce new policies designed to produce a longer-term solution to the general political problems of the province. In either case, it would be each Community's expectation of what would accompany and follow Direct Rule, rather than the measure itself, which would govern their reactions.

The Assumptions

4. We take it that, in introducing Direct Rule, Her Majesty's Government would be guided by the following assumptions -
   i. The efforts of the security forces against the IRA would continue under Direct Rule as long as the IRA's campaign of violence lasted; action against Protestants would be taken if their reaction was a violent one.
   ii. The search for a solution would continue on the basis that an active, permanent and guaranteed role must be found for the minority in the life and public affairs of the province.
   iii. If the North and South wished to form a united country Her Majesty's Government would not obstruct that solution. Reunification would be acknowledged as an honourable and legitimate aim, but one which could only be achieved by consent of the people of the North.
   iv. Direct Rule would be a temporary measure until such time as other arrangements could be made.
We further assume that these points would be made in the public statement issued at the time of the introduction of Direct Rule, which would also explain the working arrangements.

The Current Contingency Plans for Direct Rule

5. These provide for a Minister (or the Governor) to be vested with full authority for all existing responsibilities of the Northern Ireland Government. He would

exercise this authority through existing departmental machinery, including the civil service departments in Belfast, supported by a suitable staff of his own. It might be necessary to introduce personnel from Britain, possibly even on a large scale.

PROBABLE FIRST REACTIONS TO THE INTRODUCTION OF DIRECT RULE

The Current Protestant Mood

6. There is a degree of general recognition among Protestants that it is now impossible to return to the system which prevailed hitherto. The Protestant position has been eroded by the increasing involvement of Westminster and the gradual Unionist retreat before pressure for reform. The successes scored by the Army have not lifted Protestant spirits as much as might have been expected and many seem cautious and uncertain about the future, including the future viability of Stormont. At the same time the continued level of violence may just possibly be beginning to make some see the need for a negotiated settlement with the Catholics rather than violent measures against the IRA whenever they reassert themselves. While unemployment has been a constant factor in the lives of many, and a relatively modest increase or decrease is not therefore likely greatly to affect the mood of Protestant workers, many of the middle class are worried about the economic implications of a continuance of the present situation. The middle class, moreover, together with an increasing number of the working class, are weary of violence and disenchanted with the present politics and politicians of Northern Ireland. These people feel that if changes are not made, the present type of violent campaign will recur in a few years even if the IRA should be defeated now. They are not clear about what changes are needed, and many look to increasing integration with the South through the EEC to provide a long-term answer, but the fact that the need for change is seen, and that men like Boal and Paisley are beginning to discuss, however obliquely, the political nature of Ireland as a whole, is a sign of hope.

The Overall Protestant View

7. Most Protestants would see Direct Rule as putting an end to their position as the permanently dominant power in Northern Ireland. They would therefore attach the highest importance to a pledge by Her Majesty's Government that integration with the South could take place only in accordance with the will of the majority in the North and also to a continued security effort to give substance to that pledge. Nevertheless, many Protestants would fear that Direct Rule was a first step towards reunification. Their basic aim has been to preserve what they see as the Protestant way of life and their basic fear that this would be impossible in what they regard as a theocratic Republic. So far this has meant keeping power in Protestant hands, the continued dominance of the Unionist Party and the prevention of those who wish to alter the status of Northern Ireland from achieving or sharing power. If the nature of the Republic were to change, in particular so as to remove elements in the constitution which give the Roman Catholic Church a special position, the idea of reunification might become more acceptable to Protestants. At present, however, they believe the only way of preserving their identity is to keep power in their own hands. Rule from Westminster in whatever form would breach this safeguard. Moreover, there is widespread scepticism among Protestants about the ability of Whitehall/Westminster to match the wiles of the Irish Catholics, North or South, as well as uncertainty about the will of Her Majesty's Government to support the Protestant case.

General Protestant Reactions

8. Protestant reactions to the introduction of Direct Rule in hypothetical circumstances are inherently hard to assess, and our information about their moods and resources remains scanty. It is probable that the nature and extent of their immediate reaction would be largely determined by 2 things –
   a. the security situation at time of its introduction;
   b. their confidence that Her Majesty's Government would stand by their pledge about reunification with the South embodied in the 1949 Act.

These two considerations might interact. If the security situation were bad and the IRA claimed that the introduction of Direct Rule was a victory which would be followed by more violence and eventual reunification, then there would be a danger that the Protestants might, whatever Her Majesty's Government said, believe the IRA claim and react with violence in the first place against the Catholics but possibly also against the security forces. If the security situation was good, many Protestants would see no advantage for themselves in the introduction of Direct Rule and might be led by extremist propaganda to believe that it showed Her Majesty's Government's intention to go back on its word about reunification. Again violence might be the result. The Protestant reaction would probably be calmest if Direct Rule were introduced at a time when IRA violence had ceased but their capacity for violence remained unimpaired and there seemed a high risk of its resurgence in the not too distant future. In these circumstances the Protestants would probably be ready to wait and see what occurred.

9. Should Direct Rule be introduced in circumstances where Protestants reacted violently, there is reason to believe that any armed resistance to the security forces that they offered would probably be of manageable proportions, provided that Her Majesty's Government could bring home to them that there was no question of their being reunited with the South against their will. The Protestants have arms, and an organisational nucleus in the Ulster Special Constabulary Association and the Orange Order. The existence of the vigilante groups and recent Protestant restraint shows organised discipline and control. The UDR contains trained men some of whom might join Protestant bands in an emergency. The Protestants would, nevertheless, be reluctant to take on the Army, and so far lack a coherent programme or a leader to rally to in opposition to Direct Rule. There is no new Carson on the horizon at the moment, and we believe it unlikely that such a leader would emerge in response to Direct Rule. The Protestants could not expect to get much support in Westminster if they resisted Direct Rule forcibly; on the contrary, they might conclude that such resistance might encourage public demands in Britain for the withdrawal of the Army. They would find themselves in a quandary and might see their only practical

course of action to lie in the declaration of an independent Protestant Ulster. The idea of UDI has already its emotional attractions for some, but few Protestants would be prepared to take practical steps towards it in the face of opposition from the Army. An economically prosperous and politically stable independent Northern Ireland is virtually impossible to envisage as the end result of defiance of the United Kingdom.

10. Violence is more likely to be triggered off if the circumstances in which Direct Rule was imposed gave colour to IRA propaganda that it was a prelude to early reunification, and led Protestants to believe that it would not preserve their way of life. Although Protestants would be very reluctant to take on the security forces in an attempt to frustrate Direct Rule they could attack the Catholics as an instinctive emotional reaction if driven to desperation, and this would in turn lead to clashes with the security forces. So far as can be judged now, it is unlikely that violent conflict would last for more than a few weeks and improbable that it would be widespread. Even in the worst case, Protestants would be likely to react by destroying capital assets and utilities and in some cases by emigration, together with a civil disobedience campaign, rather than by mounting and sustaining an IRA-type campaign of their own. It is also possible that some at least would decide to come to terms with the South. Many Protestants would in any case believe that the threat of armed opposition, coupled with a civil disobedience campaign, was a better bargaining counter to use with London than actual armed resistance.

The Civil Service and Judiciary

11. In most probable circumstances, the very great majority of the Northern Ireland Civil Service and Judiciary, whatever their regrets for the past and fears for the future, would be likely to co-operate with Westminster. The Court system, however, might be disrupted by refusal of Protestant juries to convict Protestants or by intimidation of witnesses.

The RUC

12. The RUC would find themselves in a more difficult position than the Civil Service or Judiciary. Some senior members could well take early retirement. Whatever the circumstances the RUC would be likely to remain a cohesive force and to continue to play its part in maintaining Law and Order. But we believe that if Direct Rule were introduced at a time when most Protestants failed to see its justification, the RUC would be less ready to co-operate with the security forces. The effect of this could be serious, particularly in the Intelligence field, as it would be likely to coincide with the need to devote more effort to the Protestant target while maintaining coverage of the Catholics.

The Catholics

13. Catholic demands from many quarters have widened in scope since 1969 and now include, as a minimum, the destruction of Stormont and an end to the Unionist Party's monopoly of power. The institution of Direct Rule would arouse hopes among Catholics North and South that these aims were on their way to realisation and would be welcomed as a blow against the Unionist Party. Like the Protestants, however, many Catholics distrust Westminster and believe that Irish affairs ought to be managed by the Irish. They would expect that Her Majesty's Government would swiftly come forward with proposals for political advance. Meanwhile the civil disobedience campaign would be maintained as a means of pressure on Her Majesty's Government, particularly for an end to internment.

Catholics and the Security Situation

14. Reactions in the Catholic Community to Direct Rule would be deeply influenced by the security situation and the policies adopted by Her Majesty's Government to meet it. Many in the Catholic enclaves at present see the Army as operating to repress the Catholics as a Community, not just against the IRA, on behalf of continued Protestant domination. To some degree, they see this as the result of Stormont dictating policy to Westminster and to this

extent might regard Direct Rule as providing the chance for a new policy to develop. If Direct Rule had to be imposed when the security position was serious the need for continued action against the IRA would confirm many Catholics in the belief that Her Majesty's Government are inherently oppressive towards them. The prospects would clearly be better if the security situation were well in hand. The Catholics would in that event expect the cessation of IRA activities to be accompanied by action to remove from Protestant hands the arms which they see as a threat to the Catholic Community.

The Social Democratic and Labour Party

15. The Social Democratic and Labour Party (SDLP) would share the hopes of many Catholics that Direct Rule was the prelude to major political changes. It is doubtful, however, whether the Party would be prepared to take or respond to any immediate constructive initiative following its introduction. The SDLP is in some disarray and does not have a consistent policy.

The IRA

16. The Brady IRA have always welcomed the prospect of Direct Rule as heralding the "final round" with British imperialism. Their hope would be to exploit the situation through violence, keeping their hold on their supporters by the use of intimidation where necessary. They might be tempted to extend violence to Great Britain. If trouble were to develop between the security forces and Protestant mobs this would rebound to the operational advantage of the IRA.

17. The Goulding leadership are less disposed to violence than the Bradyites and have spoken against the prospect of Direct Rule on the grounds that it would "reduce democracy". Their long-term aim is to achieve positions of influence through existing political bodies and then to overthrow the system from within by violence if necessary, thus ushering in the "People's Republic". The Goulding IRA have been heavily involved in the civil disobedience campaign and would probably wish to concentrate on stepping up this rather than on attacking the security forces. They would be the more disposed to take

this line, and might persuade some Brady supporters to follow them, if the security situation had become stabilised and there was a risk that militant IRA action could alienate the Catholic Community by putting at risk the chances of political advance through negotiation with Her Majesty's Government and Protestants. They, also, would continue to maintain cohesion using intimidation where necessary.

The Republic

18. Lynch would welcome Direct Rule if he believed it to be the prelude to radical change in the North. His long-term aim is, and will continue to be, reunification, perhaps under a new constitution. He and other Ministers have spoken in vague terms since 1969 about the need for radical changes in the constitution and laws of the Republic to accommodate a substantial non-Catholic minority. Lynch has proposed inter-party talks in Dublin about what those changes might be. In the short term Lynch wants first the abolition or complete transformation of the present Stormont system (without which step, he believes, the minority can have no confidence that they will never again be subjected to a permanent Unionist regime): secondly, some public hint by Her Majesty's Government that they look in the long term towards reunification: and thirdly a change of emphasis on the security front from military action against the IRA to an attempt to win back the confidence of the minority by demonstrating the impartiality of Her Majesty's Government. This Lynch believes to entail not merely the abolition of the present Stormont system, but changes in the present policies of internment, cratering and arms searches. Lynch's aims are shared by all parties in the Republic and are unlikely to change. Lynch has a strong political interest in seeing the present situation brought to an end: it weakens his own position as against the extremists in his own party and outside; it threatens the spread of violence, perhaps involving Irish Security Forces, along the Border; and it is already starting to bring about a deterioration in the internal situation in the Republic which must eventually endanger the democratic system. Above all, he believes that the IRA cannot be defeated purely by military

means. In principle, therefore, Lynch would probably be prepared to welcome (and later support) Direct Rule provided that it satisfied, or promised to satisfy, his major short-term aims.

19. We cannot be sure what sort of Government might follow if Lynch were to go. But it is probable that it would be either less effective or less accommodating.

Attitudes Once Direct Rule Has Been Introduced

20. While Direct Rule could provide a breathing space it will not, by itself, do much more, and the breathing space would be likely to be short. Both Catholics and Protestants would see it as important not so much in itself but in what they believe it would lead to. If no major political initiative were taken fairly soon after its introduction the disillusionment currently felt by most Catholics with Westminster would deepen, especially if operations against the IRA continued. Neither Community, in effect, is likely to trust Westminster for long and while Direct Rule could provide the opportunity for radical change by removing the Unionists from power at least temporarily, the chance could be a fleeting one and its advent could be judged only according to moods in the province at the time. An Annex discusses the reactions of people in Northern Ireland to the main courses of action which they believe Her Majesty's Government might take following the introduction of Direct Rule, depending on what Her Majesty's Government says at the time.

ANNEX TO JIC(A)(71) 54

WHAT MIGHT BE EXPECTED IN THE NORTH TO FOLLOW
DIRECT RULE

1. There are a number of courses of action, consistent with the assumptions of this paper (paragraph 4) which Her Majesty's Government might announce at the time of the imposition of Direct Rule or which the Communities in Northern Ireland might be led to expect. The spectrum of possibilities is a wide one, but people in Northern Ireland would probably see these reduced in general

terms to three options for Her Majesty's Government: the restoration of an independent Stormont together with constitutional devices to protect the interest of the minority; radical changes indicating an intention that Northern Ireland should in the future be fully integrated into the United Kingdom; and changes similar to those in the first alternative but including elements suggesting a desire to facilitate a closer relationship with the Irish Republic. There would in practice probably be little difference between the second and third possibilities in terms of the actual reforms introduced. Reactions will be chiefly determined by what the Communities understand Her Majesty's Government's ultimate intentions to be. As regards the reaction of the Northern Ireland Civil Service and the RUC, in particular, we consider that our assessment in paragraph 11 and 12 of the main report is likely to remain valid under each option.

Restoration of an Independent Stormont

2. Even if the IRA were forced to abandon violence and were discredited with the Catholic working class, the Catholics would not acquiesce in continued Unionist rule. The SDLP and Catholic moderates are not totally blind to the need eventually to come to terms with the Protestants, but civil disobedience and their withdrawal from Parliamentary and other office would be likely to continue so long as they believed Stormont would remain permanently dominated by the Unionist Party.

3. It would be possible to devise constitutional means of protecting the interests of the minority in Stormont. Nonetheless, the Unionist Party would, if it held together, be able to retain a permanently dominating position in any elected central decision-making body like Stormont. In these circumstances non-sectarian parties would have little influence. A period of peace and the implementation of current reforms, together with Faulkner's "green paper" proposals, could perhaps do something to alter this situation and permit the emergence of parties based on the general, rather than the communal, interest. But the hope would be a slim one. Without radical reform a resurgence of violence in the

next few years would be looked on as a virtual certainty even if the IRA can be suppressed this time round.

Northern Ireland Permanently Integrated into the United Kingdom

4. This might take a number of forms but the essential points would be the complete subordination of Stormont to Westminster and the transfer of responsibility for security. It would be possible on this hypothesis to secure by legislation at Westminster the introduction of various reforms in Northern Ireland similar to those in the previous alternative, in order to protect the position of the minority. Nevertheless Protestants might well fear that concessions to Catholics would lead in the end to reunification and their becoming a minority in the South, while Catholics might continue to see reunification as their only guarantee in the long run from domination by the Protestants. The touchstone, so far as Protestants were concerned, for judging whether reforms were or were not a step towards reunification would be whether Stormont, under whatever name, remained and whether they thus retained the power to decide this basic question. Catholics would judge the situation similarly. All would turn on how Her Majesty's Government expressed their policy towards reunification.

Reforms Looking Towards Eventual Reunification

5. This alternative would include reforms similar to those indicated above, and also institutional measures to encourage co-operation with Dublin. The Catholics would be encouraged to co-operate in Direct Rule and to negotiate seriously with the Protestants about what arrangements should follow if they believed this could open the way to reunification in the longer term. Most Catholics probably would not press for it immediately, partly because of the immense problem of integrating the Protestants into the Republic and partly because of the economic and social benefits of continued British citizenship. As a long-term aspiration, however, it would be important, and steps towards it, however small, would undercut the appeal of the IRA and diminish the risk of resumed violence after the end of the current

campaign. Nor would most Protestants be likely to react with violence if it became evident that Her Majesty's Government's ultimate and long term aim was to negotiate with the South. One possible effect of Direct Rule might indeed be to encourage the discussion that has just begun about the possible future constitution of a united Ireland. If it became apparent to both Communities in Northern Ireland that Her Majesty's Government was prepared to encourage such a debate, Catholics would probably be prepared to co-operate, while Protestants could perhaps overcome their present fears of an immediate sellout to the Roman Catholic South.

RESTRICTED

UK EYES ONLY

JIC (A) (71) 54

THE PROBABLE REACTIONS TO THE INTRODUCTION OF DIRECT RULE IN NORTHERN IRELAND

...

DISTRIBUTION

UNITED KINGDOM

Cabinet Ministers (if approved by the Secretary of the Cabinet)
Secretary of the Cabinet
Secretary, Counter Subversion Committee
Chiefs of Staff: to take note
Metropolitan Police Office, Mr P E Brodie
Ministry of Defence: D of DOP
Secretary, Defence Policy Staff
Director, Communications
Electronic Security Group
Joint Intelligence Committee (A)
Joint Intelligence Committee (B)
Secretary, Official Committee on Northern Ireland (For issue to Committee)
Secretary, Official Committee on Northern Ireland

Sub-Committee on Contingency Planning (For issue to Committee)

MILITARY COMMANDS

Secretary CICC (West)
Secretary, UK Cs-in-C Committee

UNITED KINGDOM NORTHERN IRELAND AUTHORITIES

Director of Operations, Northern Ireland (Lieut-Gen Sir Harry Tuzo)
Director of Intelligence, Northern Ireland
UK Representative, Northern Ireland (Mr H F T Smith)

FOREIGN AND COMMONWEALTH POST

Dublin, BE

Cabinet Office
7 January 1972

Notes

1. Eunan O'Halpin, '"A Poor Thing but Our Own": The Joint Intelligence Committee and Ireland, 1965–72', *Intelligence and National Security* 23/5 (2008), pp. 665–6.
2. Eunan O'Halpin, 'The Value and Limits of Experience in the Early Years of the Northern Ireland Troubles, 1969–1972', in Robert Dover and Michael S. Goodman (eds), *Learning from the Secret Past: Cases in British Intelligence History* (Washington, DC: Georgetown University Press, 2011), pp. 189–90.
3. Initially, these assessments overwhelmingly focused on the nationalist groups.
4. 'The Situation in Northern Ireland to the end of 1971', 10 September 1971, JIC(A)(71)44, TNA: CAB 186/9.
5. Prime Minister to Home Secretary, 24 September 1971, TNA: PREM 15/481.
6. Home Secretary to Prime Minister, 4 October 1971, TNA: PREM 15/482.
7. Cabinet Secretary to Prime Minister, 'Northern Ireland', 5 October 1971, TNA: PREM 15/482.
8. Confidential annex to Chiefs of Staff minutes, 26 October 1971, CoS 36th Meeting 1971, TNA: DEFE 4/261.
9. 'The Probable Reactions to the Introduction of Direct Rule in Northern Ireland', 6 January 1972, JIC(A)(71)54, TNA: CAB 186/9.
10. Cabinet Secretary to Prime Minister, 'Northern Ireland, Annex: Detailed Elements of the Proposed Reform', 26 January 1972, TNA: PREM 15/1001.
11. The Home Secretary's plan involved more of a direct approach from Westminster. This included reassurances regarding the border, a redefinition of the powers of government in Northern Ireland and a change in the composition of the government.

12. Cabinet Secretary to Prime Minister, 'Northern Ireland', 19 January 1972, TNA: PREM 15/1001.
13. William Beattie Smith, *The British State and the Northern Ireland Crisis, 1969–73: From Violence to Power-Sharing* (Washington, DC: United States Institute of Peace Press, 2011), p. 192.
14. Paul Carmichael and Robert Osborne, 'The Northern Ireland Civil Service under Direct Rule and Devolution', *International Review of Administrative Sciences* 69/2 (2003), p. 207.

17

THE FALKLANDS WAR

ON 2 APRIL 1982, Argentina invaded the Falkland Islands. Although the ensuing war lasted only until mid-June, it became the defining event of Margaret Thatcher's long premiership. Sir Frank Cooper, permanent under-secretary at the Ministry of Defence, believed that Thatcher 'regard[ed] it as the high peak of her whole prime ministerial life'.[1]

The invasion famously took Thatcher by surprise. 'The war', she recalled, 'was very sudden' and 'no one had predicted the Argentine invasion more than a few hours in advance.'[2] The factors explaining this make the Falklands War a highly instructive case study when considering intelligence and policy. The threat framework constructed by intelligence between the mid-1970s and early 1982 allowed the Falklands to escape ministerial attention. The JIC failed to provide warning and ministers were caught unawares.

The Argentine threat to the Falkland Islands had long been on the JIC's agenda. The committee concluded as early as March 1965 that invasion was unlikely, and this pattern continued throughout the mid-to-late 1970s when JIC assessments became more regular as tension increased.[3] Throughout this period, JIC members were in consensus and broadly argued that Argentina would not do anything rash until faced with a clear breakdown in negotiations.[4] Moreover, the JIC had established a model whereby escalation would occur gradually. Argentine intentions towards the Falklands, however, remained a low priority until October 1981 – and even then additional resources were not found to meet the growing importance.[5]

The last full JIC assessment before the invasion came in July 1981. According to the Franks inquiry, it had 'considerable influence on the thinking of Ministers and officials'.[6] Demonstrating continuity with previous assessments, the JIC judged that Argentina still sought sovereignty of the Falklands. Once again, however, intelligence suggested that Buenos Aires hoped to achieve this through peaceful means – but would turn to force as a last resort. Although noting some concerning trends, the JIC ultimately concluded that 'extreme Argentine reactions' were not imminent.[7] Unfortunately, the JIC paper remains classified and a Freedom of Information request has proved unsuccessful. This is surprising given that the conclusions have already been summarised in detail by Lawrence Freedman in his official history.

Nonetheless, the JIC paper proved influential in policy circles. It shaped government thinking. Firstly, the assessment reinforced the Foreign Office assumption that Argentina would follow the standard escalation path, beginning with the withdrawal of services.[8] Nicholas Ridley, the FCO minister with responsibility for the Falklands, echoed these conclusions just days after the report was published. He warned that if negotiations broke down, the UK 'must expect retaliatory action', beginning with withdrawal of Argentine services and escalating in the longer term towards 'some sort of military action'.[9]

Secondly, the JIC assessment influenced ministers and senior officials when they discussed a draft paper for the Defence Committee in early September 1981. Reinforced by the intelligence assessment, the draft paper recommended three choices of action ranging from opening negotiations with Argentina without the islanders' consent to setting contingency preparations in motion. Officials decided that it was a poor moment to put such unpalatable decisions to the Defence Committee, not least because the Argentine government was changing and more talks were due in December. Accordingly, the draft paper turned into a minute on the current situation.[10]

Thirdly, the MoD explicitly built on JIC conclusions. On receiving the report, defence officials judged that there had been a marginal increase in the threat, 'but not enough for us to alter our position from 1979'.[11] The following September, they did, however, compose a paper considering the defence implications of seeking to deter or counter by military means options available to Argentina which had been put forward by the JIC. The MoD's conclusion is worth quoting at length:

> Military measures to deter or counter Argentine military action against the Falkland Islands would require the despatch to the area of additional forces, primarily naval, and possibly on a substantial scale. Any such deployment would be costly and pose considerable logistic difficulties. To deter or repel even a small scale invasion would require a significant commitment of national resources, at the expense of commitments elsewhere, for a period of uncertain duration. To deal with a full scale invasion would require naval and land forces with organic air support on a very substantial scale, and the logistic problems of such an operation would be formidable.[12]

Fourthly, the JIC assessment created a threat framework which influenced ministerial thinking up until the invasion. As late as 24 March 1982, Lord Carrington and Thatcher were still reliant upon on the JIC's July assessment. Indeed, the Foreign Secretary explicitly informed his Prime Minister that Argentine options remained as set out in the JIC paper. Moreover, the threat levels and model of escalation also remained in place. Military action might take place as a final resort if negotiations broke down, but the more immediate response would see Argentina cutting off essential services to the islands.[13] Influenced by the JIC's model and framework, no meeting of the Defence Committee was held to discuss the Falklands during this period, and there was no reference to the islands at Cabinet level until 25 March.[14]

It is perhaps surprising that the JIC's July 1981 assessment and model remained in place for so long. The Latin America Current Intelligence Group met eighteen times between July 1981 and March 1982 – but did not discuss the Falklands. On four separate occasions officials considered whether or not to update the JIC assessment, but invariably decided against it. When assessing the Argentine threat to the Falklands, the Assessments Staff relied on four criteria. Firstly, progress in Argentina's dispute with Chile over the Beagle Channel; secondly, the political and economic situation in Argentina; thirdly, the state of interservice rivalry in Argentina; and fourthly, Argentina's perception of the prospects of making progress by negotiation. Information received after July 1981 was not thought to indicate any significant change in these factors.[15]

This approach opens up the JIC to two counts of intelligence failure: perseveration and an overreliance on secret intelligence. For example, the British ambassador in Argentina, Anthony Williams, sent an acute warning to the Foreign Office in autumn 1981. Based largely on open sources, the warning did not break the committee's cognitive rigidity. Overly dependent on secret intelligence, officials in London were not persuaded.[16] Similarly, the acquisition of power by Leopoldo Galtieri in December 1981 did not warrant a new assessment or a challenge of the existing intelligence consensus. The change of government was discussed neither in the 'Weekly Survey of Intelligence' nor in a JIC note. Officials broadly assumed that Galtieri would maintain the position of his predecessor, thereby making the crux of the JIC's 1981 paper valid.[17] Again this is surprising as, to achieve the presidency, Galtieri was forced to rely upon the support of the Argentine navy, whose commander-in-chief held a particularly hardline view about Argentine claims to the Falklands. Other new intelligence was also assessed within this framework. Accordingly, single pieces of material were dismissed on the grounds that each did not increase the risk beyond the JIC's report of July 1981.[18] The JIC was left unaware of a top secret Argentine national security directive circulated in January 1982. This stated that the junta 'resolved to analyse the possibility of the use of military power to obtain the political objective'.[19]

The Franks inquiry criticised the Joint Intelligence Organisation for overemphasising secret intelligence, which was more reassuring about prospects of early moves towards confrontation. Whitehall's central intelligence machinery overlooked open source intelligence and the weight of the Argentine press campaign in 1982. For example, the JIO dismissed material arising from the press by believing it was probably designed to exert pressure on the UK in negotiations.[20] The Falklands War emphasised the importance of a genuinely all-source intelligence assessment machine.

At the end of March 1982, the Latin America Current Intelligence Group put together an immediate assessment at very short notice. It was so highly classified that only Thatcher and her most senior colleagues saw it. Although concerned with events in South Georgia, where Argentina had established a presence, it concluded that the possibility of Argentina escalating the situation by landing a military force on another dependency of the Falklands could not be ruled out. According to the CIG, however, Argentina did not wish to be the first to adopt forcible measures. Once again, the model of escalation beginning with diplomatic pressure remained in place. Thatcher was left feeling deeply uneasy by the JIC assessment but still did not expect an imminent invasion. Uncertainty reigned. Only afterwards did a separate piece of intelligence, obtained through an intercept, confirm that an Argentine task force was on its way to the islands. A gloomy and confused atmosphere descended on Thatcher's room in the House of Commons.[21]

The JIC did not predict the Falklands invasion. The Prime Minister was 'deeply disturbed' about the JIC's performance. She summoned Patrick Wright, the newly appointed Chairman, to Chequers to be 'dressed down at considerable length for failing to predict the attack'. The meeting left Wright in need of 'a very strong drink'.[22] The JIC did, however, assess the situation once underway. This was done through current intelligence and immediate assessments. From January 1967, the JIC's current intelligence was augmented with special assessments and notes. The former covered important issues of immediate interest, whilst the latter examined longer-term matters of less urgency or expanded on a topic already covered by a special assessment. In September 1974, immediate assessments replaced special assessments. They remain classified.[23]

The JIC was the key provider of intelligence to the War Cabinet. Shortly after the invasion, the committee decided to disseminate a daily intelligence briefing which included sections on Argentine military dispositions and intentions, as well as reaction from other Latin American countries and the Soviet Union. The JIC issued a total of seventy-five daily assessments and twenty-three more detailed notes between 4 April and 18 June. Although the committee met twice a week during the war, the bulk of the work was conducted by the Latin America CIG. As Lawrence Freedman points out, the greatest challenge was not content but timing, given that Argentina was four hours behind London.[24]

One JIC immediate assessment of the Falklands War has, however, slipped through the net after being sent to the Americans. It is reproduced below.[25] Prepared by the Latin America CIG a couple of weeks after the invasion, it offers a unique insight into JIC current intelligence. The assessment was received through the top secret cable known as UMBRA, which signified highly sensitive communications or signals intelligence. It also sheds intriguing light on the relationship between the UK and the US. American attempts to show impartiality over the conflict caused 'incessant irritation' in London. The document reveals how Britain anxiously awaited the American response to an Argentine request to access the civilian Landsat satellite so as to provide images of the

Falklands area. According to the CIG, the political ramifications of American agreement would be far greater than the military. From 21 to 23 April, NASA duly programmed the civilian Landsat satellite to take the required pictures. From the American perspective, Landsat was a civilian programme without intelligence value. If the US acquiesced to British requests then it would jeopardise the project by implying it had espionage functions.[26]

The CIG assessed that the quality of images from Landsat would not offer the Argentines much intelligence. Britain expressed concern to Washington nonetheless. After some negotiation, America decided to use technical problems as a reason for not giving satellite material to Argentina. The following month, however, some material was transmitted to Buenos Aires. It revealed little.[27]

As well as creating a threat framework upon which policymakers relied, the JIC's performance (especially prior to the invasion) had longer-lasting implications. Although Franks ultimately cleared the JIC of failing to provide warning, the inquiry recommended a number of reforms to the committee's structure. Franks argued that the chair of the JIC should be a full-time position and a more critical and independent role. Consequently, he recommended that the Chairman should be appointed by the Prime Minister and be a member of the Cabinet Office.[28] This challenged JIC tradition, whereby the Chairman had long been drawn from the Foreign Office. In practice, Franks's recommendation did not make a great deal of difference and several subsequent Prime Ministers have chosen to appoint Chairs from the Foreign Office.[29]

```
                    TOP SECRET CODEWORD

                  WHITE HOUSE SITUATION ROOM

PAGE 01 OF 02              DTG: 171715Z APR 82  PSN: 044079
JIC JIR 1011 SIT276        TOR: 107/1910Z
DISTRIBUTION: NONE /001

[...]
INFO CSE


TOP SECRET [...] - DELICATE SOURCE - (UNITED KINGDOM
CLASSIFIED)

                                        DATED 17 APRIL 1982

[...]
THE FOLLOWING IS AN IMMEDIATE ASSESSMENT/JIC(82)(IA)29
PREPARED BY THE LATIN AMERICA CURRENT INTELLIGENCE GROUP
AT THEIR MEETING WHICH ENDED AT NOON ON 17 APRIL 1982
```

FALKLAND ISLANDS - 17 APRIL 1982 - TOP SECRET UMBRA - DELICATE SOURCE (UNITED KINGDOM CLASSIFIED)

MAIN POINTS

A LARGE PART OF THE ARGENTINE FLEET IS BELIEVED TO BE AT SEA. ARGENTINA HAS REQUESTED LANDSAT PHOTOGRAPHIC COVERAGE OF THE FALKLAND ISLANDS FOR 21-23 APRIL. TERRORIST ORGANISATIONS HAVE THREATENED BRITISH CITIZENS AND INTERESTS IN ARGENTINA AND URUGUAY. ARGENTINA HAS PREPARED A DRAFT NOTE FOR INVOKING ACTION UNDER THE RIO TREATY. THE SOVIET UNION IS REPORTED TO BE READY TO OFFER ARGENTINA SHIPS, AIRCRAFT AND LAND BASED MISSILES IN EXCHANGE FOR GRAIN. THE ARGENTINE FOREIGN MINISTRY HAS DENIED IN A TELEGRAM TO THE ARGENTINE EMBASSY IN VENEZUELA THAT THE SOVIET UNION IS PROVIDING INTELLIGENCE MATERIAL. THE HIGH LEVEL OF SOVIET PHOTOGRAPHIC COVERAGE OF THE AREA IS UNUSUAL.

ARGENTINE MILITARY

1. A GROUP OF FOUR ARGENTINE WARSHIPS WAS NOTED TO BE ABOUT 70 MILES SOUTH EAST OF THEIR BASE PORT OF PUERTO BELGRANO ON THE EVENING OF 16 APRIL; THEY WERE POSSIBLY INVOLVED IN GUNNERY FIRING AND TACTICAL EXERCISES. WE BELIEVE ANOTHER GROUP OF SHIPS WHICH PROBABLY INCLUDES THE AIRCRAFT CARRIER, IS AT SEA. WE DO NOT KNOW ITS POSITION. THERE IS NOW EVIDENCE THAT SHORT RANGE GROUND TO AIR MISSILES HAVE BEEN SITED CLOSE TO PORT STANLEY AIRFIELD.
2. ARGENTINA, WHICH IS A SUBSCRIBER TO THE LANDSAT PROJECT, HAS MADE A REQUEST TO THE UNITED STATES FOR THE LANDSAT PHOTOGRAPHIC SATELLITE TO BE TASKED TO COVER THE FALKLAND ISLANDS ON 21-23 APRIL. THE SATELLITE WAS DESIGNED TO PROVIDE NO INFORMATION OF MILITARY VALUE AND IT PRODUCES VERY LOW RESOLUTION PHOTOGRAPHS (80 METER). THE COVERAGE WOULD BE LIMITED TO THE FALKLAND ISLANDS THEMSELVES AND A FEW MILES OF SURROUNDING SEA. WE DOUBT WHETHER ARGENTINA WOULD BE ABLE TO DERIVE ANY MILITARY INFORMATION OF VALUE FROM THIS REQUEST. THE POLITICAL SIGNIFICANCE WOULD OUTWEIGH THE MILITARY.

ARGENTINE INTERNAL.

3. THREE BRITISH JOURNALISTS HAVE BEEN ARRESTED IN ARGENTINA APPARENTLY ON CHARGES OF SPYING. REPORTS INDICATE THAT

> TERRORIST ORGANISATIONS AND OTHER POLITICALLY MOTIVATED GROUPS FROM LATIN AMERICA MIGHT TAKE ACTION IN BRITAIN OR AGAINST BRITISH MISSIONS ABROAD. THE STAFF OF THE BRITISH EMBASSY IN MONTEVIDEO ARE AT PARTICULAR RISK.
>
> INTERNATIONAL REACTIONS
>
> 4. THE ARGENTINE FOREIGN MINISTRY HAS PREPARED A DRAFT NOTE TO THE PRESIDENT OF THE PERMANENT COUNCIL OF THE OAS REQUESTING A SPECIAL MEETING TO HOLD CONSULTATIONS ON ACTION UNDER THE RIO TREATY. (SUCH CONSULTATIONS IN THE OAS GOVERNING BOARD MAY PRECEDE A MEETING OF FOREIGN MINISTERS OF THE RIO TREATY STATES, ACTING AS THE RIO TREATY ORGAN OF CONSULTATION). THE MINISTRY HAS NOT AS YET INSTRUCTED ITS REPRESENTATIVE TO PRESENT THE NOTE; WE DO NOT CONSIDER THAT ARGENTINA IS LIKELY TO DO THIS WHILE MR HAIG'S MISSION CONTINUES.

Notes

1. Frank Cooper quoted in Peter Hennessy, *The Prime Minister: The Office and Its Holders since 1945* (London: Penguin, 2001), p. 412.
2. Margaret Thatcher, *The Downing Street Years* (London: HarperCollins, 1993), p. 173.
3. *Falkland Islands Review: Report of a Committee of Privy Counsellors* (Franks report), Cmnd. 8787 (London: HMSO, 1983), paras 19, 305.
4. Lawrence Freedman, *The Official History of the Falklands Campaign, Vol. I: The Origins of the Falklands War* (London: Routledge, 2005), p. 156. For an overview of the various JIC assessments see Franks report, paras. 50, 77.
5. Freedman, *The Origins of the Falklands War*, p. 155; Franks report, para. 311.
6. Franks report, para. 306.
7. Ibid., para. 95; Freedman, *The Origins of the Falklands War*, p. 137.
8. Freedman, *The Origins of the Falklands War*, p. 151.
9. Ridley to Carrington, 20 July 1981, Thatcher Foundation Archive.
10. Freedman, *The Origins of the Falklands War*, p. 137.
11. Ibid., p. 148.
12. Falklands: MOD draft paper, 'Defence Implications of Argentine Action against the Falkland Islands', 14 September 1981, TNA: PREM 19/643.
13. Carrington to Thatcher, 24 March 1982, PM/82/23, Thatcher Foundation Archive.
14. Hugo Young, *One of Us* (London: Macmillan, 1989), p. 262.
15. Franks report, paras 307–8.
16. Richard Aldrich, *GCHQ: The Uncensored Story of Britain's Most Secret Intelligence Agency* (London: HarperPress, 2011), pp. 392–3.
17. Freedman, *The Origins of the Falklands War*, p. 156.
18. For examples see Franks report, para. 151; note by H. Lowles (DIS), 10 March 1982, Thatcher Foundation archive.
19. Charles Moore, *Margaret Thatcher: The Authorized Biography, Vol. 1: Not for Turning* (London: Allen Lane, 2013), p. 661.

20. Franks report, para. 316.
21. Ibid., para. 310; Freedman, *The Origins of the Falklands War*, pp. 206–7; Moore, *Margaret Thatcher*, p. 665.
22. Moore, *Margaret Thatcher*, p. 670.
23. National Archives, 'CAB 189 Cabinet Office: Central Intelligence Machinery: Joint Intelligence Committee: Assessments and Notes', http://discovery.nationalarchives.gov.uk/SearchUI/Details?uri=C15827 (last accessed 11 November 2013).
24. Lawrence Freedman, *The Official History of the Falklands Campaign, Vol. II: War and Diplomacy* (London: Routledge, 2005), p. 28. This volume offers good descriptions of some of the JIC assessments throughout the war.
25. JIC(82)(IA)29, 17 April 1982; see also Carlos Osorio, Sarah Christiano and Erin Maskell (eds), 'Reagan on the Falkland/Malvinas: "Give [] Maggie enough to carry on ..."' National Security Archive website, 1 April 2012, http://www.gwu.edu/~nsarchiv/NSAEBB/NSAEBB374/ (last accessed 11 November 2013).
26. Ibid., pp. 165, 384–5.
27. Ibid, pp. 384–5.
28. Franks report, para. 319.
29. Len Scott, 'British Strategic Intelligence and the Cold War', in Loch K. Johnson (ed.), *The Oxford Handbook of National Security Intelligence* (New York: Oxford University Press, 2012), p. 146.

18

CHANGING REQUIREMENTS AT THE END OF THE COLD WAR

'NOTHING IS ETERNAL in this world.'[1] Mikhail Gorbachev's words of June 1989 about the Berlin Wall proved prophetic: it was torn down the following November. Germany reunified just under a year later. In 1990, Russia declared sovereignty from the Soviet Union and was quickly followed by other members of the communist bloc. After nearly half a century of Cold War, the fall of the Soviet Union was remarkably swift. This rapidity, however, belied the huge significance. It marked a major shift in international politics.

The end of the Cold War had a major impact on the British intelligence community. For the entire careers of most serving intelligence officers, the Soviet Union and international communism had been the primary target of their activity. Unsurprisingly, the JIC had spent the bulk of its existence watching Moscow, counting nuclear weapons and assessing the likelihood of future wars. And yet between 1989 and 1990, that threat suddenly crumbled. It was a rare cause for a typically understated JIC celebration. On hearing that the Soviet Communist Party had been proscribed, Sir Percy Cradock, Chairman of the JIC, invited his colleagues on the committee to join him for champagne. Raising his glass, Cradock toasted: 'We didn't have a war, and we did win.'[2]

Western intelligence agencies were caught off guard by the manner in which the Soviet Union collapsed. The CIA, however, has staunchly defended its record. Releasing many of its national intelligence assessments and estimates from the period for scrutiny, the agency has attempted to counter criticisms that the end of the Cold War was an intelligence failure. Even so, a number of senior American officials, from Lawrence Eagleburger, US Secretary of State in 1992, to Robert Blackwell, the CIA's Soviet specialist in the 1980s, have since admitted to being taken by surprise.[3]

British policymakers must have been surprised too, for the JIC seemingly did not foresee the Soviet bloc's implosion.[4] On 8 December 1989, Charles Powell, Margaret Thatcher's foreign policy adviser, confessed: 'We are finding that we are almost daily being taken by surprise by the pace of developments in the Soviet Union and Eastern Europe.'[5] In stark contrast to the Americans, however, the British government has refused to release any JIC document relating to the end of the Cold War. It is therefore unclear where the JIC went wrong and how its assessments were used by policymakers. Younger members of the Assessments Staff were keenly aware of the importance of the changes made by Gorbachev, but it appears the 'grandees' who dominated the JIC were more sceptical.[6] One potential explanation, put forward by Cradock, looks to the JIC's obsession with missile counting and a consequent tendency to overlook broader economic and political indicators.[7] Detailed analysis however, is a task for future historians.

What is abundantly clear, however, is that the end of the Cold War dramatically changed the landscape of security. It ushered in a new era of instability and uncertainty. In the absence of the long-standing Soviet threat, intelligence actors faced a fundamental reappraisal of priorities and requirements. They had to determine the nature and direction of any new threats, whilst becoming more flexible so as to meet increasingly diverse targets. Forced to justify their existence in the post-Cold War world, this, in practice, meant severe budget cuts. MI5 was forced to make compulsory redundancies for the first time since the end of the Second World War. Similarly, by 1995, GCHQ's budget had been slashed by £200 million a year. MI6 did not escape either. The Treasury inflicted poorly handled compulsory redundancies on the service. Overall staff levels dropped by 25 per cent, with cuts to senior management going even deeper. This left MI6 with a notably young senior management team. Young talent also formed part of the drive towards flexibility. Instead of retaining permanent and expensive assets on the ground across the world, MI6 sought to insert officers at short notice into a target country.[8]

The end of the Cold War also led to a new era of openness and oversight of the intelligence services. The British intelligence machinery emerged from the shadows. Whitehall's 'open government' programme included the gradual release of JIC documents for the first time in history. Meanwhile, the 1994 Intelligence Services Act placed MI6 and GCHQ on a legal footing for the first time. The Act also created the Intelligence and Security Committee (ISC). This was, and remains, a committee of senior parliamentarians (now chaired by Sir Malcolm Rifkind) and is charged with overseeing the expenditure, administration and policy of the UK's intelligence agencies.

The document reproduced below illustrates these two core themes: changing priorities and increasing oversight. It is an extract from the first ISC annual report, which draws heavily on testimony from the diplomat Paul Lever, then JIC Chairman. Half a decade on from Cradock's champagne toast, Lever was well aware of the shift in intelligence requirements that had taken place. He informed the new oversight committee that the United Kingdom now faced challenges that were a great deal more varied than those which had characterised the Cold War. Termed 'functional' topics, these myriad threats included terrorism, nuclear proliferation, international sanctions, and serious organised crime (such as drug trafficking and money laundering). Towards the end of the

1990s, the challenges of peacemaking and humanitarian interventionism had likely been added to the list. It was a decade of greater uncertainty in terms of threats – sandwiched between the dominance of the Cold War and the so-called war on terror. Lever's was a similar sentiment to that expressed more poetically by a former US Director of Central Intelligence, James Woolsey. He famously stated in 1993 that 'having slain the Soviet dragon, the intelligence community now found itself in a jungle full of snakes'.[9]

Lever, however, emphasised the JIC's lack of complacency towards the more traditional threats. The JIC assessed that neither Russia nor any other state belonging to the former Soviet Union posed a direct military threat to the United Kingdom. Despite this, it was certainly not forgotten that Russia still possessed a nuclear arsenal, vast strategic capabilities and the largest armed forces in Europe. Interestingly, Stella Rimington, Director General of MI5, reported that Russian espionage against the United Kingdom was again on the rise by 1995. Similarly, the conflict in Northern Ireland was another threat which transcended the end of the Cold War – although this is unsurprising given its disconnection to the Soviet Union and international communism. Nonetheless, it remained high on the JIC agenda and MI5 was able to approach the Irish challenges with renewed vigour.

Given that the JIC was responsible for tasking Britain's intelligence agencies, Lever's articulation of the changing nature of the threat is important. As outlined in the annexed document, in the mid-1990s the committee set requirements annually prior to ministerial endorsement. The JIC's assessment of the changing priorities in the post-Cold War world therefore had ramifications for targeting and the activity of the individual agencies.

Placing the JIC at the apex of the British intelligence machinery, the ISC report is again interesting because it indicates how each intelligence agency responded to the JIC's changing priorities. Despite the challenges of uncertainty, change and budget cuts, the heads of MI5, MI6 and GCHQ all recognised the importance of refocusing their efforts. Accordingly intelligence on eastern Europe was dramatically slashed, as revealed in the document.

Demonstrating the new oversight regime, the ISC's report reached John Major, the Prime Minister. It was then laid before Parliament. Major responded by expressing his encouragement that the British intelligence community had responded rapidly and with flexibility to the changing world scene since the end of the Cold War.[10] This document also recalls the last full decade in which the JIC retained an important coordination function for the UK intelligence community, something which it no longer enjoys.[11]

Intelligence and Security Committee
Annual Report 1995

Chairman:
The Rt Hon Tom King CH MP

Intelligence Services Act 1994
Chapter 13

Presented to Parliament by the Prime Minister
by Command of Her Majesty
MARCH 1996

Our work so far

Background

12. We set out first and foremost to build up our knowledge of the Agencies' individual roles, working methods and current priorities. In our Interim Report in the Spring,* we identified our first major subject for enquiry as:

> "how the Agencies have adapted in general to the new situations post-Cold War and, in particular, how tasks and the priorities attached to them have altered, and whether the resources now provided are appropriate to those tasks and used in a cost-effective way"

and gave a number of other major issues on which we proposed to focus as our work developed. These included:
- the extent to which it is appropriate to try to maintain a 'global reach' in intelligence terms;
- increasing resource pressures and their effects on Agency capabilities and staff;
- the extent to which the Agencies are able to maintain their 'core' capabilities and their major investment patterns and commitments;
- the protection afforded to Agency information and operations;
- the Agencies' work with the police and other enforcement bodies in the UK, and their relationships with the civil community;
- how the Agencies are coping with the ever increasing flow of openly available information.

---

* Cm 2873, May 1995, paragraph 10–11.

13. It is possible to approach all these questions from several different directions: structures and organisational responsibilities, resources and funding, and questions bearing on operations. We decided first to look in the round at the post-Cold War world; address in some detail the reduction in the military threat posed by the former Soviet Union (FSU), and the consequent resource allocation decisions taken in the Agencies; and focus in addition on some of the 'functional' issues,* in particular work against serious organised crime,† on which the Agencies have increasingly been tasked by Government and on which they are now concentrating significant proportions of their effort.

Tasking the Agencies

14. We examined the systems for tasking the Agencies. The UK's requirements for the collection of secret intelligence are set annually by the Cabinet Joint Intelligence Committee (JIC), and endorsed by Ministers.‡ Intelligence targets are divided into three broad priorities which reflect the importance of particular policy objectives and the significance of secret intelligence in helping to achieve them.§ These requirements are elaborated in a series of 'Guidelines' papers, which enable SIS and GCHQ to plan the allocation of their resources in more detail. At the working level, the Agencies meet regularly with customer departments to ensure that they are meeting their needs. Outside this formal framework, customers put forward proposals for new or amended requirements, or downgradings or deletions, at any time.¶ The Security Service does not, as yet,** have 'customers' in the same sense as the other two Agencies, but its priorities in terms of threats to national security, and the Service's plans to counter them, are examined and validated each year by a sub-committee of the Cabinet Official Committee on Security, and approved by Ministers.††

The changing nature of the threat

15. The Chairman of the JIC told us that the past few years had seen a significant shift in the overall balance of intelligence requirements. With the ending of the Cold War, activity has moved away from traditional NATO-Warsaw Pact concerns towards a more varied range of threats to, and opportunities for, British interests at home and abroad. Increased emphasis is now placed on what are termed 'functional' topics, such as terrorism, the proliferation of weapons of mass destruction, serious

---

* See paragraph 15.
† See paragraphs 26–30, and footnote 25 on page 16.
‡ Evidence from the Cabinet Office, December 1994.
§ Evidence from the Chairman of the JIC, May 1995.
¶ Evidence from the Cabinet Office, December 1994.
** See paragraphs 26–29.
†† Evidence from the Cabinet Office, December 1994.

organised crime* (which is taken to include drug trafficking, money laundering and other international financial crime) and international sanctions.†

16. Attention, however, continues to be paid as a matter of the highest national order of priority to some of the more 'traditional' concerns, in particular Russia. The JIC has assessed that neither Russia nor any of the other FSU states currently poses any direct military threat to the UK or to NATO.‡ Russia, however, retains both a formidable strategic capability and the largest conventional armed forces in Europe; and Russian military equipment, which is of generally high quality, is being aggressively marketed around the world. Intelligence customers' needs are, therefore, set increasingly in the context of risks of instability and proliferation concerns. Other high priority tasks include the UK's continuing intelligence needs in relation to Northern Ireland following the 1994 cease-fires; the conflict in the former Yugoslavia, where British forces are operationally deployed; and certain countries in the Middle East. Lower down the priority list, intelligence needs in several regions of the world including Africa and South-East Asia have been considerably scaled down.§

The Agencies' response

17. **It is a measure of the significant shifts in the Agencies' efforts over the past few years that SIS now devotes only about *** of its operational effort to Russia and the other FSU states**, as against almost *** at the height of the Cold War,¶ this being a reduction of about two thirds. The Service considers its current effort to be the absolute minimum that it can safely devote to the target. For GCHQ, **about *** of the total Sigint effort is still devoted in one way or another to work on Russia (about a half of the previous level).**** ***.

18. Only rarely in the Agencies' history have they had to face the major difficulties that are involved in significant shifts of effort and resources. The disintegration of the Soviet Union, however, was followed rapidly by the Gulf War. This led to a rapid, relatively short term, increase in SIS effort devoted to Iraq and other targets in the Middle East, and to a steady increase in counter-proliferation work. Since that time, the longer-lasting Balkan crisis has led to the Service devoting a significant proportion of effort to a target against which there had previously been very little work. These increases, and others designed to meet 'functional'†† requirements, in turn necessitated balanced reductions across other areas and, on occasion, the closure of less essential SIS stations abroad.‡‡

19. GCHQ's reallocation of resources over the same period followed a similar

---

* See paragraphs 26–30.
† Evidence from the Chairman of the JIC, May 1995.
‡ Evidence from the MOD, October 1995.
§ Evidence from the Chairman of the JIC, May 1995.
¶ Evidence from SIS, March 1995; evidence from the Chief of SIS, May 1995.
** Evidence from Director of GCHQ, May 1995.
†† See paragraph 15.
‡‡ Evidence from the Chief of SIS, May 1995.

pattern, with the fall in effort against the FSU mirrored by significant increases in effort on the Middle East and the Balkans, and work on other regions of the world staying roughly constant. Among 'functional' topics, there was increased emphasis on work on counter-proliferation, terrorism and serious organised crime in particular. GCHQ has also been altering the balance of expenditure between manpower costs and technical facilities, placing increased emphasis on developing a flexible resource which can quickly be deployed against alternative targets as priorities change.*

20. For the Security Service, a significant reduction in the overall 'intelligence threat' posed by the former Warsaw Pact states allowed a consequent reduction to less than half the operational resources required five years ago.† We have been told, however, that covert intelligence activity against the UK by Russian intelligence services is now once again on the increase.‡ This has led in turn to the reinstatement of some resources that had previously been moved to other areas of work.

21. Taken together with parallel reductions in the effort necessary to counter subversion, these changes meant that resources could be released to work against Irish terrorism, at a time (1992) when the Service was taking on the lead role in countering Republican terrorism on the British mainland. Monitoring Irish terrorist groups and their supporters has involved just under one half of the Service's operational resources over the past couple of years, and will continue to do so 'for at least the next year' in order to produce intelligence in support of the Government's conduct of the peace process.§

22. **The scope of these changes presents major challenges of leadership and management for all three Agencies. The Agency Heads have each made clear to us that they recognise the crucial importance of the most sensitive handling of the reassignments and, in some cases, compulsory redundancies that have proved necessary. We welcome these assurances.**

23. In view of these challenges, we also asked a number of questions on, and intend to pursue further, the methods of appointment of the Heads of the Agencies, with particular regard to the identification of successors to Sir John Adye as Director of GCHQ and Mrs Stella Rimington as Director-General of the Security Service. **We have already stressed to the Foreign and Home Secretaries respectively the importance, in senior Agency appointments, of a conscious effort to include candidates from outside as well as inside these organisations, which tend by their occupation to be somewhat removed from the normal exchanges that exist between other departments. The Hurn Review of GCHQ¶ shows how outside experience can be most usefully brought to bear.**

---

* Evidence from the Director of GCHQ, May 1995.
† Evidence from the Security Service, October 1995.
‡ Evidence from the Security Service, May 1995; evidence from the Director-General of the Security Service, May 1995.
§ Evidence from the Security Service, May 1995; evidence from the Director-General of the Security Service, May 1995.
¶ See paragraph 4.

24. We conclude that there have been significant and unprecedented changes since the end of the Cold War in the tasks all three Agencies are required to undertake for Government. Each has had to respond rapidly and with flexibility to these changes; all must be prepared for further changing demands in the years ahead. The reductions in the Agencies' work on the former Soviet Union are appropriate to the changing nature of the threat, and have released resources to work on the newer 'functional' targets such as proliferation and serious organised crime.

25. We further conclude that the Security Service will need to keep under close review the resources it devotes to work against Russian espionage. On work against the hazard of Irish terrorism, we support the Service's decision to keep deployed about one half of its total operational resources on this work for at least the next year, and recommend that the recent assumption of responsibility by the Service for the lead in work against Republican terrorism on the British mainland should be maintained.

Notes

1. Mikhail Gorbachev, quoted in Benjamin B. Fischer (ed.), *At Cold War's End: US Intelligence on the Soviet Union and Eastern Europe, 1989–1991* (CIA, 1999), available at https://www.cia.gov/library/center-for-the-study-of-intelligence/csi-publications/books-and-monographs/at-cold-wars-end-us-intelligence-on-the-soviet-union-and-eastern-europe-1989-1991/art-1.html#rtoc8 (last accessed 11 November 2013).
2. Percy Cradock, *In Pursuit of British Interests: Reflections on Foreign Policy under Margaret Thatcher and John Major* (London: John Murray, 1997) p. 121; Percy Cradock quoted in Max Hastings, 'Heroes of the war that wasn't', Telegraph website, 5 March 2002, http://www.telegraph.co.uk/culture/books/historybookreviews/3574020/Heroes-of-the-war-that-wasnt.html (last accessed 11 November 2013).
3. David Arbel and Ran Edelist, *Western Intelligence and the Collapse of the Soviet Union, 1980–1990: Ten Years That Did Not Shake the World* (London: Frank Cass, 2003), p. xii.
4. Richard J. Aldrich, *GCHQ: The Uncensored Story of Britain's Most Secret Intelligence Agency* (London: HarperPress, 2011), p. 465. Christopher Andrew has stated that it took MI5 by surprise – historians can assume that it also therefore took the JIC by surprise (Christopher Andrew, *The Defence of the Realm: The Authorized History of MI5* (London: Allen Lane, 2009), p. 771).
5. Powell (Strasbourg) to Wall (FCO), also copied to Robin Butler (Cabinet Office), 8 December 1989, RS 020/2/3, Document 70, in Patrick Salmon, Keith Hamilton and Stephen Twigge (eds), *Documents on British Policy Overseas, Series III, Vol. VII: German Unification, 1989–90* (Abingdon: Routledge, 2010).
6. Gordon Barrass, *The Great Cold War: A Journey through the Hall of Mirrors* (Stanford, CA: Stanford University Press, 2009), p. 410.
7. Richard J. Aldrich, review of Percy Cradock: *Know Your Enemy: How the Joint Intelligence Committee Saw the World* (London: John Murray, 2002), *International History Review* 15/1 (2003), pp. 216–18.
8. Andrew, *The Defence of the Realm*, p. 780; Gordon Corera, *The Art of Betrayal: Life and Death in the British Secret Service* (London: Weidenfeld and Nicolson, 2011), p. 316; Aldrich, *GCHQ*, p. 495.

9. James Woolsey, statement before the Permanent Select Committee on Intelligence, US House of Representatives, 9 March 1993.
10. Major to King (chairman, ISC), 26 March 1996, reproduced in *Intelligence and Security Committee Annual Report, 1995*, Cm 3198 (London: HMSO, 1995).
11. This was transferred in 2009 to the National Security, International Relations and Development Committee Official Subcommittee on Intelligence (NSID(I)(O)).

19

WAR IN IRAQ: WEAPONS OF MASS DESTRUCTION

BEFORE THE TURN of the twenty-first century, very few people outside Whitehall's security and intelligence circles had heard of the Joint Intelligence Committee. This was soon to change. In the aftermath of the invasion of Iraq, the JIC exploded into the public consciousness amid deep controversy. The committee acquired unprecedented media coverage and its Chairman briefly became a household name.

The Iraqi weapons of mass destruction (WMD) saga is undoubtedly the most famous, indeed infamous, episode in the JIC's long history. Tony Blair's government publicly drew upon its intelligence to justify a controversial war against Saddam Hussein's Iraq. That intelligence has since been subjected to no fewer than four inquiries. It is now widely acknowledged that the intelligence was deeply flawed.

The JIC had been monitoring Iraqi WMD and strategic weapons programmes since the First Gulf War. Assessments initially downplayed Saddam's capabilities, so long as Iraq lacked external support. UN inspections, however, later revealed that Iraq's pre-1991 nuclear programme was more advanced than the JIC had realised. Underestimation of Iraq's weapons programme led to overcorrection in the early 2000s. It must be remembered that this is a highly specialised field of intelligence analysis and the same people involved in 1991 were present in 2002. They did not want to be wrong twice.[1]

Towards the end of the 1990s, the JIC assessed that the weapons inspectors had curtailed the vast majority of Iraq's 1991 WMD capability. Some biological and chemical weapons, however, apparently remained hidden and the JIC grew increasingly suspicious about Iraq's ballistic missile programme as the decade progressed. Shortly after the turn of the century, the JIC grew more concerned still. Although acknowledging limited sources, the committee warned that Iraq was becoming bolder in its pursuit of WMD.[2]

Intelligence on Iraqi WMDs since 2001 must be placed in its broader context. It should not be forgotten that policymakers who read JIC reports on the subject also received swathes of intelligence on other matters. These included the

A. Q. Khan network of nuclear proliferation and Osama bin Laden's apparent desire for unconventional weapons. When read together, they made a pattern of intelligence that led policymakers to feel they were facing a creeping tide of proliferation by the start of 2002. Having read the JIC intelligence assessments, Tony Blair, for example, believed that states pursuing WMDs, including Iraq, had become 'very determined'. Moreover, they were states that 'you would not want to have this type of stuff because of their unstable and repressive nature and there were certainly suggestions [of] the potential link with terrorism'.[3]

Meanwhile it is important not to overlook the sheer surprise created by the terrorist attacks on America. Officials on both sides of the Atlantic had simply not seen them coming. A new sense that anything was possible permeated Whitehall along with a feeling that the enemy now occupied an alien intellectual world. Uncertainty reigned. Planes flying over Westminster were watched with an uneasy sense of dread as officials feared further attacks in the weeks after 9/11.[4]

September 2001 also changed the policy context. Iraq's WMD programme had not necessarily accelerated, but Anglo-American tolerance had evaporated.[5] Policymakers moved away from containment towards pre-emption. In September 2002, the government published its evidence surrounding Iraqi WMD. The role of the JIC was important and, between March and September, the committee had disseminated three assessments. The third and most important has been declassified and is reproduced here.[6]

Dated 15 March 2002, the first assessment was commissioned by the Foreign and Commonwealth Office to aid policy discussions on Iraq, and considered the status of Iraqi WMD programmes. This assessment was followed by another on 21 August 2002. This time prepared at the request of the Ministry of Defence, it considered firstly Iraq's diplomatic options to deter, avert, or limit a US-led attack; and secondly Saddam's military options to face such an attack. The key assessment, however, followed on 9 September 2002. Entitled 'Iraqi Use of Chemical and Biological Weapons – Possible Scenarios', it was designed to inform military and contingency planning. Accordingly, its conclusions were inherently precautionary. By mid-September therefore, policymakers were under the impression that Iraq sought to pursue its WMD programme. At the time, there was evidence of Iraqi development of ballistic missiles, some evidence of Iraq's ability to produce biological weapons in a mobile laboratory, and some inferential evidence of chemical capabilities.[7] Much of this intelligence was retrospectively criticised and some of it withdrawn.

In the late summer of 2002, Blair's government grew increasingly concerned about the public debate in the UK. The media presented military action as being imminent. Accordingly, the press and parliamentarians sought answers to why Britain was seemingly planning to invade Iraq. To alleviate the pressure, Blair decided to release more information on Iraqi WMD into the public domain.[8] This decision was almost unprecedented. Although governments had a history of releasing sanitised intelligence to selected media outlets (for example through the Cold War Information Research Department), it was the first time any government had explicitly drawn on JIC material to justify action to the British public. There is one known parallel from the committee's history, however. In 1964, Britain was under pressure in the United Nations after bombing Yemeni territory in what was perceived as an imperial misadventure. The JIC was commissioned to compile a publishable dossier implicating the Egyptians in the conflict to help justify Britain's policy stance. It drew on some fairly flimsy intelligence to support this preconceived objective. It is unclear, however, whether the report was issued publicly (at the UN) under the authority of the JIC.[9]

Blair's infamous dossier was commissioned on 3 September. According to Lord Butler, the JIC's September report 'exercised considerable influence' over the government's dossier. Both were prepared at practically the same time. As Butler has pointed out, the dossier incorporated the precautionary conclusions from the JIC report but omitted the caveats.[10] The September dossier was, and remains, divisive.

A string of government inquiries have dismissed any allegations that intelligence was knowingly embellished by the government. The Intelligence and Security Committee, for example, noted that the dossier had in fact been endorsed by the JIC.[11] Similarly, Butler's review dismissed accusations that the government misused intelligence to explicitly make a case for war. The JIC Chairman, John Scarlett, believed that the dossier did not make the case for anything. Similarly, Jack Straw, the Foreign Secretary, stated that the dossier was simply designed to meet the public demand for 'intelligence-based information'.[12] The policymakers did not fabricate or 'sex up' intelligence to make a case for an unpopular war. At worst, they pushed the available intelligence to its credible limits by exaggeration, artful selection and ignoring caveats.[13]

The problems arose in the foreword to the dossier and Tony Blair's performance in Parliament on the day of publication. One former defence intelligence official, a particularly forceful critic of this episode, has argued that 'while the dossier itself was a fair summary of the JIC's conclusions over the years, the Executive Summary painted an overstark picture, while the Prime Minister's foreword went completely over the top'.[14] Meanwhile, when addressing MPs on the day of publication, Blair reinforced the impression that there was firmer and fuller intelligence underpinning the dossier. He personally assured Parliament that the intelligence was 'extensive, detailed, [and] authoritative'.[15] Lord Butler has since acknowledged that the British public 'have "every right" to feel misled by their Prime Minister.'[16] With hindsight, Tony Blair regrets writing the foreword. He should have just published the sanitised intelligence.[17]

Of course, it has since been revealed that both JIC intelligence and the dossier were wrong. No WMD have been found in the Iraqi desert. In December 2004, the JIC reviewed the extent to which its intelligence underpinned the dossier. The results were published by the ISC and are worth quoting at length:

a. Nuclear weapons – The 2002 JIC judgement that 'Iraq is pursuing a nuclear weapons programme. But it will not be able to indigenously produce a nuclear weapon while sanctions remain in place' was wrong in that Iraq was not pursuing a nuclear weapons programme, but correct on Iraq's nuclear ambitions and its inability to produce a nuclear weapon under sanctions.
b. Ballistic weapons – In 2002, the JIC judged that 'Iraq retains up to 20 Al-Hussein ballistic missiles'. This has not been substantiated. The 2002 JIC judgement that 'Iraq has begun development of medium-range ballistic missiles over 1,000km' has been partially substantiated: the ISG[18] found that Iraq had authorised its scientists to develop missiles with ranges in excess of the 150km UNSC [United Nations Security Council] limit (a number of which were destroyed under UNMOVIC [United Nations Monitoring, Verification and Inspection Commission] supervision before the war), and had designs for missiles with ranges up to 1,000km.
c. Chemical weapons (CW) – In 2002, the JIC judged that 'Iraq may retain some stocks of chemical agents ... Iraq could produce significant quantities of mustard within weeks, significant quantities of Sarin and VX [nerve agents] within months, and in the case of VX may already have done so.' Although a capability to produce some agents probably existed, this judgement has not been substantiated. The ISG found that Saddam intended to resume a CW effort once sanctions were lifted.
d. Biological weapons (BW) – In 2002, the JIC judged that 'Iraq currently has available, either from pre-Gulf War, or more recent production, a number of biological agents ... Iraq could produce more of these biological agents within days.' The ISG found that Iraq had dual-use facilities which could have allowed BW production to resume, but not within the timeframes judged by the JIC, and found no evidence that production had been activated. The ISG found that Saddam probably intended to resume a BW programme if and when the opportunity arose.
e. Intentions and scenarios – In 2002, the JIC judged that 'Saddam ... might use CBW ... against coalition forces, neighbouring states and his own people. Israel could be his first target.' Although reporting which informed this judgement was subsequently withdrawn, based on Iraq's actions pre-1991 and during the first Gulf War this would have remained a reasonable judgement.[19]

The Iraq WMD story also sheds light on the JIC's friends and allies. The intelligence communities in Australia, Denmark, France, Germany, Israel and many other countries got it wrong, triggering waves of inquiries in parallel to the Butler review. Like Britain, many countries were influenced by the fact they had underestimated Iraqi WMD stocks in 1990-1. Determined not to be wrong a second time they too overcorrected. Only the Canadians called it right – perhaps the finest moment in the history of Ottawa's intelligence assessments machine. [20]

Although flawed, the dossier episode represented a remarkable effort to put JIC material into the public domain. Intended to explain, by drawing on intelligence, why the government was treating Iraq as a policy priority, the plan backfired. The most infamous event in the committee's history, Iraq has come to define public perceptions of the JIC. Indeed, yet another inquiry into the decisions underpinning the invasion of Iraq began in 2009. Iraqi WMD form an important case study in producer–consumer relations and mistakes were undoubtedly made. Using declassified documents, readers can make up their own minds about the levels of politicisation or misuse. It is important, however, not to allow this episode to cloud judgements of the committee's long and (generally) impressive history.

TOP SECRET *Declassified 2004*

JIC Assessment, 9 September 2002

IRAQI USE OF CHEMICAL AND BIOLOGICAL WEAPONS – POSSIBLE SCENARIOS

Key Judgements
I. Iraq has a chemical and biological weapons capability and Saddam is prepared to use it.
II. Faced with the likelihood of military defeat and being removed from power, Saddam is unlikely to be deterred from using chemical and biological weapons by any diplomatic or military means.
III. The use of chemical and biological weapons prior to any military attack would boost support for US-led action and is unlikely.
IV. Saddam is prepared to order missile strikes against Israel, with chemical or biological warheads, in order to widen the war once hostilities begin.
V. Saddam could order the use of CBW weapons in order to deny space and territory to Coalition forces, or to cause casualties, slow any advance, and sap US morale.
VI. If not previously employed, Saddam will order the indiscriminate use of whatever CBW weapons remain available late in a ground campaign or as a final act of vengeance. But such an order would depend on the availability of delivery means and the willingness of commanders to obey.

IRAQI USE OF CHEMICAL AND BIOLOGICAL WEAPONS – POSSIBLE SCENARIOS

This paper assesses possible scenarios for Iraqi use of chemical and biological weapons and takes account of new intelligence that has recently become available on Iraq's intentions. It has an intelligence cut off point of 4 September.

1. Recent intelligence casts light on Iraq's holdings of weapons of mass destruction and on its doctrine for using them. Intelligence remains limited and Saddam's own unpredictability complicates judgements about Iraqi use of these weapons. Much of this paper is necessarily based on judgement and assessment.

2. Iraq used chemical weapons on a large scale during the Iran/Iraq War. Use on the same scale now would require large quantities of chemical weapons and survivable delivery means in the face of overwhelming US air superiority. Iraq did not use chemical weapons during the Gulf War. Intelligence suggests that Iraq may have used the biological agent, aflatoxin, against the Shia population in 1991. We do not believe that Iraq possesses nuclear weapons and there is no intelligence that Iraq is currently interested in radiological dispersal devices.

Chemical and biological capabilities

3. Based on intelligence on the nature of Iraqi CBW weapons, known delivery means, continuing procurement activity, and experience from previous conflicts, we judge that:
- Iraq currently has available, either from pre Gulf War stocks or more recent production, a number of biological warfare (BW) and chemical warfare (CW) agents and weapons;
- following a decision to do so, Iraq could produce significant quantities of mustard agent within weeks; significant quantities of the nerve agents sarin and VX within months (and in the case of VX Iraq may have already done so). Production of sarin and VX would be heavily dependent on hidden stocks of precursors, the size of which are unknown;
- Iraq could produce more biological agents within days. At the time of the Gulf War Iraq had developed the lethal BW agents anthrax, botulinum toxin and aflatoxin. Iraq was also researching a number of other agents including some non-lethal (incapacitating) agents;
- [...];
- even if stocks of chemical and biological weapons are limited, they would allow for focused strikes against key military targets or for strategic purposes (such as a strike against Israel or Kuwait);

- Iraq could deliver CW and BW agents by a variety of means including free fall bombs, airborne sprays, artillery shells, mortar bombs and battlefield rockets;
- Iraq told UNSCOM in the 1990s that it filled 25 warheads with anthrax, botulinum toxin and aflatoxin for its Al Hussein ballistic missile (range 650km). Iraq also admitted it had developed 50 chemical warheads for Al Hussein. We judge Iraq retains up to 20 Al Husseins and a limited number of launchers;
- Iraq is also developing short-range systems Al Samoud/Ababil 100 ballistic missiles (range 150km plus) – One intelligence report suggests that Iraq has 'lost' the capability to develop warheads capable of effectively disseminating chemical and biological agent and that it would take six months to overcome the 'technical difficulties'. However, both these missile systems are currently being deployed with military units and an emergency operational capability with conventional warheads is probably available;
- Iraq may have other toxins, chemical and biological agents that we do not know about;
- the effectiveness of any CBW attack would depend on the method of delivery, concentration of the target, dissemination efficiency, meteorological conditions and the availability of suitable defensive counter measures.

Other recent intelligence indicates that:
- production of chemical and biological weapons is taking place;
- Saddam attaches great importance to having CBW, is committed to using CBW if he can and is aware of the implications of doing so. Saddam wants it to dominate his neighbours and deter his enemies who he considers are unimpressed by his weakened conventional military capability;
- Iraq has learned from the Gulf War the importance of mobile systems that are much harder to hit than large static sites. Consequently Iraq has developed for the military, fermentation systems which are capable of being mounted on road-trailers or rail cars. These could produce BW agent;
- Iraq has probably dispersed its special weapons, including its CBW weapons. Intelligence also indicates that chemical and biological munitions could be with military units and ready for firing within 20-45 minutes.

Intentions for use

4. Intelligence indicates that Saddam has already taken the decision that all resources, including CBW, be used to defend the regime from attack. One report states that Saddam would not use CBW during the initial air phase of

any military campaign but would use CBW once a ground invasion of Iraq has begun. Faced with the likelihood of military defeat and being removed from power, we judge that it is unlikely there would be any way to deter Saddam from using CBW.

5. We judge that several factors could influence the timing of a decision by Saddam to authorise the use of CBW weapons:
- the availability of stocks of CW and BW agents;
- the survivability of his delivery means. Many are vulnerable. Once a military campaign is underway the pressure will increase to use certain assets before they are destroyed;
- the survivability of command and control mechanisms. The method and timing of such decision making is unknown. Intelligence indicates that Saddam's son Qusai may already have been given authority to order the use of CBW. Authorising front line units to use chemical and biological weapons could become more difficult once fighting begins. Saddam may therefore specify in advance of a war the specific conditions in which unit commanders should use these weapons e.g. once Coalition forces have crossed a particular geographical line;
- the reliability of the units in question. Late in any military campaign commanders may not be prepared to use CBW weapons if they judge that Saddam is about to fall.

Possible scenarios: pre-emptive use before a conflict begins

6. The aim of a pre-emptive strike would be to incapacitate or kill Coalition troops in their concentration areas. Intelligence indicates that Saddam has identified Bahrain, Jordan, Qatar, Israel and Kuwait as targets. Turkey could also be at risk. Both chemical and biological weapons could be used; biological agents could be particularly effective against such force concentrations. But the use of CBW weapons carries serious risks and Saddam will weigh up their military utility against the political costs. Use of CBW weapons would expose the lies and deception about Iraq's WMD capabilities, undermining Iraqi diplomatic efforts and helping build support for rapid and effective US action. Saddam might also consider using non-lethal agents in a deniable manner; whilst it would be difficult to quickly establish a clear attribution of responsibility, Saddam could not be sure of the US reaction to an outbreak of a non-lethal disease.

7. The early, widespread use of CBW or non-lethal agents would affect Coalition military planning; disruption of the build-up of personnel and material could delay operations. On balance however we judge that the political cost of using CBW weapons would outweigh the military advantages and that Saddam would probably not use CBW weapons pre-emptively.

Possible scenarios: use during the ground phase of a conflict

8. There is no intelligence on specific Iraqi plans for how CBW would be used in a conflict. Large numbers of chemical munitions would need to be used to make a major battlefield impact. BW could also be used although it is less effective as a tactical weapon against Coalition units than CW. But the use of even small quantities of chemical weapons would cause significant degradation in Coalition progress and might contribute to redressing Coalition conventional superiority on the battlefield. Iraq could make effective use of persistent chemical agents to shape the battlefield to Iraq's advantage by denying space and territory to Coalition forces. Booby-traps and improvised explosive devices could be used as chemical and biological weapons to inflict local losses in urban areas. It is also possible that Saddam would seek to use chemical and biological munitions against any internal uprising; intelligence indicates that he is prepared to deliberately target the Shia population. One report indicates that he would be more likely to use CBW against Western forces than on Arab countries.

Drawing Israel into the conflict

9. Launching a CBW attack against Israel could allow Saddam to present Iraq as the champion of the Palestinian cause and to undermine Arab support for the Coalition by sowing a wider Middle East conflict. [...] One intelligence report suggests that if Saddam were to use CBW, his first target would be Israel. Another intelligence report suggests that Iraq believes Israel will respond with nuclear weapons if attacked with CBW or conventional warheads. It is not clear if Saddam is deterred by this threat or judges it to be unlikely [...].

Unconventional use of CBW

10. Although there is no intelligence to indicate that Iraq has considered using chemical and biological agents in terrorist attacks, we cannot rule out the possibility. [...] Saddam could also remove his existing constraints on dealing with Al Qaida (extremists are conducting low-level work on toxins in an area of northern Iraq outside Saddam's control). Al Qaida could carry out proxy attacks and would require little encouragement to do so. Saddam's intelligence agencies have some experience in the use of poisons and even small-scale attacks could have a significant psychological impact. Intelligence indicates that Saddam has specifically commissioned a team of scientists to devise novel means of deploying CBW.

Possible scenarios: at the death

11. In the last resort Saddam is likely to order the indiscriminate use of whatever chemical and biological weapons remain available to him, in a last attempt to cling on to power or to cause as much damage as possible in a final act of vengeance. If he has not already done so by this stage Saddam will launch CBW attacks on Israel. Implementation of such orders would depend on the delivery means still remaining, the survivability of the command chain and the willingness of commanders to obey.

Notes

1. Richard Aldrich, 'Whitehall and the Iraq War: The UK's Four Intelligence Enquiries', *Irish Studies in International Affairs* 16 (2005), p. 77.
2. Lord Butler of Brockwell, *Review of Intelligence on Weapons of Mass Destruction: Report* (London: The Stationery Office, 2004), pp. 43–5, 52, 55.
3. Tony Blair quoted ibid., p. 63.
4. Private Information.
5. Butler, *Review of Intelligence on Weapons of Mass Destruction*, p. 70.
6. Readers are strongly recommended to also examine Lord Butler of Brockwell, *Review of Intelligence on Weapons of Mass Destruction, Annex B: Intelligence Assessment and Presentation: From March to September 2002* (London: The Stationery Office, 2004), pp. 163–76.
7. Butler, *Review of Intelligence on Weapons of Mass Destruction*, pp. 72–5.
8. Ibid., p. 72.
9. Rory Cormac, *Confronting the Colonies: British Intelligence and Counterinsurgency* (London: Hurst, 2013), pp. 130–1.
10. Butler, *Review of Intelligence on Weapons of Mass Destruction*, p. 80.
11. Ibid., pp. 76–8; Aldrich, 'Whitehall and the Iraq War', pp. 80, 82.
12. Butler, *Review of Intelligence on Weapons of Mass Destruction*, pp. 76–8.
13. For an overview of the various schools of thought regarding the dossier see Steven Kettell, 'Who's Afraid of Saddam Hussein? Re-examining the "September Dossier" Affair', *Contemporary British History* 22/3 (2008), p. 409.
14. John N. L. Morrison, 'British Intelligence Failures in Iraq', *Intelligence and National Security* 26/4 (2011), p. 515.
15. Anthony Seldon, *Blair Unbound* (London: Simon and Schuster, 2007), p. 140.
16. Lord Butler quoted in Peter Taylor, 'Iraq: The spies who fooled the world', BBC News website, 18 March 2013, http://www.bbc.co.uk/news/uk-21786506 (last accessed 13 November 2013).
17. Tony Blair quoted in *The Iraq War: Regime Change*, BBC Two, 29 May 2013.
18. Iraq Survey Group, a multi-national fact-finding mission sent to Iraq after the invasion to search for WMD.
19. Intelligence and Security Committee, *Annual Report, 2004-2005*, Cm 6510 (Norwich: HMSO, 2005), pp. 23–4.
20. Jean Chrétien, *My Years as Prime Minister* (Toronto: Knopf Canada, 2007), pp. 306–13.

20

WAR IN IRAQ: AFTERMATH[1]

ON 19 MARCH 2003, American-led forces invaded Iraq. Less than six weeks later, speaking alongside a banner that read 'Mission Accomplished', President Bush triumphantly declared victory over Saddam Hussein. Yet British combat operations in the country only ended in 2009. The aftermath of the invasion saw a series of vicious insurgencies sweep across Iraq. Accordingly, British forces swiftly became embroiled in a difficult counterinsurgency campaign against Shia militia in southern Iraq. In addition to attacking the British, rival militant groups fought each other for power within the regional vacuum. Like the Americans elsewhere in Iraq, British planners and security forces were unprepared.

Broader questions must therefore be asked of intelligence. The role of the JIC was not limited to establishing whether Iraq had WMD (as discussed in the previous chapter). The committee also issued assessments on the aftermath of the invasion. For example, Clare Short, Secretary of State for International Development, commissioned a JIC paper at the start of 2003. She asked the committee to assess the situation in southern Iraq before and during an invasion, as well as to predict what might happen after any military action. The final report, issued on 19 February 2003 – one month before the invasion – is reproduced here. Overall, the JIC warned of an unpredictable security and political situation. It predicted a high risk of revenge attacks against former regime officials as well as a settling of scores between armed tribal groups in the region. The committee also warned that the Shia population needed to be involved in any future government of Iraq to ensure popular support for the post-Saddam administration. It played down concerns about Iranian-inspired terrorism as unlikely. There is no mention of al-Qaeda or Osama bin Laden.

The JIC highlighted five policy implications of its assessment. In doing so, it drew the government's attention to the importance of swift humanitarian aid, peace enforcement and winning over the local population. Further intelligence followed. In March 2003, the JIC cautioned that al-Qaeda might have 'established sleeper cells in Iraq to be activated after the coalition operation'.[2] The following month, the committee warned policymakers that 'in the short term, for many Iraqis the details of the post-Saddam political process will be less important than a restoration of public order and the start of reconstruction'. Putting the issue incredibly bluntly, the JIC stated that 'the Iraqi population will blame the coalition if progress is slow. Resentment could lead to violence.'[3]

JIC assessments reached the Prime Minister. The committee's Chairman, John Scarlett, made formal presentations of JIC material to the Cabinet's Defence and Overseas Policy Committee, chaired by Tony Blair. Although these meetings were fairly infrequent, they did include discussions of Iraq. In addition, Scarlett regularly met with officials from the Prime Minister's Office and ensured that Blair was kept updated on the latest intelligence. Indeed, Scarlett made a point of notifying David Manning, Blair's foreign policy adviser, of the assessment reproduced here. Unfortunately, Scarlett cannot recall Blair's reaction to the committee's 'blunt' conclusions. David Omand, then Intelligence and Security Coordinator, suspected that this assessment was received as 'part of the flow'. JIC material continued to regularly reach Number 10 as the war progressed. From mid-March, a 'War Cabinet', composed of an inner group of senior ministers, met daily. Every morning Scarlett began each meeting with an update of JIC intelligence. Although the JIC's assessment on southern Iraq could perhaps be considered as too little too late, questions of insurgency and al-Qaeda sat heavily on the JIC's agenda once the war was underway.[4]

Referring to the JIC's conclusions, Blair later recalled that the situation in southern Iraq was 'obviously going to be unpredictable'. The JIC's warnings were 'right and important' but given the overwhelming Shia dominance in the region, the Prime Minister thought it would be an 'easier' area of operation for Britain than elsewhere in Iraq. The committee's assessment certainly did not put Blair off operating in Basra and the south.[5]

Clearly the post-war planning fell short. Indeed, Tony Blair has openly admitted that this was a 'failing'.[6] There are two interpretations, however, regarding the JIC's role. The first is that the government acted upon intelligence assessments and did engage in planning, but the intelligence was flawed. The second is that the government ignored intelligence and planning was severely underdeveloped. Unsurprisingly the then Prime Minister subscribes to the former. He maintains that planning did take place. But according to Blair, it was unfortunately working on flawed assumptions that Iraq had a functioning bureaucracy and civil service. Moreover, plans overly focused on humanitarian and environmental issues related to the possibility of the use of chemical and biological weapons.[7] Interestingly, both of these misassumptions can be seen in the JIC document produced below. On the former, the committee wrote of 'engaging the remains of the state bureaucracy in the South'. Such surviving networks of influence formed a group with which the JIC thought the British could work. On the latter, the committee specifically concluded that 'we will have to deal with large numbers of displaced and hungry people, possibly contaminated or panicked by CBW use, at a time when the UN is not fully prepared'.

Similarly, the JIC assessment can be accused of being vague and open to various interpretations. Its conclusions on Iran serve as a case in point. The JIC optimistically predicted that Iran was unlikely to be aggressive, and yet it also warned of Iranian meddling in Iraqi affairs and noted links between Tehran and armed Shia groups in the south of Iraq. Blair himself has pointed out that the JIC got it wrong and one can arguably sympathise with him for being poorly advised. The JIC admitted that its intelligence on the region was limited. On the other hand, however, one can criticise Blair for not taking the JIC's warnings seriously enough. Blair accuses his critics of using excessive hindsight. The JIC assessment made some prophetic points, but arguably only when the reader has the benefit of seeing what actually happened in Iraq. Indeed, Blair maintains that intelligence did not anticipate the eventual situation in Iraq.[8]

The second interpretation suggests that the government ignored intelligence assessments and neglected planning. With hindsight, Blair has conceded that Britain could have planned more thoroughly for the rise of al-Qaeda in Iraq. In May 2002 intelligence warned that al-Qaeda had sent Abu Musab al-Zarqawi (who went on to become leader of al-Qaeda in Iraq) into the country, but little was done about it.[9] In terms of broader post-war planning, Britain left a great deal to the Americans.[10] Despite the JIC's assessments on southern Iraq, the Coalition Provisional Authority (CPA) unashamedly focused its political and reconstruction efforts on Baghdad, leaving the south, according to a former British official operating in Iraq, 'in danger of being starved of resources'. Meanwhile, the CPA's short-lived predecessor, the Office of Reconstruction and Humanitarian Assistance, was branded an 'unbelievable mess' by London's new envoy in Baghdad, John Sawyers.[11] In April 2003, the deputy chief of the Defence Intelligence Staff told the House of Commons: 'I am not aware of anything from my knowledge where we explicitly looked at how we should deal with policing in the aftermath of conflict.'[12]

Warnings from the JIC were certainly reinforced by other messages. Major General Tim Cross, the British officer tasked with reconstruction, was so concerned that on his return from a planning discussion in Washington in February 2003, he insisted on briefing the Prime Minister. 'I did not believe postwar planning was anywhere near ready.' Part of the problem was deep divisions within Blair's Cabinet. Neither Clare Short nor Gordon Brown wished to devote significant resources to a war that they found distasteful, still less to cleaning up its aftermath.[13]

British civil-military reconstruction efforts did see some initial moderate successes. The Emergency Infrastructure Plan, headed by the Department for International Development (DfID), funded the rebuilding of schools and hospitals. Distribution of money, however, was haphazard and efforts were effectively dissolved in 2004 as the security situation deteriorated. It was three long years until the Foreign and Commonwealth Office, Ministry of Defence and DfID established a formal agency to coordinate British reconstruction efforts.[14] In the words of one analyst, Britain and the US operated 'on the fly'.[15]

The JIC did warn of potential hostilities in southern Iraq. Intelligence noted the importance of winning popular support through reconstruction efforts. However, it was somewhat vague and open to various interpretations. The British government lacked a sufficiently detailed assessment on the post-conflict situation whilst those assessments it did have appear to have been produced only fairly late in the day. This shaped government planning to an extent. Yet the government must also carry its fair share of responsibility. Warnings did eventually appear.

~~TOP SECRET~~ DECLASSIFIED

JIC Asesssment, 19 February 2003

SOUTHERN IRAQ: WHAT'S IN STORE?

Key Judgements

I. The Iraqi forces currently guarding Southern Iraq are a relatively weak first line of conventional defence. They face rapid defeat. There is little evidence so far that the Iraqis are preparing for a hard-fought defence of Basra and other urban centres.

II. Southern Iraq is the most likely area for the first use of CBW against both coalition forces and the local population.

III. Coalition forces will face large refugee flows, possibly compounded by contamination and panic caused by CBW use. They may also face millions of Iraqis needing food and clean water without an effective UN presence and environmental disaster from burning oil wells.

IV. Iran does not have an agreed policy on Iraq beyond active neutrality. Nevertheless Iran may support small-scale cross-border interventions by armed groups to attack the Mujahideen e-Khalq (MEK). The Islamic Revolutionary Guards Corps (IRGC) will continue to meddle in Southern Iraq. Iranian reactions to a coalition presence in Southern Iraq remain unclear, but are unlikely to be aggressive.

V. Post-Saddam the security situation in the South will be unpredictable. There is a high risk of revenge killings of former regime officials. Law and order may be further undermined by settling of scores between armed tribal groups.

VI. Popular support for any post-Saddam administration in the South will depend on adequately involving the Shia in the government of Iraq as a whole as well as engaging the remains of the state bureaucracy in the South, local tribal leaders and Shia clerics in local government.

> **Policy Implications:**
>
> UN authorisation for a post-Saddam administration will be crucial.
> We may have to deal with post-Saddam issues in Southern Iraq while fighting continues elsewhere. Offensive military action, provision of humanitarian aid and peace enforcement may have to be pursued simultaneously.
> We will have to deal with large numbers of displaced and hungry people, possibly contaminated or panicked by CBW use, at a time when the UN is not fully prepared.
> We will need to use all available means now and in future to win over the population and networks of influence in Southern Iraq.
> We will need to avoid unhelpful intervention by the Iranians by doing what we can to take account of their interests and concerns, especially about the Turks, Kurds and MEK.

This paper was commissioned by OD Sec to look at the situation in Southern Iraq and what might happen there before, during and after any coalition military action. The paper covers Iraqi military disposition, likely Iraqi regime and popular reactions, Iranian policy and the possible political landscape in Southern Iraq post-Saddam.

Introduction

1. We have limited intelligence on the particular conditions of Southern Iraq. Where possible we have tried to show how Southern Iraq may differ from other parts of the country, but in order to give as full a picture as possible of the conditions there, we have also referred to intelligence describing conditions prevailing throughout the country.

Iraqi Military Dispositions

2. Southern Iraq is currently defended by the III and IV Corps of the regular Iraqi army. Security in the main urban centres is maintained by Iraq's many security organisations. Unlike Central and Northern Iraq the regular army is not reinforced in the South by divisions of the elite Republican Guard, which are forbidden by UNSCR 949 from moving into the No Drive Zone south of the 32nd parallel. We

> **Southern Iraq: Basic Facts**
> *Estimates suggest roughly 9 million people live in the nine provinces south and east of Baghdad (see map). The largest town is Basra (population 1.5 million). The area is populated by a wide variety of Arab Shia. Roughly half of Iraqi oil production comes from the oil fields of Southern Iraq. Southern Iraq includes Shia Islam's two holiest cities, Najaf and Kerbala and Iraq's only coastline, including the large port at Um Qasr.*

previously judged that once military action begins, widespread lack of loyalty to the regime will become clear throughout Iraq. Reporting shows the regime particularly concerned about the lack of loyalty of the Shia, who make up a majority of conscripts in the regular army. The absence of the Republican Guard coupled with the regular army's low morale, poor equipment and limited training mean **the forces guarding Southern Iraq are a relatively weak first line of conventional defence. They face rapid defeat in the face of a massive military onslaught.**

3. [Intelligence] from mid-January indicates most elements of the 14th Infantry Division of IV Corps, supported by artillery, have redeployed southwards around al-Qurnah, a key town located at a strategic road junction. Other reporting indicates the redeployment of elements of the 18th Infantry division southwards to the Faw peninsula in mid-January, apparently to counter a possible amphibious landing there. [...] We know little about Iraqi plans for the defence of Basra, but there is as yet no sign of preparations for a hard-fought defence of this or other urban centres in Southern Iraq.

Iraqi Response to an Attack

4. Reporting indicates that the regime has contingency plans for a regional military command structure, if a coalition attack severed central control from Baghdad. Saddam has appointed his cousin Ali Hassan al-Majid as regional commander of the southern sector of Southern Iraq (covering the provinces of Basra, Dhi Qar, Maysan and Al-Muthanna) with authority over all forces in the area. Iraqi practice in the Iran/Iraq war suggests this would include tactical control over CBW. Ali is a loyal member of Saddam's inner circle. He was a brutal Governor of occupied Kuwait in 1990/91. He also played a leading role in suppressing the Shia uprising in 1991 and Kurdish rebels in the late 1980s (using chemical weapons against the Kurds). His appointment may reflect an Iraqi leadership view that a particularly loyal and ruthless figure is needed to take command in the South in a crisis, both to suppress the Shia and to maintain discipline among the Iraqi forces. The relative weakness of Iraq's conventional forces in the South and the fact that those forces will face the brunt of a coalition ground attack mean **Southern Iraq is the most likely area for the first use of CBW against both coalition forces and the local population.**

5. We previously judged that as a last resort Saddam may seek to pursue a scorched earth policy, including the destruction of oil wells. There is no conclusive intelligence on Iraqi plans but they could:

• defend oil wells against attack;

• set fire to them to stop production, cause pollution and disrupt coalition forces; and

• cause long-term, possibly irreparable, damage to prevent others benefiting from future production.

The potential environmental disaster, coupled with the possible use of CBW against coalition forces and the local population, could cause widespread panic and contamination. This could result in hundreds of thousands of displaced persons and refugees, many needing immediate help.

> **Systems currently deployed in Southern Iraq with possible CBW capabilities**
> –at least 20 155mm-artillery pieces (range: up to 39km).
> –at least 10 BM-21 multiple rocket launchers (range: 20km).
> –at least 2 Ababil-100 missile units (range: 150km)

6. [...] Interruption of food supplies under the Oil for Food (OFF) programme, upon which 60% of the Iraqi population depends, could boost the number of displaced persons and refugees throughout Iraq. There may be strong international demands for the immediate provision of food and clean water to millions of Iraqis as well as an immediate environmental clean-up operation. Tackling such problems in Southern Iraq will be complicated by possible CBW contamination. While UN contingency planning has started, some UN officials and outside observers question whether the UN will be fully ready to meet these requirements. The UN will be particularly badly placed if a humanitarian disaster occurs in the South while fighting continues in close proximity.

Shia Reactions

7. Reporting has previously indicated that **the regime is concerned about a Shia uprising in the South after the outbreak of hostilities.** One report from August 2002 indicates Iraqi plans to use CBW in Southern Iraq to cause mass casualties among the Shia in the event of a US-led attack. The regime would seek to pin the blame for the resulting high level of casualties on the coalition. Another report noted the concerns of the close relatives of senior Shia clerics that the regime might attempt to arrest or assassinate senior Shia clerics in the event of war.

8. Recent reporting confirms our judgement [...] that the Shia will be cautious in opposing Saddam until they see the regime is finished and its capability to retaliate is substantially weakened. The experience of 1991 will be a major influence. The Shia will fear the regime's use of CBW to crush any uprising and will also remember that their earlier expectations of support from external forces were dashed. Even if the initial severity of any coalition attack makes clear that the regime is finished, the Shia may still fear what the regime could do to them in its dying days. As in 1991, the timing and scale of any uprising is likely to vary between localities, depending upon the level of local tribal and religious leaders' encouragement. Overall we judge **there will be no immediate, unified Shia response to a coalition attack.**

Iranian policy

Badr Corps
The Badr Corps is trained and equipped by the Iranian Islamic Revolutionary Guards Corps (IRGC) and based in camps in Iran. We assess it to be at least 3-5000 strong, but with the addition of reservists this may increase up to 20,000. The Badr Corps operates in Southern, Central and Northern Iraq (There have been reports of a recent incursion in Northern Iraq).

9. Iranian aims in Iraq include preventing refugee flows across its borders; ensuring a leading role for its proteges among the Iraqi Shia (the Supreme Council for an Islamic Revolution in Iraq [SCIRI] and its armed wing the Badr Corps); minimising the size and duration of a US presence post-Saddam; and destroying the Mujahideen e-Khalq (MEK), an armed terrorist opposition group supported by Saddam's regime. Iran has interests throughout Iraq, but may consider it has greatest influence to pursue them in the South through armed Shia groups, such as the Badr Corps.

10. Intelligence on Iranian activity [...] indicates that in early 2003 **the Iranians have increased their support for Shia opposition groups and have upgraded their intelligence effort targeted at Southern Iraq.** [...] Their national and cultural ties to other Iraqi Arabs outweigh their religious links to Shia Iran. [...] Iran has accepted that there is little support among Iraqi Shia for an Iranian-style theocratic regime.

11. [...] If the coalition does not deal with the MEK, Iran may make limited cross-border rocket attacks on them. [...] The Iranian Revolutionary Guard Corps (IRGC) might act to undermine any post-Saddam peace that did not take Iran's concerns into account. Recent reporting indicates that the IRGC is continuing to support incursions of the Badr Corps into Iraq. We judge that both Iranian conservatives and reformers are anxious to avoid provoking a US-led attack on Iran. We therefore assess that **Iranian-inspired terrorist attacks on coalition forces are unlikely, unless the Iranians thought the US had decided to attack them after an Iraq campaign.**

12. The Iranians have espoused a policy of "active neutrality" on Iraq. But this is not well developed and there is little regime agreement on what "active" means. The regime is pre-occupied with domestic concerns and is not in a strong position to project its power into Iraq. Different elements of the regime may pursue very different policies. Hardliners will oppose co-operation with a US-led post-Saddam regime. Some moderates, however, will wish to establish a good working relationship with the international community to ensure Iran plays a major role in reconstruction. The Iranians will react negatively, however, if they feel we are attempting to marginalize them.

The Political and Security Landscape post-Saddam

13. We know very little about the Iraqi Shia. [...] They are not politically organised above the local, tribal level and there are no clear candidates for overall Shia leadership. They are very diverse, straddling the urban/rural and secular/Islamist divides. They have had little opportunity to discuss their preferred political arrangements. **Shia politics post-Saddam therefore look highly unpredictable.**

14. Saddam's regime has centralised power and stifled opposition. The only networks of influence in the South that exist outside of the Ba'ath party are the tribes and the followers of some of the senior Shia clerics. Once the regime has collapsed, coalition forces will find the remains of the state's bureaucratic structures, local tribal sheikhs and religious leaders. There will also be a number of fractious armed groups, some strengthened by arms seized during the collapse of the regime. The external opposition will attempt to assert authority, but only those with armed forces on the ground or support from senior Shia clerics, such as SCIRI or Da'wa, another Shia Islamist group, are likely to succeed to any extent. [...]

15. Given that the Shia in Southern Iraq have borne the brunt of regime oppression since 1991, there is a high probability of revenge killing of Ba'ath officials, both Sunni and Shia. This could be particularly widespread and bloody, if the regime collapses quickly and few Ba'ath officials have the chance to escape. Beyond that the extent of any further breakdown of law and order is difficult to predict. But there will be large numbers of armed groups and some potential for tribal score-settling, including between those who have opposed and collaborated with Saddam's regime. There may also be competition for limited food. Overall there is a risk of a wider breakdown as the regime's authority crumbles. There are no indications, however, of Shia preparations for an all-out civil war against Sunni Iraqis. Coalition forces may be forced to impose peace in Southern Iraq, including the disarmament of armed groups. As we previously judged Iraqis may not welcome coalition military forces, despite welcoming the overthrow of Saddam. **The establishment of popular support for any post-Saddam administration cannot be taken for granted.** It could be undermined by:

- damage to holy sites;
- major civilian casualties;
- lack of a UNSCR authorising a post-Saddam administration;
- heavy-handed peace enforcement;
- failure to meet popular expectations over humanitarian aid and reconstruction;
- failure rapidly to restore law and order;
- failure to involve the Shia adequately in a post-Saddam administration; and
- failure to be seen to run the oil industry in the interests of the Iraqi people.

16. There are factors, however, that could work in our favour:
• surviving networks of influence with whom we could work, including remains of state bureaucracy and food-distribution networks, tribal leaders and religious figures; and
• receptivity of the population to information from external media and leaflet drops.

Notes

1. This chapter was written before the Iraq inquiry led by Sir John Chilcot reported.
2. 'Sir David Omand, Transcript', Evidence to the Iraq Inquiry, 20 January 2010, p. 40.
3. JIC, 'Iraq: The Initial Landscape Post-Saddam', 16 April 2003.
4. 'Sir John Scarlett, Transcript', Evidence to the Iraq Inquiry, 8 December 2009, pp. 13, 14, 15, 24; 'Sir David Omand, Transcript', Evidence to the Iraq Inquiry, 20 January 2010, pp. 15, 17.
5. 'Rt Hon. Tony Blair, Transcript', Evidence to the Iraq Inquiry, 21 January 2011, pp. 120–1.
6. Ibid., p. 122.
7. Ibid., p. 123.
8. Ibid., pp. 121, 153.
9. Ibid., p. 151.
10. See Peter Mandelson and Tony Blair quoted ibid., pp. 122, 123–4.
11. Andrew Mumford, *The Counter-insurgency Myth: The British Experience of Irregular Warfare* (Abingdon: Routledge, 2012), pp. 128–9.
12. 'Evidence of Mr Martin Howard, Lt General John McColl, Major General Nick Houghton and Major General Bill Rollo, 26 January 2005', in House of Commons Defence Committee, *Iraq: An Initial Assessment of Post-conflict Operations, Vol. II: Oral and Written Evidence*, HC65-II (London: The Stationery Office, 2005).
13. 'Post-invasion Iraq: The Planning and the Reality after the Invasion from Mid-2002 to the End of August 2003 – A Witness Statement by Major General Tim Cross CBE', 7 December 2009, http://www.iraqinquiry.org.uk/media/39160/timcross-statement.pdf (last accessed 12 November 2013).
14. Mumford, *The Counter-insurgency Myth*, p. 130.
15. Andrew Rathmell, 'Planning Post-conflict Reconstruction in Iraq: What Can We Learn?', *International Affairs* 81/5 (2005), p. 1031.

21

THE JOINT INTELLIGENCE COMMITTEE AND THE NATIONAL SECURITY COUNCIL

On becoming Prime Minister in 2010, David Cameron quickly began tinkering with Britain's national intelligence and security apparatus. Desperate to distance himself from his Labour predecessors, Cameron's much-vaunted ideas revolved around establishing a new National Security Council (NSC). He wasted little time, creating the body less than a week after the election. The inaugural meeting was held on 12 May 2010 to discuss Afghanistan, Pakistan and the terrorist threat to the UK.

The NSC is chaired by the Prime Minister himself – a keen consumer of intelligence. Other members include the Deputy Prime Minister, the Chancellor of the Exchequer, the Foreign Secretary, the Home Secretary, the Defence Secretary and the International Development Secretary. Bringing the intelligence and policy worlds closer together, the JIC Chairman and the heads of all three intelligence agencies also regularly attend meetings (as does the Chief of Defence Staff – although the Chief of Defence Intelligence unfortunately does not). Unlike its various predecessors (under both Tony Blair and Gordon Brown), the formal NSC meets regularly every week. It is supported by an official-level committee, known as the National Security Council (Official). In addition to attending the weekly NSC, the JIC Chairman also attends the NSC(O). The new format institutionalises the relationship between intelligence and policy. It formalises instant policy impact.

Unsurprisingly, Cameron's reforms have affected the workings of the JIC and the Joint Intelligence Organisation (JIO) more broadly. Peter Hennessy, a particularly experienced Whitehall watcher, has gone as far as to argue that the impact has been

> at least as important as the 1957 and 1968 developments and, perhaps, even on the scale of 1940–1 when Winston Churchill used the demands of total war to bring the JIC fully and continually into the highest councils of the Second World War machine after an indifferent first five years of its institutional life.[1]

Since 1936, Britain's central intelligence machinery has evolved to acquire an impressive and prestigious status at the heart of Whitehall.

The NSC raises important questions about the committee's role and future direction. Does it slightly eclipse the JIC? Is the JIC in danger of being forced to take a back seat? Or does such institutionalised contact with senior policymakers leave the JIC in enviable shape? Whitehall insiders are quick to point towards the latter, saying that the two bodies complement each other well and that the NSC has given the JIC a new lease of life.[2]

The JIC was not in great health in the 2000s. Tony Blair was uninterested in intelligence unless it conformed to his world view. With the spectre of Iraq hanging heavily, the JIC found it difficult to engage the Prime Minister in its work. Even before the WMD fiasco, Blair's informal 'sofa government' style posed a problem for the 21st-century JIC. His Chief of Staff, Jonathan Powell, has since dismissed the committee as producing 'lowest-common-denominator-type reports, hedging their bets and failing to give a clear steer in any direction'. Accordingly, some policymakers sought to bypass the JIC altogether and receive more raw intelligence. Unsurprisingly, the JIC learnt different lessons from the Butler review. It was keen to limit Blair's access to this raw material.[3]

The JIC fared little better under Gordon Brown – another broadly uninterested consumer. He removed the committee's long-standing remit for the day-to-day coordination of the intelligence community. In late 2009, Brown also abolished the long-standing Permanent Secretaries Committee on the Intelligence Services, which oversaw the dialogue between intelligence priorities and budgets, transferring its remit to the national security machinery. In the same year, JIC meetings temporarily became fortnightly for the first time in its history. Even after weekly sessions were resumed, attendance by the heads of MI6 and GCHQ remained patchy. The committee had lost some of its shine.[4]

Successive chiefs of MI6 reported that the JIC's status had diminished. In November 2008 for example, John Scarlett made it clear that 'the JIC priorities are not gospel as far as SIS is concerned'.[5] Just under two years later, his successor, John Sawers, publicly downgraded the JIC further still. He described the committee's role as merely offering 'context' to intelligence information. Sawers went on to emphasise that he did not answer to the JIC, reporting instead to the NSC.[6]

The NSC reforms have since redefined the JIC's role and place within Whitehall. This, however, was not without problems and, although welcoming the creation of the NSC, the Intelligence and Security Committee expressed concerns. How would the JIC fit into the new system? One particularly muddy area involved setting priorities and requirements, for which the JIC had long held responsibility. Cameron's NSC and National Security Strategy potentially challenged this. Indeed, the latter included a separate assessment of priority threats, whilst, towards the end of 2010, the JIC was instructed merely to 'contribute to the formulation' of national intelligence requirements.[7] Meanwhile, the chief of MI6 declared that 'we take our direction from the National Security Council'.[8] It should be noted, however, that these National Security Strategy priorities were compiled with assistance from certain JIC members and the JIO more broadly.

The situation remained complicated. In addition to the NSC and (theoretically) the JIC, intelligence agencies also took direction from the Strategic Defence and Security Review, their own existing agency strategic objectives, and Treasury targets. With no single tasking process, the potential for contradiction and confusion was rife.[9]

A review was desperately needed. In January 2011, therefore, the Prime Minister and the Cabinet Secretary, Gus O'Donnell, commissioned a report into the situation. They asked Alex Allan, the JIC Chairman, and National Security Adviser Peter Ricketts (himself a former JIC Chairman) to examine the impact of the NSC on the workings of the JIC. The task was conducted by Paul Rimmer, chief of the Assessments Staff, and Ciaran Martin, then of the Cabinet Office's Intelligence and Security Secretariat.[10]

Rimmer and Martin's report was issued ten months later and signed off by the Prime Minister himself. Its recommendations are reproduced below. As a result of the review, the JIC now operates on two levels: principals and sub-principals. Senior members (the principals), including the heads of the intelligence agencies, meet only monthly (although they can attend other meetings if they so wish). In theory they focus on key issues relevant to the National Security Council. By contrast, the sub-principals (less senior members or representatives of the directors) meet more regularly, supposedly to discuss papers of less immediate concern, issues of interest to one particular department, and tactical short-term issues. Insiders believe the new practice works well, albeit slightly differently from how the review initially suggested. In reality, the deputy-level meetings tackle the normal JIC agenda (including the important issues), whilst the principal level takes a more strategic view.

Some context here is necessary. This is not the first time in the committee's history that the JIC has operated on two levels. In the late 1940s and into the mid-1950s the JIC was also split into director- and deputy-director-level meetings. The same departments were represented on both, simply at a slightly lower level. It operated in a similar manner to that prescribed by Rimmer and Martin.

The new arrangements potentially undermine community cohesion, which has traditionally been a vital but intangible function of the JIC. The presence of the agency heads at meetings is useful in binding the joint intelligence community together – so important in the committee- and consensus-oriented British system. It remains to be seen whether monthly meetings will attenuate this long-held function. One could also argue that the agency heads' presence at the NSC undermines the role of the JIC Chairman. It is, of course, the latter's responsibility to represent the voice of the intelligence community. NSC meetings do, however, start with an overview of the latest JIC intelligence, following which the Prime Minister and others ask questions and offer feedback. The agency heads are there in an operational capacity and in case they are asked to take action.

Whilst there is an argument that agency heads are too busy for both committees, this is also about natural human behaviour. The heads of the three security and intelligence agencies 'are in attendance at the NSC and are invited to speak, and they speak frequently'. Although they always enjoyed good access to Downing Street, the NSC has given them greater opportunity to talk to ministers and the Prime Minister. Naturally, they prefer to attend weekly NSC meetings rather than the weekly JIC. Perhaps their new elevation is symptomatic of the growing importance of intelligence generally over the last two decades within the UK system.[11] More cynically, the NSC also operates as a marketing tool for each intelligence agency to promote its work to the highest consumers in the land.

The review clarified issues of agenda setting. As its principal consumer, the NSC agenda now broadly drives that of the JIC. Accordingly, the NSC(O) has become a key, but not the sole, setter of JIC papers. Demonstrating continuity with JIC tradition, the committee's assessments can still be tasked and sponsored by departments to meet their own priorities. However, Whitehall's JIO will challenge these if they are out of kilter with overall NSC requirements. The JIC is now docked squarely beneath the NSC. Whilst increasing impact, this creates a problem dubbed the 'tyranny of the tactical'. The JIC must keep pace with myriad NSC requirements. NSC direction can potentially skew intelligence towards myopic short-termism by neglecting longer-term strategic issues on which no immediate policy decision is necessary. This is an issue of which the committee must be aware as it settles into the new system.

The National Security Strategy sets the broad strategic direction of intelligence and the JIC then offers more detailed prioritisation. This is then overlaid by the NSC, which dictates the more immediate repositioning of resources in response to developing events. The ISC has welcomed this change and clarification.[12] It should also be noted that the NSC has now discussed those priorities established through the JIC process, thereby giving them formal ministerial endorsement.

Although this sounds complicated, Iain Lobban, the director of GCHQ, has described how it works in practice:

> The Joint Intelligence Committee has continued to provide us, through its Requirements and Priorities process, with our annual priorities and focus. That tends to be quite a stable, quite a static, process. Then the National Security Council, with its weekly rhythm gives an opportunity for a more dynamic flexing of the system and of the information required from the agencies.[13]

It should also be noted, however, that despite this close monitoring of the committee's agenda, the JIC is also expected to provide early warning of issues of its own accord. This seems somewhat optimistic. Policymakers want the best of both worlds.

The Rimmer–Martin review also shaped the presentation and dissemination of intelligence. According to Peter Ricketts, the JIC had become too 'stately and formal' over the years. Assessments needed to be much faster, more nimble and more flexible.[14] The JIC now offers fewer memoranda. Lengthy papers which characterised the Cold War era are a thing of the past. Almost like a consultancy company, it instead provides a more diverse range of tailored products to meet consumer needs. Building on Lord Butler's recommendations, these publications are more accessible to senior readership, including the Prime Minister himself.

The most controversial aspect of the review concerned the JIC's relationship with policy. Closer relations enhance relevance and policymakers' access to intelligence. Senior ministers can now see where intelligence comes from, whilst it can simultaneously be inspiring for the intelligence community to witness its product being debated at the highest level. The NSC gives impact to intelligence and ensures it passes the 'so what' test. This is vital. No matter how accurate or insightful, an unread intelligence assessment is pointless.

Closer relations, however, risk politicisation and the abuse of intelligence. Debating the issue in the House of Lords, Peter Hennessy expressed concern that 'some of the key elements of the JIC tradition might fade under the new dispensation'. JIC analysts should not 'fall into the trap either of advocacy or of telling their customers what they wish to hear'.[15] Defending the system, William Hague has refuted such warnings. The Foreign Secretary argued that JIC papers do not say 'Well then, these are the policies that follow from that [assessment]'. The committee, therefore, does not present a 'blurring of the lines'. Although Hague's defence went some way to alleviating ISC concerns about the subject, the committee still felt compelled to issue a warning: 'It is imperative that policy implications and analytical judgments remain separate in any intelligence assessment provided to Ministers.'[16] To be fair, the JIO was always alive to these issues. For a variety of reasons, JIC papers no longer contain a policy implications box.

The JIC is now closely tied to the most senior policymakers in the land. Building on the committee's ascent of the Whitehall hierarchy since 1936, the new reforms put the JIC in a potentially impressive position. The committee is at the forefront of providing essential intelligence decisions to support policy at the highest levels of government. This is a far cry from the days of Suez when its reports were marginalised. Its future is certainly brighter than it was a decade ago. At the same time, moreover, the JIC model has been much admired by Britain's allies over the last seventy years. As Hennessy warns, 'Its tradition [...] should never be allowed to slip towards the margins.'[17]

Supporting the National Security Council (NSC): The central national security and intelligence machinery

The establishment of a National Security Council (NSC) was one of the earliest decisions of this Government and represents one of the most significant changes to the national security and intelligence machinery at the centre of British Government in recent years.

In January 2011, the Prime Minister and the Cabinet Secretary asked the National Security Adviser and the Chairman of the Joint Intelligence Committee to review how the central national security and intelligence machinery and structures can best support the NSC, building on the Butler report of 2004. The terms of reference for the review can be found on the Cabinet Office website.

In summary, the **key recommendations** from the review are:

On the role of the Joint Intelligence Committee:

i. **The NSC's priorities should be the lead driver of the JIC agenda**, following as closely as possible the NSC's agenda and timetable. The NSC (Officials) meeting (NSC(O)) is best placed to oversee the tasking of the JIC, in line with its core role of setting strategic direction for the NSC. The NSC(O) should therefore task the JIC. However, the JIC must retain the latitude to provide early warning on issues outside of the immediate cycle of the NSC agenda.

ii. **The needs of the NSC are best supported by the JIC meeting in two formats, at a Principals and a Sub-Principals level.** This will better balance high level strategic judgments on NSC priorities with those less immediately before the NSC, of importance to policy Departments or more tactical short term assessments. So senior JIC members should meet monthly as "JIC Principals" to focus on key NSC issues, judgements and papers. Otherwise the JIC should meet at a Sub-Principals level to agree papers in between.

iii. **The JIC should produce a wider range of tailored intelligence products. The number of full JIC papers should be reduced, and replaced by more current briefs and summaries**, making them more focussed and more accessible to the Prime Minister/Ministerial readership.

On the UK's wider assessment capability:

iv. **The wider assessment capability, including Defence Intelligence (DI) and the Joint Terrorism Analysis Centre (JTAC), should be put more directly at the disposal of the NSC where appropriate.** The Cabinet Office's Chief of Assessment (CoA) should be responsible for commissioning materials from the wider assessment capability to support NSC discussions and those of its sub-committees, as well as signing off, or "kitemarking", the product to go to the NSC.

v. **The leadership of the Joint Intelligence Organisation should be charged with ensuring that the collective business plans of HMG's assessment bodies align** with the NSC's priorities. This is in line with the SDSR commitment on assessment. It will need to be done in a way that respects the operational independence and links to other organisations of those assessment bodies.

vi. **In supporting the NSC, the policy implications of analytical judgements should be identified in significant assessments given to Ministers.** This could be achieved through closer working between assessment and policy expertise in the Cabinet Office while respecting the independence of intelligence assessment from policy.

vii. **The Joint Intelligence Organisation should implement the recommendations of its open source audit**. This includes recruitment of a dedicated information specialist to improve the way that the JIO exploits open source, and its ability to support the use of open source material across the intelligence community.

On briefing intelligence to Ministers:

viii. **Clearer processes should be established to ensure that Ministers receive timely, well-chosen and auditable intelligence reports consistent with the principles set out in Lord Butler's report of 2004.** These should also enable everyone handling intelligence for Ministers to understand what sets it apart from other reporting, to understand the range of intelligence products, and to know where to go to for training and guidance.

Notes

1. Peter Hennessy, *Distilling the Frenzy: Writing the History of One's Own Times* (London: Biteback, 2012), p. 94.
2. Private information.
3. Jonathan Powell, *The New Machiavelli: How to Wield Power in the Modern World* (London: Vintage, 2011), p. 286; private information.
4. Philip Davies, *Intelligence and Government in Britain and the United States: A Comparative Perspective, Vol. 2: Evolution of the UK Intelligence Community* (Santa Barbara, CA: Praeger, 2012), pp. 306–7; Hennessy, *Distilling the Frenzy*, p. 95.
5. Sir John Scarlett quoted in Mark Phillips, 'Failing Intelligence: Reform of the Machinery', in Michael Codner and Michael Clarke (eds), *A Question of Security: The British Defence Review in an Age of Austerity* (London: I. B. Tauris, 2011), p. 262.
6. Davies, *Intelligence and Government in Britain and the United States*, p. 308; Sir John Sawers, 'Britain's Secret Front Line', speech to the Society of Editors, 28 October 2010.
7. Davies, *Intelligence and Government in Britain and the United States*, p. 309.
8. Intelligence and Security Committee, *Annual Report, 2010–2011*, Cm 8114 (Norwich: The Stationery Office, 2011), p. 40.
9. Ibid., pp. 40, 4; Intelligence and Security Committee, *Annual Report, 2011–2012*, Cm 8403 (Norwich: The Stationery Office, 2012), p. 11.
10. Hennessy, *Distilling the Frenzy*, p. 94.
11. Joint Committee on the National Security Strategy, *First Review of the National Security Strategy 2010*, HL Paper 265 / HC 1384 (London: The Stationery Office, 2012),

para. 93, available at http://www.publications.parliament.uk/pa/jt201012/jtselect/jtnatsec/265/26506.htm#a19 (last accessed 12 November 2013).
12. Intelligence and Security Committee, *Annual Report, 2011-2012*, p. 12.
13. Iain Lobban quoted ibid.
14. Peter Ricketts quoted ibid., p. 11.
15. Lord Hennessy of Nympsfield, December 2011, quoted in *Distilling the Frenzy*, p. 99.
16. Intelligence and Security Committee, *Annual Report, 2011-12*, pp. 9-10, 13.
17. Hennessy, *Distilling the Frenzy*, p. 99.

22

THE SYRIAN CIVIL WAR

THE SELF-IMMOLATION OF a Tunisian street vendor in late 2010 sparked turmoil across the Middle East. A series of turbulent uprisings have since swept the region, deposing leaders in Tunisia, Libya, Egypt and Yemen. Protests in Syria, beginning in the spring of 2011, gradually escalated into a protracted and militarised civil war pitting President Bashar al-Assad's forces against armed rebels.

The security situation deteriorated throughout 2012 and 2013, creating a humanitarian emergency and a spiralling refugee crisis. By September 2013, the United Nations estimated that two million Syrians had been forced to leave their country. A further four and a quarter million had been displaced within Syria.[1] Meanwhile, evidence of chemical weapons attacks – a self-proclaimed 'red line' for President Obama – piled up on government desks. On the morning of 21 August 2013, a particularly heavy chemical attack indiscriminately killed hundreds of civilians in east Damascus. David Cameron, Britain's Prime Minister, sought military intervention.

With developments moving at a fast pace in the last week of August, intelligence became central. In deliberating military intervention, governments needed to know whether Assad's forces had in fact used chemical weapons, who actually ordered this use, and why. With Parliament recalled ahead of a vote on the principle of military intervention, Cameron's government made a striking decision. Echoing Tony Blair eleven years earlier, the Prime Minister decided to publish Joint Intelligence Committee material. Accordingly, the Cabinet Office released the JIC's conclusions on the reported use of chemical weapons in Damascus alongside a covering letter from the committee's Chairman, Jon Day. These are both reproduced below.

Intelligence and Iraq had proved highly controversial, thrusting the JIC into the media spotlight. Why then did Cameron seek to follow suit? In truth there was no escaping the legacy of Iraq and the WMD saga. Despite the differing contexts, its echo reverberated around the parliamentary debate about intervention in Syria. Indeed, David Cameron acknowledged that 'I am deeply mindful of the lessons of previous conflicts and, in particular, of the deep concerns in the country that were caused by what went wrong with the Iraq conflict in 2003'.[2] Similarly, Ed Miliband, leader of the opposition, stressed the need to 'learn the lessons of Iraq'.[3] This extended to issues of intelligence and proof of Syrian chemical weapons use.

David Cameron faced a similar dilemma to Tony Blair. Back in 2002, Blair was confronted by a maelstrom of media and parliamentary questions about the justification for military intervention. As discussed in Chapter 19, he opted to publish a dossier based on sanitised intelligence. Eleven years later, Cameron felt similarly obliged to publish declassified intelligence as the debate gathered pace and Britain, alongside the United States, appeared to be heading towards another unpopular military intervention.[4] Given the legacy of Iraq, Cameron's government may have felt even greater pressure to release the intelligence assessment. Indeed, the Prime Minister was all too aware that 'we must recognise the scepticism and concerns that many people in the country will have after Iraq'.[5]

Although seeking intervention, Cameron expressed caution. Fully aware that weapons of mass destruction were never found in Iraq, political leaders in both Whitehall and Washington had to be careful not to prematurely accuse Assad of using chemical weapons. Evidence had to be found. And more importantly, a wary public had to be convinced that the evidence had been found. The various investigations, from Butler to Chilcot, into flawed intelligence and politicisation surely soured public perceptions of both the value of intelligence and how policymakers used it.

As a result of these various factors, JIC material again became central. On 27 August 2013, the committee concluded it was 'highly likely' that the Syrian regime was responsible for the chemical weapons attack, which, according to the JIC, resulted in at least 350 fatalities. The reasons underpinning this assessment are clearly visible in the document below and need not be repeated here.

Despite demonstrating some similarities with intelligence regarding Iraq, the Syria assessment reveals four key differences. The government had learnt from earlier mistakes. Firstly, and most obviously, the Syria assessment was not a government dossier. It clearly maintained JIC ownership, whilst Day's letter emphasised that conclusions 'were agreed by all committee members'. These two factors allowed little room for accusations of political spin and 'sexing up' reminiscent of those that hounded Blair and Alastair Campbell in the aftermath of the Iraq dossier.

Secondly, the Syria assessment was introduced by a letter from the JIC chairman. This lies in stark contrast with Tony Blair's foreword which headed the Iraq dossier. As noted in Chapter 19, the foreword was highly criticised for stretching the available intelligence to its limits and Blair has since expressed regret at having written it all. With hindsight the former Prime Minister wished he had simply published the sanitised material. Learning from Blair, this is exactly what Cameron did. By publishing the JIC's conclusions, introduced by

Day, Cameron once again reduced the potential for criticisms of spin, politicisation and manipulation.

Thirdly, the prominent references to open-source intelligence in the Chairman's letter are noteworthy. Day attempted to emphasise how intelligence was not, for the most part, based on secret sources unavailable to the public. For example, he highlighted the 'considerable' degree of 'open source reporting' alongside the committee's consultations with experts outside government to assess whether the footage of the attack could have been faked. In doing so, the letter reveals an apparent attempt to ensure credibility, build consensus beyond the Whitehall 'securocrat' bubble, and move away from a 'trust us' attitude which might have proved unsuccessful given the mistakes over Iraq. Indeed, Cameron drew heavily upon this in the debate, telling the House of Commons that 'there is an enormous amount of open-source reporting, including videos that we can all see'.[6]

These efforts reflect Lord Butler's recommendations about mistakes in Iraq. He expressed concern about secret intelligence being given undue weight in JIC assessments and suggested 'occasional external peer review'.[7] Alongside these attempts to emphasise open-source intelligence, however, Day's letter to the Prime Minister also referred explicitly to 'highly sensitive' intelligence to which Cameron had access – this was probably a reference to signals intelligence material including intercepts of Syrian political and military traffic. A combination of open and secret sources is essential to the JIC's all-source intelligence.

Fourthly, Day's covering letter clearly states what the JIC did know and, crucially, what it did not. It acknowledges the limitations of intelligence and gives confidence ratings to the various conclusions. For example, Day conceded that the JIC had 'high confidence in all of its assessments except in relation to the regime's precise motivation for carrying out an attack of this scale at this time'. Again, this demonstrates progression from the time of Iraq when, according to Lord Butler, 'it [was] not the current JIC convention to express degrees of confidence in the judgement'.[8] Accordingly, this contrasts heavily with Blair's foreword and accompanying parliamentary performance, which reinforced the impression that firmer intelligence underpinned the dossier than was actually the case. Indeed, Cameron explicitly stated that 'I do not want to raise, as perhaps happened in the Iraq debate, the status of individual or groups of pieces of intelligence into some sort of quasi-religious cult'.[9]

How, then, did the JIC assessment impact upon policymaking? On one level, alongside published legal advice, it helped support the government's case for war. The JIC paper directly informed National Security Council discussions, whilst Day personally briefed NSC members to provide 'further background and a summary of the most recent reporting, analysis and challenge'. The JIC enjoyed direct access to policymaking at the highest level. Moreover, the day after the NSC meeting the Prime Minister explicitly quoted the committee's key judgements in the parliamentary debate. He then argued that all the evidence we have – the fact that the opposition do not have chemical weapons and the regime does, the fact that it has used them and was attacking the area at the time, and the intelligence that I have reported – is enough to conclude that the regime is responsible and should be held accountable.[10]

On another level, the JIC report also influenced parliamentarians. This is unusual in so far as assessments traditionally only influenced senior policymakers but, owing to the Iraqi precedent, it will perhaps become more common. During the parliamentary debate one Conservative MP lamented:

> On the intelligence, those of us who were here in 2003, at the time of the Iraq War, felt they had their fingers burnt. The case for war was made and Parliament was briefed on the intelligence, but we were given only part of the story and, in some cases, an inaccurate story. A summary of the intelligence has been published [on Syria], but it is the bare bones, and I urge the government in the following days to consider how more intelligence can be provided.[11]

Even Jack Straw, Foreign Secretary in 2003, conceded that 'Iraq has made the public much more questioning and more worried about whether we should put troops in harm's way, especially when intelligence is involved'.[12]

The JIC's assessment of 'highly likely', reliant on a 'limited but growing body of intelligence', seemingly did not convince MPs. One Labour member argued that '"highly likely" and "some evidence" are not good enough to risk further lives, to risk counterattack, to inflame the whole region, to risk dragging other states into this war and, at the same time, to increase the risk of terrorism on British streets.'[13] In a humiliating blow to the Prime Minister's authority, the House of Commons rejected Cameron's plea for military intervention in principle.

The parliamentary debate reveals how publishing JIC intelligence is a double-edged sword. On the one hand, it is useful for transparency and for explaining the factors driving important political decisions. On the other hand, however, intelligence rarely deals in certainties and publishing JIC material risks raising the required burden of proof beyond realistic levels. Despite this, the French government published an intelligence dossier the following week, whilst the Americans also spelt out the conclusions of their intelligence. It is too soon to say whether this is a new trend but a future role of intelligence, including that of the JIC, will perhaps be to inform public debate on key issues.

Joint Intelligence Organisation
Cabinet Office Open +44 (0)20 7276 1234
70 Whitehall
London SW1A 2AS
www.cabinetoffice.gov.uk

From the Chairman of the Joint Intelligence Committee

Ref: Jp 115

Prime Minister 29 August 2013

SYRIA: REPORTED CHEMICAL WEAPONS USE

Following the widespread open source reports of chemical weapons (CW) use in the suburbs of Damascus in the early hours of 21 August 2013, the JIC met on 25 August to agree an assessment. At a subsequent meeting on 27 August we met again to review our level of confidence in the assessment relating to the regime's responsibility for the attack. The JIC's conclusions were agreed by all Committee members. The final paper informed the National Security Council meeting on 28 August, at which I provided further background and a summary of the most recent reporting, analysis and challenge. The paper's key judgements, based on the information and intelligence available to us as of 25 August, are attached.

It is important to put these JIC judgements in context. We have assessed previously that the Syrian regime used lethal CW on 14 occasions from 2012. This judgement was made with the highest possible level of certainty following an exhaustive review by the Joint Intelligence Organisation of intelligence reports plus diplomatic and open sources. We think that there have been other attacks although we do not have the same degree of confidence in the evidence. A clear pattern of regime use has therefore been established.

Unlike previous attacks, the degree of open source reporting of CW use on 21 August has been considerable. As a result, there is little serious dispute that chemical attacks causing mass casualties on a larger scale than hitherto (including, we judge, at least 350 fatalities) took place.

It is being claimed, including by the regime, that the attacks were either faked or undertaken by the Syrian Armed Opposition. We have tested this assertion using a wide range of intelligence and open sources, and invited HMG and outside experts to help us establish whether such a thing is possible. There is no credible intelligence or other evidence to substantiate the claims or the possession of CW by the opposition. The JIC has therefore concluded that there are no plausible alternative scenarios to regime responsibility.

We also have a limited but growing body of intelligence which supports the judgement that the regime was responsible for the attacks and that they were conducted to help clear the Opposition from strategic parts of Damascus. Some of this intelligence is highly sensitive but you have had access to it all.

Against that background, the JIC concluded that it is highly likely that the regime was responsible for the CW attacks on 21 August. The JIC had high confidence in all of its assessments except in relation to the regime's precise motivation for carrying out an attack of this scale at this time – though intelligence may increase our confidence in the future.

There has been the closest possible cooperation with the Agencies in producing the JIC's assessment. We have also worked in concert with the US intelligence community and agree with the conclusions they have reached.

Jon Day

JIC assessment of 27 August on Reported Chemical Weapons use in Damascus

A chemical attack occurred in Damascus on the morning of 21 August, resulting in at least 350 fatalities. It is not possible for the opposition to have carried out a CW attack on this scale. The regime has used CW on a smaller scale on at least 14 occasions in the past. There is some intelligence to suggest regime culpability in this attack. These factors make it highly likely that the Syrian regime was responsible.

Extensive video footage attributed to the attack in eastern Damascus (which we assess would be very difficult to falsify) is consistent with the use of a nerve agent, such as sarin, and is not consistent with the use of blister or riot control agents.

There is no obvious political or military trigger for regime use of CW on an apparently larger scale now, particularly given the current presence in Syria of the UN investigation team. Permission to authorise CW has probably been delegated by President Assad to senior regime commanders, such as [*], but any deliberate change in the scale and nature of use would require his authorisation.

There is no credible evidence that any opposition group has used CW. A number continue to seek a CW capability, but none currently has the capability to conduct a CW attack on this scale.

Russia claims to have a 'good degree of confidence' that the attack was an 'opposition provocation' but has announced that they support an investigation into the incident. We expect them to maintain this line. The Syrian regime has now announced that it will allow access to the sites by UN inspectors.

There is no immediate time limit over which environmental or physiological samples would have degraded beyond usefulness. However, the longer it takes inspectors to gain access to the affected sites, the more difficult it will be to establish the chain of evidence beyond a reasonable doubt.

Notes

1. UNHCR, 'Number of Syrian Refugees Tops Two Million Mark with More on the Way', *UNHCR News*, 3 September 2013, http://www.unhcr.org/522495669.html (last accessed 5 September 2013).
2. David Cameron MP, *Hansard*, 29 August 2013, Column 1427, http://www.publications.parliament.uk/pa/cm201314/cmhansrd/cm130829/debtext/130829-0001.htm #1308298000001 (last accessed 3 September 2013).
3. Edward Miliband MP, *Hansard*, 29 August 2013, Column 1443, http://www.publications.parliament.uk/pa/cm201314/cmhansrd/cm130829/debtext/130829-0001.htm #1308298000001 (last accessed 3 September 2013).
4. An Opinium/Observer poll conducted in August 2013 found 60% of Brits opposed military intervention in Syria. Toby Helm, 'Poll finds 60% of British public oppose UK military action against Syria', *The Guardian Online*, 31 August 2013, http://www.theguardian.com/politics/2013/aug/31/poll-british-military-action-syria (last accessed 3 September 2013).
5. David Cameron MP, *Hansard*, 29 August 2013, Column 1440, http://www.publications.parliament.uk/pa/cm201314/cmhansrd/cm130829/debtext/130829-0001.htm #1308298000001 (last accessed 3 September 2013).
6. David Cameron MP, *Hansard*, 29 August 2013, Column 1437, http://www.publications.parliament.uk/pa/cm201314/cmhansrd/cm130829/debtext/130829-0001.htm #1308298000001 (last accessed 3 September 2013).
7. Lord Butler, *Review of Intelligence on Weapons of Mass Destruction* (London: The Stationery Office, 2004), p.146
8. Butler, *Review of Intelligence on Weapons of Mass Destruction*, p. 145
9. David Cameron MP, *Hansard*, 29 August 2013, Column 1437, http://www.publications.parliament.uk/pa/cm201314/cmhansrd/cm130829/debtext/130829-0001.htm #1308298000001 (last accessed 3 September 2013).
10. David Cameron MP, *Hansard*, 29 August 2013, Column 1432, http://www.publications.parliament.uk/pa/cm201314/cmhansrd/cm130829/debtext/130829-0001.htm #1308298000001 (last accessed 3 September 2013).
11. Richard Ottaway MP, *Hansard*, 29 August 2013, Column 1460, http://www.publications.parliament.uk/pa/cm201314/cmhansrd/cm130829/debtext/130829-0001.htm #1308298000001 (last accessed 3 September 2013).
12. Jack Straw MP, *Hansard*, 29 August 2013, Column 1450, http://www.publications.parliament.uk/pa/cm201314/cmhansrd/cm130829/debtext/130829-0001.htm#1308298000001 (last accessed 3 September 2013).
13. John McDonnell MP, *Hansard*, 29 August 2013, Column 1461, http://www.publications.parliament.uk/pa/cm201314/cmhansrd/cm130829/debtext/130829-0001.htm #1308298000001 (last accessed 3 September 2013).

23

THROUGH THE LOOKING GLASS: ILLUSIONS OF OPENNESS AND THE STUDY OF BRITISH INTELLIGENCE

MANY OF THE JIC's files are open. They are seemingly comprehensive and can seduce the unwary historian with a siren song of 'top secret' intelligence. Certainly a book such as this would have been impossible until relatively recently. New declassification benchmarks have resulted in a veritable archival feast for historians and political scientists.

The available records do, however, shape our understanding of the committee in certain ways. This book has predominantly drawn upon JIC memoranda. These present fascinating insights into intelligence thinking on myriad issues, as well as on intelligence successes and failures. From here, it is possible to consider the relationship between intelligence and policy throughout much of the twentieth century. However, the declassified files construct a particular narrative of the JIC's role since 1936. Firstly, they offer a narrow account of a reactive body cumbersomely dealing with long-term issues. Historians are left unaware of current intelligence and the committee's responses to crises. Secondly, the files create an impression of JIC passivity, neglecting both the committee's active and global roles. Thirdly, by focusing on the JIC at the expense of other actors operating beneath the committee, the available files skew interpretations of the Joint Intelligence Organisation as a whole. Arguably Current Intelligence Groups, staffed by amazing subject and regional specialists, were a key part of this machine, but they are not well represented in the extant archive. Above all JIC papers give a misleading sense of interdepartmental unity and intelligence hermeticism. This is not the result of some strategic government conspiracy, but merely the by-product of classification policy and a fragmented record.

Government openness

Intelligence studies are perennially dogged by a core epistemological frailty – government secrecy. At best, scholars are faced with a disjointed self-assembly kit that lacks instructions and has core pieces missing. At worst, scholars are given no pieces at all and intimidating blanket bans on declassification impede entire areas of research. In terms of the JIC, however, whole series of papers are now neatly lined up at the National Archives. Indeed, since the dark days of the Cold War, much-vaunted progress has been made regarding government openness, especially on intelligence assessment.

In July 1993 John Major's Conservative administration announced the Waldegrave Initiative on Open Government. MI6 and GCHQ were formally 'avowed' the following year. This approach formed a notably stark contrast with Margaret Thatcher's famed love of secrecy and her incessant desire to stifle debate through the wielding of the Official Secrets Act.[1] The Open Government programme oversaw the accelerated declassification of volumes of archival files to the Public Records Office, and the government proudly lauded it as nothing short of a revolution in official attitudes towards secrecy. However, the move has been criticised as a cynical, if skilful, attempt at information management by the keepers of history.[2] Intelligence scholars are all too familiar with the dreaded red stamp of exemption: 'This document has been retained under subsection 3(4) of the Public Records Act, 1958.' Moreover, certain files, notably those of MI6, remain permanently locked away. Covert action in particular remains a mostly missing dimension in British post-war history.

Ideas of open government and mutual trust supposedly expanded under the Labour governments of Tony Blair and Gordon Brown. Arguing that 'openness is fundamental to the political health of a modern state',[3] Blair brought in the much-heralded Freedom of Information (FOI) Act in 2000. The Prime Minister, however, quickly regretted his decision. He later ranted colourfully (almost quaintly) at his own innocence: 'You idiot. You naive, foolish, irresponsible nincompoop. There is no description of stupidity, no matter how vivid, that is adequate. I quake at the imbecility of it.'[4] Historians can request JIC files under the Act. As with the Waldegrave initiative and the Public Records Act of 1958, however, sensitive intelligence files are exempt from FOI releases. The Freedom of Information Act therefore does little to circumvent the distortions assessed below.

The committee's post-war assessments and minutes began to be released from 1994. The Secretary's files, which contain more detail and flavour, were slower in appearing but began to drip into the public domain from 2000. Assessments and minutes dating from 1969 were added in 2002 and declassification is now moving towards a twenty-year rule. Taken together, the committee's files appear comprehensive and they are indeed a wonderful resource. Various series span contemporary British history and offer the researcher intelligence history on a plate.

But there are problems. Levels of weeding leave professional historians with a sense of unease. It is therefore important for those wanting to fully understand intelligence history to draw upon sources outside the preselected and processed material of the National Archives.[5] Certain insiders have privately stated that writing intelligence history is pointless without full access to all records, which, outside official histories, is impossible. There is some logic in this stance, for fragmented evidence can often lead to inaccurate assumptions. And yet it is imperative to try. Intelligence history is too important to be forgotten until all records are publicly available (if that ever happens). Historians must be wary of the methodological and epistemological frailties of lazy overreliance on the government's declassification process. It is of course essential to cast one's net as widely as possible and draw upon oral history and private papers to supplement the 'history supermarket'. Occasional archival 'accidents' can illuminate these issues. The JIC paper on sigint targets reproduced in this volume was uncovered in 1987 in the India Office Records now held at the British Library but remains classified in the Cabinet Records at Kew.

That said, there is far more in the National Archives than meets the untrained eye. Regarding the JIC, overreliance on the committee's papers creates a distorted narrative of its history and role. But awareness of parallel files and dusty hidden corners of the labyrinthine archival system offers a veritable gold mine. Historians can get by on the National Archives, so long as they look beyond the obvious series and supplement their work with interviews. For example, certain reports which remain classified in the JIC series can be found declassified elsewhere (including in America), whilst other files can challenge the narrative of the JIC releases.

Constructing a false narrative

Overreliance on the declassified JIC series creates a false narrative in a number of ways. Firstly, the JIC appears cumbersome and only able to deal with long-term issues. Secondly, the JIC appears purely passive. It has no operational dimension. Thirdly, it seems an isolated body with few links to other countries, notably the United States. Fourthly, it comes across as an admirable beacon of interdepartmental harmony and reports appear hermetic. They appeal to the tidy mind.

Current vs long-term intelligence

The JIC has long engaged in current intelligence. Lord Butler outlined the committee's 'main function' as being to provide assessments on issues of both 'immediate and long-term importance to national interests'.[6] It is therefore imperative that the JIC should not be perceived solely as some cumbersome long-term body unable to respond to crises and engage with short-term problems. As far back as the early 1950s, the committee was offering weekly intelligence reviews of various global developments. These usually involved Soviet activity and were tied heavily to the ongoing Cold War. They did, however, extend to other issues, such as tension in the Middle East and insurgent uprisings.

Current intelligence proliferated from the late 1960s. Backed by the newly created Assessments Staff, the JIC began to issue increasing numbers of short-term intelligence reports known as special assessments. These were disseminated alongside 'notes', which were of a slightly longer-term nature. Special assessments formed a crucial means of monitoring ongoing developments, from the Soviet invasion of Czechoslovakia to the deteriorating security situation in Ireland.

Reliance on the JIC series leaves historians somewhat blind to this role. Current intelligence generally remains classified, but was often hot stuff appreciated by successive Prime Ministers and senior members of the Cabinet. An instructive example is found in the committee's weekly intelligence reviews. Throughout the 1950s and 1960s, the JIC issued two current intelligence products every week. The first, known as the Grey Book, was distributed to a broad mass of officials in London and overseas. The second, known as the Red Book, was far more highly classified. It went to more senior consumers – including the Queen. There is a blanket ban on historians viewing any Red Book material. JIC minutes reveal its existence but offer no real hint at content. By contrast, the Grey Book was far less sensitive. It was disseminated to all and sundry manning British posts across the world. And yet declassification remains patchy at best. Whole years are missing and there is nothing from 1966 onwards.

Regrettably, the government has consistently held back special assessments and notes. Lack of access to the latter is strange: notes released under the Freedom of Information Act appear strikingly similar in topic and nature to the declassified longer-term appreciations. Special assessments, however, incorporated Red Book material from 1967. They covered matters of urgent importance, before being discontinued and replaced by 'immediate assessments' from 1974.[7] All special assessments remain classified.

Reliance on the declassified papers rather skews perceptions of the nature of the JIC's reports. The JIC appears to be an overwhelmingly cumbersome body. The masses of declassified memoranda found in CAB 158 and CAB 186 are strategic assessments of longer-term issues, such as annual reviews of world communism. They are broad and sit at the foundation of the policymaking process, cumulatively building up consumers' background information and shaping Whitehall understanding. As Michael Herman, a former JIC Secretary and veteran watcher of the committee, has acknowledged, this of course is a crucial role of intelligence in peacetime. Long-term JIC papers help create well-informed policies.[8]

On the downside, however, such memoranda can be dense and dry, and often lacked current insight. Many of these papers took months to produce. To give just one example: an important report running to over eighty pages ascertaining the Soviet threat in the early Cold War was commissioned in January 1948. But it was not disseminated until July.[9] Although there were other papers produced in a shorter time, the declassified files do create a misleading impression that the wheels of Whitehall bureaucracy were turning very slowly indeed. The JIC files suggest that the committee was somewhat pedestrian and lacked sharp, incisive and acutely relevant policy insight.

Most importantly, in Rumsfeldian parlance, this particular missing dimension is a 'known unknown'. Historians are aware that these intelligence products exist even if we cannot see them. The government has openly acknowledged that current intelligence has long formed part of the JIC's role and has offered an overview of how the system evolved. But the sources themselves are kept tantalisingly out of reach.[10] In a recent overview of British strategic intelligence in the Cold War, Len Scott briefly mentions classified weekly output as a caveat to his broader discussion of the JIC.[11] Such awareness is important, but lack of full discussion impedes a holistic understanding of the committee's role. Unfortunately, detailed analysis remains impossible owing to a lack of sources. Historians naturally rely on the declassified papers and tend to take the archival feed as an analogue of reality. As a result the role of the JIC becomes skewed.

Passive vs active

The second distortion is perhaps more serious. It is an 'unknown unknown'. As we have seen, the JIC series create the impression that the committee was cumbersome and mostly reactive: members lacked dynamism and were not remotely interested in operational details. This is of course fair to an extent. The JIC was (and remains) fundamentally an intelligence assessment body. It spent the majority of the Cold War watching the Soviets, counting nuclear weapons and determining intentions.

Yet there is another aspect to the committee, on which the declassified JIC series are silent. Senior members, especially the Chairman, enjoyed a more operational dynamic. Firstly, this involved overseeing intelligence operations of a 'special nature'. JIC members were tasked with monitoring controversial or risky intelligence-gathering operations. This aspect of the committee's role is far from adequately revealed in JIC papers. Detailed discussion between the JIC and the Prime Minister regarding air photography in the Berlin Corridor, for example, has to be found in Ministry of Defence files.[12]

Secondly, the JIC Chairman was at the forefront of British covert action planning throughout the Cold War. He worked closely with MI6 to define the parameters, recommend action and design the new Whitehall bureaucracy for taking the covert Cold War to the Soviets. JIC Chairman Patrick Reilly was heavily involved in Whitehall's committee overseeing covert action, known as the Official Committee on Communism (Overseas), in the early 1950s. Moreover, he personally headed a working party examining proposals for covert action behind the Iron Curtain and argued in favour of limited strikes against satellite economies. It was Reilly who liaised with the Americans on covert action at the strategic level.[13]

Reilly's input began a fascinating pattern linking the JIC Chairman to covert action. Indeed, by the 1960s his successors were chairing a shadowy successor to the Official Committee on Communism (Overseas), known as the Joint

Action Committee (JAC).[14] And the overlaps between the JIC and covert action did not stop there. Senior JIC members also sat on the JAC whilst the JIC Secretary doubled up as its secretary.[15] The JIC connected with other secret operational actors too. For example, the JIC Chairman was instrumental in establishing another body tasked with instigating covert action in the Yemen during the civil war in the 1960s.[16]

The JIC Chairman was vastly influential and yet this does not come across adequately in the archives. He sat at the heart of an intricate and secret Whitehall web, and was probably third only to the Cabinet Secretary and the chief of MI6 when it came to covert activity. This gaping lacuna has important implications, which are going unnoticed because scholars are unaware that the lacuna exists in the first place. The Chairman's active role raises core questions: what is the relationship between intelligence and policy in the British system? Where does covert action sit in the intelligence–policy dichotomy? If historians are unaware that the JIC Chairman was engaged in such activity then these questions go unanswered. Moreover, certain leading scholars of intelligence machinery have erroneously suggested that the Cabinet Secretary chaired the JAC.[17] This is an easy mistake to make as there are practically no archival files on the subject. Herculean digging is required. The answers, however, *are* in the National Archives – just not in an obvious place.

Such material would not necessarily be in the JIC files anyway. Strictly speaking, covert action was not JIC activity. It is therefore important not to overemphasise the dealings of JIC members outside the committee. But there is an important point here. This activity was planned by JIC members wearing different hats – Suez is a classic example of this. One of the reasons this material was kept outside the JIC was simply to keep it more secret. Much JIC material is not particularly sensitive and the committee had a surprisingly broad distribution list. Bodies such as the JAC therefore allowed the same people to engage in a highly sensitive activity without other government departments (and future historians) ever finding out.

Whitehall vs global

The JIC files downplay the committee's global connections. They do this in three ways: firstly, there is no sense of foreign representation on the JIC; secondly, there is little detail on British liaison with former colonies post-independence; and thirdly, very few papers covering the JIC's regional outposts remain. That the CIA enjoyed regular representation on the JIC is a poorly kept secret. Historians are well aware, for example, that the CIA had an officer on the committee during the Suez Crisis. Indeed, Chester Cooper, the CIA man in question, has written a lively account of his time in London.[18] Strikingly, however, any indication of this has been erased from the archival records. The JIC minutes do not even acknowledge the presence of a CIA officer, let alone offer his name.

Cooper's role was important. Neglecting it skews understanding of Anglo-American relations in the strained days of the mid-1950s. Cooper continued his role on the JIC even when the regular diplomatic connections between London and Washington were broken. According to former JIC Chairman Percy Cradock, at one point Cooper was the sole channel of communication between the two capitals.[19] Similarly, Cooper's role was again important during the Cuban Missile Crisis. Canada, New Zealand and Australia enjoyed similar status. The allies were present at one end of the JIC table for general discussion and for certain assessments, but were waved away during others.[20] This, however, cannot be proved using archival evidence at all – such input (especially regarding the US) has been mostly wiped from the official record. The JIC's liaison role and the important input of intelligence in diplomacy are therefore neglected by historians relying on JIC papers. This is the sort of area where historians need to deploy their interview skills.

JIC files have likewise been excised of references to connections with the intelligence apparatus of other countries. The JIC was tasked 'to keep under review the organisation and working of intelligence and defence security at home and overseas [...] and to advise what changes are deemed necessary'.[21] Accordingly, the committee gradually acquired a role in colonial security. This included attempts to manage and reform the local intelligence assessment and dissemination systems.[22] There is plenty of material on such activity, including the detailed papers of JIC working groups.

It quickly vanishes, however, once the colony is approaching independence. There is very little on the role of the JIC post-independence. The Federation of South Arabia forms an instructive example. A great deal of material is available regarding JIC planning for withdrawal in 1967 but many of the relevant files regarding post-independence requirements remain classified. The released documents merely hint at some sort of offshore intelligence naval task force, the intelligence functions of the British embassy in the new South Yemen, and the need for intelligence liaison officers.[23] Perhaps more intriguingly, the countersubversion files suggest 'arrangements for "stay-behind" facilities in colonial territories which were approaching full independence'.[24] No further detail is given. The JIC's global role remains unknown.

During and after the Second World War, the JIC had a number of regional outposts. These included JIC (Far East), JIC (Germany), JIC (Washington) and JIC (Middle East). A number of smaller joint intelligence groups were also established, including one in the Gulf. Like the JIC in London, these often included representation from the US, Canada, Australia and New Zealand – again, this is not apparent from the files.[25] Although these groups answered to the local theatre commander or head of mission in the first instance,[26] they formed an important network around the London JIC. On top of this, local intelligence committees existed in colonial territories whilst foreign-run JICs were also associated with the JIC in London.

Once more, however, reliance on the archives creates a skewed view.

Overseas JIC files are held in CAB 191, but the series is notably fragmented. Many of the papers have simply been destroyed. JIC minutes do discuss issues relating to the regional JICs, including matters of structure and function, but very few regional reports have survived in the National Archives. Historians are therefore left broadly unaware of how JIC (Far East) reports, for example, fed into Whitehall intelligence assessments of south-east Asia. Yet again, the declassified JIC files create a distorted narrative of the committee's role and work: this time as an insular Whitehall actor, as opposed to a global actor with tentacles reaching all four corners of the world.

Calm vs chaos

JIC files give the false impression that the committee writes the reports. It does not. Members merely review assessments which have been drafted by specialists seconded from different government departments within the central intelligence machinery system. The JIC makes last-minute alterations before approving reports and issuing them under the JIC banner.

The declassified series concentrate almost exclusively on the committee: its minutes and final memoranda. Historians are presented with an overly linear progression from conception, through drafting, to dissemination. In the released files, JIC assessments begin with the terms of reference (neatly outlined) and the final report follows behind. The corresponding minutes reveal some light discussion about presentation and emphasis. The process appears smooth and amiable – unnaturally so. It appears excessively hermetic and the committee is presented in a unified manner.

In reality the process is messier. The central intelligence machinery takes raw intelligence, comments from the intelligence agencies, contribution from the intelligence analysts and input from the relevant policymaking departments, and places it into the bigger picture by assessing what it all actually means.[27] Committee members have the final say, and one former Chairman has described the JIC as 'the final arbiter of intelligence'.[28]

A central reason underpinning this impression is the lack of sources from the sub-JIC level. Papers of the Joint Intelligence Staff and the Assessments Staff, the bodies who actually draft the assessments, are not present in the archives. There is some material in the JIC secretariat files, but declassification of this is patchy and barely scratches the surface of the central intelligence machinery as a whole. Similarly, historians rely on the smallest of hints in the JIC memoranda themselves – papers are tagged 'revised' or 'final', for example.

The result is a distorted impression of the JIC. Historians are presented only with the neat, calm and occasionally banal apex of the central intelligence machinery. What is missing is the chaos beneath. Strategic interdepartmental intelligence does not start and finish with the JIC report and it is simplistic to talk of intelligence as a single unit. Instead, myriad processes take place beneath the final product which shape the intelligence assessment in underexplored ways. One might extend this criticism to British record preservation policy generally in the foreign, defence and security fields. Its excessive focus on elites means that we have failed to capture the locations where much of the debate took place. For example, just occasionally, minutes of the Joint Planning Staff – the engine room of British strategic thinking – surface in a forgotten file, but no central record has been preserved.

JIC assessments are the product of their environment. Those involved in writing and scrutinising the reports are under the command of their various ministries, not the JIC (although the creation of the Assessments Staff in 1968 was designed to address this). Understanding the competing pressures within the central intelligence machinery is therefore essential to understanding British interdepartmental intelligence assessments. Indeed, JIC conclusions are the product of competing agendas, diverging threat perceptions and jealous departmental turf wars. By tasking and framing issues in a certain way, a dominant department within the drafting process can dangerously alter an intelligence conclusion. Likewise, intelligence assessment is impeded if a particular department is sidelined. It is therefore important to shine a light on the corridors and back rooms of Whitehall to reveal the processes underpinning JIC assessments. Reliance on the JIC files alone renders this impossible. By looking beneath the JIC, it is possible to explore the competing conceptions behind a swathe of important issues since the Second World War.

Different departments have conceptualised security differently. In the immediate post-war period the military, for example, continuously pushed traditional defence issues upon the JIC. By contrast, the Foreign Office was keen to challenge narrow understandings of security and examine political issues. Meanwhile, the Colonial Office understood the Cold War threat in a very different way from both the military and the Foreign Office. Turf wars between the Colonial Office and the joint intelligence machinery were common throughout the 1950s. But there is no sense of this in the available JIC papers. To get a real sense of the animosity, the historian must dig through various Colonial Office files instead.

The same is true regarding the rise of terrorism in the 1970s. The core debates are not in the JIC files, they are in the equivalent Foreign and Commonwealth Office papers. Once again, JIC files offer only the final papers and historians are left ignorant of the sources, debates and bargaining which underpinned the ultimate conclusions. The processes of intelligence go unnoticed. By examining the papers of the FCO's Maritime and Transport Department, for example, the historian can start to assess how the JIC reached the conclusions it did and why intelligence grossly overestimated the threat from maritime hijacking in 1970.[29] Importantly, the government weeders are less strenuous in such seemingly mundane departmental files. There are no strict rules underpinning declassification, and a good deal of subjectivity guides the process. Accordingly a paper from MI5, MI6 or the FCO's secretive Permanent Under-Secretary's Department occasionally appears in full in the most random of places.

A government conspiracy to rewrite history?

Swathes of JIC material are now available, but overreliance on them can create a distorted impression. An important question, therefore, is whether the government has deliberately constructed a skewed narrative of the JIC. Have the weeders attempted to rewrite history through careful information management? The simple answer is no.

Any misleading accounts of the JIC are simply a by-product of broader issues. For example, one assumes that current intelligence is strictly classified because of the reliance on sensitive signals and human intelligence. Unlike the strategic longer-term JIC papers, it is much more difficult to camouflage the sources of this intelligence. This is an area in which twenty-first-century JIC papers differ from their predecessors. The longer-term JIC assessments issued during the Cold War made very little reference to the intelligence on which they drew. This is a stark contrast with the heavily annotated papers produced today. Like earlier current intelligence assessments, this development has significant implications for the future release of JIC material.

Moreover, the authorities have clearly acknowledged the JIC's long-standing involvement in current intelligence. That this particular missing dimension is a 'known unknown' renders government conspiracy highly unlikely. Similarly, the operational dimension has been classified because it is more sensitive than intelligence assessments. Any reduction of JIC members to a caricature of bean-counting passivity is a side effect. Whether or not the government should be suppressing such covert activity in the first place is another debate.

Intelligence liaison is a particularly sensitive subject, as is anything that impacts upon British relations with independent countries. It is unclear whether it is the Americans or the British who are behind the excising of the likes of Chester Cooper from JIC records. Regarding the regional JICs, it appears that the bulk of this material was destroyed during decolonisation and Britain's withdrawal from east of Suez. Again, there is no evidence of a government conspiracy to rewrite history. The final area is more confusing. It is unclear why sub-JIC documentation is not in the archives. Such material is far too important to warrant destruction, for it offers invaluable insight into the Whitehall mind in all its complexity. It reveals how threats were constructed and understood. Any government conspiracy again seems unlikely, for a lot of this material is decentralised and available in the parallel files of the JIC's constituent departments. Similarly, certain papers which are redacted in the JIC series lie buried elsewhere as a glistening prize for the intrepid historian. Scholars just need to know where to look – which is easier said than done. It can be assumed, however, that the government is aware that there is more to the JIC than the declassified material suggests. It has, after all, commissioned an official history using secret sources.

Notes

1. David Vincent, *The Culture of Secrecy: Britain, 1832-1998* (Oxford: Clarendon Press, 1999), p. 262.
2. For an early reflection on these issues see, Richard J. Aldrich, 'Did Waldegrave Work? The Impact of Open Government upon British History', *Twentieth Century British History* 9/1 (1998), pp. 111-26.
3. *Your Right to Know: The Government's Proposals for a Freedom of Information Act*, Cm 3818 (The Stationery Office, 1997), available at http://www.archive.official-documents.co.uk/document/caboff/foi/foi.htm (last accessed 13 November 2013).
4. Tony Blair quoted in Martin Rosenbaum, 'Why Tony Blair thinks he was an idiot', BBC News website, 1 September 2010, http://www.bbc.co.uk/blogs/opensecrets/2010/09/why_tony_blair_thinks_he_was_a.html (last accessed 13 November 2013).
5. Aldrich, 'Did Waldegrave Work?', p. 124; Richard J. Aldrich, '"Grow Your Own": Cold War Intelligence and History Supermarkets', *Intelligence and National Security* 17/1 (2002) p. 148. See also Richard J. Aldrich, 'Policing the Past: Official History, Secrecy and British Intelligence since 1945', *English Historical Review* 119/483 (2004), pp. 922-53.
6. Lord Butler of Brockwell, *Review of Intelligence on Weapons of Mass Destruction: Report*, HC 898 (London: The Stationery Office, 2004), p. 13.
7. 'Cabinet Office: Central Intelligence Machinery: Joint Intelligence Committee: Assessments and Notes', CAB 189, The National Archives, http://www.nationalarchives.gov.uk/catalogue/displaycataloguedetails.asp?CATLN=3&CATID=60582&SearchInit=4&SearchType=6&CATREF=CAB+189 (last accessed 13 November 2013).
8. Michael Herman, *Intelligence Power in Peace and War* (Cambridge: Cambridge University Press, 1996), p. 152.
9. 'Soviet Interests, Intentions and Capabilities', 23 July 1948, JIC(48)9, TNA: CAB 158/3.
10. 'Intelligence and Security Services: Joint Intelligence Committee Records', The National Archives, http://www.nationalarchives.gov.uk/records/research-guides/intelligence-records.htm#16184 (last accessed 13 November 2013).
11. Len Scott, 'British Strategic Intelligence and the Cold War', in Loch K. Johnson (ed.), *The Oxford Handbook of National Security Intelligence* (New York: Oxford University Press, 2012), p. 145.
12. See for example, Record of a meeting held at Admiralty House on 15 September 1960, TNA: DEFE 13/15.
13. AC(O) minutes, 1 March 1950, TNA: CAB 134/4; Robert Joyce, 'Final Meeting in London with British Foreign Office and SIS Representatives', 20 December 1951, Executive Secretariat, Psychological Strategy Board Working File, 1951-53, Box 6, RG59. We are indebted to Thomas Maguire for this file.
14. Rory Cormac, 'Coordinating Covert Action: The Case of the Yemen Civil War and the South Arabian Insurgency', *Journal of Strategic Studies*, Vol. 36, No. 5, 2012, pp. 692-717.
15. Ibid.
16. The body was known as the South Arabian Action Group. For more details see Cormac, 'Coordinating Covert Action'.
17. Clive Jones, *Britain and the Yemen Civil War, 1962-1965: Ministers, Mercenaries and Mandarins - Foreign Policy and the Limits of Covert Action* (Brighton: Sussex Academic Press, 2004), p. 111; Philip Davies, *Intelligence and Government in Britain and the United States: A Comparative Perspective, Vol. 2: Evolution of the UK Intelligence community* (Santa Barbara, CA: Praeger, 2012), p. 193.

18. Chester L. Cooper, *The Lion's Last Roar: Suez, 1956* (New York: Harper and Row, 1978), p. 70.
19. Percy Cradock, *Know Your Enemy: How the Joint Intelligence Committee Saw the World* (London: John Murray, 2002), pp. 128, 279.
20. Private information.
21. 'Charter for the Joint Intelligence Committee', 26 August 1955, JIC(55)57, TNA: CAB 158/21.
22. Rory Cormac, *Confronting the Colonies: British Intelligence and Counterinsurgency* (London: Hurst, 2013), pp. 217–19.
23. JIC minutes, 13 July 1967, JIC(67) 29th Meeting, TNA: CAB 159/47; 'Operations in South Arabia after Independence', draft Foreign Office/Ministry of Defence paper, 10 July 1967, TNA: DEFE 24/570; 'Liaison Staff' (Appendix 2 to Annex A to CINCFE33/67), 27 September 1967, TNA: DEFE 24/571.
24. Committee on Counter-Subversion in the Colonial Territories minutes, 16 March 1956, GEN. 520/1st Meeting, TNA: CAB 130/114.
25. 'Overseas Joint Intelligence Groups: Fragmentary Records', CAB 191, The National Archives, http://discovery.nationalarchives.gov.uk/SearchUI/details/redirect/?CATLN=3&CATID=60711&CATREF=CAB+191 (last accessed 13 November 2013).
26. Davies, *Intelligence and Government in Britain and the United States*, p. 16.
27. 'Transcript of Sir John Scarlett Hearing', Oral Evidence to the Iraq Inquiry, 8 December 2009, p. 18, http://www.iraqinquiry.org.uk/media/40665/20091208pmscarlett-final.pdf (last accessed 13 November 2013).
28. Cradock, *Know Your Enemy*, p. 261.
29. See for example TNA: FCO 76/18, which is a Maritime and Transport Department file discussing the terrorist threat to British shipping in 1970.

APPENDIX: CHAIRMEN OF THE JOINT INTELLIGENCE COMMITTEE

Desmond Anderson	1936–7
Roger Evans	1938
Frederick Beaumont-Nesbitt	1938–9
Ralph Skrine Stevenson	1939
Victor Cavendish Bentinck	1939–45
Harold Caccia	1945–6
William Hayter	1946–9
Patrick Reilly	1950–3
Patrick Dean	1953–60
Hugh Stephenson	1960–3
Bernard Burrows	1963–6
Denis Greenhill	1966–8
Edward Peck	1968–70
Steward Crawford	1970–3
Geoffrey Arthur	1973–5
Richard Sykes	1975–7
Antony Duff	1977–9
Antony Acland	1980–1
Patrick Wright	1982–3
Antony Duff	1983–5
Percy Cradock	1985–92
Rodric Braithwaite	1992–3
Pauline Neville-Jones	1993–4
Paul Lever	1994–6
Colin Budd	1996–7
Michael Pakenham	1997–2000

Peter Ricketts	2000–1
John Scarlett	2001–4
William Ehrman	2004–5
Richard Mottram	2005–7
Alex Allan	2007–11
Jon Day	2012–

DOCUMENT SOURCES

Chapter 2
Document 1 DCOS 4, 'Central Machinery for Co-ordination of Intelligence', 1 January 1936. TNA: CAB 54/3.
Document 2 'The Organisation of Intelligence', Report by F Beaumont-Nesbitt and cover note to Hollis, 21 December 1938. TNA: CAB 21/2651.

Chapter 3
JIC(42)304(0)(Final), 'Operation "TORCH" – Intelligence Appreciation', 7 August 1942. TNA: CAB 81/109.

Chapter 4
Document 1 V. Cavendish-Bentinck and D. Capel-Dunn, 'The Intelligence Machine. Report to the Joint Intelligence Committee', 10th January 1945, CAB 163/6.
Document 2 JIC(44)86(O), 'The British Intelligence Organisation', 3 March 1944. TNA: CAB 81/121.

Chapter 5
JIC(44)467(0)(Final), 'Russia's Strategic Interests and Intentions from the Point of View of Her Security', 18 December 1944. TNA: CAB 81/126.

Chapter 6
JIC(48)19 (0) (2nd Revised Draft) 'Sigint Intelligence Requirements – 1948', 11 May 1948, L/WS/1/1196, India Office Library and Records.

Chapter 7
Document 1 JIC(48)42(0)Final, 'Indications of Russian Preparedness for War', 18 June 1948. TNA: CAB 158/3.
Document 2 JIC(48)78(0), 'Measures to Prevent the Russians Obtaining Strategic Surprise', 16 July 1948. TNA: CAB 159/3.

Chapter 8
Document 1 JIC(50)88(Final – Revise), 'Chinese Communist Intentions and Capabilities – 1950/51', 11 October 1950. TNA: CAB 158/11.
Document 2 JIC/2162/50, 'Korea – Situation Report Number 90', 1 November 1950. TNA: DEFE 11/202.

Chapter 9
Document 1 JIC(48)104, 'Soviet Intentions and Capabilities 1949 and 1956/7', 8 November 1948. TNA: CAB 158/4.
Document 2 JIC(51)6(Final), 'The Soviet Threat', 19 January 1951. TNA: CAB 158/12.

Chapter 10
JIC(55)28, 'Colonial Intelligence and Security', 23 March 1955. TNA: CAB 158/20.

Chapter 11
JIC(56)80(Final)(Revise), 'Egyptian Nationalisation of the Suez Canal Company', 3 August 1956. TNA: CAB 158/25.

Chapter 12
Document 1 JIC(62)99, 'Likely Soviet Response to an American Decision to Invade or Bomb Cuba', 27 October 1962. TNA: CAB 158/47.
Document 2 JIC(62)101(Final), 'Soviet Motives in Cuba', 6 December 1962. TNA: CAB 158/47.

Chapter 13
JIC(64)26, 'Consequence of Deeper US Involvement or Withdrawal', 12 March 1964. TNA: CAB 158/57.

Chapter 14
JIC(68)54(Final), 'The Soviet Grip on Eastern Europe', 2 December 1968. TNA: CAB 158/71.

Chapter 15
GEN 9(70)22, 'Arab Terrorist Threat to Western Interests (Delicate Source)', JIC Middle East Current Intelligence Group report, 30 October 1970, TNA: CAB 130/475.

Chapter 16
JIC(A)(71)54, 'The Probable Reactions to the Introduction of Direct Rule in Northern Ireland', 6 January 1972. TNA: CAB 186/9.

Chapter 17
JIC(82)(IA)29, 'Falkland Islands', 17 April 1982. National Security Archive, USA.

Chapter 18
Intelligence and Security Committee, 'Annual Report, 1995', December 1995. Available via Intelligence and Security Committee website.

Chapter 19
'Iraqi use of Chemical and Biological Weapons – Possible Scenarios', JIC Assessment, 9 September 2002. Available via the website of Sir John Chilcot's Iraq Inquiry.

Chapter 20
'Southern Iraq: What's in Store?', JIC Assessment, 19 February 2003. Available via the website of Sir John Chilcot's Iraq Inquiry.

Chapter 21
'Supporting the National Security Council: The Central National Security and Intelligence Machinery', Cabinet Office report, October 2011. Available via the Cabinet Office website, https://www.gov.uk/government/publications/supporting-the-national-security-council-nsc-the-central-national-security-and-intelligence-machinery.

Chapter 22
JP 115, 'Syria: Reported Chemical Weapons Use', 29 August 2013. Available via the No. 10 website, https://www.gov.uk/government/publications/syria-reported-chemical-weapons-use-joint-intelligence-committee-letter.

BIBLIOGRAPHY

Richard J. Aldrich, 'Counting the Cost of Intelligence: The Treasury, National Service and GCHQ', *English Historical Review* 128/532 (2013), 596–627.

Richard J. Aldrich, 'Did Waldegrave Work? The Impact of Open Government upon British History', *Twentieth Century British History* 9/1 (1998), 111–26.

Richard J. Aldrich, *GCHQ: The Uncensored Story of Britain's Most Secret Intelligence Agency* (London: HarperPress, 2011).

Richard J. Aldrich, '"Grow Your Own": Cold War Intelligence and History Supermarkets', *Intelligence and National Security* 17/1 (2002), 135–52.

Richard J. Aldrich, 'Policing the Past: Official History, Secrecy and British Intelligence since 1945', *English Historical Review* 119/483 (2004), 922–53.

Richard J. Aldrich, 'Whitehall and the Iraq War: The UK's Four Intelligence Enquiries', *Irish Studies in International Affairs* 16 (2005), 73–88.

Christopher Andrew, *The Defence of the Realm: The Authorized History of MI5* (London: Allen Lane, 2009).

David Arbel and Ran Edelist, *Western Intelligence and the Collapse of the Soviet Union, 1980–1990: Ten Years That Did Not Shake the World* (London: Frank Cass, 2003).

Nigel Ashton, 'Harold Macmillan and the "Golden Days" of Anglo-American Relations Revisited, 1957–63', *Diplomatic History* 29/4 (2005), 691–723.

James Bamford, *The Puzzle Palace: America's National Security Agency and Its Special Relationship with Britain's GCHQ* (London: Sidgwick and Jackson, 1982).

Gordon Barrass, *The Great Cold War: A Journey through the Hall of Mirrors* (Stanford, CA: Stanford University Press, 2009).

Richard K. Betts, 'Politicization of Intelligence: Costs and Benefits', in Richard K. Betts and Thomas G. Mahnken (eds), *Paradoxes of Strategic Intelligence: Essays in Honor of Michael I. Handel* (London: Frank Cass, 2003).

Richard K. Betts, 'Policy-Makers and Intelligence Analysts: Love, Hate or Indifference?', *Intelligence and National Security* 3/1 (1988), 184–9.

Günter Bischof, Stefan Karner and Peter Ruggenthaler (eds), *The Prague Spring and the Warsaw Pact Invasion of Czechoslovakia in 1968* (Lanham, MD: Lexington, 2009).

Alan Bullock, *Ernest Bevin, Foreign Secretary 1945-1951* (London: Heinemann, 1983).

Peter Busch, *All the Way with JFK? Britain, the US, and the Vietnam War* (Oxford: Oxford University Press, 2003).

Peter Busch, 'Supporting the War: Britain's Decision to Send the Thompson Mission to Vietnam, 1960–61', *Cold War History* 2/1 (2001), 69–95.

Lord Butler, *Review of Intelligence on Weapons of Mass Destruction, Annex B: Intelligence Assessment and Presentation: From March to September 2002* (London: The Stationery Office, 2004).

Paul Carmichael and Robert Osborne, 'The Northern Ireland Civil Service under Direct Rule and Devolution', *International Review of Administrative Sciences* 69/2 (2003), 205-18.

Gérard Chaliand and Arnaud Blin, 'From 1968 to Radical Islam', in Gérard Chaliand and Arnaud Blin (eds), *The History of Terrorism: From Antiquity to Al Qaeda* (Berkeley: University of California Press, 2007).

Jean Chrétien, *My Years as Prime Minister* (Toronto: Knopf Canada, 2007).

Ian Clark and Nicholas J. Wheeler, *The British Origins of Nuclear Strategy, 1945-1955* (Oxford: Clarendon Press, 1989).

Chester L. Cooper, *The Lion's Last Roar: Suez, 1956* (New York: Harper and Row, 1978).

Gordon Corera, *The Art of Betrayal: Life and Death in the British Secret Service* (London: Weidenfeld and Nicolson, 2011).

Rory Cormac, *Confronting the Colonies: British Intelligence and Counterinsurgency* (London: Hurst, 2013).

Rory Cormac, 'Coordinating Covert Action: The Case of the Yemen Civil War and the South Arabian Insurgency', *Journal of Strategic Studies*, 36/5 (2012), 692-717.

Rory Cormac, 'Much Ado about Nothing: Terrorism, Intelligence, and the Mechanics of Threat Exaggeration', *Terrorism and Political Violence* 25/3 (2013), 476-93.

Rory Cormac, 'Organizing Intelligence: An Introduction to the 1955 Report on Colonial Security', *Intelligence and National Security* 25/6 (2010), 800-22.

Percy Cradock, *In Pursuit of British Interests: Reflections on Foreign Policy under Margaret Thatcher and John Major* (London: John Murray, 1997).

Percy Cradock, *Know Your Enemy: How the Joint Intelligence Committee Saw the World* (London: John Murray, 2002).

Mark Curtis, *Unpeople: Britain's Secret Human Rights Abuses* (London: Vintage, 2004).

Philip Davies, *Intelligence and Government in Britain and the United States: A Comparative Perspective, Vol. 2: Evolution of the UK Intelligence Community* (Santa Barbara, CA: Praeger, 2012).

Philip Davies, 'Twilight of Britain's Joint Intelligence Committee?', *International Journal of Intelligence and Counterintelligence* 24/3 (2011), 427-46.

Jack Davis, 'The Kent-Kendall Debate of 1949', *Studies in Intelligence* 36/5 (1992), 91-103.

Anne Deighton, *The Impossible Peace: Britain, the Division of Germany, and the Origins of the Cold War* (Oxford: Clarendon Press, 1993).

Stephen Dorril, *MI6: 50 Years of Special Operations* (London: Fourth Estate, 2000)

Robert Dover and Michael S. Goodman (eds), *Learning from the Secret Past: Cases in British Intelligence History* (Washington, DC: Georgetown University Press, 2011).

Anthony Farrar-Hockley, *The Official History of the British Part in the Korean War, Vol. I: A Distant Obligation* (London; HMSO, 1990).

Lawrence Freedman, *The Official History of the Falklands Campaign, Vol. I: The Origins of the Falklands War* (London: Routledge, 2005).

Lawrence Freedman, *The Official History of the Falklands Campaign, Vol. II: War and Diplomacy* (London: Routledge, 2005).

David French, *The British Way in Counter-insurgency, 1945-1967* (Oxford: Oxford University Press, 2011).

Robert Gates, 'Guarding against Politicization', *Studies in Intelligence* 36/5 (1992), 5-13.

Michael S. Goodman, 'Avoiding Surprise: The Nicoll Report and Intelligence Analysis', in

Robert Dover and Michael S. Goodman (eds), *Learning from the Secret Past: Cases in British Intelligence History* (Washington, DC: Georgetown University Press, 2011).

Michael S. Goodman, 'British Intelligence and the Soviet Atomic Bomb, 1945-1950', *Journal of Strategic Studies* 26/2 (2003), 120-51.

Michael S. Goodman, 'The British Way in Intelligence', in Matthew Grant (ed.), *The British Way in Cold Warfare: Intelligence, Diplomacy and the Bomb, 1945-1975* (London: Continuum, 2009).

Michael S. Goodman, 'The Joint Intelligence Committee and the Cuban Missile Crisis', in David Gioe, Len Scott and Christopher Andrew (eds), *An International History of the Cuban Missile Crisis: A 50-Year Retrospective* (Abingdon: Routledge, forthcoming).

Michael S. Goodman, *The Official History of the Joint Intelligence Committee, Vol. I: From the Approach of the Second World War to the Suez Crisis* (Abingdon: Routledge, forthcoming).

Michael S. Goodman, *Spying on the Nuclear Bear: Anglo-American Intelligence and the Soviet Bomb* (Stanford, CA: Stanford University Press, 2007).

Michael I. Handel, 'Leaders and Intelligence', in Michael I. Handel (ed.), *Leaders and Intelligence* (London: Frank Cass, 1989).

Michael Handel, 'The Politics of Intelligence', *Intelligence and National Security* 2/4 (1987), 5-46.

Peter Hennessy, *Distilling the Frenzy: Writing the History of One's Own Times* (London: Biteback, 2012).

Peter Hennessy, *The Prime Minister: The Office and Its Holders since 1945* (London: Penguin, 2001).

Peter Hennessy, *The Secret State: Whitehall and the Cold War* (London: Allen Lane, 2002).

Peter Hennessy, *The Secret State: Whitehall and the Cold War*, rev. ed. (London: Penguin, 2003).

Peter Hennessy, *Whitehall* (London: Secker and Warburg, 1989).

Michael Herman, *Intelligence Power in Peace and War* (Cambridge: Cambridge University Press, 1996).

Michael Herman, *Intelligence Services in the Information Age: Theory and Practice* (London; Frank Cass, 2001).

Michael Herman, 'The Post-War Organization of Intelligence: The January 1945 Report to the Joint Intelligence Committee on "The Intelligence Machine"', in Robert Dover and Michael S. Goodman (eds), *Learning from the Secret Past: Cases in British Intelligence History* (Washington, DC: Georgetown University Press, 2011).

Michael Herman, 'Up from the Country: Cabinet Office Impressions, 1972-75', *Contemporary British History* 11/1 (1997), 83-97.

Roger Hilsman, *Strategic Intelligence and National Decisions* (Glencoe, IL: Free Press, 1956).

Michael Howard, *Grand Strategy: History of the Second World War, Vol. IV: August 1942-September 1943* (London: HMSO, 1972).

Geraint Hughes, 'British Policy towards Eastern Europe and the Impact of the "Prague Spring", 1964-68', *Cold War History* 4/2 (2004), 115-39.

Clive Jones, *Britain and the Yemen Civil War, 1962-1965: Ministers, Mercenaries and Mandarins - Foreign Policy and the Limits of Covert Action* (Brighton: Sussex Academic Press, 2004).

Simon Kear, 'The British Consulate-General in Hanoi, 1954-73', *Diplomacy and Statecraft* 10/1 (1999), 215-39.

John Kent, *British Imperial Strategy and the Origins of the Cold War, 1944-49* (Leicester: Leicester University Press, 1993).

BIBLIOGRAPHY

Steven Kettell, 'Who's Afraid of Saddam Hussein? Re-examining the "September Dossier" Affair', *Contemporary British History* 22/3 (2008), 407–26.

Keith Kyle, *Suez: Britain's End of Empire in the Middle East*, rev. ed. (London: I. B. Tauris, 2011).

Julian Lewis, *Changing Direction: British Military Planning for Post-war Strategic Defence, 1942-1947* (London: Sherwood Press, 1988).

Ariel Merari, 'Attacks on Civil Aviation: Trends and Lessons', *Terrorism and Political Violence* 10/3 (1998), 9–26.

Charles Moore, *Margaret Thatcher: The Authorized Biography, Vol. 1: Not for Turning* (London: Allen Lane, 2013).

John N. L. Morrison, 'British Intelligence Failures in Iraq', *Intelligence and National Security* 26/4 (2011), 509–20.

Andrew Mumford, *The Counter-insurgency Myth: The British Experience of Irregular Warfare* (Abingdon: Routledge, 2012).

David Murphy, Sergei Kondrashev and George Bailey, *Battleground Berlin: CIA vs KGB in the Cold War* (London: Yale University Press, 1997).

Eunan O'Halpin, '"A Poor Thing but Our Own": The Joint Intelligence Committee and Ireland, 1965-72', *Intelligence and National Security* 23/5 (2008), 658–80.

Eunan O'Halpin, 'The Value and Limits of Experience in the Early Years of the Northern Ireland Troubles, 1969-1972', in Robert Dover and Michael S. Goodman (eds), *Learning from the Secret Past: Cases in British Intelligence History* (Washington, DC: Georgetown University Press, 2011).

Ritchie Ovendale, *The English-speaking Alliance: Britain, the United States, the Dominions and the Cold War, 1945-51* (London: George Allen and Unwin, 1985).

Mark Phillips, 'Failing Intelligence: Reform of the Machinery', in Michael Codner and Michael Clarke (eds), *A Question of Security: The British Defence Review in an Age of Austerity* (London: I. B. Tauris, 2011).

Jonathan Powell, *The New Machiavelli: How to Wield Power in the Modern World* (London: Vintage, 2011).

Andrew Rathmell, 'Planning Post-conflict Reconstruction in Iraq: What Can We Learn?', *International Affairs* 81/5 (2005), 1013–38.

Patrick Salmon, Keith Hamilton and Stephen Twigge (eds), *Documents on British Policy Overseas, Series III, Vol. VII: German Unification, 1989-90* (Abingdon: Routledge, 2010).

Len Scott, 'British Strategic Intelligence and the Cold War', in Loch K. Johnson (ed.), *The Oxford Handbook of National Security Intelligence* (New York: Oxford University Press, 2012).

Anthony Seldon, *Blair Unbound* (London: Simon and Schuster, 2007).

Raymond Smith, 'A Climate of Opinion: British Officials and the Development of British Soviet Policy, 1945-7', *International Affairs* 64/4 (1988), 631–47.

William Beattie Smith, *The British State and the Northern Ireland Crisis, 1969-73: From Violence to Power-sharing* (Washington, DC: United States Institute of Peace Press, 2011).

Brian Stewart, *Scrapbook of a Roving Highlander: 80 Years round Asia and Back* (Newark: Acorn, 2002).

Margaret Thatcher, *The Downing Street Years* (London: HarperCollins, 1993).

Edward Thomas, 'The Evolution of the JIC System up to and during World War II', in Christopher Andrew and Jeremy Noakes (eds), *Intelligence and International Relations, 1900-45* (Exeter: University of Exeter Press, 1987).

Gregory F. Treverton, *Reshaping National Intelligence for an Age of Information* (Cambridge: Cambridge University Press, 2003).

Rhiannon Vickers, 'Harold Wilson, the British Labour Party, and the War in Vietnam', *Journal of Cold War Studies* 10/2 (2008), 41–70.

David Vincent, *The Culture of Secrecy: Britain, 1832–1998* (Oxford: Clarendon Press, 1999).

Odd Arne Westad, *The Global Cold War: Third World Interventions and the Making of Our Times* (Cambridge: Cambridge University Press, 2005).

Hugo Young, *One of Us* (London: Macmillan, 1989).

J. W. Young, 'Britain and "LBJ's War", 1964–68', *Cold War History* 2/3 (2002), 63–92.

J. W. Young, 'The Wilson Government's Reform of Intelligence Co-ordination, 1967–68', *Intelligence and National Security* 16/2 (2001), 133–51.

INDEX

Adye, Sir John, 386
al-Assad, Bashar, 417, 418
al-Qaeda, 400
Assessments Staff, 3, 295

Berlin Airlift, 149
Berlin Blockade, 156, 157
Blair, Tony, 8, 389, 390, 391, 400, 401, 409, 410, 417, 418, 425
Bloody Sunday, 354
Brook, Norman, 148
Brown, Gordon, 8, 401, 409, 410, 425
Bulgaria, 318, 331
Burma, 192–5
Butler, Michael, 343

Cameron, David, 7, 409, 417, 418
Capel-Dunn, Denis, 62
carrier pigeons, 61
Cavendish-Bentinck, Victor, 31, 61, 121
Central Intelligence Bureau, 99
Central Interpretation Unit, 81–4
'Central Machinery for Co-Ordination of Intelligence' report, 1936, 11
China, 169
  economy, 174
  implications of intervention in Korea, 184
  possible courses of action in North Korea, 183
  reaction to war in Vietnam, 282
  relationship with Soviet Union, 173
Chinese Communist Army, 175

'Chinese Communist Intention and Capabilities 1950/51' report, 170
Churchill, Winston, 7, 31
CIA, 428
Colonial Office, 227
'Colonial Security' report, 229
Combined Services Detailed Interrogation Centre, 80
Cominform, 148
'Consequences of Deeper United States Involvement in Vietnam or United States Withdrawal from South Vietnam' report, 270
Cooper, Chester, 429–30
Council for Mutual Economic Aid, 324
Cradock, Percy, 380, 381, 430
Current Intelligence Groups, 3, 343, 423
Czechoslovakia, 300, 314, 328
  reform programme, 309

Dill, John, 10, 11
Dubcek, Alexander, 299

East Germany, 315, 329
Eden, Anthony, 8, 226
'Egyptian Nationalisation of the Suez Canal Company' report, 242
'Elint', 150

Finland, 134
Formosa, 198–204

France, reaction to invasion of north Africa during World War II, 35
  Ground Forces in Indo-China, 189
Freedman, Lawrence, 373, 375
Freedom of Information Act, 425
'functional topics', 384

Galtieri, Leopoldo, 374
GCHQ *see* Government Communications Headquarters
General Intelligence Requirements Committee, 99
Germany, reaction to invasion of north Africa during World War II, 37
  reunification, 380
  significance during Cold War, 156
  Soviet policy on Germany, 136
Gorbachev, Mikhail, 380
Government Code and Cypher School, 90
Government Communications Headquarters (GCHQ), 148, 342, 381, 382, 385, 410, 412, 425

Hague, William, 413
Hankey, Maurice, 10, 11, 31
Heath, Edward, 352
Herman, Michael, 6, 225, 427
Hooper, Robin, 343
Hungary, 318, 330
Hussein, Saddam, 395, 396, 398, 400, 402, 403, 404, 407
Hutton Report, 2

'Indications of Russian Preparedness for War' 1948 report, 158
intelligence, definition of, 62
Intelligence and Security Committee, 381, 391
  Annual Report 1995, 383
intelligence failures, 4–5, 157, 168, 225, 296, 374
'Intelligence Machine' report, 64
Intelligence Section (Operations), 77
Intelligence Services Act 1994, 381
Inter-Service Security Board, 78
Inter-Service Topographical Department, 75
Iraq War, 2, 399
  Iranian aims, 406

post-war planning, 400, 401
  Shia reactions, 405
'Iraqi Use of Chemical and Biological Weapons – Possible Scenarios' report, 393
IRA, 356, 358, 364
Israel, 248
Italy, reaction to invasion of north Africa during World War II, 37

Joint Intelligence Committee
  ability to adapt to developing situations, 157
  assessments of Soviet capabilities, 208
  balanced tone of forecasts, 158
  elevation to full committee status, 63
  end of the Cold War, 381
  decision to prioritise Soviet activity, 149
  discrepancies between JIC and COS statements, 209
  implications of creation of NSC, 410
  intelligence failures, 4–5, 157, 168, 225, 296, 374
  media coverage, 389
  post-war planning, 61
  prediction of Cuban Missile Crisis, 251
  purpose, 1
  relationship with NSC, 412
  relationship with government policy, 413, 424
  relationship with policy-makers, 6
  role in World War 2, 32
  warnings over Vietnam, 268
Joint Intelligence Staff, 32, 98
Joint Technical Intelligence Committee, 98

Khrushchev, Nikita Sergeyevich, 259, 262–4
Korean War, 169

Latin America Current Intelligence Group, 374, 375
Lever, Paul, 381–2
Lewis, Julian, 2
Lobban, Iain, 412
Local Intelligence Committees, 230–2

Macao, 204
Malaya, 225
Major, John, 382, 425

INDEX

Marshall Aid, 156
McArthur, Douglas, 169
'Measures to Prevent the Russians Obtaining Strategic Surprise' report, 165
MI5, 227, 381, 382
MI6, 381, 382, 410, 411, 425
Miliband, Ed, 418
mirror imaging, 4, 170, 296

Nasser, Gamal, 240
National Security Council, 409, 419
North Korea, 168
Northern Ireland, 385
   Catholics and Direct Rule, 363
   civil service, 362
   mood of Protestant community, 359–62
Norway, German invasion of, 31
   and Soviet Union, 133

Obama, Barack, 417
Omand, David, 400
open source intelligence, 374, 419
Operation Torch, 31, 33
   JIC report on, 34

Permanent Secretaries Committee on the Intelligence Services, 148
Photographic Reconnaissance Committee, 98
Poland, 137, 317, 329
political intelligence, 232
Political Warfare Executive, 84–7
Popular Front for the Liberation of Palestine, 341, 346
'Possible Soviet Response to a US Decision to Bomb or Invade Cuba' report, 254
Postal and Telegraph Censorship Department, 87
'Probably Reactions to the Introduction of Direct Rule in Northern Ireland' report, 355

Radio Security Services, 94
Reilly, Patrick, 428
Rimington, Stella, 382, 386
Rimmer-Martin review, 411, 413
Rumania, 319, 330
Russia *see* Soviet Union

'Russian preparations for war' report, 157
Russian psychology, 212
'Russia's Strategic Interests and Intentions from the Point of View of Her Security' report, 123

Scarlett, John, 2, 391, 400, 410
security intelligence, 232
Short, Clare, 399, 401
Siam, 195–8
'Sigint Intelligence Requirements – 1948' report, 150
Signals Intelligence
South Korea, 168
   United Nations Forces in South Korea, 183
'Southern Iraq: What's in Store?' report, 402
'Soviet Grip on Eastern Europe' report, 298
'Soviet Intentions and Capabilities 1949 and 1956/57' report, 210
'Soviet Motives in Cuba' report, 257
Soviet Union, 121
   atomic weapons, 150
   attitudes to use of force, 303
   and Balkans, 138
   birthrate, 130
   Black Sea, 140
   buffer states, 126
   collaboration with UK and US, 126
   demilitarisation of Japan, 128
   disarmament of Germany, 127
   fall of, 380
   and Far East, 143
   and Finland, 134
   fuel and power supply, 130–2
   industrial capacity, 132
   and Middle East, 141
   military strength, 125
   nuclear offensive, 208
   nuclear sufficiency, 209
   and Poland, 137
   policy in Eastern Europe, 304
   post-war naval policy, 146
   raw materials, 130
   reaction to war in Vietnam, 283
   relationship with Egypt, 242

Soviet Union (*cont.*)
    scientific and technical developments in 'weapons of mass destruction', 149
    standard of living, 125
    Western frontier, 135–6
    and Western powers, 139
Spain, reaction to invasion of north Africa during World War II, 34
Special Operations Executive, 92
Stalin, Joseph, 150
Straw, Jack, 391, 420
Suez Canal, 240, 413
'Supporting the National Security Council (NSC): The central national security and intelligence machinery' report, 414
Sweden, 133
'Syria: Reported Chemical Weapons Use' report, 421

Templer, Gerald, 225
terrorism, 341

Thatcher, Margaret, 7, 372, 375, 425
Tibet, 204–5

US Intelligence Community, 209

Viet Cong, 275–6, 279
Viet Minh, 189

Waldegrave Initiative on Open Government, 425
War Planning Committee, 99
Warsaw Pact, 322
Wilson, Harold, 8, 297
WMD (weapons of mass destruction), 389, 391
'Working Party on Acts of Violence Against Civil Aircraft' report, 344
Wright, Patrick, 375

'Y' Services, 91
Yugoslavia, 320, 385